People and Computers XVII – Designing for Society

Springer
London
Berlin
Heidelberg
New York
Hong Kong
Milan
Paris
Tokyo

Eamonn O'Neill, Philippe Palanque
and Peter Johnson (Eds)

People and Computers XVII – Designing for Society

Proceedings of HCI 2003

Springer

Eamonn O'Neill, BA, MSc, PhD
Department of Computer Science, University of Bath, Bath BA2 7AY, UK

Philippe Palanque, PhD
Universite Paul Sabatier, LIIHS-IRIT, 31062 Toulouse Cedex, France

Peter Johnson, BSc, PhD
Department of Computer Science, University of Bath, Bath BA2 7AY, UK

British Library Cataloguing in Publication Data
People and computers XVII : designing for society
   1. Human computer interaction – Congresses
   I. O'Neill Eamonn II. Palanque, Philippe, 1966- III. Johnson, Peter, 1950-
   004'.019
   ISBN 1852337664

ISBN 1-85233-766-4 Springer-Verlag London Berlin Heidelberg
a member of BertelsmannSpringer Science+Business Media GmbH
http://www.springer.co.uk

Typeset by: *Winder.*
Printed and bound at the Athenaeum Press Ltd., Gateshead, Tyne and Wear
34/3830-543210 Printed on acid-free paper SPIN 10945308

Contents

Preface

HCI is a fundamental and multidisciplinary research area. It is fundamental to the development and use of computing technologies. Without good HCI, computing technologies provide less benefit to society. We often fail to notice good HCI. Good HCI passes us by without comment or surprise. The technology lets you do what you want without causing you any further work, effort or thought. You load a DVD into your DVD player and it works: why shouldn't it? You take a photograph with your digital camera and without any surprise you easily transfer and view these on your computer. You seamlessly connect to networks and devices with a common interface and interaction style. Yet when HCI is wrong the technology becomes useless, unusable, disrupts our work, inhibits our abilities and constrains our achievements. Witness the overuse and inconsistent use of hierarchical menus on mobile phones; or the lack of correspondence between call statistics on the phone handset itself and the billed call time on the account bill; or the lack of interoperability between file naming conventions on different operating systems running applications and files of the same type (e.g. the need for explicit filename suffixes on some operating systems). Those programmers, designers and developers who know no better, believe that HCI is just common sense and that their designs are obviously easy to use. Often these designs are easy to use only by those who created them, if at all, begging the question of how common is their common sense?

The fact that everyone recognizes bad HCI design and yet everyone finds good HCI to be unremarkable is not a cause for concern. Why should we be surprised when the design is right? It is not magic. It is not chance. HCI design and evaluation methods, techniques, knowledge, skills, practices, guidelines and principles lead to good HCI. The product of HCI research and practices is visible in technology that works. The incidence of HCI methods, techniques and personnel in technology design and development as well as in end user organizations is high. The field of HCI has progressed from largely solving the problems created by technology designers and developers to developing and creating technologies and products with good HCI integral to their design.

However, there are still areas where our understanding may not be adequate to overcome the challenges in design and development of emerging technologies. For example, in the development of multi-modal interaction technologies it is now technologically possible to provide fine-detailed, tactile feedback, along with hi-fidelity audio and visual output. However, we still do not understand how to achieve, in some cases, awareness of three different streams of independent and meaningful information or, in other cases, an integrated single event synthesized from three streams. Furthermore, input technologies allow for gesture, eye gaze, head position and more conventional input techniques yet it is still not possible to allow users effectively to carry out multiple tasks at the same time or varying as the environmental and contextual demands change. These fundamental HCI questions concerning awareness and multitasking cut across all areas of interaction design.

We can, for example, take these issues of multi-modal input and output and relate them to safety critical issues in the design of aircraft flight deck interaction. The same technologies are available and, more importantly, the same issues of awareness and multitasking underlie the technologies' use but in far greater complexity and with far more serious concerns than they might in, say, interactive movies. Hence HCI research impacts upon the development of interaction design in safety critical as well as in entertainment application areas. We can give numerous examples like this in which fundamental issues and understanding underlie technological and application issues. Fundamental research issues also include questions relating to the nature of collaboration in multi-user interaction and context, as in the case of pervasive and mobile computing. Both collaboration and context are poorly understood concepts, yet technological developments are advancing fast in these areas and standards and guidelines are being established in advance of sound understanding. These are further examples of the more recent research challenges that HCI is tackling.

Multidisciplinarity

HCI research is necessarily multidisciplinary and requires approaches from many different disciplines and traditions to be used together to develop richer, fuller and more useful HCI theories, methods and practices. There are many barriers to multidisciplinary research and development. Many of these are caused by ignorance, prejudices and vested interests, not by the segmentation or restrictions of the problems we wish to solve and understand or the designs we wish to create.

> "The greatest enterprise of the mind has always been and always will be the attempted linkage of the sciences and humanities. The ongoing fragmentation of knowledge and the resulting chaos in philosophy are not reflections of the real world but the artefacts of scholarship."
> E. O. Wilson, Consilience.

The Humanities, Arts, Engineering and Science each contribute to the understanding of HCI, and together arrive at a common ground for the explanation and understanding of complex interactive systems and phenomena of real world importance. There is a danger in undertaking multidisciplinary work that the differences between the disciplines can make this difficult. We must not be put off by a difficult task. However, experience suggests that difficulties arise out of individuals' preconceptions about what other disciplines claim. HCI must suspend and break down these preconceptions and enable researchers and students to gain insight from the richness of each discipline's contribution to the whole picture. We must enable people to see and to create the rich tapestry of understanding and explanation we require rather than just having isolated phenomenas and partial explanations that come from knitting in the dark.

Moving Forward in HCI Research and Development

There are many difficult questions facing the HCI researcher and developer. There is nothing to be gained from maintaining or building self-imposed barriers or restrictive practices. What are the research questions that the HCI community as a whole see as necessary to the development of the next generation of computing technologies? How does the HCI community see its research developing a core understanding? What HCI research is needed to improve society? What application challenges face us? Do we have all the necessary methodological and theoretical underpinning that we need in order to develop good HCI? Are there HCI research problems that we cannot yet answer? These are just some of the questions that are asked by and of the HCI community.

HCI generic research issues include: the development of contributing theories and mappings amongst them; the development of existing and new methods and paradigms; relating practice to theory and methods, and relating theory and methods to practice; identifying domain specific methods, theories and practices vs generalizing across domains; design and development of more powerful interaction platforms and architectures; the transitions between designs — a mix of science, engineering, art and craft.

At a lower level, consider some of the current and emerging topics such as: multitasking, awareness, context, collaboration, ubiquitous and pervasive computing, interaction input/output technologies, creativity, emotion, multi-sensory/modality interaction, visualization, augmented reality.

Both lists provide us with a plethora of research and development opportunities that have both technical and theoretical implications. Researchers and practitioners are actively engaged in research and development that address these issues and contribute to the growth of HCI knowledge.

The Technical Programme

First a brief explanation as to how the papers that are included here were chosen. The intention from the outset was to limit bias and look for quality. Bias as far as possible was reduced by employing a process of anonymous reviewing and selection. Quality was attained by the use of independent peer reviewers who carefully read the full papers submitted by the authors. The full papers published in this volume have been subjected to anonymous, independent peer assessment and refereeing. The technical programme Chairs selected papers, preserving the anonymity of the authors, on the basis of the reviews. Only the highest quality and most relevant papers were chosen to be included as full papers in the programme. Fewer than 30% of the submitted papers were accepted for publication. On the basis of the selected papers, the programme sessions were identified while still preserving the anonymity of the authors. Only after the sessions and papers had been finalized did the programme Chairs know the identity of the authors. Inevitably, in a conference and proceedings that is based upon open response to publicized calls for papers, the collection of work is to some extent determined by the interests and the community of the day. There is no claim that these are the most important issues or a representative sample of the ongoing research. It is a high quality research collection that because of the length of each paper provides a deeper and fuller account of research than that which is often found in conference proceedings.

The sessions cover issues of theoretical, methodological and practical consideration. In creating the sessions, the technical programme Chairs have sought to create interesting relationships between the individual papers. The sessions have emerged from the papers and so are grounded in the papers and not a preset structure that influenced the selection or choice of the papers. The sessions are of course an imposed structure that seeks to identify and encourage interesting relationships that emerge above and beyond any single paper.

"Doing the right thing in the right place" captures relationships between activity and place. The papers in this section include and discuss issues concerning how tasks or activities are grouped together according to internal and external factors, how place influences activity and how activity, collaboration and place intersect. Each paper includes issues of activity, place and collaboration to a greater of lesser degree.

"Information Retrieval" brings together papers addressing peer-to-peer file sharing tools to support information gathering by knowledge workers, an evaluation of an interface to support structured document retrieval and the consideration of different methods of supporting the user in focusing and zooming on to objects, points and features of interest.

No conference on HCI would be complete without a session concerned with "Design Methods and Principles". In this session the papers consider novel principles and methods. The principles aspect takes the form of the application of urban design principles to navigation of information spaces. The methodological perspective considers a method for organizational and cultural analysis and user centred design in organizations.

Similarly "Evaluation methods" are a core area of HCI research. This session brings together new research on usability inspection methods and further research on a particular form of analytical evaluation known as ontological sketch models.

As HCI technologies evolve and develop, the range of input techniques to facilitate user interaction is increased. The session on "Input techniques" considers different modalities of input in terms of aspects of looking and listening, aiming and pointing and gesturing.

An emerging application domain is "E-commerce". This session includes considerations of aspects of culture and society as obstacles to e-commerce. Also the issue of identifying trustworthiness in e-commerce applications is raised.

With the development of wireless and pervasive computing technologies, sessions such as the one entitled "On the move" are a further interesting area of new research, raising many issues. These include the ability to search and browse large information spaces like the Web on mobile devices such as phones and PDAs. A further consideration is how applications are affected by the type and form of the mobile device on which they are run.

As technology reaches wider sectors of society, issues of how HCI takes account of their individual needs becomes more important. The session on "Accessibility" includes a wide selection of papers that address issues of graphics, accessibility and age differences, voice dialogues for older people, audio-tactile browsers for disabled people and an automated accessibility assessment of Web sites.

An important aspect of human interaction concerns how we express ourselves through our faces. The session "Look at me" considers how to express emotions, how to monitor and track facial expressions, and a study involving eye tracking.

All these sessions and the papers they contain present exciting new and evolving areas of HCI. The barriers that used to exist between disciplines such as computer science, psychology and social sciences are not present here. HCI has overcome these to engage in multidisciplinary research that uses and develops theories, methods and understanding in design, development and evaluation of technologies to the benefit of people and society. Since the aims and goals of HCI are high and worthy we should not be held back by the biases and prejudices of old disciplinary boundaries. This collection represents the freedom from such barriers.

Finally, we thank all the authors who sent papers to us for review. We are sorry we could not publish them all. It is a pleasure to see the volume and variety of HCI research being conducted. Also, our thanks to the vast team of reviewers who freely gave up their time and energy carefully to review all the papers. Without all of you this community of researchers would not exist and this conference would not happen. Enjoy the conference and be excited and enthused by the research in HCI 2003: Designing for Society.

Peter Johnson
Eamonn O'Neill
Philippe Palanque

June 2003

The Committee

Conference Chair	Eamonn O'Neill *University of Bath, UK*
Technical Chairs	Philippe Palanque *Université Paul Sabatier Toulouse III, France*
	Peter Johnson *University of Bath, UK*
Industry Day	Catriona Campbell *The Usability Company, UK*
Short Papers	Phil Gray *University of Glasgow, UK*
	Hilary Johnson *University of Bath, UK*
Tutorials	Laurence Nigay *CLIPS-IMAG, France*
Interactive Experiences	Panos Markopoulos *Technische Universiteit Eindhoven, The Netherlands*
	Simon Crouch
Doctoral Consortium	Lachlan MacKinnon *Heriot-Watt University, UK*
	Ann Blandford *UCL, UK*
	Steve Brewster *University of Glasgow, UK*
Posters	Nick Bryan-Kinns *Optic Experience Design, UK*
Workshops	Leon Watts *UMIST, UK*
Laboratory and Organizational Overviews	Dave Roberts *IBM, UK*
Panels	Alistair Edwards *University of York, UK*
Accessibility	Tony Stockman *QMUL, UK*
Marketing and Publicity	Tom McEwan *Napier University, UK*
Webmaster	Dave Clarke *Visualize Software Ltd, UK*
Treasurer	Peter Wild *University of Bath, UK*
Technical Support	Vassilis Kostakos *University of Bath, UK*
Student Volunteers	Jo Hyde *University of Bath, UK*
Social Programme	Rachid Hourizi *University of Bath, UK*
British HCI Group Liaison	Phil Gray *University of Glasgow, UK*
Previous Conference Chair	Fintan Culwin *South Bank University, UK*

The Reviewers

Rajarathinam Arangarasan	*Purdue University, USA*
Sandrine Balbo	*The University of Melbourne, Australia*
Gordon Baxter	*University of York, UK*
Staffan Björk	*Göteborgs Universitet, Sweeden*
Rebelo Bocianoski Irla	*Universidade Federal de Santa Catarina, Brazil*
Susanne Bodker	*Aarhus Universitet, Denmark*
Nathalie Bonnardel	*Université de Provence, France*
Norbert Braun	*Technische Universität Darmstadt, Germany*
Edwin Curran	*University of Ulster, UK*
Mary Czerwinski	*Microsoft Research, USA*
Maia Dimitrova	*Middlesex University, UK*
Emmanuel Dubois-Peyrard	*Université Paul Sabatier Toulouse III, France*
Lynne Dunckley	*Thames Valley University, UK*
Sue Fenley	*The University of Reading, UK*
Fabio Ferlazzo	*Università degli Studi di Roma La Sapienza, Italy*
Paola Forcheri	*Consiglio Nazionale delle Ricerche, Italy*
Gheorghita Ghinea	*Brunel University, UK*
Simon Grant	*Information Strategists, UK*
Tom Gross	*Fraunhofer Gesellschaft, Germany*
Hans-Juergen Hoffmann	*Technische Universität Darmstadt, Germany*
Stefan Holmlid	*Linköpings Universitet, Sweden*
Kate Hone	*Brunel University, UK*
Kasper Hornbæk	*Københavns Universitet, Denmark*
Ebba Hvannberg Thora	*Háskóli Íslands, Iceland*
Hilary Johnson	*University of Bath, UK*
Peter Johnson	*University of Bath, UK*
Timo Jokela	*Oulun yliopisto, Finland*
Pekka Ketola	*Nokia, Finland*
David Lane	*Leeds Metropolitan University, UK*
Lachlan MacKinnon	*Heriot-Watt University, UK*
Thomas Mandl	*Universität Hildesheim Marienburger, Germany*
Masood Masoodian	*The University of Waikato, New Zealand*
Rachel McCrindle	*The University of Reading, UK*
Tom McEwan	*Napier University, UK*

Elizabeth Kemp	*Massey University, New Zealand*
Philippe Palanque	*Université Paul Sabatier Toulouse III, France*
Antonia Palmer	*University of Waterloo, Canada*
Rodolfo Pinto da Luz	*Universidade Federal de Santa Catarina, Brazil*
Margit Pohl	*Technische Universität Wien, Austria*
Mark Riordan	*Dun Laoghaire Institute of Art, Design and Technology, Ireland*
Andy Sloane	*University of Wolverhampton, UK*
Jan Stage	*Aalborg Universitet, Denmark*
Mark Treglown	*University of Nottingham, UK*
Phil Turner	*Napier University, UK*
Susan Turner	*Napier University, UK*
Colin Venters	*University of Manchester, UK*
Robert Ward	*University of Huddersfield, UK*
Janice Whatley	*University of Salford, UK*
Peter Wild	*University of Bath, UK*
Marco Winckler	*Université Paul Sabatier Toulouse III, France*

Doing the Right Thing in the Right Place: Technology, Theory and Design for Multiple and Group Activities

Understanding Task Grouping Strategies

Peter J Wild, Peter Johnson & Hilary Johnson

Department of Computer Science, University of Bath,
Bath BA2 7AY, UK.

Tel: *+44 1225 386811*

Email: *{P.J.A.Wild, P.Johnson, H.Johnson}@bath.ac.uk*

This paper's concern is with the exploration of one aspect of multitasking, namely the grouping of tasks. Our own studies reported in brief within this paper and related work suggests that groupings of tasks are both possible, desirable, and occur. These grouping are behaviours that support the creation of 'sets of tasks' by some form of commonality. This commonality may refer to the tool or transformation or to facets of context such as locations or participants. In line with the assertion that task structure is a joint reflection of how a task is represented in memory and how a task is carried out in the world this paper seeks to understand the wider ramifications of such task / subtask groupings. We outline two case studies that provide supporting evidence of task groupings. From this we extract four forms of grouping that are scoped in relations to locations, deadlines, participants and roles.

Keywords: tasks, task grouping, task knowledge structures, strategies, non-obligatory goals.

1 Introduction

It is widely accepted that changes in technology, work practices and the general socio-economic environment affect the way we plan and perform tasks. A full listing of such changes is beyond this paper's scope, but examples include: the convergence of media forms in one electronic workspace; support for specialist tasks by generalists; knowledge and service work that is less constrained by the physical environment; and advances in computer power. Overall, support, opportunity and pressure for people to 'multitask' has increased. Despite rapid advances in technology, and increasing dynamics in groups and organizations, human abilities have not changed as quickly. Our capacity to deal with multiple goals and streams of information has not increased and we need to find ways of analysing and designing for these contexts. As is often the case in HCI, theory lags technological and other advances. Deeper insights into how people interleave elements across different tasks and contexts have not informed the array of technological support for such phenomena. Some work has moved us towards an understanding of multiple tasks [Cypher 1986; Smith et al. 1997]. However, the work is either fragmented or has failed to permeate into mainstream user / task / activity analysis methods.

This paper's concern is with the task structure implications of multiple tasks, although it is grounded in a wider investigation of multiple tasks. More specifically, its concern is with how sets of tasks are grouped in a manner that balances: the goals of the individual tasks; higher-level goals; against the resources and opportunities in the task environment. Our own studies, reported in brief in this paper, and related work [Smith et al. 1997], suggest that such groupings of tasks and subtasks are both possible, desirable, and occur. These groupings are behaviours that support the creation of a set of tasks based on some of some form of commonality. The commonality can refers facets of context, such as roles, deadlines, location and participants. Following from the assertion that task structure is a joint reflection of how the human cognitive system represents task knowledge and how the task is carried out in the world [Johnson et al. 2000], this paper explores the ramifications of such task groupings.

The paper continues in Section 2 by discussing structure in tasks and reviewing the theory driven approach to task analysis, Task Knowledge Structures (TKS). We move on to introduce the background and derivation of four candidate task grouping strategies (Section 3). Section 4 elaborates and discusses the candidate groupings in more detail and includes a discussion of factors that prevent groupings from being formed. Section 5 concerns itself with the implications of this work for Task Knowledge Structures. Section 6 concludes the paper and outlines future work.

2 Structure in Tasks: Task Knowledge Structures

There are a number of 'theories of task' ranging from the ethnographically informed GTA [van der Veer et al. 1996] to the execution duration orientation of GOMS [Card et al. 1983]. The primitives in each approach vary, but they all assume that a task has some form of analysable structure, that reoccurs across performers and instances of a task.

One approach to task analysis that has considered task structure in depth is Task Knowledge Structures (TKS) [Johnson et al. 2000]. TKS is a theory-based approach to the design of interactive systems. It draws on various knowledge elicitation techniques[1] to create a representation of task knowledge that is considered functionally equivalent to a user's task knowledge. TKS holds that goal / subgoal ordering is not random and that it reflects structuring principles [Johnson et al. 2000].

The theoretical basis of TKS draws on parsimonious evidence from theories of knowledge representation and direct empirical evidence from working with TKS. TKS theory holds that a TKS is a conceptual representation held in long-term memory

---

[1]The main ones used are: structured interviews, text and document analysis, observations, card sorting, and where appropriate the analyst performing the task.

and processed in working memory during task performance. As such a TKS is a reflection of two concerns. The first is how the human cognitive system represents and processes conceptual knowledge about tasks. The second is the way the task is achieved in the world, i.e. what goals are held towards the world, what opportunities exist and what constraints stand in the task's way. A TKS of a task will include information about the goals and subgoals, task-objects, actions, procedures, pre- and post-conditions strategies, the relationships between tasks and roles, as well as the centrality and representativeness of task elements[2].

In TKS theory tasks are concepts [Margolis & Laurence 1999] comprised of related components of knowledge. The relationships between the task components dictates how a task is structured, understood, organized and executed. The relationships include sharing of attributes, features or functions (thus making them similar in some way), part-whole and class-instance, relationships. These relationships are not assumed to be absolute and in most cases reflect the opportunities and constraints in the environment [Medin et al. 1997].

Theoretical and empirical work developed two task-structuring principles which provide strong empirical evidence for structure in tasks. The *categorical structuring* principle dictates that those task components that are semantically related are grouped together. This then results in a grouping of actions on those components. The *procedural dependency* principle dictates the enabling, priming, temporal and cause-effect relationships between task activities that give rise to procedural dependencies. Evidence for these principles is most manifest in the work on the PRIDE project. Experimentation provided strong supporting evidence that users will impose their own task model upon interfaces that partially or fully fail to reflect that task structure. With a badly structured interface, errors and slower task execution are partly due to the need to translate the TKS of the task into an execution path. In contrast an interactive system that fully supported the TKS of a task by obeying the principles, resulted in higher measures of objective and subjective usability.

To date, research and practice with TKS has predominantly worked from a single user, single task perspective. However, TKS's concern with the structure of tasks and the increase in computer support and group and organizational pressure for multitasking has led to an interest in applying and extending TKS to, and in contexts where, multiple tasks are performed.

2.1 TKS and Multiple Tasks

TKS has made use of a subset of the LOTOS formalism for representing temporal relationships (e.g. serialization, choice, parallelism, interleaving, Markopoulos et al. [1997] within a task, but not the temporal relationships between a set of tasks. In contexts such as those reported in this paper and elsewhere [e.g. Cypher 1986; Johnson et al. 2001; Smith et al. 1997] as well as multiple tasks, there are multiple roles, goals, pre- and post-conditions, task-objects, tools, and participants to consider. As we move beyond the single user single task perspective we note that a person may have a set of tasks whose interrelationships are more complex than the

---

[2]TKS has been applied to domains such as radiography, architectural design, and flight decks and used in cooperation with a range of interactive system development methods, including scenarios, structured design, object oriented design, OMT, UML and formal specification languages.

within and between role relationships currently modelled by TKS. Even with a set of tasks that are instances of the same class (e.g. writing a document) the priorities and deadlines that lie behind a task's performance may differ, for example writing a grant application maybe more important than updating a resume. In some domains, the order of a set of tasks may be mutable, particularly in domains that are strongly shaped by intentional, social and organizational forces.

We can also see that groupings of tasks and subtasks are both possible, desirable, and occur. The groupings can be dynamically formed in relation to the environment, or more formally planned and socially constructed. Examples of the former are grouping tasks by their location or participant. Examples of the latter are meetings that group together participants and tasks. The presence of multiple tasks entails accounting for phenomena such as task switching, suspension, interruptions and in the context of this paper, the creation of groupings of tasks. Our concern is with being able to describe, analyse, model and comprehend the structure of both the individual tasks and any groupings of tasks that occur in task planning and performance.

2.2   TKS and Strategies

In TKS strategies are configurations of behaviour that people develop to cope with constraints, requirements and opportunities in their environment. An example is the strategy Hourizi & Johnson [2001] discovered in pilot to co-pilot, and pilot to air traffic control operator in flight deck systems. A design based on this strategy was shown to significantly reduce the errors in performance of specific scenarios with the automated flight controller unit.

A key part of the characterization of strategies is that although goal driven, they are non-obligatory behaviours [Bhavnani & John 1997], the goals of the specific task goals can be achieved without their use. Their use entails that decisions be made about the use of resources in the environment, that are not immediately essential to the task. Our concern differs from Bhavnani & John [1997] in one major way. Our concern is with strategies that apply across sets of tasks, rather than with the 'low level' within-task strategies explored by Bhavnani & John [1997].

3   Derivation and Overview of the Task Grouping Strategies

Smith et al. [1997] provided several planning heuristics, two of which indicate that aspects of a set of tasks can be merged, either through the creation of composite objects that support multiple goals, or through grouping task elements by the commonality of task behaviours.

We also assume that people are capable of making groupings out of a set of tasks and we assume that the *context of task execution* has an impact on the forms of grouping that are made.

Informal evidence backs up the view that task groupings are in existence. A common example is a group of tasks whose main relationship is that they are all performed within, outside or near to a specific location. A specific example would be a person making themselves a refreshment, whist attending to 'personal needs', and picking up and dropping off their post. Another example are those people who batch a number of instances of the same task and perform them together. Photocopying, printing, searching for references, reading research papers or dealing with emails are all examples of groupings that can be informally observed in everyday task performance.

If we extrapolate from TKS's concern with the sharing of attributes, features and functions, we can argue that groupings such as these may be represented as strategies whose concern is to relate tasks based on features. The two examples given previously suggest relationships based on locational, and class-instance features. The behaviours that remain goal directed, both in relation to the goals of each individual task and the goal behind the grouping strategy (e.g. save time, minimize interruption), but are non-obligatory in that the individual tasks will not fail if they are not followed.

3.1 Overview of the Case Studies

Sections 3.2 and 3.3 provide more overviews of the two studies relevant to this paper. This subsection is concerned with outlining the rationale behind the studies.

Our starting point for the studies was a general exploratory investigation into multiple task phenomena. Our main concern was to study real world task performers undertaking multiple tasks in the contexts of multiple; tasks, roles, tools, task-objects, and goals with the attendant facets of the world such as events, interruptions, breakdowns and exceptions. The studies were part of a more general investigation in multitasking. As such task groupings were not explicitly sought by the studies, they are based on evidence and inference from the studies. Within the studies our wish was to be able to focus upon the minute-by-minute detail of a task performer and trace the longer-term aspects of multiple tasks within a larger set of tasks or defined processes. Constraints on the research process surrounded having consent to video tape the subject in order to gain a record of minute by minute behaviour, and the willingness to talk about the longer term task performance. We were able to gain consent to generate video data with one person and consent for longer-term access with another.

When we consider the studies in the light of multiple task phenomena, the research question driving this paper is:

- Are there task-structuring mechanisms that govern how a person plans and interleaves the execution of a set of similar or dissimilar tasks in their environment?

Corollaries to this question include:

C1. When are such groupings used, what are the costs and benefits associated with them?

C2. When a grouping is possible why is it not undertaken?

C3. What further theoretical constructs are needed to provide explanatory accounts of the grouping strategies?

Grouping by	Example	Data source
Deadline	Two tasks with hard and soft deadlines were performed as soon as possible.	Task order, verbal statement.
Tool	Reading of emails, writing of emails.	Explicit actions with tools, verbal statement.
Location	A number of tasks that needed to be performed outside of the office were grouped together.	Explicit gathering tools and artefacts that met the pre-conditions of the group of tasks.
Participant	A number of tasks were grouped in relation to a specific participant, whose help was needed for all the tasks.	Verbal statement.
Role	The subject cleared time for one role (research) and allocated time in her diary to focus on another role (teaching).	Explicit planning and verbal statement.
Transformation	A number of documents were placed together to be photocopied at a later time. A notable exception to this was a document considered personal and private that was copied separately.	Verbal statement.

Table 1: Candidate groupings of tasks.

3.2   Pilot Case Study

The pilot study reported here is a detailed analysis of a video recording of an hour long slice of a researcher performing a number of tasks [Wild et al. 2003c]. The researcher's role was participant observer and where necessary conversed with the subject about relevant tasks. The main source of data was the video recording, however the participant observer also had relevant background knowledge. The analysis of the video recording started with the production of complete time annotated transcript. The next phase was to examine the physical actions which led to the addition of contextual information such as artefacts and tools used as well as locations and participants. A first pass attempt describes and defines the tasks that were planned, attempted and undertaken. In turn this was presented to the participant for feedback and criticism.

The participant in question was a researcher with additional teaching duties. A key motivation was to create a block of undisturbed time in order to focus on her own project's research analysis. Furthermore, as a new staff member, she faced questions along the lines of 'how do I?' and 'where is?' The participant had 6 main roles which generated attempts to plan and execute 17 distinct tasks during the observed period. The participant was the explicit recipient of 5 interruptions by other agents. She also interrupted her own task performance on 9 occasions and she interrupted other people 14 times. These interruptions and other events meant that task suspension and switching / interleaving was common. In terms of the wider environment the

Object	Attributes
UCAS day	(date, time, start, location, expected applicants [list], expected accompanying persons [list], day_schedule (tours), SV_timetable, APP_timetable, exceptional interviews).
Course Intake	(students, expected_grades | achieved_ grades, start dates, and course).

Table 2: Objects and attributes from the UCAS day study.

Task phase	Central tasks
Phase 1: Applicant Processing.	Central tasks include, logging, choosing and sending offers to applicants.
Phase 2: UCAS day planning.	(Central tasks include, picking dates, booking rooms and catering, notifying participants).
Phase 3: UCAS day execution.	Central tasks include, setting up the room, registering the applicants.
Phase 4: UCAS day follow up.	The central task being to inform the student of the admissions tutors.

Table 3: Tasks and task phases within the UCAS study.

participant interacted with 16 different participants (35 cumulatively). Over the hour, tasks and interactions took place in 8 different locations excluding traversed corridors.[3] Much of this data is interesting in its own right [Wild et al. 2003a,c], but from the perspective of this paper we were able to identify a number of candidate groupings of tasks, presented in Table 1.

3.3   Case Study Two

Our second study was a longer term study of the planning and execution of administrating undergraduate applications (commonly referred to as UCAS). One of the UCAS day sessions was observed, and this was combined with email and document analysis and a number of informal interviews. The interviews were undertaken to both understand the tasks, clarify our understanding of the tasks and to 'test' interim task representations.

The main participant in the study was a secretary whose three roles were, undergraduate and postgraduate admissions secretary, and being a member of the general office support team. Each of these roles had a different line manager.

The UCAS tasks can be seen as the creation of two types of abstract object described in Table 2, and can be divided into four phases described in Table 3.

As well as having several UCAS days there are multiple applicants. A single applicant is never dealt with within a single time period, due to natural breaks [Smith et al. 1997] in the task of processing a single applicant. Throughout the processing there was batching of a number of activities (e.g. logging applicants) relating to

[3]Other interesting features are reported elsewhere [Wild et al. 2003a,c], namely constant re-planning, switching and suspension of tasks, alternative execution strategies and the nature of the interruptions.

around 30 applicants at a time. Because there are multiple UCAS day instances and multiple applicants there are several instances being created at any one time. In theory each applicant could attend any one of the eight UCAS days. This potential for chaos, is reigned in by initially offering candidates two dates to choose from and then dealing with exceptions.

The UCAS process also has a number of immutable deadlines set by an outside agency. To enable reporting of activities with accuracy about progress, organizational and personal deadlines are set which provide further constraints on the tasks being performed.

Overall, the tasks for each specific UCAS day temporally overlap and elements interact. There are many interesting features within this case study that are reported elsewhere [Wild et al. 2003b], including the non-negotiated delegation of tasks, how events and instances relate, and the need to distinguish generic, instance and repeated tasks. And whilst much of this data is interesting in its own right what we highlight from this study within this paper are a number of observed task groupings and observations about them:

- Grouping by role. Throughout the process, tasks that could have been grouped by other criteria were overridden by the priority and deadlines generated from a specific role.

- Grouping by deadline. Of the weekly set of tasks that the administrative assistant was responsible for a number were grouped by the deadline they most related to.

Overall in this case, groupings of tasks occurred less often, and were less dynamically formed. Furthermore, reporting requirements such as the need to report to the manager on task progress and deadlines, such as the need to pass on batches of applicants on time, provide major shaping forces for the tasks carried out.

3.4   Interim Conclusions and Candidate Groupings

There are commonalities in the nature and findings of the two case studies. They both studied people with multiple roles and tasks, had some form of layering of goals that motivated general task performance above and beyond the immediate goal of the tasks in hand. There were also several task groupings observed.

From the two case studies four candidate grouping strategies are suggested:

- Grouping by deadline. For example when several urgent tasks must be completed before a specific time, regardless of whether there are any formal relationships between them.

- Grouping by location. For example when a number of tasks are grouped by the proximity of the locations they are carried out in.

- Grouping by participant. For example when a number of tasks are grouped by the need to involve another participant in their planning or performance.

- Grouping by role. Tasks that relate to a specific role are grouped.

It is important to note that grouping by tool and transformation was dropped from consideration because conceptually it was considered difficult to distinguish groupings from each other. Furthermore, grouping by tool appears too frequently and in too coarse grain a manner to be useful. Both studies suggest that groupings are not an all or nothing phenomena, sometimes groupings will occur, but it is as important to consider how aspects of context of a task performer affect whether they actually occur. In line with the view that strategies are non-obligatory [Bhavnani & John 1997], we suggest that within TKS modelling of multiple tasks, the use of strategies to represent task groupings captures their goal-directed and non-obligatory nature.

4 Discussion of the Candidate Task Grouping Strategies

Overall we have four candidates for grouping strategies: Grouping by deadline, location, participant, and role. This section discusses these grouping strategies in more detail, providing examples from our case studies, everyday life and emphasizes the costs and benefits for the application and non-application of the strategies.

4.1 Grouping by Deadline

Deadlines along with many temporal issues relevant to the modelling of tasks are neglected by HCI. To understand more about the implications of grouping by deadlines, it is important to consider deadlines in general.

A deadline is a temporal feature that implies some form of cut-off time or date to indicate the end of, or start of tasks. Deadlines can be seen as hard or soft [Lee 1999]. Hard deadlines may reflect physical properties of the task domain such as reaction times in chemical processes. Or they reflect constraints imposed socially / organizationally to impose order onto a task environment. Missing such hard deadlines will result in some form of task failure, in physically based processes this could be disastrous. In socially or organizationally oriented tasks this could be politically embarrassing, or result in legal / financial reprimands. Soft deadlines, are less likely to reflect physical constraints and reflect personal, social or organizational priorities and values. Deadlines are set in different ways. If they are set internally, by the person, group or organization, they relate more to the entity's overall motivation, priorities and values. When set by external bodies, deadlines are much more of a constraint in the environment that needs to be considered in the longer term planning and execution of tasks. Both sorts influence the planning and execution of tasks.

A benefit of deadlines is that their setting and attainment enables state monitoring — an important facet of project management. They also serve as a motivational factor in tasks. Another benefit is to stop an endless or open-ended task, in effect by saying that in this time slot we can only do so much. Deadlines also serve to demarcate the start of subsequent activities, setting a deadline for paper submission enables paper reviewing to start, and in turn setting a deadline for reviews to come back enables programme selection.

Instances of this grouping are present within the two case studies. In the pilot study the subject had two deadlines. One hard, the booking of AV and one soft, the passing on of information to a colleague that shaped the execution order of her set of tasks. Within the UCAS case study there are numerous hard and soft deadlines. The hard deadlines are set externally by the UCAS organization and the university as a whole. These are in addition to softer deadlines set by the secretary in order to manage her time and be able to report to her manager the status of the task.

4.2   Grouping by Location

Location serves as one physical aspect of context, serving as both a 'container' for contexts, and as a factor in how tasks are grouped. At some level of description all tasks are undertaken in a location. Some locations are intrinsic to a task and its context, through the near permanent location of artefacts (desks, photocopiers, printers), work areas (wards, surgeries, meeting rooms), and social areas (e.g. reception area, private office, tea room).

Within the pilot study we saw a grouping of a number of tasks whose main grouping criteria is deemed to be those tasks that involve participants, resources, activities, that are located outside of the office. This was inferred from the implicit order of the tasks and from the gathering of tools and artefacts that were relevant to the grouping (e.g. diary task, to-do-list, security card). This form of grouping serves to save one resource, the repetitious movement of a person in their environment against other factors. Two key issues that are traded off by this grouping strategy are the costs of making alternative trips to the same location verses the availability of the resources needed for the set of tasks. In the former case, the benefit is the reduction in the number of journeys. In the latter case either the costs of setting up the grouping, or the costs of executing all the tasks in a given location, are higher than is considered acceptable. A third option is to plan the trips in relation to other tasks so that whilst the multiple journeys are made they provide a break to the main ongoing task.

In the second case study, the secretary will make multiple journeys to the same location in order to execute subtasks to meet soft deadlines. Whilst an alternative groupings of tasks could be undertaken, the overall groupings of tasks reflected roles and deadlines.

4.3   Grouping by Participant

The need to interact with another participant for a number of tasks can result in a grouping of tasks that involve that participant. There are two examples of this form of grouping within the two case studies. In the pilot one such grouping was planned, and is evidenced in explicit verbal statements, but not undertaken due to the absence of the participant. The UCAS days were planned and structured to bring together a number of different participants in different roles (applicants, parents, admissions tutor, UCAS administration assistant, lecturers, current and past students) together during the same time period. As such it can be seen as an pre-planned and refined grouping by participant.

In the first case the major trade off here is between the number of interruptions to the participant focused on in such a grouping strategy, against the costs incurred to the person making the grouping. It can be that interruption costs are minimized for both participants if this grouping strategy is used, rather than either participant going back and forth, all the tasks can be progressed within one meeting or exchange. However, the set up and execution costs of planning for a grouping such as this are potentially higher. As well as the individual pre-conditions of each task the grouping may impose resource costs of its own. The interaction between participants can refer to different tasks. A mental note to do several tasks with a particular participant may be obscured by the fine detail of each task. Reminders such as to-do-lists, diaries etc., may help ameliorate this phenomena.

A common example, when a person has to talk to an administrator, they may group a number of tasks that relate to their role(s). This pattern can be formalized through regular meetings such as those between managers and personal assistants.

Meetings with multiple participants have refined conventions and structures that support and order interaction in relation to a set of tasks, an agenda serves as an example. In this second example a potential cost is that interaction may fragment into concern with tasks that may be a benefit for the group as a whole, reducing the cost effectiveness of the meeting's set up costs.

Artefacts such as email and voice mail messages, notes, and letters enable an alternative version of this grouping. One instance of these artefacts can serve to exchange information about a range of unrelated tasks in one message. Although the immediacy, pace and opportunism of such artefacts will be different.

4.4   Grouping by Role

TKS's role construct provides a modelling concept that maps between the tasks performed and the wider organizational context. Roles reflect commitments and task responsibilities in relation to the environment around the role holder. They entail issues such as reporting and supervision. As we move into contexts where multiple tasks are present, multiple roles are an obvious phenomena to account for. In both the pilot and the follow up study each participant had many roles. And in general role strain has been identified as a contemporary issue in HCI [Beyer & Holtzblatt 1998].

Within the case study we see several examples. In the pilot study the subject was observed explicitly allocating time to a teaching role, and as mentioned a motivation behind the tasks being formed was to clear time to focus exclusively on her research. Within the second case study the secretary's attention to roles helped to shape the ordering and execution of tasks.

With multiple roles it is likely that different roles will differ in priority. Tasks within a high priority role maybe grouped (e.g. research day), or placed in time periods when interruptions are minimized. This is an example seen within study one, with the researchers overall motivation is to create a block of time where little should impinge on the high priority task of research analysis. It can also affect the opportunity to undertake other grouping strategies through the generation of deadlines.

Roles may also have specific durations, for example chairing a conference. Roles may also be mutually exclusive. Two forms of mutual exclusion can be identified, the first is generic and applies to contexts such as legal representation. People maybe able to perform as a judge, defence, or prosecution but not all three. The second form is specific and would refer to how the roles of paper writer and reviewer cannot be held by the same person in reference to a specific paper written by them.

4.5   Breaking Down Task Groupings

Corollary 2 of the main research question was "When a grouping is possible, why is it not undertaken?" It is therefore important to consider factors in the environment that can unpick these groupings. Two interrelated factors in the environment seem to help prevent the utility of grouping tasks. These are deadlines, and reporting requirements.

The presence of deadlines can act to prevent groupings from being effective strategies. For example, it would be pointless to group a set of documents to photocopy for later in the week when two of the documents need to be sent off within hours.

Reporting requirements relate to the ability to report to other participants — especially managers — the status of tasks. The reason for the deadlines in case one was to enable a colleague to report more effectively in a meeting the following week. The issue of reporting requirements is most manifest in the UCAS study: There are three roles, three different managers and a host of information and tasks to track, coordinate, distribute, delegate and report on. The ability and willingness to report on the status of a task are important. In study two tasks are performed in manner that trades off the 'travel resource' against the definitive completion of tasks.

5   Implications For Task Knowledge Structures

Awareness of grouping strategies provides further primitives with which to understand the structure and context of work and are therefore something for TKS to model when being extended to cover multiple tasks.

When considering the implications for a theory driven approach like TKS, there are two relevant issues:

1. What current concepts within TKS needed highlighting or revising?

2. What further theoretical constructs are needed to provide explanatory accounts of grouping strategies?

With regards to the first question we focus on pre- and post-conditions and roles. Pre- and post-conditions are often represented in the goal hierarchy of TKS models of tasks. In the context of multiple tasks there is a need for greater explication of pre- and post-conditions, because groupings increase the salience that they take on. There is no longer just one set of pre- and post-conditions activated during task performance. There is now a set of pre-conditions for the individual tasks in the grouping plus any conditions that have to be met for the grouping to be successful. The need to construct and maintain this set in dynamic and ad-hoc contexts has mental resource implications.

The role construct in TKS, provides a modelling concept that maps between the tasks performed and the wider organizational context[4]. Roles reflect commitments and task responsibilities in relation to the environment around the role holder. GTA [van der Veer et al. 1996] introduced the agent concept and is a useful addition to

---

[4]Its influence can be seen in similar constructs being included in GTA [van der Veer et al. 1996] and Contextual Design [Beyer & Holtzblatt 1998].

the modelling of tasks However, the notions of agency and interaction with roles are issues that need deeper consideration before being adopted within HCI. Sometimes participants will interact according to roles and sometimes by the specific agent. It is likely that this will affect what groupings of tasks are considered appropriate.

When we consider the extension of TKS, one of the main considerations for TKS is the notion of competing and overlapping goals. It is clear that just as knowledge exists at different levels, goals exist at a number of levels. Goals can differ in how abstract-concrete, general-specific or high-low level they might be. For example, when looking for a very recent and relevant journal paper that can be accessed via the Web, several goals might simultaneously be active. One goal might be to become familiar with searching the Web in general, and for journal papers in particular. Another goal could be to cause a co-author surprise in how up-to-date one is with relevant journal articles. Another goal is to contribute to the joint paper that is being written. Yet a further goal might be to receive the information before lunchtime and without trekking in the rain to the library. All of these goals are different, either in terms of their generality or specificity, some have social implications and contribute to joint work, others relate to resource limitations.

Goals can be classified as compatible or incompatible. Compatible goals can be pursued in parallel. Incompatible goals cannot be pursued in parallel but would involve some form of interleaving. Goals at different levels of abstraction can occur in parallel and are therefore another kind of compatible goal.

In general we recommend that during the analysis of the task domain and task performers the elicitation of priorities and values, role complements and conflicts is made more prominent when we consider how tasks relate to each other. This should shed insight into what the higher level goals a person has when they approach a set of tasks, potentially leading to grounded qualitative predictions about what grouping strategies they use in the planning and executing of tasks.

When we consider deadlines, we note that TKS has a rich set of temporal operators for describing and scoping the temporal relationships between subgoals [Markopoulos et al. 1997]. But as it stands TKS models represent time in a relative sense. They are not embedded in time as experience by people, whether subjectively or culturally. Deadlines are seen to be a shaping force, both within this paper and elsewhere [Lee 1999] and other temporal issues such as natural breaks need to be accounted for in the extended version of TKS.

When we consider TKS and location we note that location has been used implicitly in the use of scenarios. However locational issues need to be highlighted when modelling tasks. Our work shows that location can be used explicitly in the planning and ordering of tasks. Whilst this may be appropriate in designing support for say, planning tools, deeper insights from how people use locations, space and place [e.g. Harrison & Dourish 1996] will inform future developments within TKS.

5.1 *Reflecting or Shaping the Environment: Context vs. Categories*

In HCI the environment is often an ill defined notion. We see broad appeals to notions of situation or context, but little systematic attempts to elucidate what this means. Those that attempt to scope the discipline and environment of HCI [e.g. Dowell & Long 1998], are criticized for missing vital social elements of the task environment

[Green 1998]. In the discussion so far, we have noted that as well as the traditional elements on a TKS of a task (e.g. roles, goals, task-objects, actions) there are other facets of context that we need to consider in greater detail (i.e. deadlines, locations, and participants). However, we cannot provide a simplistic listing of these factors in an extended TKS approach. Some work in situations and context sets the scene for aspects of context [e.g. Harrison & Dourish 1996; Lee 1999], but does not contain any detailed notion of tasks and their structure. In other approaches tasks are reduced to some form of simplistic process model or as opportunistic reaction to complexity of environments. Whilst it may be possible to elucidate a model of context that is both broad and useful, subtle issues arise. One question that can be framed is whether an entity or property is part of the environment that a task is executed in, or part of the conceptual representation that drives a task. Palmer [1978] talks of representing worlds, such as the knowledge we hold in the mind and represented worlds, that is the environment that is being represented. Both the representing and represented worlds are dynamic and the interplay between them is one source of the complexity of cognition. For example sometimes an environmental factor (e.g. location) is a resource, used and traded of against other resources, sometimes a key facet of the task, and sometimes it is just an necessary, but unused aspect of context. Overall, as humans we are as much imposing a structure onto the environment as having to reflect the environment in our conceptual representations of the world. Strategies such as those presented within this paper are an example of the way this interplay between representing and represented worlds occurs.

5.2 Resources, Costs and Task Qualities

Colloquially resources refer to the means that are used when doing something. Resources are important because they are expended and conserved by people performing tasks. With reference to quality we are all familiar with management never ending quests for ISO quality. Quality, can also relate to many contemporary aspects of cognitive, social and organizational structures. More specifically within HCI we see the traditional measures of quality such as ease of learning, low number of errors and with growing interest in the quality of user experience [Preece et al. 2002].

Such notions are often used explicitly [Smith et al. 1997; Wright et al. 2000] and implicitly [Preece et al. 2002] in the literature. To date little work has attempted to elucidate resources, costs and task quality. Our discussion in Section 4 made informal reference to resources. But if task grouping strategies are non-obligatory and composed and chosen in relation to the costs and benefits, more precise use of the terms needs to be made. We are now working towards a characterization of such issues. This attempts to list common resources and task quality measures; their properties and how they relate to tasks in general, groupings in multiple tasks, and the collaborative aspects of task performance.

6   Conclusions and Future Work

We began with the observation that there is little support for multitasking, and observing that task groupings are both possible, desirable, and occur. We reported an interim analysis of two case studies that provide further evidence that groupings of tasks occur. These groupings have functional value in ensuring acceptable levels of task quality and recourse utilization, but are not essential. Rather they are strategies that are focused around the use of context in a broader sense than TKS has considered in the past.

We are keenly aware that grouping strategies are a small part of the multiple task phenomena [Wild et al. 2003a,b,c]. Included for consideration in wider discourse should be issues such as interruptions, suspension of tasks and participating in task performances with others. Nevertheless task groupings occur and have salience, being evidenced within our studies, everyday life and other HCI frameworks [Smith et al. 1997].

As we move away from examining the structure of single tasks we move into an area where, because of non-obligatory goals, tracing both the existence and implications of task groupings are difficult. It is important to be able to form explanatory accounts that are not bound to simple or surface factors of context. For example, all tasks occur in a location and in theory we could claim that everything we do is grouping by location. Similarly collaborative and cooperative activities will always involve participants. We caution against over-zealous use of the concept of grouping strategy.

With all this in mind, our current work centres around several issues. The first is further observation of these and related multiple task phenomena. The second is providing deeper explanatory accounts of the phenomena from the case studies to enable the development of something more than yet another set of design heuristics about groupings. We are also undertaking design efforts as a way, of gaining further insight. Prototype development of an interactive system that supports a number of these grouping phenomena and others (constant re-planning, interruptions, multiple execution choices, switching and suspension of tasks) is being undertaken. Feedback from these efforts will provide further insight into the way people multitask. It has also been suggested that the time management literature [Hall & Hursch 1982] may provide further insights and explanations about task ordering and grouping. And this will compose another strand in our future work.

Acknowledgements

This work is supported by EPSRC grant number GR/M97305/0. Heartfelt thanks are given to the participants in the two studies for their time and feedback. Useful and interesting comments have been made by the reviewers. We have attempted to address some of them in the paper, and address others in future work. We thank them for asking us to clarify our ideas and basis for interpretation.

References

Beyer, H. & Holtzblatt, K. [1998], *Contextual Design: Defining Customer-centered Systems*, Morgan-Kaufmann.

Bhavnani, S. K. & John, B. E. [1997], From Sufficient to Efficient Usage, *in* S. Pemberton (ed.), *Proceedings of the CHI'97 Conference on Human Factors in Computing Systems*, ACM Press, pp.91–8.

Card, S. K., Moran, T. P. & Newell, A. [1983], *The Psychology of Human–Computer Interaction*, Lawrence Erlbaum Associates.

Cypher, A. [1986], The Structure of Users' Activities, *in* D. A. Norman & S. W. Draper (eds.), *User Centered System Design: New Perspectives on Human–Computer Interaction*, Lawrence Erlbaum Associates, pp.243–63.

Dowell, J. & Long, J. B. [1998], Conception of the Cognitive Engineering Design Problem, *Ergonomics* **41**(2), 126–39.

Green, T. R. G. [1998], The Conception of a Conception, *Ergonomics* **41**(2), 143–6.

Hall, B. L. & Hursch, D. E. [1982], An Evaluation of the Effects of a Time Management Training Program on Work Efficiency, *Journal of Organisational Behaviour Management* **3**(4), 73–96.

Harrison, R. & Dourish, P. [1996], Re-Place-ing Space: The Roles of Place and Space in Collaborative Systems, *in* G. Olson, J. Olson & M. S. Ackerman (eds.), *Proceedings of 1996: ACM Conference on Computer Supported Cooperative Work (CSCW'96)*, ACM Press, pp.67–76.

Hourizi, R. & Johnson, P. [2001], Beyond Mode Error, *in* A. Blandford, J. Vanderdonckt & P. Gray (eds.), *People and Computers XV: Interaction without Frontiers (Joint Proceedings of HCI2001 and IHM2001)*, Springer-Verlag, pp.229–46.

Johnson, H., Wild, P. J., Johnson, P., May, J. & Gamble, T. [2001], Notes for the Workshop on 'Modelling Multiple and Collaborative Tasks' held at HCI'01.

Johnson, P., Johnson, H. & Hamilton, F. [2000], Getting the Knowledge into HCI — Theoretical and Practical Aspects of Task Knowledge Structures, *in* J. M. Schraagen, S. F. Chirman & V. L. Shaun (eds.), *Cognitive Task Analysis*, Lawrence Erlbaum Associates, pp.201–14.

Lee, H. [1999], Time and Information Technology, *European Journal of Information Systems* **8**(1), 16–26.

Margolis, E. & Laurence, S. [1999], *Concepts*, MIT Press.

Markopoulos, P., Johnson, P., & Rowson, J. [1997], Formal Aspects of Task-based Design, *in* M. Harrison & J. Torres (eds.), *Design, Specification and Verification of Interactive Systems'97*, Springer-Verlag, pp.209–24.

Medin, D. L., Lynch, E. B., Coley, J. D. & Atran, S. [1997], Categorization and Reasoning Among Tree Experts, *Cognitive Psychology* **32**(3), 49–96.

Palmer, S. E. [1978], Fundamental Aspects of Cognitive Representations, *in* E. Rosch & B. B. Lloyd (eds.), *Cognition and Categorisation*, Lawrence Erlbaum Associates, pp.259–303.

Preece, J., Rogers, Y. & Sharp, H. (eds.) [2002], *Interaction Design: Beyond Human–Computer Interaction*, John Wiley & Sons.

Smith, W., Hill, B., Long, J. B. & Whitefield, A. [1997], A Design-Oriented Framework for Modelling the Planning and Control of Multiple Task Work in Secretarial Office Administration, *Behaviour & Information Technology* **16**(3), 161–83.

van der Veer, G. C., Lenting, B. F. & Bergevoet, B. A. J. [1996], GTA: Groupware Task Analysis — Modeling Complexity, *Acta Psychologica* **91**(3), 297–322.

Wild, P. J., Johnson, H. & Johnson, P. [2003a], An Hour in the Life: Data and Analysis of a Pilot in Multiple Tasks, Technical Report TICKS/TKS/EMP/1, University of Bath.

Wild, P. J., Johnson, H. & Johnson, P. [2003b], People, Places and Deadlines: Data and Analysis of a Case Study in Multiple Tasks, Technical Report TICKS/TKS/EMP/2, University of Bath.

Wild, P. J., Johnson, P. & Johnson, H. [2003c], An Hour In The Life: Generating Requirements for Modelling Multiple Task Work, *in* G. Cockton & P. Korhonen (eds.), *CHI'03 Extended Abstracts of the Conference on Human Factors in Computing Systems*, ACM Press, pp.1016–7.

Wright, P. C., Fields, R. E. & Harrison, M. D. [2000], Analysing Human–Computer Interaction as Distributed Cognition: The Resources Model, *Human–Computer Interaction* **15**(1), 1–41.

Two Phenomenological Studies of Place

Phil Turner & Susan Turner

HCI Research Group, School of Computing, Napier University, Edinburgh EH10 5DT, UK

Email: *{p.turner, s.turner}@napier.ac.uk*

We introduce our initial investigations into the phenomenology of place as part of the BENOGO project. BENOGO is concerned with giving people the experience of 'being there without going there'. Employing a state-of-the-art mixture of photorealistic, real-time rendered images, three-dimensional soundscapes and augmented reality to create a sense of place. The work reported in this paper we describe as 'benchmarking', that is, establishing how people experience and describe places in the real world. We then will be able to compare the BENOGO experience with these benchmarks. This approach should be seen to be more naturalistic and relevant than the use of post hoc presence questionnaires.

Keywords: virtual reality, place, language, phenomenology.

1 Introduction

Phenomenological studies of place may, at first sight, seem a little unconnected with human-computer interaction. However, as we hope to demonstrate, they are not. As virtual reality (VR) technology matures then the design of its application, as distinct from it ability to solve computation problems become more important. One important aspect of the use of VR is to create a sense of place as distinct from an impression of three dimensional space alone. While the later is an 'external', coordinated based conception, the former is personal, subjective and filled with meaning. Harrison & Dourish [1996] have also distinguished between the two in the context of designing for collaboration. Space can be described and proscribed using geometry, place may, among other ways, be understood phenomenologically.

Dennett [1991] helpfully distinguishes between phenomenology (lower case p) which is the study of phenomena and Phenomenology (upper case p) refers to the philosophical schools of thought[1] of which there are a number. The former type of phenomenology is concerned with describing experiences as they appear in consciousness, without recourse to explanation, theory, or other assumptions. Phenomenology has a long history, Thomas Caxton in the 16th century wrote of the phenomenology of magnetism while this year will witness an academic conference on the phenomenology of particle physics. Caxton's work was pre- or atheoretic and remained that way until Maxwell and Cavendish developed a theory of magnetism. Similarly phenomenological psychology, for example, is concerned with the study of personal experience and subjective perception of phenomena rather than 'objective truths'. Dennett again usefully suggests that they could be divided or grouped into:

1. experiences of the 'external' world such as sights and sounds;

2. experiences of the 'internal' world such as daydreams, talking to oneself; and

3. affect — pains, hungers and emotional responses such as surprise or desire.

While these very different experiences could be divided and partitioned in a dozen different ways we can (probably) agree that they are direct (i.e. unmediated), subjective, personal and qualitative in nature.   Investigating place from a phenomenological perspective may provide the kind of rich, thickly descriptive accounts which are required to inform the design of virtual places. Indeed this is situation is similar to that of CSCW (computer supported cooperative work) and its use of ethnomethodology and like CSCW we are looking to language as a means to unlock these personal, subjective experiences. As Heidegger [1978] has noted "It is language that tells us about the nature of a thing ... ". In the same essay, Heidegger, demonstrates at great length, how language, the use of language and philology affords insights into the nature dwelling which he took to be central to the having a sense of place or being-there:

> "The Old English and High German word for building, buan, means to
> dwell. This signifies: to remain, to stay in a place. The real meaning
> of the verb bauen, namely, to dwell, has been lost to us. But a covert
> trace of it has been preserved in the German word Nachbar, neighbour.
> The neighbour is in Old English the neahgehur; neah, near, and gebur,
> dweller." [Heidegger 1978]

We use language to describe place, our experience of place [for example, Calvino 1997], place-less-ness [for example, Relph 1976] and what we did on our Summer holidays (see Section 4.3). But language is much more than just a descriptive tool as the work of cognitive scientists, philosophers of language and developmental psychologists have shown who have in their different ways convincingly argued that language may also affect our very cognition [for example,

---

[1]Phenomenology has two broad meanings, the first is concerned with describing experiences as they appear in consciousness, without recourse to explanation, theory, or other assumptions from other disciplines. Phenomenology also refers to a number of schools of philosophy studying the nature of being in a variety of different ways using a variety of different methods. For the purposes of this essay, we have concentrated on the former.

Clark 1997; Dennett 1991; Vygotsky 1978] among many. It may be that language may both constrain our description of place and our cognition (and/or experience) of that place, cf. the Whorf-Sapir hypothesis [Whorf 1956]. While this may be an unconscious inevitability of our everyday lives, it needs to be understood, quantified and qualified when we are faced with creating a sense of place using virtual reality (VR) technology.

The work reported here is part of the BENOGO project which is described in detail below in Section 3. The authors are part of a team tasked with understanding the experience (or phenomenology) of place by people using the BENOGO VR technology. The first part of this task we describe as *benchmarking*, that is, describing the experience / phenomenology of place in the real world which we will use as a benchmark or baseline against which we will compared the BENOGO experience. Given the timescale and constraints on the project we are carrying out this work in parallel with its technical development. At the outset of the project (indeed during the project proposal writing phase too) we decided to adopt an explicitly phenomenological perspective. While our reasons for doing so are varied they all centred on evaluating its usefulness as a potential foundation or theory upon which virtual reality / presence research might be stood.

We now move to consider these issues in more detail before briefly introducing the BENOGO project. After this we introduce our two empirical studies of language and place and conclude with a discussion of the consequences of this preliminary work for the project.

2 Three Senses of Place

Sense of place has been considered extensively in environmental psychology, sociology, geography, literary and media theory and almost certainly other domains. It is also an element of the concept of 'being-in-the-world' in phenomenological thought, for example Heidegger's extensive exploration of the verb 'to dwell'. This paper references three of the more recent and/or influential studies from environmental psychology and humanistic geography: a more extensive literature review of sense of place with relation to presence is continuing. It should be noted that much sense of place research centres on the experience and affect of long-term inhabitants of a place. The models cited here are selected as supporting more general application to the type of place experience which BENOGO may provide. However, it will be necessary to develop a model of visited, rather than dwelt-in place for BENOGO, and it is this aim that this pilot study addresses.

2.1 Relph's Model of Place Identity

Relph [1976] is much cited in the sense of place literature. Relph's key monograph takes an explicitly phenomenological and therefore holistic stance, but nevertheless defines three components of 'place identity':

- Physical setting.

- Activities afforded by the place.

- Meanings attributed to the place.

Relph describes his model as follows:

" ...the static physical setting, the activities and the meanings —
constitute the three basic elements of the identity of places.   A
moment's reflection suggests that this division, although obvious, is a
fundamental one. For example, it is possible to visualize a town as
consisting of buildings and physical objects, as is represented in air
photographs. A strictly objective observer of the activities of people
within this physical context would observe their movements much as
an entomologist observes ants, some moving in regular patterns, some
consuming objects and so on. But a person experiencing these buildings
and activities sees them as far more than this — they are beautiful or
ugly, useful or hindrances, home, factory, enjoyable, alienating; in short,
they are meaningful." [Relph 1976, p.47]

2.2   Gustafson's Tri-polar Model of Meanings of Place

This model [Gustafson 2001] draws on empirical work in the form of an interview
survey and builds on a review of earlier models. The poles of the model are listed
below — the contributing factors use Gustafson's terminology:

- Self — life-path, emotions, activities, self-identification.

- Environment — physical environment, distinctive features and events; type of
  place; localization).

- Others [i.e. other people] — perceived characteristics, traits behaviour.

Other factors such as social relations and atmosphere lie between the poles.

2.3   Sense of Place as Attitude: Jorgensen and Stedman's Proposition

Jorgensen & Stedman [2001] propose that the many interpretations of sense of place
could benefit from the treatment of sense of place as an attitude, thus drawing on
classical psychological theory. Just as any other attitude, sense of place then has
cognitive, affective and conative (behavioural) components. In this particular case,
these components are:

- Beliefs about the relationship between self and place.

- Feelings towards the place.

- Behavioural exclusivity of the place compared with alternatives.

A sense of place scale has been validated using these components with a large sample
of participants. However, the items rely on long-term familiarity with the place in
question. The empirical work discussed in the remainder of this paper uses Relph's
model of place identity to organize the reporting and discussion of findings. This has
the advantage of taking an explicitly phenomenological stance, in particular in the
prominence given to activity in relation to place.

From this brief survey of models of place we now supply a little context with
respect to the EU's 'Presence' initiative.

3 The BENOGO Project

BENOGO is a recently funded project under the European Community's Future and Emerging Technologies 'Presence' initiative. The BENOGO consortium comprises 6 academic institutions from Europe and Israel with expertise in virtual reality, photo-realistic panoramic image acquisition and rendering, the psycho-physics of visual sensing and spatial perception, and the human aspects of new technologies. This project brings together a mixture of novel technologies that will enable real-time visualization for an observer of recorded real places. The aim of the research is to develop new tools for empirical and theoretical studies of presence based on the concept of the observer's embodiment in the computationally created virtual environment. Furthermore, as real places (possibly known to the observer) with man-made and/or organic objects (like trees, foliage etc.) are otherwise hard to represent in a virtual environment, the objective is to bring about new insight into presence through comparison with the sense of presence experienced in the real world.

The BENOGO experience will be based on true-to-life visual and auditory information presented in real-time. The technology will be designed to support the observer's active exploration of the visual and auditory space, through the addition of a physical dimension to the experience. Through visual and auditory augmentation a sense of life will be added including objects for interaction. Projection technologies will range from Head Mounted Display (HMD) to large screens including a 6-sided CAVE.

The empirical research will exploit the possibilities to investigate the experience of 'being there' in relation to real places and objects The theoretical framework will be based on the concept of embodiment in conjunction with presence and sense of place. This will be investigated in terms of fidelity of experience and presentation as compared to equivalent real-word places, and physiological and neurological aspects like consistency of sensory-motor co-ordination. The framework will be developed in close interaction with, and as a guide for, technical development by focusing on the particular strengths that the technology offers as well as on its weak points. The research will iterate through 11 demonstrators to achieve these goals. In order to structure the research, four main themes have been identified. These are:

1. the acquisition and real-time rendering of places;

2. the augmentation of this rendered images with synthetic virtual reality images and 3D soundscapes;

3. an investigation in to the psycho-physiological aspects of presence; and finally, for us the most important,

4. establishing a sense of place.

   Needless to say our focus is on theme four.

4 Place and Language — Two studies

Much existing work in both place and presence research uses free-form self-reports or retrospective descriptions which are then subjected to content analysis. The pilot study follows this paradigm. In this case the written reports were retrospective: we are also currently investigating the sense of place as described *in situ*. As in any pilot study, trialling the methods used was just as important as collecting data.

There were two phases of data collection. In the first phase descriptions were elicited of a range of places of the type which might be represented in BENOGO. The second phase focused exclusively on descriptions of the glasshouse complex in Edinburgh's Botanic Gardens, since a glasshouse environment was to be used in the first of the series of BENOGO experiments with the technology.

4.1   Participants and Procedure

The participants were 18 volunteers from the School of Computing at Napier University. They comprised an administrator, a research student, six other students and ten members of academic staff. None were directly involved with the BENOGO project at the time. A data collection instrument asked participants to describe a written description of a familiar place. It provided written instructions, collected basic personal data and provided space for subjects to supply their response. In the first phase, nine places were listed from which participants could choose one; in the second phase, participants were limited to the glasshouse location. The places were local to Edinburgh. They were also of the scale which might be captured for BENOGO (for example a city square rather than the city as a whole). Finally the list contained both natural and built environments and interior and exterior settings.

They are listed below (notes in *italics* were not provided to participants):

- Inside the one of the glasshouses in the Botanical Gardens.

- Beside the lake in the Botanical Gardens.

- Inside the JKCC — *The university's main open access computing facility.*

- The main ground floor corridor at Craiglockhart (before the latest building work) — *part of a distinctive late 19th century building used until recently by the School of Computing.*

- The central atrium at Jenner's — *a large department store.*

- Charlotte Square — *a city-centre square with classical architecture, part of 18th century 'New Town'.*

- The beach at Yellowcraig — *a popular location for walks and family outings.*

- One of the narrow streets in the Old Town — *part of mediaeval Edinburgh.*

- Princes Street near Scott's monument — *part of Edinburgh's main shopping street.*

Participants were asked to provide a 150–350 word written account of the place, as if describing it to a friend who had never been there. They were further instructed "You want the friend to have as vivid an impression of the place as possible.". It was hoped that this would stimulate accounts which attempted to communicate a sense of place. Instructions otherwise were deliberately unspecific to avoid suggesting particular elements or a particular structure.

Background details were collected of gender, occupation, familiarity with the place concerned, when it was last visited, duration of residence in or around Edinburgh and age group. Permission to quote anonymous extracts from their material was obtained. No descriptions were obtained of two places on the list. The descriptions supplied were distributed as follows:

Inside the JKCC (a large new computing laboratory on campus)	4
The main ground floor corridor at Craiglockhart (a 19th century university building)	4
Inside the one of the glasshouses in the (Edinburgh) Botanical Gardens	6
Beside the lake in the Botanical Gardens	1
Princes Street near Scott's monument (the main shopping street in Edinburgh)	1
The beach at Yellowcraig (a popular location for walks and family outings)	1
The central atrium at Jenners (Edinburgh's most traditional department store)	1

4.2 Analysis

When returned, the descriptions were transcribed (if hand-written) or converted onto the plain text files required by the analysis software, ATLAS/ti[2]. They were then analysed against:

1. the Relph [1976] model of place identity; and

2. the practical dimensions likely to be of immediate relevance for the design of BENOGO demonstrators and scenarios.

4.2.1 Individual Differences

The most striking feature of the results was the differences between participants in overall richness of description, even where the same place was being described. For example, here are two accounts (in full) of Napier's computer centre, the JKCC:

Description 4: There is sunlight. It slants through the small windows and strikes the blank walls. The room is filled with about 500 computers, on benches of 12. There are ventilation grilles in the floor through which I can see deep holes. The walls at the far, high end have mysterious cabinet doors which open to reveal even more mysterious recesses. One day I'll climb in to one. Working there, there is as much isolation or contact as I need. The technicians' open-plan desk in the centre is a source of friendliness and sociability. They are always happy to chat. There is an open entrance area, carpeted but with no computers, which separates out those working from those passing through.

---

[2] The software supports qualitative content analysis of text, images and audio material, in particular the selection, coding annotating and comparison of segments of raw data. A semantic network editor allows the building and modification of theoretical models.

It has a standing computer display of the system status, which itself is often faulty. The JKCC has a feeling of noise and disquiet, and it is difficult to concentrate fully.

Description 8: The room is full of computers about 500 of them on three levels. The computers sit in bays of about 10 computers. The monitors sit on benches each has a keyboard, mouse and mouse pad beside it. the box with disk drives etc., in sits on the floor. For each computer there is a swivel chair. In the centre is an area with a technician sitting behind a counter. There are a few students dotted around using some of the machines. The walls are blue, there are sky lights. The carpets are red.

There were also notable differences between participants in the depth and amount of description devoted to the individual dimensions described below. Participant numbers are too few, however, to permit meaningful analysis against the places described and personal characteristics and background.

4.2.2   The Physical Setting

This section reports content relating to the physical features of the environment, contrasts made between the chosen place and others, and sensory modalities in the description of physical features.

The nature of objects populating the places described and the level of detail of object descriptions are difficult to categorize and naturally dependent on the place in question. That being said, inanimate objects are present in all descriptions, people in most accounts, and living non-human objects (primarily plants) are only in the descriptions of the Botanic gardens. The extracts below are typical of the treatment of inanimate objects and people:

Each tier has bays of computers. The monitors are arranged in rows. There are grey pillars. (Description 1, JKCC)

They are mostly coming and going to the refectory some with plastic cups of coffee in hand. (Description 11, Craiglockhart)

Comparisons of the place described with other places, or between different parts of the same place, are relatively common:

Everything enclosed with the garden's walls is exaggerated when compared with what lies beyond. (Description 3, beside the lake in the Botanic Gardens)

As you approach North Berwick, there are more people enjoying the beach. The atmosphere changes and even the quality of the sand changes. (Description 6, Yellowcraig)

The descriptions are overwhelmingly visual. Sound is mentioned in only six reports, touch / temperature in five and smell in two:

...you can hear lots of movement on the gravel, from cars, bicycles and people. (Description 10, Craiglockhart)

The air outside is quite chilly, so the interior of the glasshouse feels very warm. (Description 13, Botanics glasshouse)

There is a distinctive smell — a melange of wet earth, sweet rotting vegetation and the heavy non-odour of humidity. (Description 13, Botanics glasshouse)

4.2.3 Activities

All descriptions have include some type of physical activity. Most are variants on bodily movement through the environment:

...you have to dodge the shoppers and workers on their lunch break. (Description 2, Princes Street)

...students and staff moving around in the corridor... (Description 11, Craiglockhart)

There is gravel underneath, laid on sand, and this shifts pleasingly when walked on. (Description 13, Botanics Glasshouse)

Interaction with objects in the environment is less frequently described and occurs in less than half of the descriptions:

...swinging our shoes in our hands. (Description 6, Yellowcraig)

...a few students dotted around using some of the machines. (Description 8, JKCC)

Social interaction is similarly rare, and with the exception of description 1 (quoted in full above) usually relates to interaction between other people rather than the participant themselves:

...technicians trying to help users. (Description 14, JKCC)

4.2.4 Meanings and Affect

Most descriptions attribute some sort of meaning (in the Relph sense of the word) to the place or its features:

...the magnificent view of Edinburgh towering above (Description 2, Princes Street)

There is an important looking control centre, it looks like a fortress... (Description 1, JKCC)

i.e. I envy the near-fake perfection of the turf ... (Description 3, beside the lake in the Botanic Gardens)

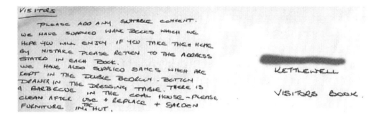

Figure 1: An image of the front page the visitors' book complete with instructions. Names are been obscured in this and next two figures.

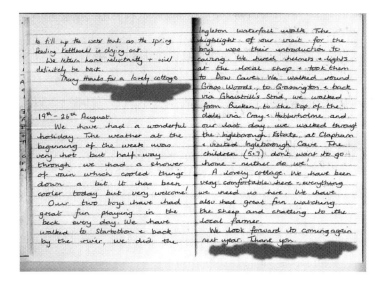

Figure 2: A longer entry covering almost two pages.

4.3   Study II: What We Did on Our Summer Holidays

As we all know there is no respite for the dedicated researcher. While on holiday in a cottage in Yorkshire (July 2002) the authors found, read and subsequently made a photocopy of the visitors' book[3] we found there. The cottage is located in the village of Kettlewell in the North Dales. The name of the village is thought to be from the old Norse for a *bubbling spring*.

4.3.1   The Visitors' Book

The visitors' book is a standard A5 notebook which has been inscribed, "**Visitors** Please add any suitable comment". The entries run from 23rd April 1994 until 13th October 2001. There are over 250 handwritten entries ranging in size from

---

[3]It has not been practical to contact the authors of the entries in the visitors' book so we have been careful not to reproduce any details which might lead to their embarrassment, identification, or cause them to pursue us through the courts.

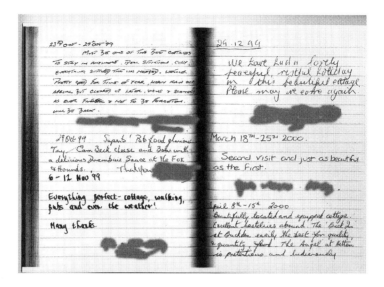

Figure 3: At the other extreme here are a pair of pages filled with 6 short entries.

2 lines to more than 3 pages. The entries are signed usually in the form Mr and Mrs Smith, Our Town, Home Counties or John, Mary, Ben (7 years old) and Rebecca (5 years old) and a drawing of a sheep. Figures 1–3 give a flavour of the contents of the book.

4.3.2 The Analysis of the Contents of the Book

On returning from holiday we took a random sample of 30 entries (approximately 12% of the total) transcribed them, saving them as plain text files to be analysed using ATLAS/t which has been described earlier. Having read the entire visitors' book we had recognized a number of recurring themes — the weather, comments on the cottage and the adjacent beck (a small stream), recommended pubs / pub food, walks and attractions. In all this pointed to the presence of a well defined genre. Following Swales' [1990] five point definition of a genre, the entries in the visitors' book meet most if not all of them. The entries are:

1. a class of communication events;

2. there is or are shared purposes to the entries — where to eat, where to walk;

3. they do vary as to their prototypicality;

4. they do appear to be constrained to a limited set of recurrent topics; and

5. have afforded us insight into the experiences of Kettlewell.

We now revisit the categories of description we identified in the first study.

4.3.3   The Physical Setting

This section reports content relating to the physical features of the environment, contrasts made between the chosen place and others, and sensory modalities in the description of physical features:

> "We have had a wonderful week. Walks, food & drink and above all rest! The weather has been perfect for walking. The best walk for views we did was from Kettlewell — to Arncliff and back — bit of a 'route-march' but well worth it."
> 15th April 1995

> First visit to North Yorkshire, scenery wonderful (even when the hills were covered by the mist!!). Weather changeable, but cottage always had a cosy welcome. Children enjoyed 'fishing' in the beck. All recommended pubs well worth a visit. Cottage tea-room in Kettlewell visited frequently, lovely food and atmosphere.
> 13th August 1994

Again, the descriptions are overwhelmingly visual although the weather does feature frequently.

4.3.4   Activities

Not surprisingly for a holiday venue, visitors are directed to participate in festivals, walk or drive to places of interest:

> A very attractive and well equipped cottage in a superb location. We enjoyed a rare 'dry' week with sunshine at the beginning and end of the week. Superb walking country with walks starting right at the door. Highlights of the week included the walk up Great Whernside via Hag Dyke and returning along Top Mere Road and seeing a Dipper feeding in the beck outside the kitchen window while I was eating my breakfast. Asgarth Falls are worth a visit but not so Settle! Enjoyed the scones in the Dales Kitchen in Grassington as well as an evening meal in the Devonshire Arms.
> 19th September 1998

> "A very pleasant and comfortable cottage in an ideal location. Our visit coincided with the Kettlewell Scarecrow Festival in aid of the local school. It was great fun to see all the different scarecrows popping up throughout the village. The scenery in this part of Yorkshire is great — particularly with Sun glittering off hill tops. However, if it is raining (and it sometimes does) and you don't mind driving, the Calderdale Industrial Museum in (Halifax), the Museum of Film and Photography (Bradford) and Urdale Glass (Masham) are all well worth visiting."
> 20th August 1994

"We had a good week staying in Kettlewell. The weather was mixed, more good than bad though. We visited many places during our stay including: Ilkley, Otley, Settle, Harrogate, etc. We also went to Malham and climbed to the top of Malham Cove, the view was well worth the climb. We enjoyed a very nice meal at the 'Old Hall' in Threshfield. We hope to return again."
5th September 1998

4.3.5 Meanings and Affect
Most visitors describe their stay as beautiful, wonderful and so forth:

"Our second visit and just as beautiful as the first."
18th March, 2000

"We would just like to say thank you. Everything has been perfect."
3rd October 1998

4.3.6 Individual Differences
There are, of course, numerous examples of differences between the entries from the cottage's visitors varying in length, lyrical quality, detail, sophistication of expression and a dozen other things. However despite this diversity they most fall into the same broad style or genre which we discussed earlier. One explanation for this is presence of all other visitors' description. We read the book and it is likely that everyone else visiting the cottage did so too.

5 Discussion

Let us leave this — did you say what you call it. 'Hill? suggested Pippin. 'Shelf?' Step?' suggested Merry. Treebeard repeated the words thoughtfully. 'Hill.' Yes, that was it. But it is a hasty word for a thing that has stood here ever since this part of the world was shaped. [Tolkien 1954, p.75]

At the outset of this paper we made it clear that we are interested in benchmarking the phenomenology of place; knowing what it is to experience a sense of (real) place will allow us insights what it is to:

1. design a virtual place; and

2. to evaluation / understanding the phenomenology of such a virtual place.

So what have we learnt?

5.1 Place vs. Space
We have not been surprised to find that descriptions of place are not the same as descriptions of space, nor our we convinced by the occasionally encountered shorthand 'place = space + meaning'. The creation of place from space is not an additive process but as Relph among others suggests, sense or place is an elusive, evanescent quality which is much more than the addition of its components, however well these are defined.

5.2 Language

Language presents more problems than opportunities for this research. Language is used to describe our sense of place but may in itself affect our experience of space [for example, Whorf 1956]. Are we preconditioned to report place in 'conventional' ways, for example, what we write on holiday postcard, the travel articles we read in the Sunday supplements and what Relph (ibid.) describes as 'inauthentic' experience of place. We also seem constrained to largely confine our description to the visual medium. As Dennett [1991] has shown our use of visual metaphor is inescapable — you see.

5.3 The Phenomenological Approach

As we expected, the phenomenological description have proved to be rich and interesting but we should also add unwieldy and difficult to generalize from, except to say descriptions of place are personal and individual. We should also note that these studies have highlighted a number of methodological problems in adopting such an approach. It may prove to be practically impossible to framing a question or line of enquiry without leading people (i.e. influencing their response). We also note that individual differences between people with respect top their linguistic style and ability is an important factor which we cannot (nor wish to) factor out.

5.4 Consequence for the BENOGO Project

While we are confident that the BENOGO project will solve the problems of creating a sense of photorealistic space augmented with a soundscape, the challenge of creating a sense of place is significantly more problematic. In essence how do we introduce (personal) meaning into a technical solution? One line of research which does present itself as a potential candidate is the field of environmental psychological specifically the design of meaningful *built space*.

Acknowledgements

We gratefully acknowledge the financial support of the EU Presence programme.

References

Calvino, I. [1997], *Invisible Cities*, Vintage Classics.

Clark, A. [1997], *Being There*, MIT Press.

Dennett, D. C. [1991], *Consciousness Explained*, Penguin.

Gustafson, P. [2001], Meanings of Place: Everyday Experience and Theoretical Conceptualizations, *Journal of Educational Psychology* **21**(1), 5–16.

Harrison, R. & Dourish, P. [1996], Re-Place-ing Space: The Roles of Place and Space in Collaborative Systems, *in* G. Olson, J. Olson & M. S. Ackerman (eds.), *Proceedings of 1996: ACM Conference on Computer Supported Cooperative Work (CSCW'96)*, ACM Press, pp.67–76.

Heidegger, M. [1978], *Basic Writings*, Routledge, Chapter Building Dwelling Thinking, pp.343–65. Edited by David Farrell Krell.

Jorgensen, B. S. & Stedman, R. C. [2001], Sense of Place as an Attitude: Lakeshore Owners Attitudes towards Their Properties, *Journal of Environmental Psychology* **21**(3), 233–48.

Relph, E. [1976], *Place and Placelessness*, Pion Books.

Swales, J. M. [1990], *Genre Analysis*, Cambridge University Press.

Tolkien, J. R. R. [1954], *The Lord of the Rings: The Two Towers*, Harper Collins. 2002 printing.

Vygotsky, L. S. [1978], *Mind In Society: The Development of Higher Psychological Processes*, Harvard University Press. Edited by Michael Cole, Vera John-Steiner, Sylvia Scribner, Ellen Souberman.

Whorf, B. L. [1956], *Language, Thought and Reality*, MIT Press.

The Interaction Character of Computers in Co-located Collaboration

Mattias Arvola

Department of Computer and Information Science, Linköping University, SE-581 83 Linköping, Sweden

Tel: *+46 13 285626*

Fax: *+46 13 142231*

Email: *matar@ida.liu.se*

URL: *http://www.ida.liu.se/~matar/*

An INTERACTION CHARACTER refers to a coherent set of qualities of the actions that an application mediates. Examples of such characters include the 'computer as a tool' and the 'computer as a medium'. This paper investigates INTERACTION CHARACTERS of applications used in co-located collaboration. Three qualitative cases have been investigated: consultation at banks, interaction design studio work, and interactive television usage. Interviews, observations, and workshops, as well as prototype design and testing, were conducted as part of the case studies. The results show that the INTERACTION CHARACTER may change swiftly in the middle of usage, which means that people are using the systems quite differently from one moment to the next. One way to increase the flexibility of a system is to facilitate those shifts between different INTERACTION CHARACTERS, by for instance letting people use the system as a tool one minute, and as a medium or a resource the next.

Keywords: interaction character, use quality, co-located collaboration, flexibility, interaction design, interactive television, bank consultation.

1 Introduction

Interaction designers and researchers need a wide variety of concepts that they can use to describe and analyse the use of the products that they are designing or studying. Too few concepts may make researchers and designers of human–computer interaction (HCI) insensitive to the nuances of the situation and the uniqueness of every design case. Some language of interaction design is indeed necessary, and commonly used concepts like usability, learnability, effectiveness, efficiency, user satisfaction, and consistency are part of that. They help in making different qualities of systems-in-use visible and allow us to compare products by discussing their properties, but other aspects of systems-in-use are also important and need to be highlighted [Löwgren & Stolterman 1998; Bratteteig & Stolterman 1997; Levén & Stolterman 1995; Cross 1995; Stolterman 1991; Lawson 1980].

This article presents a qualitative collective case study where the concept INTERACTION CHARACTER is applied in the study of three quite different settings of co-located computer usage. In short, INTERACTION CHARACTER describes the kind of actions a system is designed to allow, support, and afford. The settings are customer meetings at banks, an interaction design studio at a university, and interactive television usage in living rooms. The purpose is to further refine the concept originally coined by Löwgren & Stolterman [1998], who in their turn based it on an article by Kammersgaard [1988] on perspectives of human-computer interaction. Co-located usage is very interesting in relation to INTERACTION CHARACTER since the concept has been developed with the premise of a single user operating a single computer connected to a network. The applicability and limits of the concept are therefore put to test by looking at co-located collaborative usage of computers. This paper describes the INTERACTION CHARACTERS for applications in co-located collaboration.

2   Theoretical Background

The work presented in this paper falls within a tradition of action-theoretic positions in human–computer interaction. It is closely related to activity theory [Leontiev 1978; Nardi 1996a; Wertsch 1998], and distributed cognition [Hutchins 1995]. In activity theory, the basic unit of analysis is a mediated activity where human action is performed by means of artefacts. The three cornerstones of an activity are the subject who performs actions; the mediating artefact; and the object that action is directed towards. The activity is also driven by motives in order to reach some outcomes. This is, however, not the entire picture. It is worth noting that activities are not stable; they change in an almost fluid way over time, and one consequence of that is that the object in one activity may be a mediating artefact in the next. Since every action is situated in an organizational context, other agents, their work, and motives are also affecting the action. In addition, procedures, norms, and artefacts, which have evolved within the history of an institution, explain why an activity is performed in a certain way. A more thorough description is provided by, for example, Wertsch [1998] and Nardi [1996a].

In distributed cognition, actions are seen as part of a system where cognitive work is distributed over individuals and artefacts, and also distributed over time. Culture precedes cognition, since cognitive behaviour is not only a property of the individual, but also an emergent property of the joint human-artefact ensemble. The artefacts themselves are, furthermore, physical embodiments of culture and history. Culture therefore provides the structural resources for action. Distributed cognition places the goals of a cognitive system as a whole in focus, while activity theory has the objectives and actions of the conscious individual as point of departure Nardi [1996b]. That makes them two sides of the same coin; activity theory is more interactional while distributed cognition is more oriented towards the structural foundations of cognition and action.

2.1 Use Qualities

A computer system that mediates the users' actions as part of a larger cognitive system or organization, can be said to have many different qualities, or properties, in its usage. Some of the qualities are objective and others are not. Some are social and yet other qualities are subjective. Another aspect of use qualities of an artefact is their level of abstraction. They can be at a high level, functioning almost as dimensions of use. Examples include, the SCOPE OF ACTIVITY that can be performed by means of the system; the CHANGEABILITY in terms of freedom to change the form, structure, or functionality of the system; and the INTERACTION CHARACTER in terms of what kinds of actions the system is designed to allow, support, and afford. Others are more specific descriptions of how the system is, or how it should be. These specific 'use qualities' can be expressed in the form of adjectives or short phrases like AFFORDABILITY, EFFECTIVENESS, ELEGANCE or INTEGRATION. All of these statements about how a computer system is or should be in its use can be utilized for specifying and assessing design solutions. Use qualities in the form of design objectives can, for example, be ordered in a dependency hierarchy using the objectives tree method [Cross 2000; Arvola 2003]. Howard [2002] argues that abstract non-quantified objectives help in retaining the focus on overall aspects of use qualities, before details cloud the picture.

Some final words about how multi-faceted use qualities are: Every action or even the entire activity of using a system has practical, social, and aesthetic aspects. Some actions are more easily described as being practical, social or aesthetic, while other actions are more complex and can be described from any of these three perspectives. Therefore when a user, designer, or other stakeholder of a computer system argue that the system ought to be, for example, 'reliable', its RELIABILITY should be assessed from a practical, a social, and an aesthetic perspective. Other perspectives such as affective values, construction or ethics may (and should!) also be applied to the usage of any artefact [Ehn & Löwgren 1997; Howard 2002; Holmlid 2002; Arvola 2003].

2.2 Interaction Character

One of the higher order use qualities that a system can be said to have is its INTERACTION CHARACTER. A character is a coherent set of specific qualities, as Janlert & Stolterman [1997] defines it. They argue that designing a computer system with consistent character, regarding behaviour and appearance, provides support for anticipation, interpretation, and interaction. When an application changes its behaviour temporarily it can be said to change mood. INTERACTION CHARACTER is here defined as a coherent and relatively stable set of qualities of the actions that an artefact mediates. Actions, in turn, consist of a purposeful subject who induces change in an object by means of a mediating artefact.

Löwgren & Stolterman [1998] elaborate Kammersgaard's [1988] ideas about perspectives on human–computer interaction, by coining the concept of INTERACTION CHARACTER ('handlingskaraktär' in Swedish). Kammersgaard views them as perspectives that a designer or user may apply to a system-in-use in order to highlight certain aspects of it. Each application or component can, at any given point in time, be seen as a system component, a dialogue partner, a tool, a medium, or as an arena. This list of characters is not seen as exclusive, but rather provides a starting point for discussions about INTERACTION CHARACTERS.

The first character that they describe is that of the application as a *system component*. In the systems perspective, both users and applications are part of a larger system (for example a business) that tries to accomplish something. Standardized tasks can be allocated between human and human, as well between human and machine for optimal performance. The organization is the agent who is performing actions by means of people and technology, and the activity is directed towards business objectives.

The second character is that of the application as a *dialogue partner*. In this perspective, a dialogue is held between the application and the user. The dialogue is preferably conducted on the user's terms and human-human communicative behaviour is therefore used as a benchmark [Qvarfordt 2003]. Written and spoken natural language is the primary form of interaction, and feedback that allows meta-communication is important. Quite often the dialogue partner can be represented as an agent of some kind. The actions of a user are directed towards an objectified application by means of natural language. The application then performs the actions that the user has requested.

The third character is that of the application as a *tool*. Given this perspective there must be a material to which the user can apply the tool, in order to produce a result. The relation between artefact and user is highly asymmetrical and control is an important use quality. It is preferred if the tool can become almost invisible to the user so that he or she only sees the activity. For example, a carpenter does not use a hammer, but is rather hammering. The hammer is invisible until there is some kind of breakdown in the activity, for instance if the carpenter hits a finger or if the shaft breaks. The artefact itself then comes into focus and moves from being the mediating artefact into being the object. Transparency of the interface then becomes important so that the user can understand what went wrong, recover from the error, and return to the activity of production. Most production-oriented applications can today be seen as tools.

The fourth character is that of the application as a *medium*. This perspective on a computer application has spread with the growth of the Internet. An application with the character of a medium promotes and allows human-human communication, either in the form of one-to-one communication such as e-mail or in the form of one-to-many as in online newspapers. Another distinction relevant to media is whether they are synchronous or asynchronous. The difference between a tool and a medium is that the object of the activity is not a material but rather one or several other people.

In the light of the changes that came with the Internet, Löwgren & Stolterman added one character to Kammersgaard's original quartet. They call the fifth character the *arena*: a computer-generated stage where actors are represented by avatars and act in relation to other actors. Immersion is important and a rich set of ways to interact with each other is sought. The arena can be described as a stage for social action, where the avatars are like puppets to the users, and they may have varying degrees of autonomy.

3 Method

The three cases, consultation at the bank, interaction design studio work, and interactive television (iTV) usage, were chosen because they represent quite different situations of use with quite different computer systems. They are, however, all situations where several users collaborate whilst being co-located. Due to their dissimilarity, common features are more likely to represent a more general condition. Within the cases, a collection of methods has been used. Workshops, observations, interviews, and questionnaires have been utilized, as well as prototype design and testing. The overarching research method is however a qualitative collective case study [Stake 1994] where three settings of co-located collaboration are compared: consultation at the bank, an interaction design studio, and interactive television usage. The empirical work in these three settings includes around 115 hours of interviews and observations, and about 35 hours of workshops, with 49 informants all in all.

3.1 Procedure in the Bank Case

The focus of the studies conducted at the bank was identification of use quality requirements for a teller system [Holmlid 2002]. In total, 40 hours of workshops, and 30 hours of observation and situated interviews were conducted. Initially the use of the teller system was modelled in 14 *workshops* with learning developers at the bank. Several tentative models of use quality were developed, and a new course in using the teller system was designed within the bank organization. The participants were two active researchers functioning as usability experts and interaction designers, a project leader at the bank, a bank employee who had developed a previous online course for the teller system, and a developer who had implemented the course. In addition, five clerks at four branches were tracked on two occasions for half a day. The researcher took part of their work, took notes, and asked questions. In total, 30 hours of *observation* let us learn more about their work and allowed us to ask probing questions about episodes that took place. Finally, a project team at the bank analysed the transcribed field notes from the interviews and the observations during three 3-hour *workshops*. The team consisted of three learning developers and three in-house system developers that all had experience of bank work. One researcher facilitated the workshops while another researcher took notes and manned the video camera. Our own analysis was also informed by the interpretations made in these workshops.

3.2 Procedure in the Studio Case

A field study in an interaction design studio at a university was conducted. The specific research focus was on events where students used resources individually and then jointly, before returning to individual use. In an e-mail *questionnaire*, the students in the design studio were asked to describe events where the work in the studio was fun and events where it was tiresome and boring. The reason for using this questionnaire was to get an idea about what the students cared about when they were in the studio. This set the frame for further observations. Five out of six students answered the questionnaire. During the course of one design assignment, a researcher worked in the studio by a desk, and did *situated interviews* as well as *observation*. Interviews were conducted as the opportunity arose in the observation and they were triggered by events that took place. A total amount of 20 hours was spent on observing the work of the six students and the two teachers, and field notes were continuously taken.

3.3   Procedure in the Interactive Television Case

Two interactive television prototype systems were developed, in order to study properties of such systems-in-use [Arvola & Holmlid 2000; Arvola 2003; Rimbark 2002]. As part of that work, interviews were conducted, both situated in peoples homes and in simulated home environments after trials of the prototypes. Situated interviews conducted in people's homes were made as *technology tours* [Baille et al. to appear], where people were asked to show and tell what technology they have and how they use, or do not use, it. In total, 56 hours of technology tours were made in eight homes. None of these homes had interactive television at this date. Field notes were taken during all interviews and most of them were audio recorded (some informants did not want to be recorded). 3-hour long situated interviews have been conducted with five informants. Two of them were male and three were female. Two informants were academics of age 28, and three of them were middle-aged with children who had left home. One of these interviews was conducted as a group interview with a married couple. In addition, interviews have been conducted with four elderly people about the technology that they had in their homes. Two were women and two were men. The elderly got disposable cameras, which they could use to document technology that they encountered. The researcher met with the four elderly in their homes on three occasions, and each informant was interviewed for ten to twelve hours in total.

During *prototype testing*, 21 users were observed during usage, and interviewed afterwards about their experiences. In total, 7–8 hours of observations and semi-structured interviews were made during these tests. The ages of the participants ranged between 21 and 30 years, and half of them were male and half were female. All of them were considered to be early adopters, with a high degree of computer experience. The tests took place in environments that looked like somebody's home but evidently were not. The first prototype was a quiz game, and eight users tested it in pairs. They were interviewed afterwards one by one. The second prototype was a news on-demand service, and it utilized two remote controls for simultaneous input. Five pairs of users tested it, and they were interviewed in pairs after the session. One initial session was also held with three participants that surfed online news with one remote control. Field notes were taken during all observations and interviews, and six of the ten sessions were audio or video recorded. The test sessions, including interviews, lasted from 30 minutes up to one hour.

4 Case Setting I: Consultation at the Bank

In customer meetings at the bank that was under study, a consulting clerk and one or two customers met together in the clerk's personal office. The clerk used a PC with the screen turned away from the customers, and both customer and clerk utilized pen and paper. Their objectives were to get the customers' economy in order and perhaps make some changes. The clerk also wanted to keep a good relationship going with the customer and make profit for the bank.

In the offices that were observed, the clerk sat so that he or she could meet the customers when they arrived at the doorway. On the desk they placed the documents that they were to go through during the meeting and the clerk often turned to the PC in order to get the latest information about interests and similar figures. If the meeting was about a loan the clerk would have to do extensive input to the system and was during this time turned partly away from the customers. The back of the office was for papers and files that the clerk used in his or her individual work.

A meeting was usually prepared in advance so that the clerk could guess what it would be about if he or she had not been told. Then the clerk printed out the forms, the information, and the documents that it would probably be necessary to go through together with the customer. Quite often they asked the customer to read or prepare something from one meeting to the next. The collaboration was to a high degree controlled by the clerk, but questions from the customer usually led their cooperative activity in unanticipated directions. The customer could see all the documents and forms that were lying on the table and by that draw conclusions about what they had to go through during the meeting. The clerk and the customers also cooperated by helping each other to keep face. Clerks were concerned that the customers felt at ease with confiding in them and felt that their economic situation is quite common; the customer must not be embarrassed. The clerk often had to ignore the customer when there was much input into the system or when he or she had to go to the printer. The clerk would then frequently ask the customer to forgive the non-attention and the customer usually made it clear that he or she completely understood: "After all, we've all had to work with computers, haven't we."

5 Case Setting II: Interaction Design Studio

In the interaction design studio that was studied, six to eight students worked together. They had their own PCs and their own desks were covered with sketches and personal items. Two design teachers sat in private offices in the same corridor, and they could, if they wished, see the students through the large windows between the corridor and the studio. Within the studio the students could see and overhear each other and cooperate at the white-board or the shared large table, or at someone's desk. The white-board was also used for projection from the shared PC, which had extra accessories such as CD-writer, drawing tablet, and scanner. Near the white-board and the shared table were also bookshelves with books on design and HCI. The students considered themselves to be there to do design and deliver before the deadline, and also to learn to do design by reflection and discussion. They also wanted to have fun and enjoy each other's company, while experiencing a flow of creativity in the group. Sometimes the students considered the studio to be too noisy with people that just fooled around and were not inspired to work. The teachers' objectives were to see every student and his or her abilities and skill in order to find ways to strengthen the student, as well as facilitating a good, creative, and friendly atmosphere in the studio. The teachers also had other courses to teach and other things to do.

The students and the teachers could easily see what others were working on by glancing at the sketches and the printed screen shots that the students had on their desks. The possibility to see what the others were working on provided a ground for unplanned interaction and chat about their work. This created an opportunity to be helpful as well as to get help from other students. Talking to others about their work was also an inspiration for the individual student. After these shorter periods of group work it went back to individual work again (see also Bellotti & Bly [1996] and Geisler et al. [1999] for similar observations).

Students often talked across the room from desk to desk and others that were in the room were free to join the conversation. Sometimes they stood next to someone working on-screen, and if the collaboration was tighter they had the opportunity to go to the shared table in the middle of the room in order to discuss and make joint sketches. Students also presented their work for each other and for the teachers more formally at the end of each design assignment. They usually did that by using the projector to show their demo or prototype, while the others sat around the shared table. During these "critique and focus sessions" the teachers and students probed the rationale for the design products as well as the process, and the objective of the sessions was peer learning.

6   Case Setting III: Interactive Television

While watching television (at least in Sweden), people are usually seated in the couch in the living room, unless they simply have it turned on in the background while they do other things. Television is often viewed in the company of others, either with friends or family. During working days, 75% of the time in front of the television is spent together with others. That figure is almost 80% during weekends [Ellegård 2001]. The family include children, parents, partners, grandparents, and so on. The exact constellation of the household may vary from single person households, to large families, or friends sharing an apartment, or perhaps elderly with visiting children and grandchildren.

It was observed during the tests of the iTV-prototypes that the television screen was a natural focus of attention. A single remote control was used for interacting with the television set and the set-top box, but in the technology tours it was noticed that that there usually were other remote controls lying on the table. Viewers reported that they often conducted other activities in front of the television screen; for instance chatting, eating, drinking, knitting, reading, or even surfing the Internet on a laptop. Users of iTV basically had three joint motives when they were lying or sitting on the couch: taking it easy, being together, and/or being entertained. They may also have had individual motives as suggested by the different side activities.

The activity in front of the television set was represented in the constellation of things in the living room. If there were cookies and tea on the table the people present were probably eating and drinking. If someone had the remote control then everybody could see that that person was in charge of the viewing experience. The way a blanket was lying on the couch indicated the degree of relaxation and so on. These things were open for interpretation by anyone who entered the room, and that person could then adjust his or her own private agendas so that individual activities did not come into conflict.

In the technology tours it was observed that the television usually was in front of a wall. There was a table a couple of meters away from the television screen, and on the other side of that table there was commonly a couch. On one or both sides of the couch there could be room for an armchair. The remote control was lying on the table where it was accessible for everybody, near a person in the couch, or in the hand of a person. Some larger living rooms had different parts for different kinds of activities, for instance a large dinner table, a small coffee table, or perhaps a desk or a bureau. In smaller apartments there was a bed or a sleeping alcove in the same room. The exact arrangement of the living room depends on the architecture of the home, on the activities that are undertaken in the room, and also on the generation that the residents belong to.

While testing the iTV-prototypes it was noted that the remote control owner often spoke out aloud about what he or she was doing. If he or she did not, the other people in the couch had trouble following the interaction. The others often lost interest in what was going on on the screen. The remote owner sometimes excused him or herself for extensive surfing. Occasionally the others in the couch told the remote owner what to do. When the remote owner felt that he or she could not decide what to do, the remote was usually handed over to another person. Sometimes the other person also asked for the remote control. When the remote was lying on the table it was considered to be free for anyone to access and manipulate, but only if that person was equal in the home: a guest in a household may hesitate to reach for the remote if not invited. In the design of iTV-prototypes it was assumed that that two remote controls was better than one, in order to facilitate the shifts of control and hence distribute control. The drawback was that it was not easy to see who was in charge of the shared screen and that tended to create screen wars and users that are annoyed with each other [Rimbark 2002; Arvola 2003].

7 Results

A common INTERACTION CHARACTER in all three settings was that of the *application as a tool*. The interaction with the application was in focus, and the interaction between people became secondary. In the case of iTV that meant that the person who did not have the remote control lost interest. In the interaction design studio students often worked by themselves and the applications were then in tool usage. The system as a tool was also an INTERACTION CHARACTER that appeared at the bank. During the extensive time spans of data input into the system, or when there was a breakdown, the clerk was forced to ignore the customer. The customer then started to look into the roof and the clerk excused him or herself for ignoring the customer, in order to help the customer regain face. The computer was then objectified and thereby entered as a topic into the conversation. When the computer is used as a tool during the meeting, the customer becomes a distraction for the adviser. This is a problem when the use of the computer is in this character for too long. The application as tool is for this reason the least wanted INTERACTION CHARACTER during a customer meeting.

During the customer meeting, the most preferred INTERACTION CHARACTER is instead the *application as a resource*, which is a variant of the tool. The social interaction is in focus when using an application as a resource, while the software interaction is secondary. For the tool it is the other way around. When an application is a resource rather than a tool, the clerk can attend to the customer rather than the system. A resource is only backing up the user in his or her main work. In this case the main work is to listen to the customer, in order to end the meeting with a signature on a contract.

Another INTERACTION CHARACTER that was observed in all three settings was a variant of the medium: the *application as a common resource*. When an application is a common resource, the interplay between the participants is in focus while the application feeds that interaction. The difference between a common resource and a medium is that the former inputs something to a dialogue, while the latter mediates or acts as an intermediary in a dialogue. Just as with the resource, it is the social interaction that is in focus, but in contrast to the resource the common resource is available and controlled by all participants and not only by one. They are also using it with joint or overlapping motives. At the bank, the printouts from the systems worked as common resources and occasionally the clerks turned their screens towards the customer in order to explain or show something. In the interaction design studio students often showed something to another student in order to get comments. They view it, point, and discuss in order to coordinate their work and give feedback. During critique and focus sessions they sat together using a projector to show a prototype. They also made printouts and sat by the shared table to sketch and discuss. During all these episodes the applications were used as common resources. When users of iTV played a game on the television screen or when they surfed news together, the applications were used also as common resources for conversations and the content of the applications fed the dialogue with topics. This is also an example of the application as a common resource.

While remaining within one INTERACTION CHARACTER, an application sometimes changed *mood of control*. Applications could sometimes be in *turn-taking control*; one of the participants controlled the interaction at one time but could later on turn over the control to another participant. Sometimes that individual asked for the control and at other times the control-owner simply turned it over. If the joint use of an application continued for some time a practice of turn-taking usually developed. This was particularly clear in the case of interactive television where there usually is only one remote control. This only happened with printouts from applications at the bank, and not with the applications themselves, due to the expert-client relationship. In the interaction design studio, applications could be in turn-taking use when two students sat together in front of one screen. At some times, especially when applications and printouts were used as common resources they were also seen to be in *parallel control* by all users. More commonly they were 'backseat driven' in *mediated control*; other participants told the control-owner what to do. Sometimes the clerks turned the screen towards the customer to show something or explain. The clerk then distributed control to the customer, and invited him or her to be a backseat driver while the clerk took on a supporting role. That meant that a number of design considerations of bank secrecy and the tension between private and public became important. Occasionally in the interaction design studio, a student stood behind another student while he or she was working, and commented on what the primary user was doing. Sometimes the bystander told the primary user what to do. For instance: "What if you write it like this ... " The application is then used as a tool with mediated control, or backseat driving. For users of interactive television backseat driving was also common. For example, one user told the other what news article to choose.

Applications were often used in many different ways. The INTERACTION CHARACTERS were not stable. The iTV-appliances sometimes changed rapidly from being a medium with content in focus, to a common resource that fed the social interaction of the users and was used with equal control. In addition, people in front of an iTV-appliance will enter and leave the activity (for example to make coffee), and the subgoals of the activity may vary as the activity goes on. The iTV-appliances could also be a tool for carrying out an action without concern of others. They were switching between turn-taking control, parallel control (when that was made possible by means of two remote controls), and mediated use. At the bank, applications were seen to switch between common resource, resource, and tool. A clerk talked to a client using the application as a resource by glancing at some figures, and only moments later it was a tool for entering information. When the clerk turned the screen or made printouts it became a common resource. In the studio, students worked with their applications in many different ways in a pattern similar to the bank clerks' usage.

8 Discussion

The results show that there are variants of the medium and the tool, which play a role in co-located use of applications. It is different to use a system while being co-located with others, and to use a system in solitude. The results also showed that the shared control over an application could change between different users in three different ways: turn-taking control, parallel control, and mediated control. The systems studied in this paper did, however, not support very fluent and swift changes between different INTERACTION CHARACTERS and different moods of control. It was cumbersome for users to use a system in different ways. A number of workarounds and insufficient strategies were used: printouts, turning screens with the risk of exposing things, using a system as tool and ignoring other people, and so on.

More field studies are needed in order to evaluate how applications work for people outside the laboratory. In real life, goals and motives shift constantly and the environment of the interaction also changes. For instance, people enter and leave activities, which means that software changes between being in joint use and individual use. This transforms the activity in a fundamental way and the INTERACTION CHARACTER changes. If the application does not support a certain kind of character or control mood, it is likely to hamper the naturalness of people's social interaction as well as the practical usage of the application. Janlert & Stolterman [1997] argue that a consistent character is important for users' interpretation, anticipation, and interaction with an application. That consistency should apply to every action across all INTERACTION CHARACTERS that the application may have in its usage. If the entire system is to be SNAPPY, every action that is performed must be SNAPPY. One could, however, claim that an application should belong mainly to one INTERACTION CHARACTER, but the results in these studies indicates that it is more rewarding to view each component of an application as being able have different INTERACTION CHARACTERS. This is in accordance with Kammersgaard's [1988] argumentation. It is the job of the designers to decide which ones should be supported and afforded in different situations of use.

8.1 Designing Flexible Applications

A consequence for design is that changes in INTERACTION CHARACTER may be a means for reaching flexibility in computer usage. A design problem that was encountered in the bank setting was that of designing systems that do not force the clerk to be rude and ignore the customer. A solution is to allow users to change INTERACTION CHARACTER. A clerk who can decide whether a system should be a common resource with parallel control, a tool with individual control, or a passive resource, can adapt to the current needs of the social situation. A user interface that is distributed over multiple display surfaces with different input and output units may solve this. If the applications at the bank were flexible in this manner the need for printouts would probably decrease, and therefore the bank would save time not only for the clerks but also for the customers. In addition, the clerk would not have to ignore the customer and then apologize.

In the case of iTV it was observed that users who did not interact with the application lost interest. In order to solve that, two remote controls were introduced, but that only led to interference. If users could choose which INTERACTION CHARACTER to use at any given time this problem would be solved. Again, multiple screens are part of the solution. If there are displays where users may individually pursue their own goals whilst being physically close to each other, their goals of entertainment, laid back interaction, relaxation, and togetherness can be met. They would also have the opportunity to move information objects between all screens, both public and private.

The students in the interaction design studio would also benefit from a system where they could display information anywhere. In such a system they could instantly move their objects of work from their own screen to another student's screen, to the common table, or to the white-board.

It does seem reasonable that supporting fluent changes of INTERACTION CHARACTERS and changes between control moods would increase flexibility and allow users to reach temporary goals that suddenly appear in co-located collaborative activities.

8.2 Future Research

The next step for this research is to implement and field-test computer systems with interfaces that are distributed over many different devices, and where information can be 'thrown' between the multiple displays. The idea is to allow users to switch INTERACTION CHARACTERS at will depending on present individual or joint goals. The system will consist of personal devices as well as shared devices and it will be tested in several situations of use, including the interaction design studio and consultation meetings.

8.3 Conclusions

This paper has described how systems used in co-located collaboration were used as tools, resources and common resources. They were also used with different moods of control: turn-taking control, parallel control, and mediated control. The system as a common resource and the system as a resource can be seen as variations of media and tools respectively. The design decision of which INTERACTION CHARACTERS to support and afford in different situations of use will to a large degree decide the entire scope of actions that a system can be used for. The systems studied in this paper did not support fluent changes in INTERACTION CHARACTER. It was cumbersome for users to use a system in different ways. A number of workarounds and insufficient strategies were used: printouts, turning screens with the risk of exposing things, using a system as tool and ignoring other people, and so on. One way to build flexible systems for co-located collaboration is to allow users to fluently switch between different INTERACTION CHARACTERS. Future research on field studies of such flexible systems is welcome, in order to determine their value and the design considerations involved.

Acknowledgements

I wish to thank the other researchers that have been involved in the empirical field work and design work that has set the ground for this paper: Stefan Holmlid, Magnus Rimbark, and Patrik Ernfridsson. I would also like to thank Jonas Lundberg for helpful comments on earlier versions of this paper, and Genevieve Gorrell for improving my English.

This work has been supported by The Graduate School for Human–Machine Interaction (HMI), and The Swedish Research Institute for Information Technology (SITI).

References

Arvola, M. [2003], Good to Use! Use Quality of Multi-user Applications in the Home, Technical Report, Linköping University. Linköping Studies in Science and Technology, Licentiate's Thesis No.988.

Arvola, M. & Holmlid, S. [2000], IT-artifacts for Socializing: Qualities-in-Use and Research Framework, *in* L. Svensson, U. Snis, C. Sørensen, H. Fägerlind, T. Lindroth, M. Magnusson & C. Östlund (eds.), *IRIS 23 "Doing IT Together": Proceedings of the 23rd Information Systems Research Seminar in Scandinavia*, Laboratorium for

Interaction Technology, University of Trollhättan/Uddevalla, pp.1293–1301. Available at http://iris23.htu.se/proceedings/PDF/78final.PDF (last accessed 2003.05.26).

Baille, L., Benyon, D., Macaulay, C. & Peterson, M. G. [to appear], Investigating Design Issues in Household Environments, *CognitionTechnology and Work* .

Bellotti, V. & Bly, S. [1996], Walking Away from the Desktop Computer: Distributed Collaboration and Mobility in a Product Design Team, *in* G. Olson, J. Olson & M. S. Ackerman (eds.), *Proceedings of 1996: ACM Conference on Computer Supported Cooperative Work (CSCW'96)*, ACM Press, pp.209–18.

Bratteteig, T. & Stolterman, E. [1997], Design in Groups and All that Jazz, *in* M. Kyng & L. Mathiassen (eds.), *Computers and Design in Context*, MIT Press, pp.289–315.

Cross, N. [1995], Discovering Design Ability, *in* R. Buchanan & V. Margolin (eds.), *Discovering Design: Explorations in Design Studies*, University of Chicago Press, pp.105–20.

Cross, N. [2000], *Engineering Design Methods: Strategies for Product Design*, third edition edition, John Wiley & Sons.

Ehn, P. & Löwgren, J. [1997], Design for Quality-in-Use: Human–Computer Interaction meets Information Systems Development, *in* M. Helander, T. K. Landauer & P. V. Prabhu (eds.), *Handbook of Human–Computer Interaction*, second edition, North-Holland, pp.299–313.

Ellegård, K. [2001], Lockropen ljuder: Komhem, Working paper ISRN LiU-TEMA-TWP–230-SE, Department of Technology and Social Change, Linköping University. ISSN 1101-1289. Available only in Swedish.

Geisler, C., Rogers, E. H. & Tobin, J. [1999], Going Public: Collaborative Systems Design for Multidisciplinary Conversations, *in* N. A. Streitz, J. Siegel, V. Hartkopf & S. Konomi (eds.), *Cooperative Buildings: Integrating Information, Organizations, and Architecture. Second International Workshop CoBuild'99*, Vol. 1670 of *Lecture Notes in Computer Science*, Springer-Verlag, pp.89–100.

Holmlid, S. [2002], Adapting Users: Towards a Theory of Use Quality, Technical Report Linköping Studies in Science and Technology, Dissertation No. 765, Linköping University.

Howard, M. V. [2002], Supporting Design for Quality-in-Use through Abstract Usability Objectives, *in* G. Dai (ed.), *Proceedings of APCHI 2002, 5th Asia Pacific Conference on Computer Human Interaction*, Science Press, pp.199–209.

Hutchins, E. [1995], *Cognition in the Wild*, MIT Press.

Janlert, L.-E. & Stolterman, E. [1997], The Character of Things, *Design Studies* **18**(3), 297–314.

Kammersgaard, J. [1988], Four Different Perspectives on Human–Computer Interaction, *International Journal of Man–Machine Studies* **28**(4), 343–62.

Lawson, B. [1980], *How Designers Think*, The Architectural Press.

Leontiev, A. N. [1978], *Activity, Consciousness and Personality*, Prentice–Hall.

Levén, P. & Stolterman, E. [1995], Turning Visions into Values — Information Systems Design as Vision Management, *in* B. Dahlbom, F. Kämmerer, F. Ljungberg, J. Stage & C. Sørensen (eds.), *IRIS 18 "Design in Context": Proceedings of the 18th Information Systems Research Seminar in Scandinavia*, Vol. 7 of *Gothenburg Studies in Informatics*, Göteborg University, pp.377–88. Available at http://iris.informatik.gu.se/conference/iris18/iris1836.htm (last accessed 2003.05.26).

Löwgren, J. & Stolterman, E. [1998], *Design av informationsteknik — materialet utan egenskaper*, Studentlitteratur. Available only in Swedish.

Nardi, B. A. [1996a], Activity Theory and Human–Computer Interaction, *in* B. A. Nardi (ed.), *Context and Consciousness: Activity Theory and Human–Computer Interaction*, MIT Press, pp.7–16.

Nardi, B. A. [1996b], Studying Context: A Comparison of Activity Theory, Situated Action Models and Distributed Cognition, *in* B. A. Nardi (ed.), *Context and Consciousness: Activity Theory and Human–Computer Interaction*, MIT Press, pp.69–102.

Qvarfordt, P. [2003], User Experience of Spoken Feedback in Multimodal Interaction, Technical Report, Linköping University. Linköping Studies in Science and Technology Licentiate's Thesis No. 1003.

Rimbark, M. [2002], Do's and Dont's in Applications for Co-surfing News, Master's thesis, Linköping University. LiU-KOGVET-D-02/02-SE. Available at http://www.ep.liu.se/exjobb/ida/2002/002 (last accessed 2003.05.26).

Stake, R. E. [1994], Case Studies, *in* N. Denzin & Y. Lincoln (eds.), *Handbook of Qualitative Research*, Sage Publications, pp.435–54.

Stolterman, E. [1991], Designarbetets dolda rationalitet — En studie av metodik och praktik inom systemutveckling, Dissertation1 UMADP-RRIPS 14.91, Department of Informatics, Umeå University. Available only in Swedish.

Wertsch, J. V. [1998], *Minds as Action*, Oxford University Press.

Information Retrieval

How Knowledge Workers Gather Information from the Web: Implications for Peer-to-Peer File Sharing Tools

Jennifer Hyams & Abigail Sellen

Hewlett-Packard Labs, Filton Road, Stoke Gifford, Bristol BS34 8QZ, UK

Email: *jen_hyams@yahoo.co.uk, abigail.sellen@hp.com*

The success of peer-to-peer (p2p) music sharing has no doubt contributed to assumptions that individuals' PCs are a vast untapped resource of assets just waiting to be unlocked by such systems. This includes the push for opening up our file spaces at work to allow peers access to previously inaccessible information with minimum effort. We wished to explore the potential value of these ideas and to test some of the assumptions underlying them, the motivation being that we believed the issues raised by this investigation would be important to those developing p2p information sharing tools. We do this by looking at the flow of information in and out of 16 knowledge workers' file spaces in the context of carrying out Web information gathering tasks at work. In doing this we find that the file spaces used for knowledge work are more like 'workbenches' than 'archives' and that the information held within them is fundamentally different in content and organization to that which knowledge workers place in shared information spaces such as the Web. Knowledge workers work on their information to make it shareable to specific audiences yet this information is found side by side on the 'workbench' with unshareable information. This leads us to question the potential value of enabling people to open up their file spaces without having regard to the reusability of this information for others.

Keywords: peer-to-peer, knowledge workers, information life cycle, information sharing, Web use, information gathering.

1 Introduction

The rise and subsequent fall of the music file sharing site, Napster, not only created great furore in the music industry and new dilemmas for copyright law, it also raised awareness of the potential popularity for new kinds of tools and applications which work in a decentralized way. These new models of computing, known more generally as 'peer-to-peer' (p2p) computing, hold out the promise of opening up previously unused or inaccessible resources from the "vast untapped resource of personal computers owned by ordinary people" [Kubiatowicz 2003].

While there is some dispute over the proper definition of p2p architectures, this vision is one in which the role of server-based networks is either minimized or bypassed altogether, allowing people to directly share resources (be they storage, cycles or content) between people, or more accurately between people's individual PC's. These concepts take different forms. For example, grid computing describes the ability to share processing power and storage capacity across institutional borders and across clusters of individual computers. Other concepts are more clearly directed at the ability to share multimedia files, bookmarks, educational materials, work-based documents or other kinds of information, usually within specific communities or groups — for example, http://www.Kazaa.com, http://www.neurogrid.net, http://edutella.jxta.org, http://www.groove.net and Hyperclip [Sato et al. 2002].

One aspect of this that interests us is how this vision is beginning to spark new ideas for sharing information. This includes the idea that, with an owner's permission, you might be able to look into and use files from your peer's PC. For example:

> "... most of the files in today's companies are on PC's, not servers, and peer-to-peer can let you see all these storage assets as one big distributed file space. A work group member might even be able to find the sketch of an idea you've just begun on your PDA." [Breidenbach 2001, para.26]

The idea of allowing others access to your 'workspace', to work in progress, and to unique documents labelled and organized in ways that support personal use, is fundamentally different to the successful Napster-like models that have been used to share completed, static, often commercially created, predictable content, that has been specifically moved into a folder for sharing. As [Bricklin 2000] argues, the reason Napster works is not merely that it uses p2p computing but that:

> "... the information being downloaded is never changed. The files shared with Napster are not news feeds — they are more likely the works of dead musicians."

There does in fact seem little justification for assuming that other types of personally owned content will be successfully shared through p2p computing purely because of the success of Napster. Rather than leap to that conclusion, however, we wished to explore these issues more systematically.

1.1 Approach and Focus

Although several groups are developing new tools to facilitate the sharing of other kinds of content (such as Edutella, Groove and Hyperclip), the focus of our research was led by the questions being raised by groups from our own laboratory. For example, we have been working on new concepts intended to allow people to more easily share the benefits from the information they gather and organize from the Web [Banks et al. 2002]. Such tools would allow people to seek out peers with similar interests or expertise and to learn from the information they gather and use.

This then raises questions such as: What kind of information do people gather from the Web? How is it used? How is it kept? How is it modified? What aspects of it might be usefully shared with others? By examining these issues, we hoped to uncover both opportunities and obstacles in developing such systems, and to shed light more broadly on the issues that people developing p2p information sharing systems must consider. Our approach was to begin by looking at how knowledge workers do this. Knowledge workers, by definition, are people who spend a great deal of their time gathering, analysing, modifying and creating content. We also know that the Web is a key resource from which information is gathered by these workers to be kept and integrated with the personally-owned content on their PCs [Sellen et al. 2002].

1.2   Existing Research

The literature does provide us with an overview of information gathering and sharing tasks as they are carried out by knowledge workers, although not generally with an eye toward the design of information sharing tools.

Web-based information gathering is defined quite specifically as using the Web to purposefully find and collate information around a specific topic or theme. It is an interesting activity in the context of knowledge workers because earlier work [Sellen et al. 2002] has shown that this is the main and most important kind of Web activity that they carry out. Such activities very often involve sets of questions, ill-defined questions, or questions that are formulated in the course of carrying out a task. Information gathering is very different from some of the other kinds of Web activities knowledge workers do (such as fact finding) being generally more time-consuming and complex.

Some of these findings have been supported more generally, [Bates 1989; Hearst 1999; Pirolli & Card 1995; Turner 1997; Markus 2001; Paepcke 1996], the literature showing that information gathering is an iterative process, involving changing goals and the use of multiple sources, to gather together new ad-hoc collections of information. Those studies that have concentrated on the Web have indicated the advantage of domain knowledge, Web searching skills and the reuse of previously discovered sources upon the efficiency and effectiveness of gathering [Hoelscher & Strube 1999; Wexelblat & Maes 1999]. Resulting information can end up fragmented, residing in different formats and places, [Jones et al. 2001; Kamiya et al. 1996], not only on PC's but on paper, [Harper 1998], and in knowledge workers' heads, [Kidd 1994]. Kidd also suggests that the seemingly chaotic organization of information during this process, which shows large individual differences [Berlin et al. 1993], is personally meaningful and allows the owner to use information, to be informed by it and to gain 'knowledge' which may then be incorporated into new documents.

The methods by which individuals share the resulting knowledge, skills and gathered information from such tasks with others has also been studied, [Paepcke 1996; Berlin et al. 1993; Jones et al. 2001; Markus 2001; Wexelblat & Maes 1999; Bannon & Bødker 1997]. This literature indicates that information sharing is different and easier between close work colleagues or those who have shared knowledge and purpose than between loosely coupled colleagues, novices and experts or those who wish to reuse information for other purposes. Sharing between individuals is often observed within organizations or disciplines and it has been argued that information shared in this way preserves shared context and interpretations in a way that information shared through a central knowledge base, accessible to a wider audience, does not [Bonifacio et al. 2002; Iamnitchi et al. 2002].

There have been a number of applications developed to support the sharing of information gathering processes [Wexelblat & Maes 1999] as well as sources, content and products [Kamiya et al. 1996; Takeda et al. 2000]. They may also support the discovery of individuals with similar interests or purposes and actively alert users to relevant information shared by others [Takeda et al. 2000]. Amongst the criticisms of some of these applications is that they may force the sharer to carry out extra work such as organizing information into a different structure [Bonifacio et al. 2002]. This contrasts with the claims that p2p systems actually offer the opportunity to reduce the work done by sharers by allowing them to continue to gather, organize and use information using their own familiar tools and workspaces yet allow others to access this information with little or no extra effort being required [Kanawati & Malek 2000].

However Markus [2001] and Bannon & Bødker [1997] suggest that unless effort is taken in documenting information in a way that is reusable by different types of users for different purposes, others may have great difficulty in reusing that information. The implication is that enabling people to make information from personal workspaces easily accessible to others may or may not be of value.

It is clear from the literature therefore that these tasks can generate a multitude of documents throughout the process we define as information gathering. Yet we know little about what is shared, how it is shared and to whom it is of value. The literature suggests that work needs to be done in order to make information shareable and that the degree of work may depend upon the intended audience. Yet, we know little about what this work is or whether this work has already been carried out on personally owned information. We therefore aimed to investigate the potential for sharing personally owned information, in particular knowledge-based products, by studying what knowledge workers keep or create on their PC's as part of their work, what they currently do and don't share with regard to their personal stores of information, by looking at the way in which they share, and by looking at whom they share with.

2 Method

An exploratory approach was taken, capturing a rich amount of data using retrospective 'walkthrough' interviews. Although some basic summary statistics were carried out, the data were primarily analysed qualitatively using thematic analysis [Aronson 1994].

No.	Job Title	Age Range	Yrs on Web
1	Customer Support (IT)	35–44	8
2	Information Resource Manager (Charity)	35–44	6
3	Education Officer (Charity)	25–34	10
4	Network Support Analyst	25–34	7
5	Territory Manager (Sales)	25–34	6
6	Development Manager (IT)	25–34	5
7	Games Producer	35–44	5
8	Graphic Artist	25–34	2
9	Architect	25–34	5
10	Lecturer and Union Representative	45–54	8
11	Government Policy Adviser	35–44	4
12	Building Historian and University Lecturer	55–64	4.5
13	Research Scientist	25–34	11
14	Government Planning Manager	25–34	2
15	Information Research Analyst	25–34	6
16	Researcher	35–44	6

Table 1: Summary description of participants.

2.1 Participants

Participants were recruited through email advertisements distributed via local mailing lists. These asked for knowledge workers, defined as people whose paid work involves significant time gathering, finding, analysing, creating, producing or archiving information, where 'information' is anything from documents to drawings to multi-media files. From these respondents, 16 different knowledge workers were selected, across a diverse range of knowledge work, who were regular users of the Web for their work tasks. Regular Web use was defined as use of the Web at least 4 times in a typical working day.

Overall, participants had an average of 6 years of Web experience (ranging from 2 to 11 years), 4.5 years of experience of Web information gathering (ranging from 9 months to 10 years) and 6.5 years of experience in their current professional domain (ranging from 1 to 17 years). The resulting pool of people is summarized in Table 1.

2.2 Procedure

Each participant took part in a videotaped interview at their workplace, in front of their PC. Having been given the definition of information gathering [Sellen et al. 2002], they were asked to identify five or six information gathering tasks using the Web from the past couple of weeks (using their history list if needed).

Participants were then asked to verbally 'walk-through' at least two of their tasks, most in fact covering more than this. Each participant started off by explaining the task they had carried out from how, when and why it was initiated up until how it was completed (or up to the current point). They were also asked to open up browsers, bookmarks, email, paper folders and so on to show how they had extracted, created or moved information in each task. Not only did this support participants in recalling their tasks, it also provided additional data such as paper print-outs. Asking to be shown the artefacts being described also provided a simple, if crude, method by which the reliability of the retrospective accounts could to some extent be checked. Participants were also prompted with questions during the interview to elicit discussion about what they did and why, such as:

> Was this a typical task?
> Where did the information come from and how was it found?
> What was extracted?
> How was it used and why?
> Was anything saved, recorded or created?
> Has this been shared or could this be shared?
> Where, how and with whom was it shared?
> Would it be useful to reuse anything?

2.3   Data and Analysis

Data, in the form of videotaped interviews, were transcribed with the addition of notes concerning the artefacts shown to the interviewer and captured on video or paper (e.g. bookmarks, Web pages, printed documents). This material was then analysed task by task using thematic analysis. This involved categorizing the data using two broad themes or frameworks, driven by the literature, the data and the research aims. The first, "the life cycle of information gathering" (consisting of starting points, browsing and reading, extracting, storing and archiving and reuse) reflects the background literature and is largely based upon Turner [1997]. The second, 'information sharing' (consisting of motivations and barriers to sharing, recipients and methods of sharing, and the work to make information shareable) was largely derived from the data. Together, the analysis within these two frameworks provides both an overview of information gathering tasks as well as the detail regarding the focus of the research: information sharing. Consistent with the analysis, the findings are presented within these two frameworks, presenting comments, behaviours, artefacts and so on that are related to particular stages of the life cycle and to the components of information sharing.

3   Findings

Overall, 120 tasks were collected from the 16 participants (an average of 7.5 tasks per person, ranging from 3 to 14). Time spent doing these tasks ranged greatly from 15 minutes to 6 hours a day depending upon the stage of a project.

The majority of tasks (94) were examples of information being gathered for a specific current task such as gathering materials for a children's workshop, preparing a talk for a conference or getting ideas for a new computer game. However, some of the tasks (26) involved gathering information to satisfy a more ongoing interest such as regularly searching for organizations with similar interests, keeping up to date with what competitors were doing, or gathering illustrations or articles on a particular subject.

Unsurprisingly, while the Web was our central focus, in reality it was often one of many resources called upon in these tasks. In many cases, information was gathered from other people and other document sources such as books, magazines and journals. Having said that these knowledge workers tended to rely heavily on the Web citing quick and easy access to a vast repository of information as now essential to their current work practices.

3.1 The Life Cycle of Information Gathering

Before looking more closely at the issues of sharing, we need first to look in more detail at how these information gathering tasks were carried out, or what we might call the 'life cycle' of this kind of process. Some interesting trends emerged when we looked at where participants started their search and where the products of these tasks ended up.

3.1.1 Starting Points

For most of these tasks (76 out of 120), participants started off with known Web sources (e.g. an organization's Web site, an online database or a specific newsgroup) as opposed to Web search engines (used exclusively in 29 tasks), although sometimes they used a combination of the two (occurring in 15 tasks). A known source is a Web site that the participant may or may not have visited before but knows is there. They may know about sources through previous Web searching, through word of mouth recommendation or by anticipating that familiar real world sources such as people, publications or organizations will have an online presence. Comments suggested that through experience of use participants learnt about the information in a source, the domain and topics covered, the quality and accuracy of the information and the ease with which this information could be accessed. We could tell that at least half of the known sources had been visited before because they were accessed via bookmarks or self-authored Web pages.

With regard to search engines, participants used these either when they could not think of a useful known source or when they tried and failed to find the information they needed. They also tended to go straight to search engines when the topic of information was unfamiliar. What the data show then, is that these knowledge workers more often than not stayed within familiar domains and used familiar resources to begin their information gathering tasks. Knowledge gained about particular sources was reused in order to find and select a starting point for a task.

3.1.2 Browsing and Reading

Once a Web task had begun, participants looked through many different kinds of information, seeking information not only relevant to the topic at hand, but also anything they found new, interesting, comprehensive, accurate, up to date and well presented. This process almost always involved multiple sites, and could take place over hours, days or even weeks.

One interesting aspect of this was that the learning was often in the gathering. Many participants talked about picking up knowledge throughout the whole process of information gathering such as gaining background information, getting to know important keywords, and learning specific pieces of information as they went from site to site. It was common to hear the study participants talk of starting their searches wide to understand the bigger picture of a topic before focusing in on detail:

> "I start off fairly wide and then hone it down to particular events so then if I find something useful, started off at the 1750's, got 1700's time line, particularly got interested in slightly later, ... and then I do a search on (name of historical event) and hone it down so you've got information, quite a lot of information on particular, literally a particular day if possible." (Games Producer)

Not only were they picking up domain knowledge through this process, they were also developing their search strategies and skills. Comments suggested that such skills were perceived as essential in being able to carry out knowledge workers' work effectively.

3.1.3   Extracting

In addition to the implicit process of information extraction that went on in almost all of the tasks, participants also explicitly extracted pieces of information from the Web by copying and pasting into documents, saving whole documents as files, printing, bookmarking, archiving in email, making written notes or saving in personalized Web folders.

For example, the Customer Support person typically sought advice both from colleagues (via email, phone and face-to-face conversations) as well as searching the Web in order to find solutions to customer problems. Good sources of Web information would be kept as a bookmark possibly later being incorporated as a link on his personally authored intranet page. In addition, gathered information from various sources would sometimes be copied and pasted into a Word document. This document might be emailed to a person who would place it either on the intranet or on the Web depending on his instructions. Associated email messages were kept including the attached documents. In addition, he often saved many downloaded files or patches from the Web on his hard drive. Those that he was able to distribute would later be moved to the server for his colleagues to access.

As this illustrates, in addition to the information kept in the heads of the knowledge workers, any particular information gathering task could have associated with it several different informational 'by-products' in different formats, residing in different places. Any of these by-products could be reformatted or otherwise modified or transformed more than once. Some of these were transient or temporary, and others were useful in and of themselves. Some of these by-products were shared and others were not. Understanding how they are related and where they have come from may be quite complex.

3.1.4   Storing/Archiving

Figure 1 provides a snapshot of where these by-products ended up in participants' own information spaces. For example, URLs most commonly ended up in bookmarks, 'Other' sorts of information (such as text or images) most commonly ended up in the documents kept in personal folders. In general it was more common for information to end up in 'personal spaces' that were only accessible to the

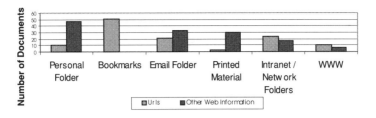

Figure 1: Graph showing the number of 'documents' containing either URLs or other extracted Web information ending up in various different storage places.

participant (i.e. personal, email and bookmark folders on the hard drive or personal folders on the network), than for information to end up in 'shared spaces' that were also accessible to others (i.e. intranet pages, shared network folders or public Web pages). It was also evident from both comments and observation that these personal and shared spaces differed in both content and organization.

With regard to content, information stored in personal spaces was described both as 'personal' (i.e. non-work) and as work information that was not 'useful' or 'relevant' to anyone else. Information may be held temporarily, in draft form or be being kept as a record of a task that has been done. Personal spaces can also be used as a dumping ground for information that does not belong anywhere else or is not appropriate to put in a shared space. Personal non-work information does not tend to be hidden away, a concern should other people suddenly have access to a personal space.

With regard to organization, although personal spaces may be described by participants as fairly organized by topic or project, it was pointed out by one individual that someone else trying to use this information would at least need to know "what I was doing and what I was supposed to be doing" (Games Producer). Indeed there was evidence of "cheating a lot" (Architect) when it came to personal organization, in that information that strictly did not 'fit into' a folder's category may be put there and similarly information that could be filed was not. By contrast, shared spaces demanded more consistent organization so that others could find information easily. Multi-contributor shared network spaces meant things might be more 'tricky' to find. In one case contribution to a shared database was controlled. This was not to do with the organization but to do with controlling the quality and amount of information that was shared, illustrating other factors are also important.

What this suggests is that participants utilized different spaces in different ways. One consequence of this is that the information in personal and shared spaces differs in its content and organization.

3.1.5 Re-use
A final issue which interested us was the potential reusability of the resulting collection of Web-derived information on gatherers' desks, PCs, and networks. Here the findings were quite striking. While participants often reused sites and sources as starting points, in only 3 of 120 cases was any content or were any documents

from past projects reused. In addition, when asked, participants said they expected to reuse information in future projects in only 12 of 120 cases.

It was quite clear then that these knowledge workers were creating bespoke products on a project-by-project basis. The way information was gathered, extracted and modified was done for the specific purpose to hand, and that purpose changed with each new project. As the Education Officer put it:

> "[The Web] is a good base of resources, … [you] will want to take pieces of it … It's not even a jigsaw, like cooking almost, you take all these relevant bits and you mix them together to make your own recipe."

By contrast, what these knowledge workers were reusing were the sources of information (and the knowledge of how to find them) together with the skills of gathering information, something they learned from long experience. For example, the Games Producer described methods of searching and extracting information that he used again and again over years of doing research. As he put it:

> "Its only when I see somebody who hasn't had [my] background try to research something that I find out that actually I'm quite good at this."

3.2 Information Sharing

Turning from the life cycle of such tasks, we now look closer at the sharing of information in such tasks.

3.2.1 Motivators and Barriers to Sharing

When we asked participants about their initial intentions, in 71 of the 120 tasks (60%) they said they were expecting to share some part of the output of their tasks. About two-thirds of these cases were driven by obligations (such as a request for information or an expectation on both sides that information will be shared, often laid down by routines or work practice). In the remaining third, participants intended to share with recipients who were not necessarily expecting anything from them. Reasons for this self-initiated sharing were often to do with promoting oneself or the organization, placing work obligations onto someone else or informing the recipient of something they ought to know. In addition to these 71 tasks where participants expected to share, there were 9 further cases in which the intention to share developed during the task (afterthought sharing).

Interestingly, there were many factors involved in why some information was not shared. In some cases, participants were restricted by copyright or company confidentiality restrictions. In other cases, participants wished to keep personally relevant information confidential (e.g. the Territory Manager was concerned that some of his bookmarks revealed his interests and where he banked or shopped). Some participants were unsure as to whom might find it useful (e.g. the Researcher copied information into an email to share with work colleagues and then deleted it, not being sure whether it would be useful or interesting to colleagues). Additionally not knowing how to share, or the effort involved in sharing, could influence whether something was shared (e.g. the Information Resource Manager wanted to share bookmarks but could not remember how to do this. And similarly, the Research

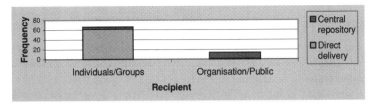

Figure 2: Graph illustrating how often information was shared with individuals / groups vs. organizations/general public.

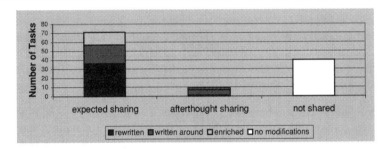

Figure 3: Number of tasks in which people shared information as expected or as an afterthought or in which information was not shared. Also shown is whether the information was rewritten, written around, enriched or unmodified.

Scientist said he would have liked to share more information on his Web page but having to pass this information through a colleague to make the alterations, had not got around to doing so).

3.2.2 Recipients and Methods of Sharing

Sharing was most often with individuals or small groups, and this was done mainly through methods that delivered information direct to the recipient(s) (i.e. via email, fax, memo or face-to-face). On fewer occasions, sharing was with the larger organization or the public, this being done mainly via central repositories (the Web, Intranet or central database or store). This is illustrated in Figure 2.

3.2.3 The Work to Make Information Shareable

One of the issues we were most interested in was what, if anything, tended to be done to the extracted Web information in the case of information intended to be shared vs. that not intended for sharing.

We found that information intended for sharing was always modified after it was extracted, whereas this was very unlikely to occur in information that was not shared (Figure 3). Specifically, we found that shared information could be modified three ways, none of which was mutually exclusive. It could be:

- rewritten;

- written around; or

- enriched at the point of delivery through the attachment of extra information.

In this last case, we mean that participants talked of adding context to, or explaining the information they were delivering through conversations, e-mail, faxes or memos at the point of handing it over.

The important point to note here is that shared information was modified in ways that non-shared information was not. This is not to say that no work was associated with personal information, but rather that this work was largely mental work (e.g. reading and comprehending), or work at the point of extracting the information which was limited to filtering, categorizing and organizing the information as opposed to modifying its content in any way.

So what exactly was being accomplished through modification? Looking more closely, we can see that there were many ways in which the information was being re-designed to make it easy to understand and to use by its recipients. This is illustrated by a quotation from the Education Officer:

> "you know teachers have not got time for anything really ... and they keep getting told to do new things and so if you're making it easy, they're going to use it. So I mean especially for education, it's a really useful tool, the Internet, ... information is what I am in the business of, information finding, it is an absolute nightmare ... there must be ways of making it more useful for them (teachers)."

While the idea of recipient design is certainly not new, going back to Harvey Sacks in the 1960s [Sacks 1992], it is interesting to look at what this means in terms of sharing Web information. There were many ways in which this took place:

Checking and filtering: During the gathering process itself, participants checked and filtered information to ensure its usefulness. Information was checked for accuracy against other sources (e.g. experts, other Web pages, own knowledge or colleagues), and judgements were made as to whether the information was of good quality and up to date. Participants also talked of only sharing information from sites that were trusted or familiar.

Translating, modifying and organizing: After extracting information, participants changed or re-organized information to ensure that it was easy to find, use and understand. This was done by:

- Changing the information format, size or language. File formats were changed to those that the recipient was most likely to be able to access or use (e.g. from CAD to bitmap; from digital to print). File sizes were cut (by zipping, removing content or reducing resolution of images). There were even examples of translating content into a recipient's native language.

- Simplifying. Information was sometimes simplified to suit its readership and a recipient's concerns. For example, language was simplified for use by children or information was cut down to its bare essentials, to reduce time and effort in scanning information, and to make it relevant to a recipient's request.

- Guiding by highlighting, organizing, signposting and explaining. Several types of cues were added to information to guide the reader. This ranged from highlighting important information, to organizing and structuring information in clusters, to inserting headings and labels. Sometimes, this included adding more explicit 'signposts' (such as step by step instructions on how to navigate the information or by adding descriptions of which link to choose for what). Sometimes it included overviews or summary explanations telling the recipient what the information was for and why they were sharing it.

Enriched delivery: We also saw that added messages, explanation or discussion often took place at the point of delivery, even if this was not done physically but in the digital realm (e.g. through email). These findings are consistent with other studies that show that information, such as documents, are often discussed with the recipient at the point of delivery [Harper 1998] in order to put them in context.

Maintaining and updating information: Finally, even after information was made available to others, sharing information on a persistent basis (either through HTML pages or regular email bulletins) also placed a burden of maintenance upon the participant. This meant there was a need to regularly add new information, update old information and check links on Web or intranet pages.

Therefore our participants expected to and did share information in a substantial proportion of their information gathering tasks despite a variety of factors that could act as barriers to sharing. Information was usually shared with individuals or groups using methods that allowed information to be delivered directly to the recipient(s). Although some form of work was carried out on the information gathered in the tasks, the work carried out on shared information was fundamentally different in nature and extent when compared to that carried out on non-shared information.

4 Implications and Conclusions

To conclude, there are several key points to take from these findings, each of which has implications for p2p information sharing:

The knowledge workers in this study more often than not dealt with familiar topics and used familiar resources to begin their information gathering tasks. By implication, we can assume that since knowing the source of information is so important in the Web gathering process, then likewise, p2p knowledge sharing systems will need to make explicit some important aspects of the source of p2p information. For example, it may be important to know aspects of the person from whence the information came (e.g. what their expertise is) as well as details about how and from where they gathered their information.

Knowledge workers learn from the process of searching and gathering. By implication, if users are given access to the products of someone else's search efforts (essentially bypassing their own search and gathering processes) it is conceivable that they might also bypass the opportunity to do some of their own implicit learning. Access to the products of someone else's work might therefore ultimately be shown to be a less effective way of gaining knowledge than doing one's own information gathering work.

Any given information gathering task may have associated with it many different kinds of informational by-products. Some are transient or intermediate products and some are more properly 'end' products. Some are Web-based and some are not. Some exist in the digital world and some are physical. Thus, by-products of these kinds of tasks are part of an 'information ecology' where the relationship between artefacts over time and space may be important to understand. The implication here is that looking at any one document or piece of information may not be useful without looking at the bigger picture, or without understanding how it has come to be. As pointed out by [Kidd 1994], this contextual knowledge may be in the head of the person who has created the information, but may not necessarily be obvious to an outsider looking 'in'. This is related to the next point.

Personal and shared spaces are used differently, the content and organization of the information being found in personal information spaces being fundamentally different to that being kept on shared spaces such as the Web. Personal spaces are akin to 'workbenches' whereas shared spaces are more like 'archives'. The implication is that p2p systems that tap into personal spaces are, as predicted, likely to unlock information that is fundamentally different to that found in archives, central repositories or the Web. By their very nature they may not be browseable or searchable in the same way as archives are. Therefore traditional p2p mechanisms for file sharing may not be appropriate for sharing information in workplaces. This is aside from questions raised in the following points as to whether this content is actually of any value to other people.

Information that has been gathered with a specific task in mind is rarely repurposed or reused for new tasks. This then begs the question: If information gathered by an individual is not perceived to be usable in the future by its owner, to what extent can any of these products be reused or repurposed by other people? By implication they will have to have similar purposes or tasks to hand. This suggests that p2p tools need a way of allowing users to effectively specify and match these across users.

Knowledge workers often shared information as part of their information gathering tasks and this was mostly to individuals and groups using methods that delivered information directly to the recipients. This implies that at least some products from these tasks are usable and shareable with peers [which is consistent with the findings that information tends to be shared within small communities of interest, Iamnitchi et al. [2002]. However, p2p systems may benefit from looking at ways in which information can be directly delivered to recipients in response to an explicit request or through identifying recipients who have an interest or need for the information. This would be more consistent with the way that knowledge workers currently share information as opposed to models where information is placed in an area such as the Web for people to find and gather for themselves.

The work carried out on non-shared information is not the same in nature or extent as the work carried out to make information shareable, where information is prepared with specific recipients or audiences in mind. Given some information will have been prepared for sharing and others will not have, it will not be obvious how to distinguish between the two let alone identify within a workspace those documents which match the needs of any particular recipient. Designers of p2p knowledge sharing tools might usefully learn by looking at the kind of work that is done to make information shareable by others. Some of this work might be done automatically, but some may not. It is likely, given the nature of these modifications, that the experience gained in the process of gathering, using or creating a knowledge-based product in turn provides much of the knowledge required to effectively prepare this information for sharing. In any case, merely enabling access to another person's information will not be enough to leverage the knowledge between them.

By studying knowledge workers' Web information gathering tasks we have highlighted both constraints and opportunities for the design of p2p information sharing systems. This work can be treated not only as a set of cautionary notes about some of the underlying assumptions of such systems, but also as pointing towards ways in which such tools might be developed in new ways. While we have focused on Web-based information gathering, we believe these results have more general application for the sharing of information across individuals, whether it is derived from the Web or not. Ultimately, the generalizability of these data, as well as specific design solutions will depend on a more extensive programme of user research than is reported here.

Acknowledgements

We thank all the knowledge workers who took part in this study both for their openness and their insights. Thanks also to Richard Harper and Martin Merry for comments on an earlier draft.

References

Aronson, J. [1994], A Pragmatic View of Thematic Analysis, *The Qualitative Report* **2**(1). Available at http://www.nova.edu/ssss/QR/aindex.html (last accessed 2003.05.26).

Banks, D., Cayzer, S., Dickinson, I. & Reynolds, D. [2002], The ePerson Snippet Manager: A Semantic Web Application, Technical Report HPL-2002-328, HP Labs.

Bannon, L. & Bødker, S. [1997], Constructing Common Information Spaces, *in* J. Hughes, W. Prinz, T. Rodden & K. Schmidt (eds.), *Proceedings of ECSCW'97, the 5th European Conference on Computer-supported Cooperative Work*, Kluwer, pp.81–96.

Bates, M. J. [1989], The Design of Browsing and Berrypicking Techniques for the Online Search Interface, *Online Review* **13**(5), 407–31.

Berlin, L. M., Jeffries, R., O'Day, V., Paepke, A. & Wharton, C. [1993], Where Did You Put It? Issues in the Design and Use of a Group Memory, Technical Report HPL-93-11, HP Labs.

Bonifacio, M., Bouquet, P. & Traverso, P. [2002], Enabling Distributed Knowledge Management: Managerial and Technological Implications, *Novatica and Informatik/Informatique* **3**(1), 23–9.

Breidenbach, S. [2001], Feature: Peer-to-peer Potential, Network World Fusion: http://www.nwfusion.com/research/2001/0730feat.html (last accessed 2003.05.26).

Bricklin, D. [2000], Thoughts on Peer-to-peer, http://www.bricklin.com/p2p.htm (last accessed 2003.05.26).

Harper, R. H. R. [1998], *Inside the IMF: An Ethnography of Documents, Technology and Organisational Action*, Academic Press.

Hearst, M. A. [1999], User Interfaces and Visualization, *in* R. Baeze-Yates & B. Ribeiro-Neto (eds.), *Modern Information Retrieval*, ACM Press, Chapter 10, pp.257–323.

Hoelscher, C. & Strube, G. [1999], Searching on the Web: Two Types of Expertise (poster abstract), *in* F. Gey, M. Hearst & R. Tong (eds.), *SIGIR'99 Proceedings of the 22nd Annual International ACM SIGIR Conference on Research and Development in Information Retrieval*, ACM Press, pp.305–306.

Iamnitchi, A., Ripeanu, M. & Foster, I. [2002], Locating Data in Small-World: Peer-to-Peer Scientific Collaborations, *in* P. Druschel, F. Kaashoek & A. Rowstron (eds.), *Peer-to-Peer Systems: First International Workshop IPTPS 2002*, Vol. 2429 of *Lecture Notes in Computer Science*, Springer-Verlag, pp.232–41.

Jones, W. P., Bruce, H. & Dumais, S. T. [2001], Keeping Found Things Found on the Web, *in* H. Paques, L. Liu & D. Grossman (eds.), *Proceedings of ACM's CIKM'01, the Tenth International Conference on Information and Knowledge Management*, ACM Press, pp.119–26.

Kamiya, K., Röscheisen, M. & Winograd, T. [1996], Grassroots: A System Providing a Uniform Framework for Communicating, Structuring, Sharing Information, and Organizing People, *Computer Networks and ISDN Systems* **28**(7–11), 1157–74.

Kanawati, R. & Malek, M. [2000], Informing the Design of Shared Bookmark Systems, *in* J. Mariani & D. Harman (eds.), *Proceedings of RIAO 2000, Content-based Multimedia Information Access*, Centre de Hautes Etudes Internationales d'Informatique Documententaire (CID) / Centre for Advanced Study of Information Systems (CASIS), pp.170–80. Available via http://citeseer.nj.nec.com/414039.html (last accessed 2003.05.26).

Kidd, A. [1994], The Marks are on the Knowledge Worker, *in* B. Adelson, S. Dumais & J. Olson (eds.), *Proceedings of the CHI'94 Conference on Human Factors in Computing Systems: Celebrating Interdependence*, ACM Press, pp.186–91.

Kubiatowicz, T. [2003], Extracting Guarantees from Chaos, *Communications of the ACM* **46**(2), 33–8.

Markus, L. [2001], Toward a Theory of Knowledge Reuse: Types of Knowledge Reuse Situations and Factors in Reuse Success, *Journal of Management Information Systems* **18**(1), 57–93.

Paepcke, A. [1996], Information Needs in Technical Work Settings and their Implications for the Design of Computer Tools, *Computer Supported Cooperative Work* **5**(1), 63–92.

Pirolli, P. & Card, S. K. [1995], Information Foraging in Information Access Environments, *in* I. Katz, R. Mack, L. Marks, M. B. Rosson & J. Nielsen (eds.), *Proceedings of the CHI'95 Conference on Human Factors in Computing Systems*, ACM Press, pp.51–8.

Sacks, H. [1992], *Lectures on Conversation*, Vol. 1 & 2, Blackwell. Edited by Gail Jefferson.

Sato, H., Abe, Y. & Kanai, A. [2002], Hyperclip: A Tool for Gathering and Sharing Meta-data on Users' Activities by Using Peer-to-peer Technology, http://www.cs.rutgers.edu/~shklar/www11/final_submissions/paper12.pdf (last accessed 2003.05.26).

Sellen, A. J., Murphy, R. & Shaw, K. L. [2002], How Knowledge Workers use the Web, *in* D. Wixon (ed.), *Proceedings of CHI'02 Conference on Human Factors in Computing Systems: Changing our World, Changing Ourselves*, *CHI Letters* **4**(1), ACM Press, pp.227–34.

Takeda, H., Matsuzuka, T. & Taniguchi, Y. [2000], Discovery of Shared Topics Networks among People — A Simple Approach to Find Community Knowledge from WWW Bookmarks, *in* R. Mizoguchi & J. K. Slaney (eds.), *PRICAI 2000: Topics in Artificial Intelligence — 6th Pacific Rim International Conference on Artificial Intelligence*, Vol. 1886 of *Lecture Notes in Artifical Intelligence*, Springer-Verlag, pp.668–78.

Turner, K. [1997], Information Seeking, Retrieving, Reading and Storing Behaviour of Library-users, http://citeseer.nj.nec.com/264174.html (last accessed 2003.05.26).

Wexelblat, A. & Maes, P. [1999], Footprints: History-rich Tools for Information Foraging, *in* M. G. Williams & M. W. Altom (eds.), *Proceedings of the CHI'99 Conference on Human Factors in Computing Systems: The CHI is the Limit*, ACM Press, pp.75–84.

Evaluation of a Prototype Interface for Structured Document Retrieval

Jane Reid & Mark D Dunlop[†]

Department of Computer Science, Queen Mary, University of London, London E1 4NS, UK
Email: *Jane@dcs.qmul.ac.uk*

[†] *Department of Computer and Information Sciences, University of Strathclyde, Glasgow G1 1XH, UK*
Email: *Mark.Dunlop@cis.strath.ac.uk*

Document collections often display either internal structure, in the form of the logical arrangement of document components, or external structure, in the form of links between documents. Structured document retrieval systems aim to exploit this structural information to provide users with more effective access to structured documents. To do this, the associated interface must both represent this information explicitly and support users in their browsing behaviour. This paper describes the implementation and user-centred evaluation of a prototype interface, the RelevanceLinkBar interface. The results of the evaluation show that the RelevanceLinkBar interface supported users in their browsing behaviour, allowing them to find more relevant documents, and was strongly preferred over a standard results interface.

Keywords: search result & hyperlink graph visualization, searching & browsing, information retrieval, Web search engines, usability evaluation.

1 Introduction

Document collections often display structural characteristics. Structure can be found both within an individual document (e.g. a report may contain sections and subsections) and between documents (e.g. Web documents may be connected by hyperlinks). Structured document retrieval (SDR) aims to combine structural and content information in order to improve retrieval effectiveness [e.g. Brin & Page 1998; Kotsakis 2002; Wilkinson 1994], cut down the amount of time and effort a user spends in identifying relevant information [e.g. Fuhr & Großjohann 2001; Roelleke 1999], and reduce time and disorientation caused by lack of proximity of related document components in results interfaces [e.g. Chiaramella et al. 1996].

Structural information can be exploited at several stages of the information retrieval process: firstly, the indexing stage, where document components are identified and indexed as separate, but related, units [Cleveland et al. 1984; Tenopir & Ro 1990]; secondly, the retrieval stage, using passage retrieval [e.g. Salton et al. 1993], data modelling approaches [Burkowski 1992; Navarro & Baeza-Yates 1995], or aggregation-based approaches [e.g. Frisse 1988; Dunlop & van Rijsbergen 1993; Lalmas & Moutogianni 2000; Roelleke et al. 2002]; and, thirdly, at the results presentation stage, using visualization techniques such as TileBars Hearst [1995], fisheye views [Furnas 1999] and expand/collapse operations [e.g. Hertzum & Frøkjær 1996], or grouping of related objects (e.g. Google's use of sub-lists in an otherwise traditional-style ranked document list; Northern Light Search's clustering interface).

The method that is investigated in this paper, however, focuses on exploiting users' natural browsing behaviour by employing the concept of *best entry points*. A best entry point (BEP) is a document component (or whole document) from which a user can obtain optimal access, by browsing, to relevant document components [Chiaramella et al. 1996; Kazai et al. 2001]. The use of BEPs is thus intended to support the information-seeking behaviour of users, and enable them to gain more effective and efficient access to relevant information items.

Two methods of employing the concept of BEPs are currently being investigated. In the first approach, results presentation is explicitly focused by presentation of BEPs, rather than relevant components. This approach is achieved through the use of *focused retrieval*, which derives relevance scores for each document component based on the aggregation of the component itself and its structurally related components. This information may be used in conjunction with a set of heuristics to derive BEPs from a traditional ranked list of document components produced by an SDR system [Kazai et al. 2002]. Only these explicit BEPs are then presented to the user. In the second approach, standard relevant document components are presented to the user. However, the interface is designed to support users identify implicit BEPs within the results list quickly and easily, i.e. document components from which the user can easily and quickly browse to other relevant document components.

This paper describes the implementation and initial evaluation of a prototype interface for supporting SDR, the RelevanceLinkBar (RLB) interface. The work discussed here involved the implementation of the RLB interface on the Web, using the Google interface as a basis. A user-centred experimental evaluation was then carried out to evaluate the potential ability of the interface to support explicit or implicit use of BEPs. The evaluation compared the effectiveness, efficiency and usability of the RLB interface with the standard Google interface.

Section 2 describes the RLB interface in detail. Section 3 outlines the elements of the experimental design: the participants, tasks, experimental methodology and data collection methods. Section 4 presents the main results of the experiment in terms of the interface's effectiveness, efficiency and usability within the context of its aim to support the use of BEPs. Both quantitative and qualitative analysis of data was performed. We close with conclusions and further work in Section 5.

2   The RelevanceLinkBar Interface

In this section, we discuss both the generic properties of the RLB interface, and its implementation in the specific context of this experiment.

The RLB interface (see Figure 1) is a prototype interface that employs a novel visualization technique based on a standard ranked results list, but additionally providing the explicit representation of any links found within the document; the motivation behind RLB is similar to that of Hearst's [1995] TileBars interface. This information is provided, for each document surrogate, in the form of a bar of boxes, each of which represents an individual link. Each link box is coloured to represent the degree of relevance of the corresponding linked document. The degree of relevance of each link could be calculated using one of many possible criteria, e.g. the presence or absence of query terms in the linked document, or the appearance of the linked document in the ranked list. Each bar thus provides three pieces of information: firstly, the total number of links contained in a document; secondly, the degree of relevance of each of those links; and, thirdly, a graphical representation of the distribution of the links within the document, with relation to each other. The assumption behind the representation of the link distribution is that it will facilitate the identification of documents, or document components, that display a high concentration of relevant links. By positioning the mouse pointer over an individual link box, any available information about the linked document, e.g. document title or keywords, can be viewed.

The interface is intended to support users' information-seeking behaviour in two main ways. Firstly, it is intended to enable more efficient browsing by its explicit representation of contained links. Secondly, it is intended to improve the quality of document surrogates as predictors of document relevance, by providing information that will allow users to assess quickly the potential usefulness of a document as a starting-point for further investigation. It is thus an ideal candidate interface to support effective, implicit identification of BEPs for an SDR system. The user has two main browsing strategies open to him: to click on the URL belonging to a document directly represented in the ranked results list, and browse from there, or to progress indirectly to a linked document by clicking on one of the RLB link boxes.

For this work, the RLB interface was constructed on top of the Google ranked results list interface. The RLB was implemented as a Java servlet querying Google (initially through HTML parsing of results, and now using the Google API). The experiment reported in this paper used two versions of the Google interface:

Plain: A slightly reduced version of the standard Google interface.

RLB: Identical to plain except for the addition of relevance link bars.

Figure 1: The RelevanceLinkBar Interface.

Both versions used the same servlet for querying and were coded, as far as possible, to have comparable search times. Once the top 100 Google search results had been retrieved, each entry in the top 10 was post-processed as follows:

1. The target page was loaded by the Java servlet.

2. The page was parsed to extract its list of links.

3. Each of these links was then annotated with the position of its target page in the original top 100 search results.

Once annotated links had been produced for the top 10 search results (or a preset time limit had expired), the servlet returned the results as a plain or RLB page, depending on the interface version. For the RLB interface, each annotated link was translated into a box on the RelevanceLinkBar, with the darkness of the box being determined by the closeness of the link destination to the top of the Google Top100. Although this prototype servlet implementation slows searching to some degree, any future implementation would be based at a search engine site, where much of the information is stored locally. The RLB link bar itself is composed by repetition of four small images, and uses plain HTML. The impact of the RLB on query execution time would, therefore, be negligible.

An initial technical evaluation of the RLB interface was carried out, with the aim of verifying the claim that it offers additional and distinct information from a standard ranked results interface. A sample of 19 queries from MetaSpy.com was submitted to Google, and 100 documents were requested in the results set. RLBs were then calculated for the resulting ranked document list, according to the method described above. The data were examined for a correlation between document ranking and the percentage of relevant links contained within each document. There was no noticeable correspondence between these two measures, confirming that the concept of RLBs offers additional information not available from a standard ranked document list. The next stage was to perform a user-centred experimental evaluation in order to examine the characteristics of the RLB interface in more detail.

3   Experimental Design

The overall purpose of the experiment was to evaluate the ability of the RLB interface to support users in the use of BEPs. This involved a comparison of the RLB interface with the plain ranked results interface, in terms of effectiveness, efficiency, usability and overall user satisfaction. The following sub-sections discuss in more detail the participants, tasks, experimental methodology and data collection methods.

3.1   Participants

Twelve participants were recruited, and a pre-questionnaire (Questionnaire A) was issued to all participants, in order to elicit information on personal and educational background, domain knowledge, collection knowledge and general information-seeking preferences and strategies. It was also used to collect descriptions of four real information needs per participant, two of which were later selected by the experimenter as the basis for experimental tasks for that participant (Section 3.2).

Of the 12 participants, 5 male and 7 female, and the average age was 25 (youngest 22, oldest 36). Eleven of the 12 were students and 1 was a desktop publishing employee. The students were mostly from a computer science background (7 participants), with some from civil engineering (2) and information technology (2). On a five-point scale, 11 of the 12 participants described both their experience with computers and their experience with Internet tools as excellent (point 1 on the scale) or good (point 2). Seven of the 12 used the Web on a daily basis, and all participants used it at least once a week. Ten of the 12 participants had used Google; other previously used search sites were Yahoo and Lycos.

Participants were also asked some general questions about their usual information-seeking preferences and strategies. The first question in this category was intended to establish the participants' criteria for a successful search. Four participants stated that they preferred to be presented with only highly relevant documents, while seven aimed to find most of the relevant documents available. This indicates that the participants were (unusually) biased towards a recall-oriented search, rather than a precision-oriented search. The majority of participants consciously employed both query-based and browsing strategies in the course of their information-seeking, with only 1 participant claiming to use querying exclusively, and only 2 claiming to use browsing exclusively. Half the participants stated that, when faced with a ranked document results list, they examined the documents sequentially, according to the ranked order, while 5 stated they examined the documents selectively. One participant stated that he combined these two strategies. Participants were also asked for reasons why they might consider a document to be non-relevant: common reasons were the language and age of the document, and the quality of the information contained within it.

3.2 Tasks

After a short period exploring each interface, each participant was allocated 4 tasks in total, 2 for completion during the first stage of the experiment and two during the second stage. Half of these tasks (one for each stage) were based on information needs gathered from the participants themselves in Questionnaire A. The other tasks were simulated, i.e. generated by the experimenter. This design was adopted in order to provide some tasks for which the participants should be highly motivated to find the answers, and some for which results could be compared across participants. The simulated tasks, which were chosen to be of general interest, i.e. not requiring any specialist knowledge or understanding, were:

1. I would like to find information on Greek philosophy and philosophers. I would like to read about the philosophers of ancient Greece (e.g. Aristotle and Plato) and their work. This is a general interest of mine.

   Search statement: Greek philosophy and Greek philosophers.

2. I have to write a report on the Seven Wonders of the World. I have been asked to give a good description of each (e.g. where they are located, the history of them, why they are considered wonders, etc.).

   Search statement: Seven Wonders of the World.

3.3 Experimental Methodology

The experiment was divided into two main stages: a usability evaluation and a functionality evaluation. Both interfaces were used in both stages of the experiment. We wished to assess both the participants' first impressions of the interface and their opinions after they had used the interface for a period of time. It was, therefore, decided to run the usability evaluation first, in order to collect users' first impressions. Any confusion or remaining queries could then be answered before the second stage of the experiment, the functionality evaluation. This would avoid any bias in our functionality results due to lack of knowledge about the interface.

A within-subjects design was followed, with each participant undertaking both experimental conditions in both stages of the experiment. Each participant was allocated 4 tasks in total, two for completion in the first stage of the experiment (one real and one simulated), and two for the second stage (one real and one simulated). The participants were assigned to experimental conditions so that half of them performed a real task followed by a simulated task in the first stage, then a simulated task first followed by a real task in the second stage. The other 6 participants performed the real and simulated tasks in the opposite order. Different sets of tasks were used for Stages 1 and 2 of the experiment, in order to avoid learning effects. Since the participants all had previous experience of using both Web search engines and the RLB interface itself (from practice sessions), it was not deemed necessary to

	User Tasks	Participant	Experimenter
Stage 1	Usability task 1 Usability task 2	Questionnaire A (*background*) Questionnaire B (*usability*)	
Stage 2	Functionality task 1 Functionality task 2	Recording Form A (*relevance*) Questionnaire C part 1 (*functionality*) Recording Form A (*relevance*) Questionnaire C part 2 (*functionality*) Questionnaire C part 3 (*preference*)	Recording Form B (*observation*) Recording Form B (*observation*)

Table 1: Summary of experimental methodology.

alternate the order of the experimental conditions themselves, so the participants all used the RLB interface first, and the plain interface second.

3.4 Data Collection

Background information about the participants was collected by a pre-questionnaire (Questionnaire A, see Section 3.1). There were 2 further questionnaires: a usability questionnaire (B), and a functionality questionnaire (C). In addition, two recording forms were employed: a relevance recording form (Recording Form A) used by the participants, and an observation form (Recording Form B) used by the experimenter. Table 1 shows a summary of the experimental methodology and data collection methods.

The usability questionnaire (B) was intended to elicit opinions on the learnability, ease of use, and good and bad points of the interface, together with suggestions for improvements and a preference for one of the two systems.

On the relevance recording form (Recording Form A), participants recorded their order of assessment of the documents in the results list and their assessment of the relevance of each individual document (relevant, partially relevant or non-relevant). They also recorded their desired ordering of the documents, i.e. the order in which they would like to have viewed the documents originally.

At the same time, the experimenter recorded her observations (Recording Form B) of the number of visited links, the number of steps a participant took to fully explore an individual document, the number of unreliable links encountered and the total amount of time spent on each document.

After each task in Stage 2, the participants filled in part of a functionality questionnaire (Questionnaire C), which elicited information regarding their satisfaction with the results for that particular task.

Ease of use of RLB	
Straightforward	4
Ambiguous	7
Totally confusing	1

Link reliability	
Reliable	9
Relatively reliable	3
Completely unreliable	0

Table 2: Usability results.

Finally, the user was asked to restate an overall preference for one of the two interfaces (in Questionnaire C).

3.5   Results and Analysis

The results are presented under 5 main headings, each section corresponding to one of the questionnaires or forms. Where appropriate, results are given across all tasks, and across simulated tasks only. In order to check that participants were equally motivated when performing simulated tasks as real tasks, the amount of time the participants spent on each type of task was analysed. For real tasks, the total amount of time spent was 104 minutes 4 seconds (mean 8 minutes 40 seconds per task). For simulated tasks, the total amount of time spent was 86 minutes 28 seconds (mean 7 minutes 12 seconds per task). This difference was found to be non-significant at $p <= 0.10$ using a parametric T-test, thus showing that participants treated both types of task with equal seriousness.

3.6   Usability Analysis

Participants were firstly asked to rate the RLB interface on a 3-point scale for 2 questions: how straightforward and easy to use it was, and how reliable the links were. The results are shown in Table 2.

Participants were then asked to state up to 5 good points and 5 bad points of each interface. Although a broad variety of opinions were displayed here, some of the common views expressed were as follows:

- The plain interface was described as simple to use (5 participants), providing sufficient information (4) and a familiar interface (3). However, 3 participants pointed out that browsing is necessary to find relevant information.

- The RLB interface was praised for its indication of relevant links (7 participants), economy of space (2), time-saving support for browsing (2), and the additional information provided by the link bar (2). However, 2 participants stated that the use of colour was not a good indicator of relevance and 2 stated that the pop-up boxes for individual links did not provide enough information.

It is clear from the participants' stated interface preferences that the value of the additional information provided by the RLB interface, together with its ability to allow users faster access to relevant information, outweigh the disadvantages of the interface.

	RLB		Plain	
Relevant documents found	5.50	(4.83)	4.83	(3.50)
Partially relevant docs found	2.42	(2.50)	2.33	(2.00)
Non-relevant found	1.66	(2.00)	2.58	(4.33)

Table 3: Mean documents found per relevance category.

3.7 Relevance Assessment Analysis

Analysis of the participants' relevance assessments was based on data gathered from Recording Form A, which was filled in by the participants as they completed each of the two tasks in the second stage of the experiment. The analysis focused on comparison of the number of relevant, partially relevant and non-relevant documents found using the RLB interface vs. the plain interface. This analysis was performed across all tasks, and then across the simulated tasks only. The statistical test used was the parametric t-test (related for within-subject, used across all tasks, and unrelated for between-subjects, used across simulated tasks only).

Table 3 shows the mean number of documents found per relevance category over all searches with a given interface and, in parentheses, over only the simulated tasks. Significant results are shown in *emphasis* ($p <= 0.10$).

In summary, participants found significantly less non-relevant documents with the RLB interface than the plain interface. The results also indicate that participants found more relevant and partially relevant documents with the RLB interface; however, this finding was only significant for relevant documents found during simulated tasks.

3.8 Ranking Correlation Analysis

Participants were asked to state two rankings on Recording Form A: firstly, the order in which they assessed the documents, and, secondly, the order in which they finally decided that they would like to have originally seen the documents. The system's ranking of the retrieved documents was also logged. Correlations between these rankings were then investigated by means of Spearman's Rank Correlation with the following aims:

- The system ranking / order of assessment correlation was analysed in combination with the participants' stated preference for judging document rankings sequentially or selectively (Section 4.1), in order to identify which interface provides better support for selective examination of documents.

- The order of assessment / final ranking correlation examined which interface provides better support for participants in identifying a good order of assessment of documents.

- The final ranking / system ranking correlation examined which interface better matched the participants' retrospective evaluation of document relevance.

	RLB	Plain
Overall satisfaction		
	RLB	Plain
Very Satisfied	7	4
Satisfied	4	8
Dissatisfied	1	0

Contribution to problem resolution	RLB	Plain
Substantial	7	6
Good	4	5
Little	0	1
Very little	1	0
Nothing	0	0

Table 4: Results from functionality analysis.

None of these correlations were found to be significant, indicating no difference in performance between the two interface variants ($p <= 0.025$). Overall, participants were slightly more likely to disagree with the system ranking of the RLB interface than the plain interface, which may indicate that the display of links provided by the RLB encouraged participants to seek an alternative order of assessment. Participants may have been inhibited from making a more consistent attempt to identify implicit BEPs by the small number of retrieved documents and the strong influence of presentation order in this context [Purgailis Parker & Johnson 1990]. This supposition is supported by the sequential assessment of documents, over both interface variants, by several participants who had previously stated a preference for selective assessment.

3.9 Functionality Analysis

Participants were asked to rate their experience of each of the interfaces after they had performed the task using that interface. They were asked to comment on their satisfaction with the results, what contribution the results had made to the resolution of the problem, and whether it was worth the time spent. Participants were asked, at the end of the experiment, to express a preference for one interface. This preference was then compared with the preference expressed after Stage 1 of the experiment (usability evaluation) to see if their opinions changed with greater exposure and experience.

Table 4 shows overall satisfaction with the results and how much users felt the results contributed to resolution of the problem. Eleven of the participants using the RLB interface and all participants using the plain interface stated that the time they had spent on their searches had been worthwhile. 10 of the 12 participants stated a final preference for the RLB interface over the plain interface.

One participant, performing a real task using a very general search statement on the RLB interface, experienced considerable problems, which she attributed to the interface; this dissatisfaction is reflected in the results presented here. However, it was later determined that the problem lay with the task, and would, therefore, have been replicated if repeated on the plain interface.

In summary, the RLB interface showed slightly higher levels of overall satisfaction and satisfaction with the individual search results, and was strongly preferred over the plain interface.

	RLB		Plain	
Links visited	18.67	(18.83)	14.75	(14.83)
Total steps	37.83	(38.67)	29.58	(29.67)
Time spent (min:sec)	8:50	(9:29)	7:02	(7:51)

Table 5: Observational results.

3.10 Observation Measure Analysis

The experimenter observed 3 main measures in the course of the experiment: the number of links the participants visited during the session, the number of steps involved in each task, and the time spent in evaluation of the retrieved documents. Again, the parametric T-test was used to test for statistical significance.

Table 5 shows the results — none of which were statistically significant ($p <= 0.10$). The, albeit non-significant, differences can be partially explained by the observation that some participants first followed the main links from the retrieved list (ignoring the RLB bar) and browsed to other links from within these documents. They then returned to the retrieved list and followed links from the RLB, resulting in another visit to the same pages. This appeared to be a way of checking the accuracy and reliability of the RLB interface, so this effect could be reduced by further experience with the interface.

In summary, although participants did spend more time and effort on the RLB interface, this difference was not significant, and the participants appeared to judge any additional effort worthwhile.

4 Conclusions and Further Work

This paper has introduced the RelevanceLinkBar (RLB) interface for supporting structured document retrieval, described a prototype implementation of the interface, and presented the results of an initial user-centred evaluation. The results of the evaluation show that users found more relevant, and less non-relevant, documents when using the RLB interface compared to a standard Web search interface.

The evaluation failed to prove that the RLB interface is suitable for the implicit identification of BEPs. This was demonstrated by the lack of correspondence between the order of document assessment and the final user ranking, showing that the interface did not significantly support effective identification of BEPs by the participants. This result requires further investigation using a larger scale experiment with more than 10 retrieved documents per query, as the small size of the retrieved set may have artificially discouraged participants from scanning the results list selectively in order to find best entry points.

The results did show, however, that the interface provided good support for browsing, as evidenced by the increased use of links and the qualitative feedback elicited from the participants. We can conclude, therefore, that the interface should prove effective when used in conjunction with explicit representation of BEPs. A further experiment to test, directly, the validity of this conclusion should be carried out.

Finally, although the RLB interface was preferred to the standard interface by 10 of the 12 participants, improvements are required in order to ensure that the interface is both reliable and usable. More information in the pop-up boxes for individual links in the RLB would be useful, e.g. document title or brief surrogate. The graded relevance links did not always appear to support users effectively in their identification of relevant documents, so further investigation of the use of degrees of relevance for links representation is recommended. Other variants of the RLB, e.g. showing only relevant (or partially relevant) links, should be implemented and evaluated, in order to assess what combination of information best supports users in their information seeking behaviour. In addition, in order to support both effective browsing behaviour and effective navigation, the RLB could continue to be shown throughout the examination of the main documents from the retrieved list and the documents linked from those. This could be achieved by presenting the RLB for each of the main documents in a separate window, while linked documents are being examined. Further experiments to evaluate all the above variations will be required.

Acknowledgements

The main experimental work described in this paper was carried out at Queen Mary, University of London during summer 2001 by Zoi Gkaranatsi, as fulfilment of the project component of the MSc in Advanced Methods in Computer Science. The project was partly supported by The Royal Society international exchange programme.

References

Brin, S. & Page, L. [1998], The Anatomy of a Large-scale Hypertextual Web Search Engine, *in* H. Ashman & P. Thistlewaite (eds.), *Proceedings of the Seventh International World Wide Web Conference (WWW7)*, Vol. 30(1–7) of *Computer Networks and ISDN Systems*, Elsevier Science, pp.107–17. See also http://www7.scu.edu.au/.

Burkowski, F. J. [1992], Retrieval Activities in a Database Consisting of Heterogeneous Collections of Structured Texts, *in* N. Belkin, P. Ingwersen & A. M. Pejtersen (eds.), *SIGIR'92 Proceedings of the 15th Annual International ACM SIGIR Conference on Research and Development in Information Retrieval*, ACM Press, pp.112–25.

Chiaramella, Y., Mulhem, P. & Fourel, F. A. [1996], A Model for Multimedia Information Retrieval, Technical Report Fermi ESPRIT BRA 8134, University of Glasgow.

Cleveland, D. B., Cleveland, A. D. & Wise, O. B. [1984], Less than Full Text Indexing using a Non-Boolean Searching Model, *Journal of the American Society for Information Science* **35**(1), 19–28.

Dunlop, M. D. & van Rijsbergen, C. J. [1993], Hypermedia and Free Text Retrieval, *Information Processing and Management* **29**(3), 287–98.

Frisse, M. [1988], Searching for Information in a Hypertext Medical Handbook, *Communications of the ACM* **31**(7), 880–6.

Fuhr, N. & Großjohann, K. [2001], A Query Language for Information Retrieval in XML Documents, *in* D. H. Kraft, W. B. Croft, D. J. Harper & J. Zobel (eds.), *SIGIR'01,*

Proceedings of the 23rd Annual International ACM SIGIR Conference on Research and Development in Information Retrieval, ACM Press, pp.172–80.

Furnas, G. W. [1999], The Fisheye View: A New Look at Structured Files, *in* S. K. Card, J. D. Mackinlay & B. Shneiderman (eds.), *Readings in Information Visualization: Using Vision to Think*, Morgan-Kaufmann, pp.312–30. Reprinted from: Furnas G. W. (1981) The Fisheye View: A New Look at Structured Files, Bell Laboratories Technical Memorandum 81-11221-9.

Hearst, M. A. [1995], TileBars: Visualisation of Term Distribution Information in Full Text Information Access, *in* I. Katz, R. Mack, L. Marks, M. B. Rosson & J. Nielsen (eds.), *Proceedings of the CHI'95 Conference on Human Factors in Computing Systems*, ACM Press, pp.59–66.

Hertzum, M. & Frøkjær, E. [1996], Browsing and Querying in Online Documentation: A Study of User Interfaces and the Interaction Process, *ACM Transactions on Computer–Human Interaction* **3**(2), 136–61.

Kazai, G., Lalmas, M. & Roelleke, T. [2001], A Model for the Representation and Focussed Retrieval of Structured Documents based on Fuzzy Aggregation, *in Proceedings of the 8th Symposium on String Processing and Information Retrieval (SPIRE 2001)*, IEEE Computer Society Press, pp.123–35.

Kazai, G., Lalmas, M. & Roelleke, T. [2002], Focussed Structured Document Retrieval, *in Proceedings of the 9th Symposium on String Processing and Information Retrieval (SPIRE 2002)*, IEEE Computer Society Press, pp.241–7.

Kotsakis, E. [2002], Structured Information Retrieval in XML documents, *in* G. B. Lamont, H. Haddad, G. Papadopoulos & B. Panda (eds.), *Proceedings of the 2002 ACM Symposium on Applied Computing (SAC'02)*, ACM Press, pp.663–7.

Lalmas, M. & Moutogianni, E. [2000], A Dempster–Shafer Indexing for the Focussed Retrieval of a Hierarchically Structured Document Space: Implementation and Experiments on a Web Museum Collection, *in* J. Mariani & D. Harman (eds.), *Proceedings of RIAO 2000, Content-based Multimedia Information Access*, Centre de Hautes Etudes Internationales d'Informatique Documententaire (CID) / Centre for Advanced Study of Information Systems (CASIS), pp.442–56.

Navarro, G. & Baeza-Yates, R. [1995], A Language for Queries on Structure and Content of Textual Databases, *in* E. A. Fox, P. Ingwersen & R. Fidel (eds.), *SIGIR'95 Proceedings of the 18th Annual International ACM SIGIR Conference on Research and Development in Information Retrieval*, ACM Press, pp.93–101.

Purgailis Parker, L. M. & Johnson, R. E. [1990], Does Order of Presentation Affect Users' Judgement of Documents?, *Journal of the American Society for Information Science* **41**(7), 493–4.

Roelleke, T. [1999], POOL: Probabilistic Object-oriented Logical Representation and Retrieval of Complex Objects — A Model for Hypermedia Retrieval, PhD thesis, University of Dortmund.

Roelleke, T., Lalmas, M., Kazai, G., Ruthven, I. & Quicker, S. [2002], The Accessibility Dimension for Structured Document Retrieval, *in* F. Crestani, M. Girolami & C. J. van Rijsbergen (eds.), *Proceedings of the 24th European Colloquium on Information Retrieval Research (ECIR'02)*, Vol. 2291 of *Lecture Notes in Computer Science*, Springer-Verlag, pp.284–302.

Salton, G., Allan, J. & Buckley, C. [1993], Approaches to Passage Retrieval in Full Text Information Systems, *in* R. Korfhage, E. Rasmussen & P. Willett (eds.), *SIGIR'93 Proceedings of the 16th Annual International ACM SIGIR Conference on Research and Development in Information Retrieval*, ACM Press, pp.49–58.

Tenopir, C. & Ro, J. S. [1990], *Full Text Databases*, Greenwood Press.

Wilkinson, R. [1994], Effective Retrieval of Structured Documents, *in* W. B. Croft & C. J. van Rijsbergen (eds.), *SIGIR'94 Proceedings of the 17th Annual International ACM SIGIR Conference on Research and Development in Information Retrieval*, ACM Press, pp.311–7.

Comparing Speed-dependent Automatic Zooming with Traditional Scroll, Pan and Zoom Methods

Andy Cockburn & Joshua Savage

Human-Computer Interaction Lab, Department of Computer Science, University of Canterbury, Christchurch, New Zealand

Tel: *+64 3 364 2987*

Fax: *+64 3 364 2569*

Email: *{andy,jps42}@cosc.canterbury.ac.nz*

Speed-dependent automatic zooming couples the user's rate of motion through an information space with the zoom level — the faster the user moves the 'higher' they fly above the work surface. Igarashi & Hinckley [2000] proposed using the technique to improve scrolling through large documents. Their informal preliminary evaluation showed mixed results with participants completing scrolling tasks in roughly the same time, or more slowly, than when using traditional methods. In this paper, we describe the implementation and formal evaluation of two rapidly interactive speed-dependent automatic zooming interfaces. The ecologically oriented evaluation shows that scrolling tasks are solved significantly faster with automatic zooming in both text document and map browsing tasks. Subjective preferences and workload measures also strongly favour the automatic zooming systems. Implications for the future of scrolling interfaces are substantial, and directions for further work are presented.

Keywords: navigation, scrolling, zooming, speed-dependent automatic zooming, evaluation.

1 Introduction

Scrolling, panning and zooming are used to navigate through information spaces that are too large to be conveniently displayed within a single window. While scrolling and panning move the workspace within the window, zooming alters its scale. Because zooming changes the proportion of the workspace shown in each window, more scrolling is necessary when zoomed in, less when zoomed out. Most systems for browsing text and graphical documents support scrolling and zooming, and many also support panning.

Until recently, there had been surprisingly little research into understanding and improving the psycho-motor performance of scrolling. Zhai & Selker [1997] showed that mouse-driven scrolling can be improved through the use of isometric controls that vary scroll rate with force. Hinckley et al. [2002] showed that scrolling is accurately modelled by Fitts' Law [1954] even though it involves acquiring targets beyond the edge of the screen, and that mouse-wheel scrolling is improved by acceleration algorithms. These findings aid the theoretical understanding of scrolling, but they do not alter its basic behaviour. Consequently, they do not address the fundamental limitations of scrolling.

One of these limitations, identified by Igarashi & Hinckley [2000], is the disorientation caused by excessive visual flow when scrolling rapidly. In long documents a small movement of the scrollbar thumb causes a large movement in the document, and the rapid rate of change can be too great for the user to perceive, resulting in a visual blur. Although users can ease this problem by altering the zoom level before and after scrolling, doing so involves tedious interface manipulations.

Igarashi & Hinckley proposed speed-dependent automatic zooming (SDAZ) as a solution. SDAZ automatically varies the zoom level dependent on the scroll rate. When scrolling quickly the display is zoomed out, and when stationary or scrolling slowly the display is zoomed in, as shown in Figure 1. An informal preliminary study (n = 7) of the technique found that in Web and map browsing tasks, the efficiency with SDAZ was, on average, the same or slightly worse than traditional scrolling methods. Subjective preferences were also divided. Their paper and their prototype implementations[1] provide dramatic and compelling demonstrations of the technique. There is, however, a risk that their results were adversely affected by the informal nature of the evaluation and by implementation compromises that were necessary to aid rapid and fluid interaction in their Java prototypes.

This paper describes a formal evaluation of speed-dependent automatic zooming in support of everyday document navigation tasks. Section 2 describes the design and implementation of our document and map browsing applications. The experimental design and results are presented in Section 3 and 4. Results are discussed, compared with related work, and used to direct further work in Section 6. Conclusions are presented in Section 6.

2   Document and Map Browsing Applications

Igarashi & Hinckley described five prototype SDAZ applications: a Web browser, a map viewer, an image browser, a dictionary browser, and a sound editor. The image browser, dictionary browser and sound editor were not promising (as discussed in Section 6), so they evaluated only the Web browser and the map viewer.

---

[1] A demonstration applet is available at www-ui.is.s.u-tokyo.ac.jp/~takeo/java/autozoom/autozoom.htm

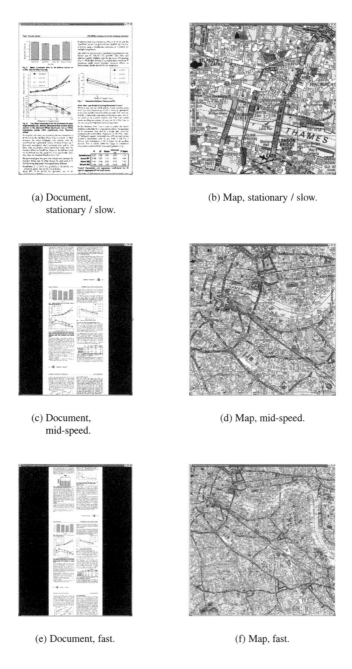

(a) Document,
stationary / slow.

(b) Map, stationary / slow.

(c) Document,
mid-speed.

(d) Map, mid-speed.

(e) Document, fast.

(f) Map, fast.

Figure 1: Slow, medium and fast scrolling with our document and map browsers. Short video clips of the system in operation are available at http://www.cosc.canterbury.ac.uk/~andy/liter.html. The map images of subfigures b, d, and f are copyright © Collins Bartholomew Ltd 2003. Reproduced by kind permission of Harper Collins Publishers. http://www.bartholomewmaps.com.

Their prototypes were written in Java, and required various implementation compromises to achieve rapid and fluid interactivity. In the Web browser, plain text was rendered as simple horizontal lines when zoomed out, and when zooming in only discrete font-sizes were available. Although they experimented with well-known zoomable user interface toolkits Pad++ [Bederson et al. 1996] and Jazz [Bederson & McAlister 1999], their performance was too slow. Their map browser was also limited because it used an artificially synthesized map to ease implementation and aid performance. They state "Although this prototype allows the user to experience zooming and panning in a multi-scale environment, an implementation using real map data would be necessary to obtain further insights."

Our implementations are written in C using the OpenGL graphics libraries, allowing graphics hardware acceleration to provide smooth and fluid animation at more than 50 frames per second. These frame rates are possible using standard graphics cards available on consumer-level computers. The capability of consumer-level graphics hardware is emphasized by Rhyne [2002], who reports that the United States Department of Energy uses standard PCs with consumer-level graphics cards for scientific visualization. Because OpenGL renders objects in 3D, the automatic zooming effect is easily implemented by moving the viewpoint away from the workspace surface.

The relationship between the zoom level and scroll speed is determined by the same formula in both the document and map browsing applications: shown in Equation 1. Zoom level indicates the perceived distance from the document; hence if the zoom level is high the document appears further away (smaller).

$$zoomlevel = k \times scrollspeed - threshold \qquad (1)$$

The constant k affects the rate of change of the zoom level. The minimum value for the zoom level is zero (fully zoomed in), which applies when the cursor is stationary or moving slower than the threshold value. To begin scrolling the user presses the left mouse-button over the document and drags in the direction they wish to scroll (up or down in the document browser, any direction in the map browser). Displacing the cursor further from the initial selection point increases the scrolling speed (the value of *scrollspeed* in Equation 1). Releasing the mouse-button stops scrolling, and the zoom level is fluidly returned to zero through a rapidly animated 'falling' effect. The falling effect is also used to limit the rate that the user can zoom into the document, reducing disorientation. Without it the display can immediately change between fully zoomed-out and fully zoomed-in when the user changes direction by 180 degrees.

2.1   Document Browser

The document browser views portable document format (PDF) and postscript (PS) files: see Figure 1a,c,e. The zoom level is determined through Equation 1, where the scroll speed is determined as follows:

$$scrollspeed = \left| Y_{ip} - Y_{cp} \right| \qquad (2)$$

where Y_{ip} and Y_{cp} represent the initial and current y-coordinates of the mouse.

A velocity scrollbar shows the scrolling speed and direction. When stationary, the velocity indicator is centred in the scrollbar, and when scrolling upward/downward at full speed the indicator is at the top/bottom of the scrollbar. Two additional marks in the velocity scrollbar indicate the threshold scroll speed beyond which zooming occurs.

In the implementation, each PDF or PS page in the document is converted to a separate Truevision Targa[2] (TGA) file for easy texture mapping in OpenGL. Splitting the document into separate pages increases performance because unseen pages do not need to be rendered.

2.2 Map Browser

The map browser, shown in Figure 1b,d,f, behaves similarly to the document browser, except scrolling occurs on two dimensions rather than one. The zoom level is determined through Equation 1, with the scroll speed determined as follows:

$$scrollspeed = \sqrt{(Y_{ip} - Y_{cp})^2 + (X_{ip} - X_{cp})^2} \qquad (3)$$

where Y_{ip}, Y_{cp}, X_{ip}, and X_{cp} represent the initial and current x and y-coordinates of the mouse.

When the user begins scrolling a red cross appears in the centre of the display and a vector shows the speed and direction of movement. When scrolling rapidly the view is zoomed out, revealing large areas of the map (see Figure 1f).

The implementation is similar to the document browser, with large maps constructed from separate TGA image files (normally OpenGL has a maximum image size limit of 2048×2048 pixels).

2.3 Experimental Design

The experimental objective was to compare the efficiency, preferences, and general usability issues of speed-dependent automatic zooming with traditional scrolling techniques. To increase ecological validity, the traditional interfaces were standard commercial applications — Adobe's Acrobat Reader[3] version 5 for document browsing tasks, and Paint Shop Pro[4] version 5 for map browsing tasks. Both of these interfaces support traditional scroll, pan and zoom facilities.

The experiment was a $2 \times 2 \times 2$ repeated measures factorial design, and was repeated for document and map browsing tasks. The dependent measure was task completion time. The three factors were as follows:

Interface type: The levels of this factor were the speed-dependent automatic zooming interfaces and their traditional equivalents (Acrobat Reader or Paint Shop Pro).

Task type: When document browsing the two levels of this factor were 'locate a picture' and 'locate a text heading', and they involved finding specific items in the document. When map browsing the levels were 'locate from direction' and

[2] http://www.truevision.com
[3] http://www.adobe.com
[4] http://www.jasc.com

'locate from path'. The map browsing tasks involved finding named schools when the search was cued with a compass direction or with a route to follow (such as a named street or river).

Scroll distance: The levels of this factor were 'short' and 'long' distance. In short tasks the target was approximately five pages or five map squares from the initial location. Long distance targets were approximately 20 pages or 20 map squares from the initial location. This factor was intended to show whether one interface was particularly suitable to short or long scrolling activities.

The repeated-measures design reduces the number of participants required for statistical power. It also reduces the impact of variation between participants — a participant with particularly good hand-eye co-ordination, for instance, is likely to perform well with both interfaces.

2.4 Participants

Twelve volunteer participants (eleven males, one female) took part in the experiment. All were graduate level computer science students in their early twenties. None had previously used speed-dependent automatic zooming interfaces. All frequently used Acrobat Reader and half had previously used Paint Shop Pro 5.

Because speed-dependent automatic zooming creates fluid and dynamic visual effects, it was possible that experience with computer games would influence its use. Three participants reported that they never played computer games, three stated that they played between one and three hours a week, four played between five and ten hours a week and two played more than twenty hours each week. The results, reported in Section 4, suggest that game-playing experience was not a major factor in performance or subjective preferences.

Each participant's involvement in the experiment lasted approximately forty minutes, including training time.

2.5 Materials

The experiment was run on a 1.2GHz AMD Athlon computer with 640MB of RAM and a Geforce 4 MX Video card. The 19″ IBM display was set to a resolution of 1024×768 pixels. Input was provided through a standard Logitech 3-button mouse, which was cleaned after each evaluation. All experimental software ran under the Windows XP operating system. Timing data was recorded using a stopwatch.

Acrobat Reader, shown in Figure 2, provides a variety of interface features for scrolling, panning and zooming. When the magnifying glass tool is selected (shown selected in the tool bar of Figure 2) each left mouse-button click magnifies or diminishes the document by approximately 25%. The 'View' menu and the pop-up context menu (shown in Figure 2) provide a variety of shortcuts for setting the zoom level. Scrollbars allow horizontal and vertical scrolling as normal (no horizontal scrolling was necessary in the tasks). The 'Continuous' view option was used in the evaluation, which means that dragging the scrollbar thumb dynamically displayed page motion. Panning is achieved by selecting the 'hand' tool and dragging with the left mouse button.

Figure 2: Zooming and panning controls in Acrobat Reader.

Paint Shop Pro also provides a variety of zooming and scrolling features. Normal horizontal and vertical scrollbars are available on the bottom and right sides of the window. A shortcut scroll/zoom technique is possible by clicking on the image with the left or right buttons to zoom in or out. This simultaneously zooms and centres the display on the clicked location. A panning tool, similar to that in Acrobat Reader, allows the workspace to be panned without zooming.

The document used for the document-browsing tasks was a 157 page Masters Thesis (PDF format), consisting of nine chapters and two appendices. The map browsing tasks used a large Auckland City road map. Experimental tasks with Acrobat Reader were initially displayed at a 'Fit to Width' level (approximately 125% zoom) which is a comfortable reading size. In the map browsing tasks the initial zoom level was set so that individual street names were clearly legible. These zoom levels were similar to the initial stationary zoom levels with the SDAZ interfaces.

The NASA Task Load Index (TLX) worksheets [Hart & Staveland 1988] were used to measure subjective assessments of workload in the tasks. Responses to six measures were taken using a five-point Likert scale, from 1 (low) to 5 (high). The measures were 'mental demand', 'physical demand', 'temporal demand', 'effort', 'performance', and 'frustration level'. The participants read explanations of these measures before using the worksheets.

2.6 Procedure

The document browsing tasks were completed first to better prepare participants for the 2D map tasks. The order of exposure to other factors was counter-balanced to minimize learning effects. Half of the participants used the SDAZ interfaces first, half the traditional interfaces first.

Each participant completed ten document-browsing tasks using both the SDAZ and Adobe Acrobat Reader interfaces. Two sets of ten similar document navigation tasks were created. The task sets consisted of two training tasks and two tasks in each combination of distance (long and short) and task type (locate picture and locate text heading). The task sets were also counter-balanced across interfaces, so that half of the participants used each set with each interface.

Each interface was described to the participants before they used it, and they were then allowed five minutes of practice. The training tasks were used to ensure that the participants understood how to use the interface, and to familiarize them with the mechanism for presenting tasks. One training task was a long distance 'locate picture' task, and the other was a long distance 'locate text heading' task. Timing data from the training tasks was discarded.

All tasks were presented to the user in a display in the top right-hand corner of the screen. The evaluator first read the task description to the participant, and they were then asked to read the task aloud. An example 'locate picture' task was 'Locate the picture of the green world globe up from your current location', and an example 'locate text heading' task was 'Locate the Software Visualization heading below your current location'. The participants were informed that the clock would stop when they read aloud the first word of the picture caption or the first word below the section heading. They were also told that if they became lost they could ask to have the starting location identified, but that the task time would continue to run.

The ten map browsing tasks were similarly administered. The first training task was a long distance 'direction' task and the second was a long distance 'path' task. An example 'direction' task is 'Locate Wairau Intermediate School in Sunnynook, North West of here'. An example 'path' task is 'Follow State Highway 16 north. When you meet State Highway 1, follow it west to the Auckland Institute of Technology'. All long distance 'path' tasks included a junction such as that in the example. The remaining eight tasks consisted of two tasks in each combination of distance and task type.

After completing the tasks with each interface the participants used the NASA-TLX worksheets to assess their workload. Finally, they were asked to state which interface they preferred for browsing documents and maps.

3 Results

The participants had no obvious problems with the experimental method or with adapting to the SDAZ interfaces.

Across both the SDAZ and traditional interfaces, and across short and long distances, the mean time to complete document-browsing tasks was 12.4s (s.d. 5.8s), slightly faster than the mean for the two dimensional map-browsing tasks at 17.5s (s.d. 9.0s).

Timing data in the document and map browsing tasks was analysed using a $2\times2\times2$ analysis of variance with repeated measures.

3.1 *Document Browsing*

Participants completed the tasks significantly faster with the SDAZ interface (mean 10.9s, s.d. 5.3s) than with Acrobat Reader (mean 14.0s, s.d. 5.8s): $F_{1,11} = 16.9$, $p < 0.01$. On average, the SDAZ interface reduced the task time by 22%.

As expected, short distance tasks were faster than long distance ones ($F_{1,11} = 35.3$, $p < 0.01$), with short and long means of 8.3s (s.d. 4.7s) and 16.6s (s.d. 6.2s). There was no interaction between interface type and distance

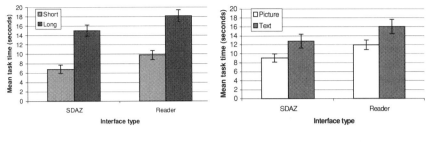

(a) Interface type by distance.   (b) Interface type by task type.

Figure 3: Mean task times for document browsing. Error bars show ±1 standard error.

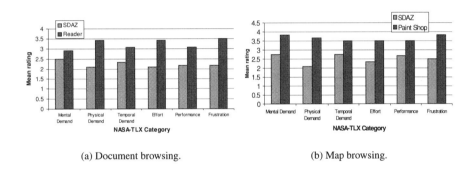

(a) Document browsing.   (b) Map browsing.

Figure 4: Mean responses to NASA-TLX workload assessments using five-point Likert scales.

$(F_{1,11} < 0.01, p = 0.94)$, indicating that performance with the SDAZ and Reader interfaces deteriorated similarly as task distance increased (see Figure 3a).

The two task types were also reliably different from one another $(F_{1,11} = 12.3, p < 0.01)$, with pictures being located more rapidly than titles: means of 10.5s (s.d. 5.1s) and 14.4s (s.d. 7.8s) respectively. The larger size and greater visual distinctiveness of pictures compared to titles explains this effect. There was no interaction between interface type and task type $(F_{1,11} = 0.09, p = 0.77)$ indicating that performance with the SDAZ and Reader interfaces deteriorated similarly between the task types (see Figure 3b).

Responses to the NASA-TLX worksheets showed that the participants rated task loads more lightly with the SDAZ interface. Figure 4a shows the mean responses to questions on the mental, physical and temporal demand of the tasks, and on the effort, performance and frustration levels. In all cases, the SDAZ interface has a lower workload rating than Acrobat Reader.

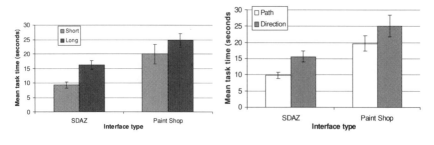

(a) Interface type by distance.   (b) Interface type by task type.

Figure 5: Mean task times for map browsing. Error bars show ±1 standard error.

Finally, all but one of the participants stated that they preferred the SDAZ interface, and several made comments such as 'all scrolling should work like this!' The one participant who preferred the Reader interface objected to being 'forced' to zoom out when scrolling. He stated that he would have preferred the technique if there had been an option to freeze the zoom level while scrolling.

3.2 Map Browsing

The participants were significantly faster with the SDAZ interface than with Paint Shop Pro: $F_{1,11} = 38.9$, $p < 0.01$. On average, the SDAZ interface was 43% faster, with SDAZ and Paint Shop means of 12.7s (s.d. 7.2s) and 22.3s (s.d. 14.4s) respectively.

As in the document browsing tasks, short distance tasks were faster than long ones ($F_{1,11} = 5.5$, $p < 0.05$), with means of 14.6s (s.d. 13.3s) and 20.4s (s.d. 10.7s). Also reflecting the document browsing tasks, performance in short and long distance tasks deteriorated similarly for both interface types (see Figure 5a): $F_{1,11} = 0.37$, $p = 0.6$.

The 'locate from path' task type was completed more rapidly than 'locate from direction', with means of 14.4s (s.d. 10.1s) and 20.3s (s.d. 13.8s) respectively: $F_{1,11} = 5.6$, $p < 0.05$. This effect is explained by the relative simplicity of following obvious landmarks (such as a road) to a location, rather than following a relatively crude compass direction. Performance with both interfaces deteriorated similarly between 'locate from path' and 'locate from direction' task types, as shown in Figure 5b: $F_{1,11} < 0.01$, $p = 0.9$.

The NASA-TLX worksheet responses showed uniformly lower workload ratings with the SDAZ interface (see Figure 4b). All of the participants stated that they preferred the SDAZ interface.

3.3 Observations and Comments

Several participants commented that the traditional scroll, pan and zoom mechanisms were 'too separate', requiring several interface manipulations with different controls for essentially the same task. Consequently, the participants felt 'busy' with interface adjustments (increasing their Physical Demand ratings on the NASA-TLX worksheets) or they accepted the long scrolling distances associated with the default zoom level (increasing their Frustration level). The participants' annoyance at the separation of controls was particularly notable when map browsing because two separate scrollbars were needed for horizontal and vertical scrolling.

The abrupt transitions between discrete zooming levels with the traditional interfaces also caused problems. The absence of animation between the pre- and post-magnification views meant that the participants had to reorient themselves with each zoom action. This problem was particularly notable with Paint Shop Pro because of its zoom centring property — many participants expected the clicked location to remain in the same place, rather than move to the centre of the display.

In the first moments of exposure to the SDAZ interfaces, some of the participants made light-hearted comments that they expected it to induce motion sickness or to make them dizzy. None of the participants mentioned dizziness or motion sickness later in the experiment.

One criticism of the SDAZ interfaces was that the participants missed the spatial orientation normally provided by scrollbars. The location of the scrollbar thumb allows users to quickly determine their approximate spatial location within a document. Similarly, the thumb can be used to rapidly move to the start/end of the document and other approximate locations. This useful information can be easily added to SDAZ interfaces.

4 Discussion and Related Work

4.1 Comparison with Igarashi & Hinckley's Results

Why did our experiment produce strong results in favour of speed-dependent automatic zooming when Igarashi & Hinckley's [2000] preliminary evaluation indicated that it was little different or worse than traditional schemes? There are several potential explanations:

Implementations: Our C and OpenGL systems exploit the high frame-rates and fluid animation available through graphics hardware. This avoids some of the implementation compromises necessary to achieve rapid interaction in Igarashi & Hinckley's Java-based systems. In their document browser zoomed-out views of text were depicted as horizontal lines rather than miniaturized fonts, and discrete font sizes were used to simulate dynamic font scaling. In their map browsing evaluation an artificially generated map was used rather than a real one. It is possible that subtle differences between our implementations and theirs explain the discrepancy between results. In particular, differences in frame-rate are important in dynamic and fluid interactive presentations, as demonstrated by the poor quality of low frame-rate video.

Experimental Objectives: Igarashi & Hinckley's primary objective was to describe their fascinating new interaction technique. Their experiment was intended only to provide initial impressions of the technique's effectiveness. With different experimental objectives, and with greater statistical power from wider participation, they may have been able to discriminate between performance with the interfaces.

Competing Interfaces: We compared our SDAZ interfaces with commercial implementations of traditional systems (Adobe Acrobat Reader and Paint Shop Pro), and all interfaces were controlled using a mouse. In their document browsing tasks, Igarashi & Hinckley compared SDAZ with a mouse-driven unspecified Web browser. They do not mention whether their Web browser supported zooming, but images in their paper suggest that it did not. It is possible (though we believe unlikely) that Acrobat Reader's zooming facilities caused slower performance in our evaluation, and that this accounted for the comparative efficiency of SDAZ.

In Igarashi & Hinckley's map navigation tasks both interfaces were controlled using a joystick, allowing users to pan and zoom concurrently when using traditional interfaces. Our mouse control, however, required scrolling and zooming to be carried out either in series (using discrete zoom adjustments, then scrolling) or in a combined action (using Paint Shop's centring zoom). Although the contrasting input devices may have contributed to the divergent results, mouse input remains the standard on desktop computers.

Task Types: Igarashi & Hinckley's map browsing tasks involved locating a white dot in an artificial terrain. The dot was continually visible in a small 'global radar' in the corner of the display. These tasks test abstract target acquisition, and in later work Hinckley et al. [2002] showed that scrolling performance conforms to Fitts' Law [1954]. Our tasks, in contrast, include the extraction of meaningful information from different levels of magnification. Evaluations based on abstract theoretical behaviour and on ecologically oriented tasks are both equally important in understanding the strengths and weaknesses of new interaction techniques. We intend to investigate both in our further work.

Participants: Differences between the participant pools may also have affected the results. All of our twelve participants were expert computer users (graduate level Computer Science students), and all but three regularly played computer games. Igarashi & Hinckley's participants were all 'good' or 'average' computer users, and four of the seven reported that they played computer games 'sometimes', 'almost every day' or 'frequently'. Although four of Igarashi & Hinckley's participants were female (compared to only one of ours), there was no notable difference between male and female performance in the data they present. We intend to conduct further evaluations with a broad participant pool to clarify whether SDAZ techniques remain effective for less experienced users.

4.2 Related Work

As desktop computers increase in power, automatic zooming techniques such as fisheye views and SDAZ are becoming increasingly viable. The main icon panel in the MacOS X desktop[5], for instance, provides a dynamic fisheye that automatically magnifies icons as the cursor approaches.

This mainstream deployment of automatic zooming has prompted research into their use. McGuffin & Balakrishnan [2002] show that the acquisition of expanding targets conforms to Fitts' Law, and that selection time depends primarily on the final target size, even when the expansion begins very late in the movement towards the target. Gutwin [2002] describes a fisheye view 'hunting' problem in which dynamic distortion causes users to miss their targets because they move most rapidly when the cursor is near. He shows that acquisition times can be improved through 'speed-coupled flattening' which removes the distortion effect when the cursor moves rapidly. The distortion is reapplied when the user decelerates and stops the cursor on final target approach.

There have also been several ecologically oriented evaluations of automatic zooming techniques. Bederson [2000] evaluated 'fisheye menus' as an alternative for selecting targets from long menus. With fisheye menus, items are magnified (displayed in a large font) when near the cursor, and diminished when far from it. The technique was faster than two types of scrolling menu, and about the same as cascading menus. Schaffer et al. [1996] showed that a 2D graphical fisheye allowed faster navigation through hierarchically organized networks than traditional full-zoom techniques. Finally, Tan et al. [2001] showed users were able to acquire and move targets in a virtual 3D scene more rapidly when using a 'speed-coupled flying and orbiting' system that varied height above a 3D world with speed. The concept of coupling speed with height was first described by Ware & Fleet [1997] who evaluated a variety of schemes for automatically adjusting velocity from the user-controlled height in 'fly-by' visualizations.

4.3   Scope, Limitations and Further Work

Igarashi & Hinckley used five categories to discuss appropriate and inappropriate domains for speed-dependent automatic zooming — size of the data space, type of the data, frequency of access to the data, input device, and user level:

Size of the data space: We agree that SDAZ is best used for intermediate sized data spaces. In small data spaces (between one and four times the amount displayed in a single screen) traditional scrolling is sufficient, and in large data spaces (thousands of screens full) searching methods are needed. We are currently investigating ways of adapting SDAZ to extremely large data spaces.

Type of the data space: Although we agree that SDAZ is appropriate for navigating through spatial information, we are not convinced that it is 'difficult to apply to symbolic information such as a dictionary'. Their unsuccessful dictionary browser provided a scrolling list of words. Words were removed from the list when scrolling fast, but this caused confusion. We believe that SDAZ can provide a natural method for browsing symbolic data that is analogous to the way we riffle book pages (for example, when searching a physical dictionary).

---

[5]http://www.apple.com/macosx/theater/dock.html

In our further work we will develop and evaluate SDAZ in spatial, symbolic and abstract data types.

Frequency of access to the data: Igarashi & Hinckley stated that SDAZ would work best when the same data items are accessed repeatedly. Our evaluation tasks involved single accesses to data items, yet SDAZ outperformed traditional interfaces. We wish to further examine the suitable activities for SDAZ.

Input device: Igarashi & Hinckley recommended that SDAZ is particularly suited to self-centring and absolute input devices such as joysticks rather than relative pointing devices such as a mouse. Although self-centring devices may be particularly suitable for SDAZ, our evaluation shows that efficiency gains are produced with mouse-driven input.

User level: Igarashi & Hinckely recommended that SDAZ is less appropriate for novice users. Given that all our participants were expert users, we have little data to assess this recommendation, and we will investigate novice use in further work.

We will also intend to develop guidelines for the calibration of speed-dependent automatic zooming. Factors affecting the calibration of SDAZ include the perceptual issues of maximum useful visual flow at various zoom levels, and the maximum useful zoom-out level for documents of different types.

5 Conclusions

Scrolling is one of the most common activities in everyday computer use, yet there has been surprisingly little research into improving its performance.

Recently Igarashi & Hinckley proposed 'speed-dependent automatic zooming', which couples scroll rate with the zoom level. The objective was to overcome problems arising from excessive visual flow when scrolling fast. Their preliminary evaluation produced disappointing results, with similar or slightly worse performance than traditional methods.

The evaluation reported in this paper shows speed-dependent automatic zooming (SDAZ) in a new light. In ecologically oriented document browsing tasks, our participants were 22% faster when using SDAZ than when using a common commercial document viewer, and in map browsing tasks the performance benefits increased to 43%. Workload assessments, preferences, and the participants' comments all amplified the efficiency and effectiveness of the automatic zooming approach.

The results suggest that Igarashi & Hinckley's invention could have dramatic implications for the future of scrolling. Our further work will continue to assess and evaluate critical factors in the success and adoption of SDAZ interfaces. Although the technique needs relatively high levels of processing power, continual improvements in processing speeds and graphics hardware will soon negate this.

References

Bederson, B. [2000], Fisheye Menus, *in* M. Ackerman & K. Edwards (eds.), *Proceedings of the 13th Annual ACM Symposium on User Interface Software and Technology, UIST2000, CHI Letters* **2**(2), ACM Press, pp.217–25.

Bederson, B. B., Hollan, J. D., Perlin, K., Meyer, J., Bacon, D. & Furnas, G. [1996], Pad++: A Zoomable Graphical Sketchpad for Exploring Alternate Interface Physics, *Journal of Visual Languages and Computing* **7**(1), 3–31.

Bederson, B. & McAlister, B. [1999], Jazz: An Extensible 2D+Zooming Graphics Toolkit in Java, Technical Report HCIL-99-07, Department of Computer Science, University of Maryland.

Fitts, P. M. [1954], The Information Capacity of the Human Motor System in Controlling Amplitude of Movement, *British Journal of Educational Psychology* **47**(6), 381–91.

Gutwin, C. [2002], Improving Focus Targeting in Interactive Fisheye Views, *in* D. Wixon (ed.), *Proceedings of CHI'02 Conference on Human Factors in Computing Systems: Changing our World, Changing Ourselves, CHI Letters* **4**(1), ACM Press, pp.267–74.

Hart, S. & Staveland, L. [1988], Development of NASA-TLX (Task Load Index): Results of Empirical and Theoretical Research, *in* P. Hancock & N. Meshkati (eds.), *Human Mental Workload*, North-Holland, pp.139–83.

Hinckley, K., Cutrell, E., Bathiche, S. & Muss, T. [2002], Quantitative Analysis of Scrolling Techniques, *in* D. Wixon (ed.), *Proceedings of CHI'02 Conference on Human Factors in Computing Systems: Changing our World, Changing Ourselves, CHI Letters* **4**(1), ACM Press, pp.65–72.

Igarashi, T. & Hinckley, K. [2000], Speed-dependent Automatic Zooming for Browsing Large Documents, *in* M. Ackerman & K. Edwards (eds.), *Proceedings of the 13th Annual ACM Symposium on User Interface Software and Technology, UIST2000, CHI Letters* **2**(2), ACM Press, pp.139–48.

McGuffin, M. & Balakrishnan, R. [2002], Acquisition of Expanding Targets, *in* D. Wixon (ed.), *Proceedings of CHI'02 Conference on Human Factors in Computing Systems: Changing our World, Changing Ourselves, CHI Letters* **4**(1), ACM Press, pp.57–64.

Rhyne, T. [2002], Computer Games and Scientific Visualization, *Communications of the ACM* **45**(7), 40–4.

Schaffer, D., Zuo, Z., Greenberg, S., Bartram, L., Dill, J., Dubs, S. & Roseman, M. [1996], Navigating Hierarchically Clustered Networks through Fisheye and Full-zoom Methods, *ACM Transactions on Computer–Human Interaction* **3**(2), 162–88.

Tan, D., Robertson, G. & Czerwinski, M. [2001], Exploring 3D Navigation: Combining Speed-coupled Flying with Orbiting, *in* J. A. Jacko & A. Sears (eds.), *Proceedings of CHI'01 Conference on Human Factors in Computing Systems, CHI Letters* **3**(1), ACM Press, pp.418–25.

Ware, C. & Fleet, D. [1997], Context Sensitive Flying Interface, *in* S. N. Spencer (ed.), *Proceedings of the Symposium on Interactive 3D Graphics*, ACM SIGRAPH, pp.127–30.

Zhai, S. Smith, B. A. & Selker, T. [1997], Improving Browsing Performances: A Study of Four Input Devices for Scrolling and Pointing Tasks, *in* S. Howard, J. Hammond & G. K. Lindgaard (eds.), *Human–Computer Interaction — INTERACT '97: Proceedings of the Sixth IFIP Conference on Human–Computer Interaction*, Chapman & Hall, pp.286–93.

Design Methods and Principles

The Application of Urban Design Principles to Navigation of Information Spaces

David Benyon & Bettina Wilmes[†]

School of Computing, Napier University, 10 Colinton Road, Edinburgh EH14 1DJ, UK

Tel: *+44 131 455 2736*

Fax: *+44 131 455 2727*

Email: *d.benyon@dcs.napier.ac.uk*

URL: *http://www.dcs.napier.ac.uk/~dbenyon*

[†] *Academic Department of Health Care of Older People, Queen Mary's School of Medicine and Dentistry, Barts and The London, 1st Floor Alderney Building, Mile End Hospital, Bancroft Road, London E1 4DG, UK*

Email: *bettina.wilmes@thpct.nhs.uk*

URL: *http://www.smd.qmul.ac.uk/hcop/staff/sta.htm*

The challenge of pervasive computing to HCI is significant. HCI theory has been dominated by 'the person using the computer', work and efficiency. In the future of pervasive computing people will be living *inside* information spaces. If we take this view then it is natural to consider how people *move through* such spaces; navigation of information space. Usage of terms such as 'navigation' have been common since the inception of the Web; Internet *explorer*, Netscape *navigator* and so on. People complain of being 'lost in hyperspace', Web sites provide 'navigation bars' and even my mobile (cellular) phone has a navigation map. In this paper we report on a novel approach to helping people navigate a Web site — a dynamic site map. In doing this we aim to implement some ideas taken from the writings of Gordon Cullen on the design of townscapes whereby he stresses the unfolding nature of interaction with a town. The bigger picture is to explore this new approach to HCI that arises from people being inside

**information spaces and to see to what extent design principles from the
built environment transfer to information spaces.**

Keywords: navigation, information space, Gordon Cullen, Web site design,
site map, urban design.

1 Introduction

Usage of terms such as 'navigation' are common in many areas of interaction design.
People complain of being 'lost in hyperspace', Web sites provide 'navigation bars'
and even my mobile (cellular) phone has a navigation map. It is a moot point
whether the idea of navigation in information spaces is a metaphor for the activities
of information searching, or whether it is a new and useful way for thinking about
human–computer interaction. However, it is the case that several authors have
transferred ideas from geographical to information spaces. Spence [1999] presents
his review of navigation as an essential part of data visualization. Chalmers [2003]
uses Hillier's space syntax to discuss issues of paths through information spaces
and Benyon has looked at the debate in several publications [Benyon & Höök 1997;
Benyon 1998, 2001]. A method for the design and evaluation of navigation has been
developed [McCall & Benyon 2003] that appears effective, particularly in 3D spaces.

The work reported in this paper is a contribution to the investigation into
navigation and information spaces. We do not, therefore review the literature on
alternative visualizations of information spaces such as cone trees. Nor do we discuss
the literature on hypertext and how to design different navigational structures. The
contribution of the paper is to illustrate how design principles and design guidance
from the built environment can be transferred to information spaces and how this
is a necessary change in HCI to deal with pervasive computing. The physics of
information spaces are different from the physics of geographical spaces and we can
do things in information spaces that cannot be achieved in geographical space. The
question that this paper addresses is to what extent design principles transfer.

One of the authors, with a background in landscape architecture, was
particularly interested in the Townscape theory of Gordon Cullen [1971]. Could it
be applied to the design of Web sites and what impact might such a theory have both
on Web site design and on the wider debate about the transfer of design principles
from the built environment to the information environment. The result is a novel
technique, a dynamic site map, that indicates size, distance and direction in the site
and further evidence that design principles from the urban environment do transfer
to electronic worlds.

After a brief introduction to the issues of navigation and Web usability, we turn
to the work of Gordon Cullen. In Section 3 we show how his theoretical framework
informed the design of the dynamic Web site map, and the reaction of people to this.
Section 4 provides a brief conclusion, setting this example of applying principles
from urban design to information space design in context.

1.1 Navigation

Throughout our everyday lives we are continuously confronted with spatial problems. The task of purchasing groceries at a nearby supermarket involves a series of very complex spatial problems starting with getting to the supermarket, locating the food within the supermarket, finding the car in the car park and finally returning home. Most of these spatial problems appear so 'trivial' to us that the ability to solve them is easily taken for granted. It is only in the case of failure (e.g. getting lost on the way to the supermarket, not finding the right pasta brand, etc.) that we may become aware of the problem-solving process and how much effort and thought we must put into the task.

As stated by Downs & Stea [1977] spatial problems occur because of the *location* someone is at, the separation or *distance* between people, places, and things, and the *movement* or co-ordination of people or things from place to place. [Downs & Stea 1977] argue that two basic types of information about the environment are needed to solve any spatial problem:

> "*whereness*, or knowledge of the spatial location of something and someone, and *whatness*, or knowledge of which things or people are at a particular location. [. . .] Included in whatness information is a subclass of information, *whenness*. We need to know not only *where* a place is and *what* is at that place, but also *when* certain things will happen there or how likely it is that things might happen there." [Downs & Stea 1977, p.39]

The key element to whereness is location, and deriving from it distance (a measure of the amount of spatial separation between two locations) and direction. The specification of location requires an identifying name and, more importantly, a location description. This can take one of two forms: state description (where something is located in terms of a well-known and commonly understood system of co-ordinates) and process description (a set of instructions telling how to get to a particular location). Both forms of location description are used in cognitive mapping, depending how the environment is organized, and how well we know and understand it. The knowing, or understanding, of location and the spatial relations between locations is defined as orientation.

Human beings have a range of strategies available when coping with spatial problem-solving, including cognitive mapping, dead-reckoning or path integration, sequential learning of linear path segments and turn angles, or controlled branch and bound search procedures [Golledge & Stimson 1997]. Downs & Stea [1977] discuss the concept of wayfinding as one class of spatial problem. They define wayfinding as the purposive movement of a person from one location to another. This process can be broken down into four sequential and interrelated steps:

- Orientation.

- Choice of a route.

- Monitoring of route (keeping on the right track).

- Discovery/recognition of the objective (arrival).

The first step, orientation, is the key one. The person identifies his or her spatial location in relation to some selected places using an orientation system with landmarks as key reference points ("If I am *here*, then X is *there*"). If the person is unable to make the necessary link between what they see around them and their 'cognitive map', they experience the feeling of being lost. The choice of a route requires the person to make a cognitive connection between his or her current location and that of the desired destination, which is then converted into a plan of actions, usually by a sequence of movements from landmark to landmark. Keeping on the right track monitors the execution of the route plan and is achieved by keeping the cognitive map tied to the perceived environment, and taking the appropriate actions at each decision point (using the aid of guiding landmarks). In order to master the final step it is essential to recognize that one has arrived. This recognition depends, again, on linking a cognitive map with the perceived environment.

This general model of navigation is broadly accepted as a reasonable representation of what people do in order to get somewhere [e.g. Passini 1992]. Within more mainstream human–computer interaction (HCI) research, Spence has proposed a 'schematic framework' for navigation which he argues is applicable to a wide range of environments, particularly for the purpose of interaction design [Spence 1999]. He proposes that navigation is 'the creation and interpretation of an internal model'. The framework consists of four cognitive activities; browsing, formation of the model, interpretation of the model and formation of browsing strategy. Spence emphasizes that his model is to inform interaction design.

1.2   Web Usability

Jacob Nielsen [2000], primarily concerned with the usability of the Web, argues that the ever-increasing size and complexity of the Web will impose a big challenge for the design of sites that can be easily accessed by everyone from everywhere. The three fundamental questions of navigation in Web sites are according to Nielsen [2000]: "Where am I?", "Where have I been?", and "Where can I go?", which essentially relate to Downs & Stea's [1977] concept of whereness. 'Whatness' concerns the content of the site.

Preece [2000] gives more specific guidelines for Web usability, which are grouped into three broad categories: *navigation, access,* and *information design.* A successful Web site is characterized by adequate and unambiguous navigation support. Good and easy access to Web material is achieved by refraining from complex URLs, and using standard hyperlink colours and good signage [McCall & Benyon 2003].

Further important navigation tools are *sitemaps* (or *spatial maps*). Especially in large Web sites it is essential to provide the user with an overview of the organization of the site. Users with lower spatial abilities may find the Web site easier to use if they are presented with a sitemap, which helps them to conceptualize the spatial relations of the site and to gain a sense of their own location relative to other part of the site. In their analysis of navigational aids in hypertext systems McDonald & Stevenson [1998] came to the conclusion that sitemaps lead to more efficient navigation behaviour. They further pointed out that sitemaps were commonly used during browsing, while indices (menus) were used more often during information search.

Most sitemaps are a diagrammatic representation of the site's structure listing the titles of individual pages and available links. In general the user is able to access individual pages or documents via the sitemap. However, a well-designed sitemap should represent more than the site's organization, the designer's aim should be to provide a strong representation of the content and structure. Nielsen [2000] strongly recommends that a sitemap should also contain a 'you are here' indicator, similar to a location map in a shopping mall and suggests:

> "a better solution would be a dynamic sitemap that indicates the page from which it was accessed and that has ways of highlighting information of interest to specific user populations." [Nielsen 2000, p.221]

There are many useful guidelines in existence to help Web site designers who are all grappling with difficult design task of large amounts of content and the minimal amounts of functionality provided by a Web browser. This is a particularly pernicious design problem and for this reason we have been looking elsewhere for inspiration. One way of helping people to find their way is by putting them in contact with other people. This is the social navigation approach [Höök et al. 2003] which includes a whole family of techniques for catching traces of others' behaviours, using recommendations, filtering and other methods for reducing a size of an information space. Another is to look at how other disciplines have solved similar problems such as the design of urban spaces.

2 Gordon Cullen

Gordon Cullen was born on 9th August 1914 in Bradford, Yorkshire. Showing already at an early age an aptitude for art he enrolled at the London School of Arts and Crafts. Persuaded that there was insufficient money to be made in fine arts, he decided to transfer to the Regent Street Polytechnic where he studied architecture to the Royal Institute of British Architects' intermediate level.

Cullen graduated in 1933 and spent the years until 1946 working as an illustrator and designer for various architectural practices amongst others the office of Raymond McGrath, the architect Godfrey Samuel (later to become Harding and Samuel), and the key architectural practice of the Modern Movement, Tecton, founded by the Russian-born architect Berthold Lubetkin. During the Second World War he joined the town planning team of Gardner-Medwin in the British West Indies. In these early years of his career Cullen worked on various smaller scale design projects as for example the Penguin Pool at London Zoo, and the Finsbury Borough Health Centre in London. Only four of his projects were ever built: a school in St Vincent (West Indies), the village hall at Wraysbury and two housing projects in London Docklands [Gosling 1996].

In the mid 1930s Cullen became a member of the MARS group (Modern Architectural Research), which was the British delegation of CIAM (Congrés Internationaux d'Architecture Modern). The group was a loosely knit society of the leaders of the Modern Movement composed of architects, engineers and writers and included Ove Arup, Marcel Breuer, Serge Chermayeff, Wells Coates, Maxwell

Fry, and Walter Gropius, as well as the Tecton group. In 1939 MARS organized an exhibition of modern architecture at the New Burlington Galleries in London, which was to have considerable influence and was a landmark in the history of architectural ideas.

The exhibition was accompanied by a manifesto *New Architecture*, illustrated by Cullen and with a foreword written by George Bernhard Shaw. Cullen's drawings took the visitor through the exhibition sequentially, illustrating that his theory of 'serial vision' as it later appeared in his book *Townscape* was already in a developing stage [Gosling 1996].

The most important change in Cullen's professional career was when he became the Assistant Editor (Art) of the influential *The Architectural Review* in 1946. *The Architectural Review* was a monthly architectural periodical with an editorial commitment to both historical scholarship and the acceptance of the Modern Movement. Many of the illustrated articles on urban studies Cullen wrote during his time at the *Review* appeared later in his book *Townscape* (e.g. Westminster Regained, Legs and Wheels, The Functional Tradition, Immediacy, Here and There).

Gordon Cullen's influence has been widespread, both nationally and internationally. One high point of his career was without doubt the publication of his 1961 book *Townscape* for which he gained much critical acclaim. *Townscape* (the 1971 edition was renamed *The Concise Townscape*) remains still in print and has been translated into German, Italian, Japanese and Spanish. It is widely used as a required text in architectural, landscape architectural and urban design schools across the world.

Even though most of Cullen's work over the six decades of his career were never realized:

> "Gordon Cullen was a true visionary, introducing many new concepts, concerning the understanding of the urban environment." [Gosling 1996, p.9]

Most of his studies were adventurous design proposals unfortunately often ignored by planners and architects when the projects were eventually realized. However, as a result of his often daring ideas Cullen became a cult figure in architectural circles and his unique three dimensional drawing techniques were copied everywhere. Throughout his career Gordon Cullen became famous for his almost philosophical visions on the urban environment and the graphic skills used to demonstrate his proposals.

All his urban studies are characterized by an:

> "objective descriptive analysis of the power and magic of a place and the personal vision of its future." [Gosling 1996, p.85]

Cullen's illustrations of the urban environment show clearly his celebration of human activity in the city with people using urban outdoor and indoor space. Both as a journalist and urban design consultant he always emphasized the importance of the individual in the urban environment and described the city as a:

"marketplace of urban contacts." [Cullen 1971, quoted in Gosling 1996, p.153]

He persistently attempted to humanize the urban scenery by stressing the importance of pedestrian priority and enjoyment.

2.1 The Townscape Theory

The article 'Westminster Regained' in the November 1947 issue of *The Architectural Review* set the starting point for Cullen's rapidly developing theories on pedestrianization and serial vision. Claiming:

> "there is only one way to enjoy what a town has to offer the eye, and that is the pedestrian's way." [Gosling 1996, p.26]

Cullen pioneered the idea of the perception of the urban environment as a piece of moving scenery. In his article he introduced a new way of viewing the city called 'serial vision' and illustrated the uninterrupted sequence of views (viewpoints) which would unfold themselves like movie stills when walking along Parliament Square. (Unfortunately the visually striking figures from Cullen's work are omitted for copyright reasons).

With his book *Townscape*, published in 1961, Gordon Cullen added another dimension to the visual analysis of the built environment. He tried to show the aesthetical art of the urban landscape from the point of view of the observer's feelings and impressions perceived through a succession of visual scenes. By focusing on the space created between the buildings he argued that there is an:

> "*art of relationship* just as there is an art of architecture." [Cullen 1971, p.7]

His main concern is one's reaction when entering or being inside these spaces and the way the built environment is perceived. His argument is that:

> "it is almost entirely through vision that the environment is apprehended; [...] vision is not only useful but it evokes our memories and experiences, those responsive emotions inside us which have the power to disturb the mind when aroused." [Cullen 1971, p.8]

The production of these emotional reactions, the so-called 'unlooked-for surplus', happens through three means — Optics (Serial Vision), Place and Content — which are strongly linked to each other. The elements of Cullen's *Townscape Theory* are described in the 'casebook' of his book and are illustrated by numerous photographs and drawings from around the world.

2.1.1 Optics (Serial Vision)

Cullen explains the concept of Serial Vision with someone travelling at a uniform speed through a town. At each turning point a new view is revealed instantaneously, which then remains visible until the next turn and subsequently a new view is exposed. Through this the scenery of towns is revealed in a series of jerks or revelation.

Examining the town from an optical approach it can be split into two elements: the *existing view* and the *emerging/revealed view*. The interplay of these two elements is ideally an accidental chain of events and results in the town becoming visible in deeper sense. For the designer this is of significant importance and according to Cullen they should aim to:

> "manipulate the elements of the town so that an impact on the emotions
> is achieved." [Cullen 1971, p.8]

The human mind reacts to contrasts and the 'drama of juxtaposition'; a long straight street, for example, has only little visual impact because the initial view is soon digested and becomes monotonous.

Taking an unrelated plan and illustrated viewpoints as an example, Cullen argues that walking from one end of the plan to another will provide a sequence of revelations. These series of sudden contrasts make an impact on the eye and bring the plan to life.

2.1.2   Place

The concept of place is concerned with one's emotional reaction to the position of their body in its environment, which in an extreme situation can induce either agoraphobia or claustrophobia. Cullen states that:

> "the human being is constantly aware of his position in the environment,
> [...] he feels the need for a sense of place and [...] this sense of identity
> is coupled with an awareness of elsewhere." [Cullen 1971, p.12]

He explains this existence of a sense of identity with the example of a person going into a room and saying to themselves the unspoken words 'I am outside IT, I am entering IT, I am in the middle of IT'.

Having established the awareness of being in IT or entering IT or leaving IT, it appears to be obvious that there must be a place outside IT. Cullen states that if there is a HERE (or HERENESS) it is indispensable to create a THERE (or THERENESS) and it is unacceptable to have one of these places without the other. It has to be noted that the interplay between these two places can take different forms; while the HERE is always known, the THERE can either be known or unknown. Either known or unknown, the THERENESS is constantly out of one's reach, but it is always THERE.

He claims that the spatial designer cannot ignore this instinctive and continuous habit of the body to relate itself to its environment. He links the concept of movement with the concept of Serial Sequence and urges that if:

> "we design our towns from the point of the moving person [...] it
> is easy to see how the whole city becomes a plastic experience, a
> journey through pressures and vacuums, a sequence of exposures and
> enclosures, of constraints and relief." [Cullen 1971, p.10]

It is the skillful relationship between the two conditions, which creates the greatest townscapes.

The concept of place is defined by a range of elements, which are concerned with the definition, restriction, manipulation of space, and the relationship of people to spaces and of spaces to each other. These components consist of:

'Possession' (with its various forms such as 'occupied territory', 'possession in movement', 'advantage', 'viscosity', 'enclaves', 'enclosures', 'focal point', 'precincts', and 'indoor landscape and outdoor room').

'The outdoor room and enclosure' (including 'multiple enclosure', 'block house', 'insubstantial space defining space', 'looking out of enclosure', and 'thereness').

'Here and there'

> **'The known here and known there'** (with 'looking into enclosure', 'pinpointing', 'truncation', 'change of level', 'netting', 'silhouette', 'grandiose vista', 'division of space', 'screen vista', 'handsome gesture', 'closed vista', 'deflection', 'projection and recession', 'incident', 'punctuation', 'narrows', 'fluctuation', 'undulation', 'closure', and 'recession').

> **'The known here and unknown there'** (with 'anticipation', 'infinity', 'mystery', and 'the maw').

'Linking and joining' (including 'the floor', 'pedestrian ways', 'continuity', and 'hazards').

2.1.3   Content

The third component of the overall townscape perception is 'content' which is concerned with the built-in quality of the urban environment and its various sub-divisions. Content is defined by the fabric of towns: colour, texture, scale, style, character, personality and uniqueness. These fabrics are used to create the individual elements of the urban space and:

> "to create symmetry, balance, perfection, and conformity." [Cullen 1971, p.11]

> "Within a commonly accepted framework — one that produces lucidity and not anarchy — we can manipulate the nuances of scale and style, of texture and colour and of character and individuality, juxtaposing them in order to create collective benefits. In fact the environment thus resolves itself into not conformity but the interplay of This and That." [Cullen 1971, p.12]

The idea of 'This and That' complements the concept of 'Here and There' and means the opposing characteristics of two elements. By establishing the idea of typicality:

> "a thing being itself" [Cullen 1971, p.62]

urban fabrics or features can be either compared, juxtaposed, or equalized ('This is That').

"For just as the interaction of Here and There produced a form of emotional tension, so the relationship of This and That will produce its own form of drama which will exist inside the overall spatial framework." [Cullen 1971, p.77]

Similar to the concept of place, Cullen names a list of characteristics, which illustrate the concept of content:

'Categories' (including 'categorical landscape', 'juxtaposition', and 'immediacy').

'Thisness' (including 'seeing in detail', 'secret town', 'intricacy', 'propriety', 'bluntness and vigour', 'entanglement', 'nostalgia', 'exposure', 'intimacy', 'illusion', 'metaphor', 'the tell-tale', 'animism', 'noticeable absence', 'significant objects', 'building as sculpture', 'geometry', and 'multiple use').

'Foils' (covering 'relationship', 'scale', 'scale on plan', 'distortion', 'trees incorporated', 'calligraphy', 'publicity', and 'taming with tact').

When Gordon Cullen wrote *Townscape* there was only a small amount of similar literature on urban design around. The year 1961 saw in addition to Cullen's book the appearance of two other influential books on urban design: Kevin Lynch's *Image of the City*, and Jane Jacobs' *The Death and Life of Great American Cities*, both published in the United States of America.

Although, according to Gosling [1996] all three books were to have a profound influence in architecture and planning schools around the world, there is a significant difference between Cullen's *Townscape* and the other two publications. Both of them lacked the graphical skills Cullen possessed and the way he used these skills for his critical reflections and convincing proposals.

Both Cullen and Lynch focused on the visual quality of a city. While Cullen was concerned with emotional experiences a city can cause, Lynch concentrated on the mental image of the city as held by its citizens. He studied the techniques of human orientation and the apparent clarity and legibility of the cityscape, which means the ease with which parts can be recognized and can be organized into a coherent pattern [Lynch 1960]. Lynch's seemingly more scientific system of analysis with its paths, edges, districts, nodes and landmarks can be easier to apply and often results in a diagrammatic representation of the urban space. On the other hand it is a very static (as opposed to moving) way of analysis, which does not consider the individual's experience when moving through the urban world. It has also been criticized for being overly objective and cognitive [Benyon 2001].

Cullen's concept of Optics or Serial Vision is probably the most important component of his theory, since up to then the dynamic experience of viewing a town was barely recognized [Gosling 1996]. His drawing of spatial sequences can almost be seen as the predecessor of modern computer animations.

Critics of the time were mainly supportive of Cullen's work and believed it to be:

"the most important title in the visual analysis of the city." [Gosling
1996, p.71]

However, despite the recognized importance of *Townscape* it has been seldom
applied in actual design work. According to Gosling:

"this lack of acknowledgement may be due to the very nature of Cullen's
lyrical and poetic prose and the evocative nature and vivid skill of his
drawings." [Gosling 1996, p.9]

In 1971, an abbreviated version of *Townscape* was published, entitled *The
Concise Townscape*. In the introduction of the new edition, Cullen complained
that architects and planners had completely misunderstood his message with their
superficial civic style of decoration using cobbles and bollards. He felt that:

"[...] the original message of *Townscape* has not been delivered
effectively." [Cullen 1971, p.13]

3 Re-conceptualizing Web Navigation

The purpose of presenting this introduction to Cullen's work is to highlight the key
concepts and the close coupling of design innovation, aesthetics and function. In
some respects concepts such as 'screen vista', 'handsome gesture', 'closed vista'
are reminiscent of Christopher Alexander's architectural patterns [Alexander et al.
1977]. These rich, socially grounded views of architecture have inspired much
discussion in computing science, notably the object patterns and more recently
interaction patterns [Borchers 2001]. In a similar way we are keen to explore how
Cullen's theoretical concepts can be applied to Web design.

3.1 Design Objectives

Much research has been done to demonstrate the similarities (and differences)
between real (physical) and information spaces, and the way people navigate through
these environments. Consequently, it is possible to argue that Web designers need
to apply a comparable design language to the one that is used by urban designers,
architects and landscape architects. Taking Downs & Stea's [1977] concept of
wayfinding and Cullen's view of townscapes as a basis, five design objectives for
Web navigation can be specified. Web navigation should aim to provide:

- A sense of place (uniqueness).

- Information on size and dimension (scale).

- Information on closeness and distance (approach).

- Information on direction and perspective.

- A sense of arrival.

The process of wayfinding [Downs & Stea 1977] is broken down into four steps:
orientation, choice of route, monitor of route, and discovery of the objective. Each of

these steps requires a certain design quality of the space. In order to orientate oneself in an environment it is necessary that the space has a series of unique, distinguishable characteristics and features. A *sense of place* is often understood as:

> "something that is of significance to people [and] refers to intangible characteristics or some immeasurable but comprehensible mix of place characteristics that makes it attractive or unattractive, but that influences people positively or negatively toward it." [Golledge & Stimson 1997, p.414]

In the real environment a sense of place is created by physical and landscape attributes as well as human environment interaction aspects. The first category includes characteristics, which are unique for that specific place, for example, architectural features, forms of land use/cover, vegetation, land form and atmospheric qualities such as light and climate. The second category is much more subjective and refers to how the environment is perceived by the individual depending on familiarity, travel frequency (experience), social and ethnic background, etc.

Golledge & Stimson [1997] argue that the concept of place generates strong psychological and emotional links between people and places, which depends on the range of experience that people have with places:

> "The sense of place incorporates not only the concepts of location and pattern but feelings of belonging, invasion, mystery, beauty, and fear. As time changes, cultures alter settings, and the sense of place, its symbolism, its meaning, its cultural significance, and even its boundaries, may change." [Golledge & Stimson 1997, p.393]

If transferring the concept of sense of place or uniqueness to the information space of a Web site, it is essential to aim for a distinguishable look and feel of the site including a clear-cut navigation strategy. Both Nielsen [2000], and Flanders & Willis [1996] promote the use of a well-designed home page as a tool for providing a sense of place and helping users to orientate themselves. This may assist the sense of arrival (see below) when coming from another Web site, however, it does not afford a sense of place which is essential for the user's orientation when navigating the site itself.

The next three design objectives can be seen as one set, since they all derive from the navigation steps 'choice and monitor of route' and are concerned with the actual extent of the space and associated spatial attributes such as closeness/distance, and direction/perspective. Although these spatial attributes are understood to be objective and can be measured by certain standards (e.g. the number of pages or the number of mouse clicks required to get from A to B), a person is likely to have an individual perception of the spatial dimensions of a site.

In order to decide on a sequence of movements from the current location to the desired destination, people need to know the dimensions of the space and which route is the most efficient one. Furthermore, it is critical that they are continuously provided with information on the remaining distance to the goal. This will give them a feeling for approach throughout the entire movement. This can be seen, for example, in serial tasks such as completing an online booking when information such as 'step 2 of 5' is provided. When moving through the site, people's perspectives of the site changes constantly, with individual targets moving into the back- or foreground. People need to be aware of these changes, in order to adjust their path if required.

If aware of it, the interplay of changing perspectives or views, can add an interesting aspect to the Web navigation experience. Following Gordon Cullen's theory on 'Serial Vision', the Web space can be split into two elements: the existing view (i.e. the view of the current locations or page) and the emerging view (i.e. the view of locations or pages directly accessible from the current one). By moving through the Web site, the user is exposed to a chain of events experiencing a constant change of view. Ideally, the entering and leaving spaces (i.e. pages) in combination with the shift in views evokes a positive emotional reaction and the Web site is experienced at a much deeper level. This follows Gordon Cullen's theory on 'hereness and thereness' and his claim that the designer needs to be aware of the existence of these to spaces. One could argue that if people know what is ahead of or immediately around them (i.e. neighbouring pages), and are able to catch a glimpse of these, they may feel curious and intrigued to find out more and subsequently move to another space.

The fifth design objective, *sense of arrival*, derives from the final step in the wayfinding process, the discovery of the goal. Once people have arrived at their desired destination they need to be made aware of their arrival. It is not enough to provide a sign 'you have arrived' (which is in architecture and landscape architecture considered to be a design failure); it is here again that the sense of place becomes important. The designer should aim to create the 'space of arrival' in a way that it becomes obvious that the goal is reached, such as a countryside mansion located at the end of an avenue.

3.2 Concept of a Dynamic Sitemap

Now with the different physics of geographical and information spaces — particularly 2D spaces such as the Web — designers cannot simply take advantage of the three dimensional properties of geographical spaces. They have to find other ways of designing for movement and a sense of hereness and thereness. Our solution was to incorporate a novel sitemap into a Web site.

The Sitemap is designed to encourage the cognitive mapping between the abstract information space and the user's mental map of the site. The key element of the Sitemap is the two-dimensional visualization of the abstract information space of a Web site using semantically organized spatial metaphors. It is aimed to reflect the size and structure of a Web site and to take into consideration the notion of movement with the aspects distance, direction and approach. People should get a feeling for the size of a site and by moving from one page to another gain a sense for the proximity or distance or indeed existence of a location. Individual pages can be accessed from the sitemap, which always displays the changing current position of the user. Deriving from the previously specified design objectives and the concept of the sitemap a more explicit design language has been worked out. The design language is divided into a spatial syntax (*spatial organization and movement*) and a semantic component (*visual characteristics/design features*).

3.2.1   Spatial Organization

Spaces, both geographical and informational, are created by the juxtaposition and interplay of spatial typologies, which can be broken down into a set of dichotomous descriptors. These contrasting spatial qualities and their relationship to each other form the framework for meaning in design and can refer to either an individual element or the whole composition. A well-considered selection of spatial typologies results in a harmonious and dynamic design. As Cullen [1971] points out, it is the 'drama of juxtaposition' and contrast to which human mind reacts and through which a city (or any other space) become a stimulating environment.

The following list of spatial qualities has been developed using various urban design and design references for guidance [Lynch 1960; Mullet & Sano 1995; Cullen 1971]. While the first category refers to the relative size of the space as a whole, the other types of grouping define the *spatial organization* of the elements within space:

- Extensiveness — smallness: the scale of the space.

- Proximity — distance ('hereness' and 'thereness'): the extent between the current location and the desired location, or any two points.

- Openness — closure: the unlimited vs. restricted freedom of activity (and movement).

- Difference — likeness: the dissimilar as opposed to similar design, function, pattern, etc.

- Intricacy — simplicity: the complex (chaotic as an extreme) vs. the uncomplicated and clear-cut (limitation of elements and design forms).

- Unity — disorder: harmony vs. chaos.

- Uniqueness — repetition: outstanding, unique element (sharp boundaries against back-ground) vs. continuity or repetition in a rhythmic interval.

- Dominance — subordination: the dominance of one element over another.

- Dispersal — clustering: spreading vs. grouping of elements of similar design.

After close examination of each spatial attribute and its significance for the development of a Web navigation strategy three typologies were selected that seem to be critical for the realization of the sitemap:

- Extensiveness — smallness.

- Proximity — distance (' hereness' and 'thereness').

- Difference — likeness.

3.2.2 Movement

In addition to the spatial organization, the notion of *movement* has been taken into account. Time and motion are considered to be the forth dimension in geographical spaces and can be seen as a third dimension in two-dimensional Web sites. Spaces are sensed in motion and over time, similar to the pedestrian or car driver moving through the urban space, the user travels (or surfs) through the Web.

According to Donald Appleyard:

> "motion can bring a sense of freedom, vividness and power to city travel. It can enliven a dead scene. And it plays a primary role in the formulation and communication of the city image, its structure and meaning, for the city is apprehend as we move through it." [Appleyard 1965, p.176]

Cullen [1971] stresses, it is only when moving through a town that people are able to interact with the space, i.e. they are either in IT or entering IT or leaving IT. In motion, the scenery is revealed in a series of jerks and revelations (serial vision); the space is split into two elements the existing view and the emerging view. A similar concept can be applied to Web spaces; with each hyperlink people are able to change direction and consequently experience a new view (i.e. page).

In geographical spaces the perception of motion may differ substantially from what is really in motion, and depending on whether it is the person's own movement or that of the surrounding things, mild illusions can occur [Appleyard 1965]. While in information space, the user moves mentally not physically through the environment. Two further conditions for the perception of motion are, as per Appleyard [1965], the perceived rate of change and duration of perception.

In Web design the amount of time allocated to an activity can be measured in mouse clicks, which results in time being equal to distance. Another aspect of time not to be ignored is the time it takes to download a site/page. Although this has a significant effect on the usability of a site it is a technical rather than navigation issue and, therefore, out with the scope of this paper. Other measures will depend on content and on how long people spend reading and viewing that content.

3.2.3 Visual Characteristics

A spatial organization as described above can be accomplished by various design features or visual characteristics, which refer to recognizable objects, group of objects or areas. They include:

- Size.

- Proximity/distance to other cues.

- Texture.

- Form/shape.

- Colour.

- Location.

Spatial Attribute	Definition	Visualization
Extensiveness — smallness	Overall size of site	Size of map
Proximity — distance ('Hereness' and 'thereness')	Distance between current and desired location (mouse clicks)	Size, proximity/distance to other cues
Difference — likeness	Categories of content	Colour, texture, location

Table 1: Mapping between Spatial Organizational Features and Design Features.

- Orientation.

- Functional class/group.

- Dominance.

While the list of design features in urban design, architecture and landscape architecture is far more extensive and may include scent, touch, sound and, of course, three-dimensional features, the focus in the implementation of the sitemap lies on visual cues. Sound as a design feature has not been investigated within the context of this work.

3.2.4 Mapping

Having defined the relevant spatial typologies and usable visual design features it is possible to create a mapping between the two components of the design language. See Table 1.

This mapping is used to visualize the semantic organization of the Web site content under the consideration of spatial attributes.

4   Implementation of the Dynamic Sitemap

The prototype of the Dynamic Sitemap has been designed for a fictional Web site containing of eight categories and 36 pages in total, including the homepage. Figure 1 shows the navigation structure of the site.

The Dynamic Sitemap is designed to reflect the structure and size of a Web site, including available links between individual pages. Furthermore, and more important, the Sitemap considers the notion of movement, with the aspects distance, direction and approach. Figure 2 shows an extract of the Dynamic Sitemap excluding the space reserved for Web content.

The individual pages of the fictional Web site are symbolized by rectangular icons, apart from the icon of the homepage which is circular. The icons are organized along a 'grid' with the homepage in the centre reflecting the structure of the site and available links between individual pages. The Sitemap shows all pages accessible within five mouse clicks; as the user moves along a path containing more than five pages additional nodes to pages emerge. This feature of 'zooming in' is important for larger Web sites, where a Sitemap, which shows the entire number of nodes, would be difficult to read.

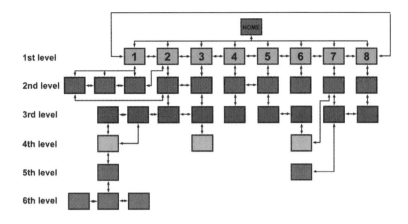

Figure 1: Dynamic Sitemap — Navigation Structure.

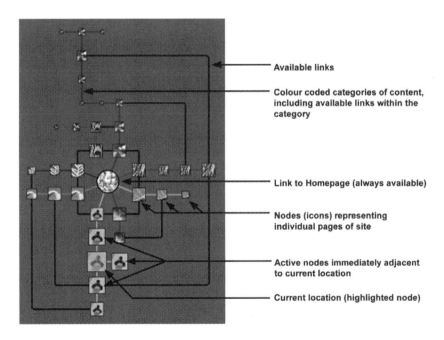

Figure 2: Dynamic Sitemap — Extract.

The pages of each content category are represented by a specific colour and background graphic. The icon indicating the user's current location is always highlighted in the category's colour; the active buttons in the immediate vicinity of the current location (i.e. neighbouring page) become highlighted when the user moves the cursor over them. The size of the icons indicates the distance between the pages and the current location; when the user moves through the site, the size of the icons alters accordingly. This feature derives from the idea of 'hereness and thereness' (distance/proximity) and gives the user a feeling of approach.

Since the Dynamic Sitemap forms part of a Web site its look and feel should follow the design of the site. For the purpose of the production of the prototype of the sitemap, a clear and almost minimalist design has been chosen. The Sitemap is located at the left side of the Web site, leaving sufficient space for the actual Web content. Because the Sitemap has been produced for a fictional Web site, there is no content included. The only indicator of changing content is the headline of the page (e.g. Category One Page One), which alters when the user interacts with the Sitemap. The content itself could theoretically also contain links to other pages. If the user selects a hyperlink via the content page, the Sitemap would then change subsequently.

5 Evaluation

An informal evaluation was undertaken with ten participants (six female, four male). After familiarizing themselves with the Sitemap and spending a while navigating through the Web site, most participants claimed to have gained a feeling for the size of the site. The majority of testers were able to orientate themselves in relation to other pages within the site and did not seem to experience a feeling of being lost. The greater part of participants felt it was very easy to move around the site and did not experience any major problems in getting to their desired destination. However, it could be observed that almost every user initially tried to select all types of icons, not only the ones which are located adjacent to the current location and have an embedded link to a page. On the other hand, in most cases, it seemed to take the participants only a short time to figure out which nodes are active and which are not. This shows that there is definitely a conflict between the design objective to represent the overall size of the Web site and the user's anticipation that every icon shown is active and can be used to access a page.

Using the Sitemap as a tool to get from one page to another came almost naturally to most participants, although not all of them were instantly aware that the appearance of the Sitemap changed throughout their interaction with it, nor did everybody understand the reasons behind it. Similarly, not all of the participants were fully conscious about the distance between the current location and the desired one, or approaching the destination. One participant noted that she thought that the size of the icons indicated the amount of content behind the icon, i.e. the larger the icon, the more content, and was confused when the sizes altered.

When discussing this issue of changing appearance with the participants after the evaluation, most of them stated that it took them a couple of minutes to notice that the Sitemap changed whenever they clicked on a node. Once informed about the rationale behind it, all of the participants were able to follow the concept and appeared to be eager to re-visit the Sitemap and to apply their knowledge. The vast majority of participants could imagine the Dynamic Sitemap as an alternative navigation tool in Web sites, and moreover, thought it was enjoyable to use and of innovative design. A further interesting result of the evaluation was that there seemed to be no significant relation between the subject's navigational performance and how they felt about the Sitemap and their knowledge of computers and the Web. Though the less experienced testers appeared to be the ones who felt the most enthusiastic about the Sitemap.

The results gained from the usability evaluation indicate that, in general, the Dynamic Sitemap can be more than useful as a navigation tool. The Sitemap is beneficial in providing the user with information on the size of the site and the changing distance between nodes (approach), which will not only help him or her perceive the spatial structure of the Web site, but also fully conceive it.

6 Conclusion

The advantage of the Web is the user's freedom of choice and flexibility of movement, but this at the same time is its problem. The freedom of user control combined with a glut of available information causes human error and finally results in a disorientated, confused and frustrated user, who is unlikely to return to a specific site or even the Web as a whole.

Similar to the process of wayfinding in a real environment, Web navigation is a conscious activity. The acquisition of navigational knowledge proceeds through developmental stages, from the initial identification of visual cues ('landmarks') to the rote memory of certain procedures ('routes') to fully formed 'survey knowledge'. Web navigation differs from navigating geographical spaces as the digital environment is characterized by a sensory degradation and a lack of many of the perceptual cues used in the real world; the physics are different. Navigational aids such as menu bars and buttons are meant to support the user in getting from one location to another. However, conventional Web navigation does not often go beyond simple one-way hyperlinks and does not take into account the user's perception and conception of the site. Web sites are still seen as a two-dimensional space and most Web designers are struggling to make that essential leap from graphic design to spatial design by adding the dimension of time and motion to it.

Gordon Cullen's 'Townscape Theory' and in particular his theory of 'Serial Vision' (or 'Spatial Sequence') is an interesting and pioneering aspect of the usage of geographical, or to be more precise, urban design principles to digital spaces. Other examples include McCall & Benyon [2003] and of course there have been many examples of using spatial interface *metaphors*. The example here has used design principles, not metaphors. Taking Cullen's concept of perceiving a space via existing and emerging views as a foundation and Down & Stea's model of wayfinding as a framework, a Dynamic Sitemap has been developed. The key element of the Sitemap is the two-dimensional visualization of intangible information space. While most conventional sitemaps are just diagrammatic representations of the structure of the site, the Dynamic Sitemap aims to reflect the size of the Web site and the users current location, and takes into consideration the notion of movement with the aspects distance, direction and approach. The results gained from the usability evaluation indicate that the Sitemap is an innovative approach to Web navigation, helping users not only to perceive the spatial structure of the Web site, but also to fully conceive the conceptual structure.

The dynamic site map is a design concept which Web designers can think about. But the contribution is more to do with the philosophy and approach. HCI needs to move away from its engineering roots and towards a design discipline. It must do this because of the challenge of pervasive computing. Soon (if not already) our job will not be concerned with engineering solutions to problems, it will be concerned with designing good experiences for people in information spaces. HCI designers will need to study architecture, urban design and landscape architecture to understand what makes a great experience in the physical environment and transfer this knowledge to the design of information spaces.

References

Alexander, C., Ishikawa, S., Silverstein, M., Jacobson, M., Fiksdahl-King, I. & Angel, S. [1977], *A Pattern Language: Towns, Buildings, Construction*, Oxford University Press.

Appleyard, D. [1965], Motion, Sequence and the City, *in* G. Kepes (ed.), *The Nature and Art of Motion*, Studio Vista, pp.176–92.

Benyon, D. & Höök, K. [1997], Navigation in Information Spaces: Supporting the Individual, *in* S. Howard, J. Hammond & G. K. Lindgaard (eds.), *Human–Computer Interaction — INTERACT '97: Proceedings of the Sixth IFIP Conference on Human–Computer Interaction*, Chapman & Hall, pp.39–45.

Benyon, D. R. [1998], Cognitive Ergonomics as Navigation in Information Space, *Ergonomics* **41**(2), 153–6.

Benyon, D. R. [2001], The New HCI? Navigation of Information Space, *Knowledge-based Systems* **14**(8), 425–30.

Borchers, J. [2001], *A Pattern Approach to Interaction Design*, John Wiley & Sons.

Chalmers, M. [2003], Informatics, Architecture and Language, *in* Höök et al. [2003], pp.315–44.

Cullen, G. [1971], *The Concise Townscape*, Architectural Press. Reprinted 2000.

Downs, R. M. & Stea, D. [1977], *Maps in Minds. Reflections on Cognitive Mapping*, Harper & Row.

Flanders, V. & Willis, M. [1996], *Web Pages That Suck. Learn Good Design by Looking at Bad Design*, Sybex.

Golledge, R. G. & Stimson, R. J. [1997], *Spatial Behavior. A Geographical Perspective*, The Guilford Press.

Gosling, D. [1996], *Gordon Cullen. Visions of Urban Design*, Academy Editions.

Höök, K., Benyon, D. R. & Munro, A. (eds.) [2003], *Designing Information Spaces: The Social Navigation Approach*, Springer-Verlag.

Lynch, K. [1960], *The Image of the City*, MIT Press. Reissued 2000.

McCall, R. G. & Benyon, D. R. [2003], Navigation: Within and Beyond the Metaphor in Interface Design and Evaluation, *in* Höök et al. [2003], pp.355–84.

McDonald, S. & Stevenson, R. J. [1998], Navigation in Hyperspace: An Evaluation of the Effects of Navigation Tools and Subject Matter Expertise on Browsing and Information Retrieval in Hypertext, *Interacting with Computers* **10**(2), 129–42.

Mullet, K. & Sano, D. K. [1995], *Designing Visual Interfaces: Communication Oriented Techniques*, SunSoft Press (Prentice-Hall).

Nielsen, J. [2000], *Designing Web Usability*, New Riders.

Passini, R. [1992], *Wayfinding in Architecture*, Van Nostrand Reinhold.

Preece, J. [2000], *Online Communities. Designing Usability, Supporting Sociability*, John Wiley & Sons.

Spence, R. [1999], A Framework for Navigation, *International Journal of Human–Computer Studies* **51**(5), 919–45.

A Method for Organizational Culture Analysis as a Basis for the Implementation of User-Centred Design into Organizations

Netta Iivari, Kaisu Juntunen & Ilkka Tuikkala

Department of Information Processing Science, University of Oulu, PO Box 3000, 90014 Oulu, Finland

Tel: *+358 8 553 1995*

Fax: *+358 8 553 1890*

Email: *netta.iivari@oulu.fi, kaisu.juntunen@mail.suomi.net, ilkka.tuikkala@oulu.fi*

Improving the position of User-centred Design (UCD) in organizations is a challenge. Organizational culture is an influential factor affecting the successes and failures of organizational improvement efforts. There does not exist studies on the effects of organizational culture in the implementation of UCD. In addition, it is difficult to find methods and theoretical models with which to reliably and systematically analyse organizational culture in the improvement efforts. This paper presents a method with which organizational culture can be analysed in the context of UCD implementation. The method was developed by experimenting with different techniques for data gathering (surveys, interviews and workshops) in 7 organizational units in 4 software development companies. The benefits and problems related to the techniques are presented. Practical guidance for doing prospective cultural analyses is offered. Finally, recommendations for the selection of a suitable UCD implementation strategy for different culture types are outlined.

Keywords: user-centred design, organizational culture, implementation of user-centred design.

1 Introduction

This paper presents results of an organizational culture analysis experimented with in the context of implementing User-centred Design (UCD) into software development organizations. UCD, defined in ISO standard 13407 [ISO 1999], is characterized by its goal of producing usable systems, and principles of user participation, appropriate allocation of functions between users and technology, iterative design and multi-disciplinary design. UCD is defined method independently in the standard. Design approaches focusing on users and usability, e.g. contextual design [Beyer & Holtzblatt 1998] and usability engineering [Mayhew 1999; Nielsen 1993] offer specific methods and techniques for carrying out the UCD activities. However, the position of UCD is often nonexistent or ineffective in software development organization. Furthermore, the improvement of the position of UCD has been widely recognized as a challenge [Axtell et al. 1997; Rosenbaum et al. 2000; Wilson et al. 1997; Vredenburg et al. 2002]. We suggest that organizational culture is a factor intertwined with organizational change effort of implementing UCD into organizations.

Organizational culture has lately been a popular focus of analysis in studies on organizational change and development [Denison & Spreitzer 1991; Lewis 1996]. The studies highlight that compatibility between the change effort and the culture is a very important criterion for success. The studies have defined compatible culture types for different kinds of change efforts, e.g. a 'group culture type' is a major facilitator of diffusion of telecommuting [Harrington & Ruppel 1999], a 'hierarchy' culture type is positively associated with the deployment of systems development methodologies [Iivari & Huisman 2001], 'adhocracy' and 'group' culture types are suitable for Total Quality Management (TQM) [Dellana & Hauser 1999], and 'adhocracy' and 'hierarchy' culture types are correlated with early adoption of intranets [Ruppel & Harrington 2001].

The studies have also showed problems to be caused by a mismatch between a unique organizational culture and an implementation effort. The studies show e.g. that a management information system implementation was resisted because the organization was presumed to have different organizational culture than it actually did [Pliskin et al. 1993], an enterprise resource planning packages implementation problems were caused by a mismatch with the values of the organizational culture [Krumbholz & Maiden 2001], and differences between the cultures of the implementers and the adopters caused difficulties in an information system implementation [Robey & Rodriquez-Diaz 1989].

However, organizational culture is a complex concept and there are many definitions of it [Smircich 1983]. Furthermore, it has been argued that it is difficult to find methods and theoretical models with which to reliably, systematically and meaningfully analyse organizational culture in relation to improvement efforts. In addition, culture studies have been carried out within a variety of research approaches. [Czarniawska-Joerges 1992; Denison & Spreitzer 1991; Smircich 1983; Zammuto & Krakower 1991]. The concept of culture is derived from the tradition of cultural anthropology. In anthropology culture denotes the socially transmitted patterns for behaviour characteristic of a particular social group. It refers to a way of life among particular people [Keesing & Strathern 1998]. The approaches for cultural studies can be divided e.g. into comparative, interpretive and clinical approaches [Iivari 2002], of which only the interpretive approach relies on the notion of culture derived from cultural anthropology.

Within the *comparative approach* culture is studied as comparable traits and dimensions. Culture is typically measured, as values, norms or attitudes. Aim is to group and profile cultures. In the *clinical approach*, on the other hand, the mode is clinical, therapeutic. Aim is to address organizational problems and dysfunctionalities, and how they contribute to the survival of organization. Culture is conceived as a tool for organizational problem solving. Finally, the *interpretive approach* relies on the tradition of cultural anthropology. Ethnography is the main method for data gathering. The researchers spend long periods of time in organizations, participate in the daily activities with the cultural members, and try to understand the culture [Iivari 2002].

Within this study *we rely on both the interpretive and comparative approaches* in the analysis of the cultures. This type of a multi-paradigmatic research into organizational cultures has been recommended. It benefits from triangulation and use of a variety of methods — the researchers can develop grounded, but general theories [Czarniawska-Joerges 1992; Denison & Spreitzer 1991; Zammuto & Krakower 1991]. We experimented with three techniques for gathering cultural data:

- organizational culture surveys;

- theme interviews; and

- workshops.

The techniques were experimented with in seven organizational units from four software development companies. The units were R&D (5), customer project (1) and documentation (1) units. After the cultural analysis we were able to suggest suitable UCD implementation strategies for the case units.

The paper is organized as follows. Next three sections present each technique for data gathering (survey, theme interview and workshop), the results achieved with the techniques, and lessons learned. The fifth section summarizes the lessons learned through the experimentation with these techniques, and suggests steps to be taken in prospective cultural analyses. Final section presents suitable UCD implementation strategies for different culture types.

2 Organizational Culture Survey

2.1 Carrying out the Phase

Within the comparative approach to organizational culture we utilized two surveys, a survey by Broadfoot & Ashkanasy [1994] and a survey based on a competing values model by Cameron & Freeman [1991]. Both surveys have been used in the context of organizational improvement efforts. Especially the competing values survey has been widely accepted and used, and researchers have defined compatible culture types for different kinds of improvement efforts [Cameron & Freeman 1991; Dellana

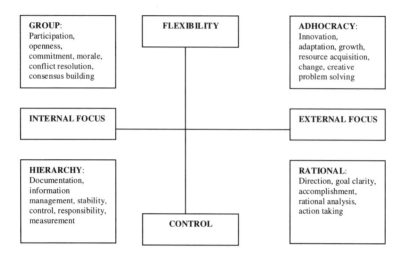

Figure 1: The competing values model [Cameron & Freeman 1991].

& Hauser 1999; Ruppel & Harrington 2001]. The Broadfoot & Ashkanasy survey has been applied in the implementation of TQM. Based on the results compatible strategies for the TQM implementation for different culture types have been defined [Kekäle 1998].

Broadfoot & Ashkanasy's [1994] survey contains 10 dimensions of organizational culture: leadership, structure, innovativeness, job performance, planning, communication, relationship to environment, humanistic values, development of individual, and socialization. Based on the survey results one can define the culture type that is either: innovative leadership; rules oriented; or relationship oriented. One can conclude that the higher scores the organization gets, the more innovative, customer oriented, flexible, unbureaucratic and individualistic the culture is.

The competing values model consists of two axes that reflect different value orientations. The vertical axis is flexibility — control dimension and the horizontal axis is internal — external dimension. By positioning organizations within the axes they can be defined within four organizational culture types: group, adhocracy, rational and hierarchical (Figure 1) [Cameron & Freeman 1991].

The group culture is based on the values and norms of affiliation. Dominant attributes are coherence, participation, teamwork and a sense of family. Organization emphasizes human resource development and values member participation in decision-making. Members' bonding to the organization is based on loyalty, long-term commitment, tradition and trust. The adhocracy type of culture emphasizes change. Growth and resource acquisition are stressed. Dominant attributes are entrepreneurship, creativity, adaptability and dynamism. Hierarchical culture type has the norms and values of a bureaucracy. It values stability and assumes that individuals will comply with organizational mandates, when roles are formally stated and enforced through rules and procedures. The dominant attributes are order, rules, regulations, uniformity and efficiency. The strategic emphasis is on stability, predictability and smooth. Finally, the rational culture type has an emphasis on competitive advantage and market superiority. Its objectives are productivity, planning and efficiency [Cameron & Freeman 1991].

Both surveys were included in one questionnaire. Seven units from four software development companies participated in the survey phase. We delivered the questionnaires to the contact persons of the units through email. They delivered the questionnaires to the personnel of the units in a weekly meeting. The personnel filled in the questionnaires in the meeting. Altogether 111 persons responded.

2.2   The Results

A report was produced of the survey results to each unit. It was sent by email to the contact persons of the units. The report presented the results of both surveys and the suggested approaches for the improvement efforts derived from the existing literature. The results were compared to the results of organizations presented in the literature, and to the results of other units participating in this study.

The suitable approaches for the improvement efforts were defined after the analysis of the culture types of the case units. For the culture types defined in the Broadfoot & Ashkanasy [1994] survey the following approaches are suggested of being suitable:

- Innovative leadership type — a soft approach.

- Rules orientation type — a hard approach.

- Relationships orientation type — a mixed approach.

The hard approach emphasizes production control aspects: systematic measurement and control of work, standardized quality systems, and statistical control mechanisms. The soft approach emphasizes soft quality characteristics, open management style, delegated customer responsibility, staff autonomy, customer satisfaction, and self-assessment tools. The mixed approach emphasizes scientific approach to one's own job, teamwork methods, and methods to assess quality organization wide [Kekäle 1998].

For the culture types defined in the competing values model the suitable implementation strategies are the following [Cameron & Freeman 1991; Dellana & Hauser 1999; Ruppel & Harrington 2001]:

Group culture: Emphasis on participation in decision-making, morale, trust, informal information sharing, employee ownership.

Adhocracy culture: Emphasis on innovation, experimenting, freedom to take risks, participation in decision making, creation and sharing of new ideas, development of individual.

Hierarchy culture: Emphasis on rules, standard procedures, process orientation, order, control, documentation.

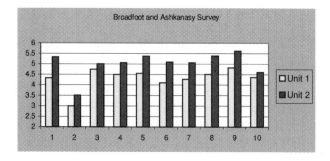

Figure 2: An example of the results from the Broadfoot & Ashkanasy survey (dimensions 1–10, scores 1–6).

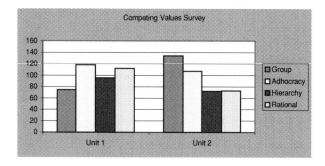

Figure 3: An example of the results of the competing values survey.

Rational culture: Emphasis on measurement, cost benefit analyses, linking the improvement effort to the business strategy and objectives.

Figures 2 & 3 present examples of the survey results of two case units.

The results of the surveys were conflicting. The units that got high scores in the group or adhocracy culture type in the competing values survey got high scores in the dimensions in the Broadfoot & Ashkanasy survey. The units that got high scores in the rational or hierarchy culture type got low scores in the dimensions in the Broadfoot & Ashkanasy survey. The units that got high scores in the Broadfoot & Ashkanasy survey, however, did not think that they represented the innovative leadership culture type. The scores they got in the dimensions in the Broadfoot & Ashkanasy survey were surprisingly high according to them.

The results are conflicting also because the group and adhocracy culture types represent the flexibility orientation, but some dimensions in the Broadfoot & Ashkanasy survey should logically get high scores instead in the control-oriented culture types, e.g. in dimensions related to planning and job performance. In addition, in the dimensions of relationship to environment and innovation the externally oriented culture types (adhocracy and rational) should get high scores, not the group culture type.

We concluded that these two surveys did not measure the same thing. The Broadfoot & Ashkanasy survey can be interpreted of measuring job satisfaction or satisfaction with the overall situation in the unit. The group culture type, focusing on loyalty, commitment and human resource practices is supposedly a culture type in which personnel has a high degree of satisfaction, loyalty and commitment towards their unit. This might be the reason the respondents gave such high scores to their unit in the Broadfoot & Ashkanasy survey.

2.3   Lessons Learned

The contact persons of the units evaluated the survey results. The results of the competing values survey were conceived to be credible. In the Broadfoot & Ashkanasy survey, the results in some dimensions, however, were surprisingly high, as mentioned earlier. The approach for the improvement efforts we proposed, based on the results from Kekäle [1998], was evaluated of being not a suitable one.

The research team evaluated the survey phase first independently, and afterwards a summary was produced. Lessons learned are presented next:

- Defining the concepts of organization and management was difficult. We used the concepts to refer to that level to which the personnel feel to belong to and of which they have enough knowledge for answering the questions.

- IT-companies were very concerned with confidential matters — a number of NDA agreements had to be assigned.

- The competing values survey provided more valid results. The Broadfoot & Ashkanasy survey, however, provided very detailed results.

3   Organizational Culture Interviews

3.1   Carrying out the Phase

The agenda for the interviews was based on the existing literature on organizational culture [Broadfoot & Ashkanasy 1994; Kekäle 1998; Schein 1985; Beyer & Holtzblatt 1998; Aaltio-Marjosola 1991]. Especially the cultural dimensions in Broadfoot & Ashkanasy's [1994] survey provided a good basis for the agenda. In addition, Schein [1985] defines five basic assumptions that characterize cultures. He also presents a list of themes within which one can analyse these basic assumptions. Beyer & Holtzblatt [1998] present ideas related to the cultural analysis while discussing the cultural and flow models in the Contextual Design methodology. Finally, Kekäle [1998] and Aaltio-Marjosola [1991] bring up the importance of the analysis of the historical background and past experiences with organizational change efforts.

The interviews were done after the survey phase. Five case units participated in the interview phase. We interviewed two types of people in the units:

- usability specialists; and

- people whose work is directly related to the unit's core mission.

Altogether we interviewed 2–3 persons in each unit. All interviews were tape-recorded and the interview team wrote down notes. Each interview lasted for two hours. In the interviews of the usability specialists we discussed the survey results and the themes in the interview agenda. Furthermore, we discussed the suitability of suggested approaches for the improvement efforts presented in the previous section. In the second type of the interviews we discussed the themes in the interview agenda without discussing the results of the survey phase.

3.2   The Results

We produced a 20-pages long report of the interview results to each unit. In the report we included theoretical background and motivation for the study, graphical presentations of cultural categories revealed through the theme interviews and a list of central observations related to the implementation of UCD in the units.

After each interview the observations from the interview were written to the post-it notes. The analysis of this material is similar to the one defined in the Contextual Design methodology [Beyer & Holtzblatt 1998]: the post-it notes were categorized in a brainstorming session in which an affinity diagram was formed. The categories were labelled. The categorization was empirical and inductive. In different units the empirical material naturally differed. However, we were able to define 7 (of 8) generic categories representing cultural characteristics of the case units. The following categories were identified:

- Relationship to larger organizational context.

- Leadership style and strategic planning.

- Innovativeness and improvements.

- Communication.

- 'Sticks and carrots' (punishments and rewards).

- Processes, methods, guidelines for work.

- Social relations.

- Usability and UCD — position and importance.

After the categorization we produced a graphical presentation of each category (an example is in Figure 4). Again, we relied on the notation of the Contextual Design methodology (the culture and flow models). The presentations did not, however, adhere strictly to the notation. Main point was to produce understandable and logical presentations of the cultural aspects prevalent in the units. The reason to produce graphical presentation was that they can be commented easily, and we wanted the interviewees to review the accuracy of the results.

Figure 4 illustrates the position of UCD in one case unit.

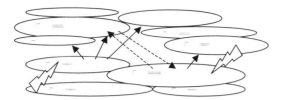

Figure 4: An example of the graphical presentation of a culture dimension.

The arrows point out communication, cooperation and coordination between the usability specialists and other stakeholder groups in the unit. The groups are illustrated as bubbles. Also perceptions about usability, UCD and users are included as bubbles in the picture. The lightning bolts represent different kinds of breakdowns and problems related to the position of UCD in the unit (e.g. no knowledge of users, usability specialists work is not visible to the rest of the personnel, senior designers have a very sceptical attitude towards the UCD activities, management does not support the UCD activities).

When the results of the interviews were compared to the survey results it seems like the competing values survey succeeded in revealing the value orientation of the units from the viewpoint of human relationships in most of the case units. However, in some units significant characteristics did not appear in the survey results. For example in one unit that got high scores in the group culture type a clear orientation towards the hierarchy type of culture 'in the ways they work' did not appear. In another unit the value orientation from the viewpoint of human relationships, on the other hand, was criticized of being incredible. The personnel felt that recent rationalization and control related to the 'ways they work' was the reason for the high scores rational culture got in their unit. They felt that their value orientation from the viewpoint of human relationships resembles the group culture type. According to them their management just 'tries to make them more rational'.

3.3   Lessons Learned

The results report was sent to the interviewees. They commented the results. Afterwards, we agreed to organize workshop sessions in the units. In these sessions the interview results were to be further validated. The interviewees gave the following feedback. The reports were clear and the results interesting. Overall, the results were conceived to be accurate. However, in some units the results were based only on two interviews and this was problematic: the results were conceived to be a caricature in which the views of the two interviewees were not consolidated enough. At least three interviews seem to be necessary.

The results provided the interviewees with new ideas and concepts with which to make sense of their environment, e.g. based on our analysis the usability specialists of one unit labelled themselves as a 'Mommy Mob', and personnel of one unit noticed that they had differing interpretations of the position of user-interface development in their unit. The interviewees got also new ideas related to their work, e.g. they gained insights of how to organize training related to the UCD (training for whom and when), and what type of cooperation is needed between the personnel of different units related to the UCD. The interviewees valued the results and wanted to discuss them with larger audience and with their management.

The research team evaluated the interview phase first individually, after which a summary was produced. Lessons learned are summarized next:

- The survey results formed an excellent basis for the interviews. We gained a lot of rich, context specific data, the agenda was logical and the discussions proceeded fluently.

- Identifying the categorization for the empirical material was laborious due to the huge amount of rich, heterogeneous data. Also the production of the graphical presentations was burdensome. However, the generic categories made the analysis phase efficient and the interview results report reusable.

- The interviewees who were not familiar with the survey results gave more 'embellished picture' of their unit than the ones who had seen the results. It is uncertain whether the survey results freed the interviewees to talk more openly or whether the results affected negatively by making the interviewees more critical towards their unit.

- The software companies were again very cautious related to confidentially issues. In one unit the tape recordings had to be left in the unit.

- Some interviewees were very frank and critical about the situation in their unit. The empirical material had to be 'filtered' before reporting it.

- Altogether, the qualitative organizational culture analysis seems to be a necessary part of any cultural study, if a sufficiently credible understanding of organizational culture is to be achieved.

4   Organizational Culture Workshops

4.1   Carrying out the Phase

Schein [1985] proposes workshops as a lightweight technique for gathering data of organizational culture. Our agenda for the workshops included graphical presentation of the interview results report in the sequence the discussion was supposed to proceed fluently. In addition, a list of observations relevant from the viewpoint of UCD implementation was included from the interview results report.

We organized the workshop sessions in four case units. 3–7 participants were present. The sessions lasted for three hours each.

4.2   The Results

The workshop sessions proved out to be very useful in validating and correcting the interview results report. In one session the participants considered the report to be too exaggerating. Some words and characterizations were to be changed. In this session not much new information was gained. The discussions were quite difficult to initiate. In other sessions, on the other hand, the results were considered to be very representative. These sessions offered, in addition, a lot of additional information. The discussions proceeded fluently and the participants spoke very openly. Finally, in all sessions the participants seemed to prefer the same approach for the improvement efforts that was considered to be suitable by the contact person — the usability specialist — of their unit.

4.3 Lessons Learned

The participants considered the issues discussed in the sessions 'really interesting'. They started planning for future actions related to these issues, which we interpret to be a very positive achievement from our point of view. The reports of the cultural analysis had been delivered to the management — they were used for initiating improvements. In addition, in one unit the workshop session and the interviews were considered to be therapeutic.

The researchers evaluated the workshop phase first individually, after which a summary was produced. Lessons learned are summarized next:

- The sessions were an efficient way to evaluate and validate the results of the interview phase.

- The agenda worked well: It was logical and the discussions proceeded fluently.

- It would have been quite difficult to discuss certain kinds of issues in a group — certain issues are too sensitive (views related to the respected types of workers or management).

- It depended a lot on the participants (or on the organizational culture of the units), whether the sessions succeed.

In some sessions the participants were communicative and open. The conversation proceeded smoothly. New information was gathered. In units, where people are used to express their opinions and discuss in groups, these sessions seem to succeed. In one session, on the other hand, the participants were more quiet and reserved. New information was not gathered much. Furthermore, the participants gave quite an 'embellished' picture of their unit. The participants were actually from the unit that got especially high scores related to the group culture type in the competing values model. Also in the workshop they seemed to be very satisfied with the current situation in their unit and they did not want to bring up any negative things of their unit. One can conclude that the culture of the unit may affect greatly whether these sessions are successful. Perhaps the workshop session is a suitable method only in a certain types of cultures.

5 Summary of the Results

We have used three different techniques for data gathering (surveys, interviews and workshops). The benefits, problems and the dependencies between the phases associated to these techniques are outlined in Table 1.

The rows present the different phases (the competing values = CV and the Broadfoot & Ashkanasy = BA). In the columns are the 1) benefits, 2) problems

Phase	Benefits	Problems	Dependences
Surveys CV BA	Relatively fast and easy way to gather cultural data. Existing literature suggests compatible strategies for the improvement efforts. CV: relatively valid results, BA: very detailed results.	BA: results difficult to interpret. Surveys provided conflicting results. Suggested strategies for the improvement efforts based on the culture types in the BA were not suitable.	The surveys are not sufficient alone, the interviews are necessary. BA: not recommended, results difficult to interpret. CV: not sufficient alone.
Interview	More thorough understanding of the culture of the units, context specific, rich data. Succeeded in identifying critical problem areas in the position of UCD. The interviewees got new ideas related to their work.	Two interviews were too few, at least three interviews needed. It is unclear how the survey results affected the interviewees: they spoke more openly or they adopted a more critical stance towards their unit.	BA: good agenda for the interviews. However, the interviewees seemed to speak more openly if they were familiar with the survey results. Workshops are still recommended for the validation of the results (or more interviews need to be done).
Workshop	The interview results were validated. In some sessions there were lively discussions and lot of new information was gained. In certain type of units the workshop seems to be a suitable method. The sessions initiated improvement actions.	Organizational culture affects the nature of the sessions? In one unit the discussions were difficult to initiate and not much new knowledge was gained. The workshop may not be a suitable method in this type of units.	Interviews are necessary as a basis? It might be difficult to initiate the discussions without the interview results. In addition, certain topics seemed to be too sensitive to be discussed in a group. Sessions in which future actions are planned should be organized separately.

Table 1: Summary of the phases of the cultural analysis.

and 3) dependences that we identified related to the phases. By presenting the dependencies, we show how the phases create a continuum.

Based on our findings we suggest the following phases for cultural analysis:

- Organizational culture survey phase — using the competing values survey.

- Organizational culture interview phase — at least three theme interviews.

- Organizational culture workshop phase — for validating the results.

We recommend using the competing values survey as a basis — as a first step — for the cultural analysis. The competing values model seems to be an efficient tool for communicating the results of cultural analysis to the organization. The model can be used as an intellectual tool for discussing the cultural aspects of the organizations.

The culture types defined in the model seem to be understandable and a useful tool for the cultural members in reflecting the cultural aspects of their organization. We do not recommend using the Broadfoot & Ashkanasy survey — it did not produce interpretable or reliable results. However, the competing values survey alone does not provide reliable results either. Qualitative approach to organizational culture is a necessary part of any cultural analysis.

Afterwards, we recommend at least three theme interviews to be done in the organizations. The organizations typically have several different organizational subcultures or stakeholder groups. These should be acknowledged, and representatives of these groups interviewed as extensively as possible. The Broadfoot & Ashkanasy survey's dimensions can be used as an agenda for the interviews. Also the position of UCD and interpretations of UCD should be discussed in the interviews. The interview results should be presented graphically to the interviewees in order that they can, and are also motivated to, comment the accuracy of the results. Feedback from the interviewees is very important.

Finally, we recommend an organizational culture workshop to be organized after the interview results report is produced. The workshops are an efficient way to validate the results and to communicate the results to a larger audience. We recommend the graphical presentations of the cultural categories of the interview results report to be used as an agenda for the workshops. The graphical presentations can be easily read and commented. The position of UCD and interpretations of UCD should also be discussed in the session. The workshops may differ in nature in organizations with different cultures. However, the workshops are recommended in every case for communication and validation.

6   Recommendations for Practice

Based on the cultural analysis one can define the culture type the case organizations represent. However, one should not rely on the organizational culture survey alone, since the surveys alone do not produce a reliable picture of the culture of the units. Instead, one should at least experiment with the feedback interviews, and/or a validation workshop. Based on the insights gained through the use of these techniques for data gathering one can define which culture type the case unit represents the most. We suggest the culture type to be defined using the culture types of the competing values model as a basis. Finally, we present again the compatible implementation strategies suggested for the different culture types in the competing values model. The recommendations are summarized in Figure 5.

For the group culture type one should select methods and tools emphasizing informal information sharing, teamwork and employee ownership. Participation in decision-making, morale and trust should be encouraged. For the adhocracy culture type one should select methods and tools emphasizing innovation, experimenting with new things, creation and sharing of new ideas, and freedom to take risks. Methods, which rely on teamwork, brainstorming and iteration of design solutions, are suitable. This culture type is an 'early adopter'. This strength should be utilized and new, innovative solutions searched for and experimented with [Cameron & Freeman 1991; Dellana & Hauser 1999; Ruppel & Harrington 2001].

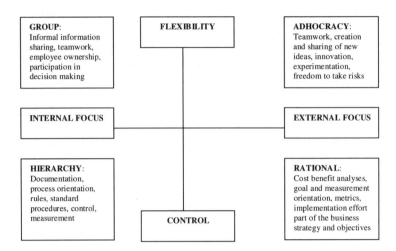

Figure 5: UCD implementation strategies for different culture types.

For the hierarchy culture type one should select methods and tools emphasizing rules, standard procedures, documentation and control (of the product and process). For example definition and implementation of a software process model in which UCD activities are incorporated, could be suitable in this culture type. In addition, process assessments and improvement programs are suitable especially for this culture type. Actually, this culture type is suitable for any kind of large-scale implementation programs, since procedures and rules for that are in place. Finally, for the rational culture type one should select methods and tools emphasizing measurement that can show the business benefits of the implementation of UCD. UCD should be linked to the business strategy and objectives. Business focus, metrics and cost benefit analyses are preferred in this culture type [Cameron & Freeman 1991; Dellana & Hauser 1999; Ruppel & Harrington 2001].

References

Aaltio-Marjosola, I. [1991], Cultural Change in a Business Enterprise: Studying a Major Organizational Change and Its Impact on Culture, *Acta Academiae Oeconomicae Helsingiensis, Series A* **80**.

Axtell, C. M., Waterson, P. E. & Clegg, C. W. [1997], Problems Integrating User Participation into Software Development, *International Journal of Human–Computer Studies* **47**(2), 323–45.

Beyer, H. & Holtzblatt, K. [1998], *Contextual Design: Defining Customer-centered Systems*, Morgan-Kaufmann.

Broadfoot, L. & Ashkanasy, N. [1994], A Survey of Organizational Culture Measurement Instruments, Paper presented at the Annual Meeting of Australian Social Psychologists.

Cameron, K. S. & Freeman, S. J. [1991], Cultural Congruence, Strength, and Type: Relationships to Effectiveness, *in* R. W. Woodman & W. A. Pasmore (eds.), *Research in Organizational Change and Development*, Vol. 5 of *An Annual Series Featuring Advances in Theory, Methodology, and Research*, JAI Press, pp.23–58.

Czarniawska-Joerges, B. [1992], *Exploring Complex Organizations. A Cultural Perspective*, Sage Publications.

Dellana, S. A. & Hauser, R. D. [1999], Toward Defining the Quality Culture, *Engineering Management Journal* **11**(2), 11–5.

Denison, D. R. & Spreitzer, G. M. [1991], Organizational Culture and Organizational Development: A Competitive Values Approach, *in* R. W. Woodman & W. A. Pasmore (eds.), *Research in Organizational Change and Development*, Vol. 5 of *An Annual Series Featuring Advances in Theory, Methodology, and Research*, JAI Press, pp.1–21.

Harrington, S. J. & Ruppel, C. P. [1999], Practical and Value Compatibility: Their Roles in the Adoption, Diffusion and Success of Telecommuting, *in* P. De & J. I. de Gross (eds.), *Proceedings of 20th International Conference of Information Systems*, Association for Information Systems, pp.103–12.

Iivari, J. & Huisman, M. [2001], The Relationship Between Organizational Culture and the Systems Development Methodologies, *in* K. R. Dittrich, A. Geppert & M. C. Norrie (eds.), *Advanced Information Systems Engineering, 13th International Conference, CAiSE 2001*, Vol. 2068 of *Lecture Notes in Computer Science*, Springer-Verlag, pp.234–50.

Iivari, N. [2002], Analyzing the Role of Organizational Culture in the Implementation of User-centered Design — Disentangling the Approaches for Cultural Analysis, *in* J. Hammond, T. Gross & J. Wesson (eds.), *Usability: Gaining a Competitive Edge, Proceedings of IFIP 17th World Computer Congress Stream 9 (TC-13 Stream)*, Vol. 226 of *IFIP*, Kluwer, pp.57–91.

ISO [1999], ISO 13407 International Standard. Human-centred Design Processes for Interactive Systems. International Organization for Standardization, Genève, Switzerland.

Keesing, R. M. & Strathern, A. J. [1998], *Cultural Anthropology*, third edition edition, Harcourt Brave College Publishers.

Kekäle, T. [1998], The Effects of Organizational Culture on Successes and Failures in Implementation of Some Total Quality Management Approaches: Towards a Theory of Selecting a Culturally Matching Quality Approach, *Acta Wasaensia* **65**. Industrial Management 1.

Krumbholz, M. & Maiden, N. [2001], The Implementation of Enterprise Resource Planning Packages in Different Organizational and National Cultures, *Information Systems* **26**(3), 185–204.

Lewis, D. [1996], The Organizational Culture Saga — From OD to TQM: A Critical Review of the Literature. Part 2 — Applications, *Leadership and Organization Development Journal* **17**(1), 12–9.

Mayhew, D. J. [1999], *The Usability Engineering Lifecycle: A Practitioner's Handbook for User Interface Design*, Morgan-Kaufmann.

Nielsen, J. [1993], *Usability Engineering*, Academic Press.

Pliskin, N., Romm, T., Lee, A. S. & Weber, Y. [1993], Presumed vs. Actual Organizational Culture: Managerial Implications for Implementation of Information Systems, *The Computer Journal* **36**(2), 143–52.

Robey, D. & Rodriquez-Diaz, A. [1989], The Organizational and Cultural Context of Systems Implementation: Case Experience from Latin America, *Information and Management* **17**(4), 229–39.

Rosenbaum, S., Rohn, J. A. & Humburg, J. [2000], A Toolkit for Strategic Usability: Results from Workshops, Panels, and Surveys, *in* T. Turner & G. Szwillus (eds.), *Proceedings of the CHI'00 Conference on Human Factors in Computing Systems*, *CHI Letters* **2**(1), ACM Press, pp.337–44.

Ruppel, C. P. & Harrington, S. J. [2001], Sharing Knowledge Through Intranets: A Study of Organizational Culture and Intranet Implementation, *IEEE Transactions on Professional Communication* **44**(1), 37–52.

Schein, E. [1985], *Organizational Culture and Leadership*, Jossey-Bass.

Smircich, L. [1983], Concepts of Culture and Organizational Analysis, *Administrative Science Quarterly* **28**(3), 339–85.

Vredenburg, K., Mao, J., Smith, P. W. & Carey, T. [2002], A Survey of User-centered Design Practice, *in* D. Wixon (ed.), *Proceedings of CHI'02 Conference on Human Factors in Computing Systems: Changing our World, Changing Ourselves*, *CHI Letters* **4**(1), ACM Press, pp.471–8.

Wilson, S., Bekker, M., Johnson, P. & Johnson, H. [1997], Helping and Hindering User Involvement — A Tale of Everyday Design, *in* S. Pemberton (ed.), *Proceedings of the CHI'97 Conference on Human Factors in Computing Systems*, ACM Press, pp.178–85.

Zammuto, R. F. & Krakower, J. Y. [1991], Quantitative and Qualitative Studies of Organizational Culture, *in* R. W. Woodman & W. A. Pasmore (eds.), *Research in Organizational Change and Development*, Vol. 5 of *An Annual Series Featuring Advances in Theory, Methodology, and Research*, JAI Press, pp.83–114.

Evaluation Methods

Changing Analysts' Tunes: The Surprising Impact of a New Instrument for Usability Inspection Method Assessment

Gilbert Cockton, Alan Woolrych, Lynne Hall & Mark Hindmarch

School of Computing and Technology, University of Sunderland, PO Box 299, Sunderland SR6 0YN, UK

Tel: *+44 191 515 3394*

Fax: *+44 191 515 2781*

Email: *{Gilbert.Cockton, Alan.Woolrych, Lynne.Hall, Mark.Hindmarch}@sunderland.ac.uk*

We describe the impact on analyst performance of an extended problem report format. Previous studies have shown that Heuristic Evaluation can only find a high proportion of actual problems (thoroughness) if multiple analysts are used. However, adding analysts can result in a high proportion of false positives (low validity). We report surprising interim results from a large study that is exploring the DARe model for evaluation method effectiveness. The DARe model relates the effectiveness of an evaluation method to evaluators' command of discovery and analysis resources. Previous work has shown that Heuristic Evaluation poorly supports problem discovery and analysis: heuristics tend to be inappropriately applied to problem predictions. We developed an extended problem report format to let us study analyst decision making during usability inspection. Our focus was on the quality of insights into analyst behaviour delivered by this extended report format. However, our first use of this format revealed unexpected improvements in validity (false positive reduction) and appropriate heuristic application. We argue that the format has unexpectedly led to more care and caution in problem discovery and elimination, and in heuristic application. Evaluation performance can thus be improved by indirectly 'fixing the analyst' via generic fixes to inspection methods. In addition, we provide the first direct evidence

of how evaluators use separate discovery and analysis resources during usability inspection.

Keywords: DARe (DR-AR) model, usability inspection methods, heuristic evaluation, usability evaluation, HCI research methods.

1 Introduction: The Discovery and Analysis Resource (DARe) Model for Usability Evaluation

The Discovery and Analysis Resource (DARe) model for Usability Evaluation distinguishes finding from keeping for usability problems. Analysts find *possible* problems (via inspection or user testing) and then either confirm them as *probable* problems (for user testing, significant), or eliminate them as *improbable* (insignificant). Analysts thus *discover* problems and then *analyse* them in separate phases of evaluation. Evidence for the DARe model and the range of resources used by usability analysts was derived from a large study [Cockton & Woolrych 2001; Woolrych 2001]. The predictive power of the model was demonstrated in a subsequent re-analysis of the study data [Woolrych & Cockton 2002].

In this paper we report the first study based directly on the DARe model. Ten groups of final year HCI students applied the standard Heuristic Evaluation (HE) [Nielsen 1994] to a local transport Web site (http://www.tyneandwearmetro.co.uk/). They reported problems using an extended version of our problem report format [Cockton & Woolrych 2001], which required them to state their discovery tactics and their reasons for heuristic use and problem elimination or confirmation. The results provide firm evidence for distinct discovery and analysis resources in usability inspection, as well as clear-cut examples of specific resources in use. For the first time, we can isolate and analyse false negatives as well as false positives.

Despite the inherent limitations of self-reporting as a research instrument, we were surprised by unexpected impacts on analyst performance. Analyst application of Heuristic Evaluation was more valid (fewer false positives) and appropriate, and (as yet) no less thorough. We discuss how explicit reporting of discovery tactics and confirmation/elimination rationales can produce highly desirable improvements in analyst performance.

Before presenting the current study, we will argue that evaluator skills are a key variable in both analytical and empirical evaluation, and that neither class of evaluation has any automatic advantages or disadvantages. Potential method benefits can only thus be ensured by careful planning and skilled execution. We introduce the DARe model as a framework for structuring planning, skill development and reflective professional self-evaluation. We then present the main study and its results, showing how a simple extension to problem reports can improve the effectiveness of multiple analysts in Heuristic Evaluation.

2 Predictive Models in Usability Evaluation

Usability evaluation methods divide into two key groups: analytical and empirical. Empirical methods [Dumas 2003] observe systems/prototypes in use. Analytical methods examine systems (perhaps via models or specifications) to identify potential (ideally, probable) usability problems. The two main approaches here are *model-based* [Kieras 2003] and *inspection methods* [Cockton et al. 2003]. The inspection method assessed in this study is *Heuristic Evaluation* [Nielsen 1994]. Both main groups of methods have potential advantages and disadvantages. However, these are not as clear-cut as often stated.

It is all too easy to make crude and shallow comparisons of analytical and empirical evaluation. The key common variable in both cases is the skill of usability specialists. Significant evaluator effects can be shown for both analytical [Cockton et al. 2003] and empirical [Hertzum & Jacobsen 2001] methods. There are no absolute differences in cost or quality between the two types of method. Analytical methods are assumed to be faster, cheaper and more flexible. Empirical methods are assumed to be more reliable. None of these commonplace beliefs stand up to examination.

All evaluations have distinct phases of planning, implementation, analysis and recommendation. Reporting can occur in all phases (test scripts, session notes, problem reports, recommendations). Planning is not automatically faster or cheaper for analytical methods, although inspection methods require less effort than model-based ones (no models to construct). Both analytical and empirical methods require system familiarization, and contextual understanding (users, goals, tasks, scenarios, domain knowledge). Empirical methods do require user recruitment and test protocol design, but these can be kept extremely simple (e.g. opportunistic 'hallway' testing, free usage, field observation). Inspection methods may require challenging recruitment and scheduling of multiple analysts.

Similarities in cost and speed apply to implementation. Managing a team of multiple analysts could be as time consuming as running several users through tests. Also, during analysis, merging analyst predictions can become as time consuming as analysing test data (especially for vague or conflicting predictions [Connell & Hammond 1999]). Indeed, if developers are present during testing, analysis can be speeded up and simplified, and even combined with agreement on necessary changes. Both method groups present challenges to speed and economy. Predictions may be too vague to support confident and detailed recommendations. User difficulties in tests may require extensive causal analysis in order to adequately ground recommendations.

Flexibility is also seen as an advantage for analytical methods, which do not require executable robust prototypes. However, neither do empirical methods, which have been applied successfully to a range of low fidelity prototypes in participative design approaches [Kuhn & Muller 1993].

Empirical evaluation can thus be fast, flexible and cheap (but at the expense of reliability Woolrych & Cockton [2001]; Barnum et al. [2003]). Analytical evaluation can be slow, inflexible and expensive, and with no corresponding increase in overall effectiveness. Thus while increased resources *can* readily result in more reliable empirical evaluation [Woolrych & Cockton 2001], this is less likely with analytical evaluation. Inspection methods are thus almost inescapably *discount* methods, because existing investment strategies (e.g. multiple analysts) have inherent limits.

Thus, extra analysts uncover more problems, but soon come to add *even more* false alarms [Woolrych & Cockton 2002]. Each extra analyst also adds to the cost of problem set consolidation and pruning. Costs keep rising and returns soon drop.

This paper addresses the challenge of increasing the effectiveness of usability inspection methods (UIMs) without increasing resource costs per evaluation. The aim is to reduce the penalties of using inspection methods in a wide range of situations where user testing is infeasible or undesirable, for example, as an input to user test planning, for driving early design iterations, or for informing change decisions in response to user testing. Usability evaluation cannot be wholly empirical, and thus analytical methods must be made more effective.

3   A More DAReing Investment Strategy for UIMs

There are two possible responses to poor UIM quality other than the discount approach of stacking analysts high and selling methods cheap. Fewer and better skilled analysts could be used (and we should be able to determine analyst skill levels). Alternatively, better methods could be developed. The choice then is: fix the analyst or fix the method? Which is better?

The *Discovery and Analysis Resource* (DARe[1]) model suggests that fixing the analyst will be more effective than fixing the method. This follows from its modelling of the middle phases of usability evaluation: implementation and analysis. The DARe model identifies distinct knowledge resources that help analysts to find possible problems (discovery resources) and others that support either confirmation of probable (or elimination of improbable) problems (analysis resources). Our first study showed that Heuristic Evaluation (HE) was never clearly a discovery resource and typically not an analysis resource. Heuristics were not being used to find possible problems, as most (61%) heuristic applications were inappropriate. 80% of the hardest to construct problems were missed, again indicating that heuristics would not lead analysts to several serious problems. Nielsen's [1994] set of ten heuristics is derived from seven factors that could only predict 30% of an eleven system corpus of 247 usability problems, so it is hard to believe that our analysts' prediction of 72% of actual problems was due to the disclosing power of heuristics. As Gray & Salzman [1998] have commented, Nielsen's studies allow nothing to be attributed to HE, instead for example, in one study [Nielsen 1992], it was experts alone who found more problems than novices, and *not experts using HE*.

Similarly, analysts in our first study failed to eliminate far too many false positives. 65% of their predictions did not transpire in a carefully designed falsification test. HE thus failed to eliminate a host of improbable problems (and many bogus ones too). Overall, HE clearly played a limited role in the discovery of possible problems and the elimination/confirmation of im/probable ones. This let us derive a conjecture that multiple analysts can improve discovery resources (since these are additive), but that they will dilute elimination analysis resources (since one bad apple can spoil the bunch), and thus increased thoroughness (hit rate) will be at the expense of lowered validity (false positive rate), and thus overall effectiveness

---

[1]In previous publications, this has been called the DR-AR model (Discovery Resources — Analysis Resources). The reason for the change should be clear.

(thoroughness×validity) will be reduced if losses outweigh gains. This turned out to be true for a retrospective analysis of our first study's data [Woolrych & Cockton 2002].

Given the importance of analyst resources in method effectiveness, it appeared that investing in analysts would have a much more immediate and reliable payback than investing in methods. We could simply see no way on improving on Nielsen's [1994] attempted grounding of heuristics in a usability problem corpus. HE, as far as we could see, was beyond repair. Analysts however, like all humans, could still be saved.

The DARe model suggests that making analysts aware of effective discovery and analysis resources could encourage them to apply knowledge resources consciously during inspections. However, to test this conjecture on the value of reflective use of known resources, we needed a better understanding of their nature. The first study impeded this in two key ways. Firstly, we derived the DARe model from that study, and thus were unprepared for separating the use of a knowledge resource for discovery from one for analysis. For example, knowledge of user tasks could lead analysts to discover a problem, but it could equally have been used to confirm it. Secondly, we had no evidence whatsoever of elimination analysis. We could see how and why many false positives *should* have been eliminated, but we had no way of seeing how any problem was confirmed or eliminated. In particular, we could not study false negatives, since HE, unlike Cognitive Walkthrough [Wharton et al. 1994], has no success cases that would expose erroneous exclusion of probable problems.

We had thus derived the DARe model from failures of elimination and discovery (and failure of HE to be involved in discoveries). The existence of confirmation was a logical dual to elimination, but again, we had no way of actually distinguishing discovery resources from confirming analysis resources. We thus designed the current study as an initial direct investigation into the nature of discovery and analysis resources in UIMs. To see resources in action, we had to extend the research instruments beyond those used in our original study.

4 A New Instrument for the Assessment Ensemble

UIM assessment requires multi-instrument research protocols. A key instrument is the structured report format [Lavery et al. 1997; Lavery & Cockton 1997], which eases subsequent merging into a single predicted problem set. Other instruments such as analyst debriefings (individual, groups, plenary) can extend or refine this problem set. Actual problem set elicitation requires further research instruments such as video recording and debriefing interviews. Ideally, test data should be systematically analysed to produce problem reports identical in format to those used by analysts. The SUPEX method [Cockton & Lavery 1999] supports such analysis.

In the current study, we extended the report format to let analysts self-report on discovery resources and confirmation/elimination rationales. A key methodological aim of the study was to establish the limits of self-reporting in this setting (theoretically, there must be limitations; practically, these must be clearly identified). However, the primary aim of the study was to gather clear evidence on the use of discovery and confirmation/elimination resources. We did not expect the new report format to radically alter analyst performance. However, the measures used in the initial study (thoroughness, validity, appropriateness) would be reapplied routinely to the current study, readily revealing performance changes.

4.1 Method

The current study follows the approach in the original study of comprehensive heuristic evaluations, using carefully designed falsification tests to validate analyst predictions [Cockton & Woolrych 2001, Figure 2]. The user tests not only address the confirmed predictions, but also ones discovered but subsequently eliminated by analysts. We thus had to develop a report format that recorded both confirmed predictions and also discoveries 'discarded' following analysis.

The report format required a more detailed record of usability problem discovery and analysis. The problem report format had four main report sections. Part 1 requires analysts to describe the problem and associated user difficulties, using the same format as the initial study. Its purpose is to positively identify the usability problem reported, with four elements providing multiple points of reference for problem merging:

Problem description: The analyst must provide a brief description (in their own words) of the problem.

Likely/Actual difficulties: The analyst must record the anticipated difficulties that the user will encounter as a consequence of the problem.

Specific contexts: The analyst is required to identify any specific contexts in which the problem may occur.

Assumed causes: The analyst should describe the cause(s) of the problem, in their own judgement.

Part 2 addresses discovery resources and methods. Two general issues are covered. Firstly, analysts must record any reflection on individual problem discovery. The purpose is to identify what method resources (if any) assisted problem discovery. HE prescribes no particular strategy for system inspection (so in what sense is it an inspection *method*?). Secondly, analysts must classify their adopted discovery method as one of four categories. These are ordered by analyst effort in terms of planning and control over the inspection processes. The ordering starts with the easiest and ends with the most onerous method:

1. **System scanning:** analysts simply 'look around the system' with no particular strategy.

2. **System searching:** a basic strategy (e.g. inspecting various links, toolbars or menu options) — effectively structured scanning.

3. **Goal playing:** involves role playing a specific user goal, for example, finding a specific piece of information.

4. **Method following:** goal playing, but walking through a preconceived method.

Part 2 also asks analysts to provide a confirmation rationale for probable problems. Part 3 of the report deals specifically with heuristic application to individual problems. Analysts must provide evidence of conformance of heuristics rather than just cite a heuristic relevant to individual performance.

Part 4 requires analysts to justify any problem elimination. The analyst is requested to clearly state why any problem initially discovered should warrant elimination, with specific reference to user impact.

31 undergraduate analysts from a final year HCI course worked in ten groups (one pair, seven groups of three and two of four) to complete a HE of a local transport Web site (http://www.tyneandwearmetro.co.uk/). All analysts used the extended problem report format. Predictions were merged into a single predicted problem set. We could then apply appropriateness measures to the set, as well as investigate the relationship between discovery methods and appropriateness, and discovery methods and elimination rates.

Appropriateness analysis followed the approach described in [Cockton & Woolrych 2001]. Briefly, appropriate heuristic applications can be determined by correspondence between predicted difficulties and/or assumed causes and applicability criteria as stated in a HE training manual [Lavery et al. 1996].

To compute other key measures such as thoroughness and validity, an actual problem set (typically from user testing) is required. Thoroughness and validity are defined:

$$\text{Thoroughness} = \frac{\text{hits}}{(\text{hits} + \text{misses})}$$

$$\text{Validity} = \frac{\text{hits}}{(\text{hits} + \text{false positives})}$$

where a *hit* is an actual problem matched by predictions, a *miss* is one unmatched by any predicted problem, and a *false positive* is a predicted problem that is not part of the actual problem set derived from user testing.

To plan user testing, two of the authors applied a card sort to the predicted problem set with the aim of isolating common site features and task steps. Falsification test scripts were then derived to systematically expose test users to site features and task steps that were predicted to be the causes or contexts of likely user difficulties. These test scripts were piloted (two obscure feature groups were initially excluded) with two test users. Test scripts were then revised to focus on unconfirmed and initially excluded problems. We thus used a simpler script to establish a core of successful predictions and then refined and extended the script to focus attention on predictions that had not been immediately confirmed. Three more test participants used the re-focused test script. The users were aged between 21 and 34, two males and three females. All had good computer/Web literacy, although the youngest claimed limited Web experience. As a result of these five users' tests, 20 actual problems were found.

A constant focus on unconfirmed predictions is essential to ensure correct ultimate coding of some predictions as false positives. This is the basis of *falsification testing* — the main aim is to maximize confidence in false positive coding. Confidence in thoroughness scores (correct predictions/all actual problems) is secondary and these are thus always maxima, i.e. further testing would reduce thoroughness scores by increasing the actual problem set. However, it should be impossible to identify how further testing could convert a false positive to a correct prediction by finally exposing the predicted problem. If this is possible, then the test script must be revised and used by further test participants.

Test user problems were either matched to predictions (hits) or to discovered problems eliminated in error (false negatives), or were added as unpredicted problems (misses) at the end of each test session. One researcher conducted the user testing, and another researcher coded problems as they arose. Post test analysis revisited problem matches and additions. Thus we could recalculate thoroughness and validity after each user test, as predictions were matched and missed problems emerged. The SUPEX method [Cockton & Lavery 1999] was not applied to test problem extraction in this or the previous study. For this study, matching was performed by two of the authors, with further checks by the other authors. In theory, improved validity could be due to more generous matching of predicted to actual problems in this study over the previous one. We need to later exclude this possibility to draw any sound conclusions from this study.

4.2   Issues with Study Comparisons

Out of curiosity, we compared appropriateness, validity and thoroughness scores at this point in the current study with those from our initial large assessment of Heuristic Evaluation. We were surprised by what we found. In order to ensure comparability, we reanalysed the initial study's data, which contained predictions from a coached single analyst and a pair of visiting masters degree students who used a combination of inspection methods. We reduced our predicted problem set to contain only predictions by undergraduate groups. This reduced the 99 analysts in 18 groups [Cockton & Woolrych 2001] to 16 groups of 96 analysts. We recalculated the scores for thoroughness (drops from 0.74 to 0.63 with the removal of only three coached analysts), validity (drops from 0.35 to 0.31) and appropriateness (drops from 39% to 31%). The 31% is for all predictions, and not just for hits only as the 39% in [Cockton & Woolrych 2001].

Thus we began by recalculating comparable scores. However, the two studies were carried out three years apart with different groups of final year undergraduates (10 groups of 31 as opposed to the initial 16 groups of 96), on different applications (drawing tool vs. Web site) and with mostly different test users (fifteen vs. five). For the comparisons of thoroughness, validity and appropriateness, the possibility of significant confounds must be excluded.

Thoroughness scores could be biased if usability problems were easier to predict for an application, misses are missed (e.g. due to mostly expert test users) or analysts are smarter. We have no evidence of the latter. Concerns over missed misses are reduced by a similar actual problem set (20, initial study = 19), so differences in overall test participant expertise have not resulted in fewer actual problems. As for ease of prediction, the fifteen hits for this study exceed the twelve for the initial study (coached analysts excluded), so if there is evidence in problems being easier to find for one application, then the current study benefits. However, we make no claims below for improved or reduced thoroughness. Still, the hit rate does impact validity scores.

	Initial Study	Current Study
Smallest set	1.0	2.0
Largest set	15.0	5.0
Median size	5.5	4.0
Mean size	5.4	3.8

Table 1: Groups' prediction set sizes.

For *validity*, analyst and test user differences between the two studies could result in bias. Again, we have no evidence that the two analyst cohorts differ in skills, and further test participants can only increase hits and thus validity (by converting false positives to hits). As long as we claim an *increase* in validity, further user testing could not undermine this. The issue is whether this is due to improved thoroughness, reduced false positives, or some combination of the two.

Validity scores depend on the hit rate and the false positive rate. Hits can only increase. However, with 20 problems revealed by five users (initial study: 19 problems by 15 users), we feel that significant increases are unlikely. Still higher thoroughness will partly explain improved validity. We must thus separate the impact of hits and false positives. As noted, the latter can only improve (i.e. decrease), so any improvements in validity reported below will be a minimum.

We also need to exclude the argument that fewer groups and analysts would inevitably result in fewer total false positives. This may be true for the complete predicted problem set, but if there is a significant drop in false positives per analyst group, then this argument will not stand.

For *appropriateness*, only analyst cohort differences could bias results. They received the same training on HE: a very similar lecture and access to the same training handbook [Lavery et al. 1996]. Possible (but unlikely) student differences apart, the only difference between the studies here was the problem format, to which we thus could attribute any differences in appropriateness. Also, we again need to exclude the argument that fewer groups and analysts would result in fewer misappropriate applications overall. If there is a significant rise in appropriate heuristic applications per analyst group, then this argument will not stand. Nor will the argument stand that application differences between the two studies eased or hindered heuristic application, since Instone [1997] could easily illustrate the use of HE for Web applications.

To conclude, while potentially confounding effects of inter-study differences are logically possible, some are no more than logical possibilities that cannot be shown to have transpired (e.g. hidden variable distorting discoverability distributions), while others could only improve the results reported in the next section (e.g. rise in validity due to further confirmation of predictions).

5   Results

Analysis of the completed problem reports resulted in an initial problem set of 37 discovered problems, of which analyst groups eliminated nine. Despite having

	Initial Study	Current Study
Lowest score	0.05	0.05
Highest score	0.37	0.20
Median score	0.11	0.10
Mean score	0.14	0.12

Table 2: Groups' thoroughness scores.

under one-third of the analysts (31 as opposed to 96) and just under two-thirds (10 as opposed to 16) of the groups relative to the initial study, the total problem discovery is almost identical (37 as opposed to 40). Table 1 shows further comparisons between prediction set sizes per group in each study. There is no significant difference between these set sizes, adding confidence to the comparability of the two studies. Given that discovered problems could be eliminated in the current study, this shows that groups did not significantly reduce their predictions when using the extended problem format.

For largest prediction sets, two groups in the initial study 'outperformed' those in the current study. They each predicted a unique problem, and thus it could be argued that thoroughness could have been higher had we used more groups. Equally though, it could have been lower if we had tested more users.

Six problems were identified during user testing in addition to the fourteen confirmed by analysts. This gives a thoroughness of 0.7, compared to 0.63 for the student groups in our initial study. Given that we have reported when and why five users aren't enough [Woolrych & Cockton 2001], we will make no claims on thoroughness until we have tested more users, despite a current difference of over 10% between the two studies. While it appears that improved validity is not at the expense of reduced thoroughness, and thus overall effectiveness (thoroughness x validity) is improved, testing a further 10 users to achieve comparability with our first study would inevitably lower thoroughness.

Table 2 compares thoroughness between the two studies. There are no significant differences here, indicating that any increase in validity will not be largely due to a raised hit rate.

The highest thoroughness score in the initial study is worth examining. The next best score was 0.21, so much of the similarity between the two studies is due to a single group of tenacious analysts. However, their validity of 0.47 would have been the third lowest in the current study, so their success here came at a price.

There were thus no significant differences for either prediction rate (despite directing analysts to eliminate improbable problems) or thoroughness (despite directing analysts to more onerous discovery resources). Both of these add credibility to two surprising significant differences.

5.1 First Surprising Impact: False Positives

Of the 28 confirmed predictions, 14 were matched to actual problems. This gives a validity of 0.5, compared to 0.31 for the student groups in our initial study. The

	Initial Study	Current Study
Lowest score	0.13	0.25
Median score	0.50	0.59
Mean score	0.52	0.59
Mean score (middle 10)	0.32	0.59
Highest score	1.00	1.00

Table 3: Group validity scores.

proportion of false positives in the merged problem set, though still high, has dropped by almost 20%. More significantly, the mean count of false positives per group halved from 3.13 (initial study) to 1.5 (current study). The difference in false positive counts between the two studies was fairly significant (*t*-test, $p = 0.0176$). We can thus exclude the argument that fewer groups and analysts would inevitably result in false positives overall, as there is a significant drop in false positives per analyst group.

Few software developers would pass over such an improvement. The reason appears to be the elimination of improbable and bogus problems, which was generally successful (totally successful in the case of bogus problems, see below). To be eliminated from the merged predicted problem set, a problem had to be eliminated by all discovering groups. There were nine such eliminated problems, of which eight cannot be associated with actual user problems (correct elimination). However one did arise in user testing, and was thus incorrectly eliminated. The ability to detect such false negatives is a valuable property of the extended report format.

A significant reduction in false positives per group did not result in a significant increase in validity per group. Table 3 compares validity scores for the two studies. They are similar until we exclude the best and worst 3 groups in the initial study (leaving the middle 10 groups). The mean drops considerably, since the loss of the worst performers cannot offset the loss of the best analysts. The failure of significantly lower false positives to be reflected in significantly higher validity is largely due to the performance in the initial study of two groups with a validity of 1 (1/1 and 4/4 predictions valid) and two with 0.67 (both 2/3 valid).

Reduced false positives were an unexpected surprise, but further user testing is required to establish whether this could be at the expense of reduced thoroughness, and ultimately, reduced effectiveness. However, there already appears to be a relationship between discovery resource usage and false positive elimination.

Analysts were far more likely to choose *system scanning* or *system searching* as their preferred method of identifying predictions (significant chi square at 0.01 level). A smaller number of predictions were made using *goal playing*. So few predictions were made using *method following* that the data relating to use of this method has limited use.

Analysts who used system scanning were more likely to keep (i.e. not eliminate) predictions, and confirmed 81% of their discovered possible problems. Analysts using *system searching* were most likely to eliminate predictions, eliminating 41% of their discovered possible problems. *System scanning* resulted in the least valid performance, with only 47% of the predictions currently confirmed by user testing. In contrast, 92% of discoveries identified through *goal playing* and confirmed as probable problems have been confirmed by user testing. So, validity for problems found via *goal playing* was double that of *system scanning*, and further user testing is unlikely to significantly close this gap.

System scanning and searching were both associated with high numbers of false positives, whilst goal playing resulted in very few, suggesting that this discovery method can support significantly more valid performance. However, goal playing is not a method that is explicitly advocated for heuristic evaluation, whilst system scanning and searching are. General education on discovery method resources here could thus have improved analyst performance by making false positives harder to find! This may seem perverse, but our data does support this, and in a way that helps us to exclude matching bias (overgenerous matching of actual to predicted problems) as a confounding cause of the improved validity scores.

More structured and user-centred discovery methods were associated with a higher elimination rate, providing clear evidence for the removal of potential false positives (in fact, there was only one false negative as a result). However, even the system scanners showed one improvement over the first study's analysts. There were no bogus problems. Neither factually or logically bogus [Cockton & Woolrych 2001] predictions were made, i.e. there were no errors of fact or recommendations based on flawed design rationales in the problem set for this study. Given that 32% of the false positives in Cockton & Woolrych [2001] were bogus, this may, combined with the clear evidence of correct eliminations, represent all of the reduction in false positives as a result of the extended report format. Our explanation is simply that the extended format makes it very difficult to report bogus problems, since reports of such problems would look very sparse in the extended format. The resulting seas of white space in a problem report probably discourages analysts from making simple false assertions that features don't exist (indeed, they instead reported correctly that they couldn't find them). The format also considerably obstructs the reporting of logically bogus recommendations, since these take the form:

"I can think of a better option because <flawed rationale>"

since the only way to get such a back to front problem report into the extended format is to leave all but the first part blank.

We are thus confident that, despite a low level of control over experimenter bias in extracting actual problems and matching them to predicted ones, the resulting data lets us exclude this as a systematic source of bias.

5.2   Second Surprising Impact: Appropriateness

Appropriateness of heuristic application rose to 57% (from 31% for all student predictions in first study), a 26% practical improvement that would be welcome in all practical settings, since inappropriate heuristic applications could result in inappropriate recommendations for design changes. Only one group in the current study scored below the overall average for the initial study (where they would have been ranked seven out of sixteen). The difference in appropriateness between the two studies was very significant (t-test, $p = 0.0018$). We can thus exclude the argument

	Initial Study	Current Study
Lowest score	0%	20%
Median score	27%	65%
Mean score	31%	61%
Highest score	80%	100%

Table 4: Groups' appropriateness scores between studies.

that fewer groups and analysts would inevitably result in fewer misappropriate applications overall, as there is a significant rise in appropriate heuristic applications per group. Thus the overall drop in misappropriate heuristic use is due to improved performance across all groups, and not just a result of having fewer groups. Table 4 compares appropriateness for the two studies.

We were also able to examine the relationship between appropriateness scores and discovery methods. Only 39% of problems found by system scanning were associated with appropriate heuristics, a rate similar to that for our initial study. For system searching, this rose to 70%, and to 73% for goal playing and method following combined. This means that we cannot completely attribute improvements here to Part 3 of the extended format, which requires heuristics to be not just named, but justified alongside confirmation rationales. Appropriate heuristic use is associated with more onerous discovery methods, which would appear to contribute to the difference between the two studies.

5.3   *Confirmation of the DARe Model*

We now have unequivocal evidence for the fit of the DARe model to analyst behaviour. Before the current study, we had only a post-hoc derivation of the model [Cockton & Woolrych 2001], with additional support from reanalysis of multiple analyst performance [Woolrych & Cockton 2002]. We now have evidence that clearly identifies different discovery and analysis resource usage.

A striking example of different discovery and analysis resources shows how carefree discovery can be combined with more sober analysis:

> "After seeing the different looking button, I decided to click on it and explore further." (Group 6, problem 6)

The report confirmed that *system scanning* was used to find this possible problem, but the confirmation rationale made clear that the button was 'unclear and misleading', with likely difficulties being confusion and inability to recover from taking this off-site link. The prediction was confirmed by user testing.

The key point is that system-centred *discovery* resources can be combined with user-centred *analysis* resources to produce successful predictions. Here, the analyst encountered a possible problem by 'playing' with the system and then empathizing with users to confirm the problem, correctly associating the problem with the heuristic *user control and freedom* (can't undo). Another associated heuristic, *consistency and standards*, was inappropriate. There were no inconsistencies here and it is not clear that there is an agreed one-size-fits-all Web standard on off-site links (just good advice that turns out to apply here).

Further striking examples arise with eliminated problems. System scanning discovered the one false negative, which was eliminated (after consideration of accessibility issues) by assumptions about user capabilities (i.e. all users were as capable as the analysts!) User testing invalidated these assumptions. In contrast, a successful elimination of a possible problem (missing back-links from a questionnaire page) was eliminated by realizing that all links into the page were from one level below the home page, and that users could thus be expected to (and did) find their way back. This possible problem was discovered by system scanning, and eliminated by knowledge of Web interaction.

The availability of clearly separated discovery, confirmation and elimination resources lets us develop educational materials that we hope can improve analyst performance across a range of usability inspection methods.

6 Discussion

In both studies, groups made similar numbers of predictions. The current study's analysts are simply more valid (significantly fewer false positives per group) and use heuristics more appropriately. Improved validity can be reasonably attributed to the impact of the extended report format that encouraged analysts to consider more structured discovery methods, to eliminate improbable problems, and to avoid bogus predictions. Reduction in false positives can be attributed to discovering fewer improbable problems or to their elimination, which was, with one exception, well considered. Although validity is much improved, it remains poor. Continued over-reliance on system scanning appears to lead analysts to more improbable problems that are less likely to be eliminated. Easily found problems, it appears, are harder to lose!

The much improved appropriateness scores are due jointly to report format requirements for confirmation and justification, and for conscious discovery and elimination. Having taken most analysts through the pain barrier of reflection, self-criticism and rational argument, they become better prepared for thinking carefully about appropriate heuristic usage. Indeed, as confirmation rationales are formed, analysts may find it easier to identify the most appropriate heuristic, where it exists.

It thus appears that we can fix the analyst indirectly via fixing the method. In this case, there was no change to the actual heuristics in use. Instead, the process of discovering and analysing problems was made more explicit. This approach could be applied to all inspection methods. In the case of Cognitive Walkthrough [Wharton et al. 1994], minimal extensions would be required to achieve this.

The extended problem report format is simpler than [Sears 1997] approach to reducing false positives with HE, by prefixing a Cognitive Walkthrough. We would argue that we can achieve comparable results without the complexity of a two phase hybrid method, which we feel could adversely impact on thoroughness. Encouraging analysts to use more structured discovery methods and to explicitly confirm or eliminate problems may be enough.

7 Further Work

This paper is an initial report from a large iterative study that will continue user testing and analyst inspections in order to fully explore the DARe model for both empirical and analytical methods. We know that as additional analysts are added and more users are tested, that there will be changes to the scores reported above, especially thoroughness, for which we make no claims other than an initial lack of apparent reduction. However, the main results reported above will not change. We thus we have not rushed through 10 further user tests in order to achieve better comparability with the initial study. In terms of the DARe model, additional users are only one discovery resource. Further usability problems can just as easily be found by changing the test scripts, by letting users prepare their own tasks, by letting users just explore the system, by field studies or by Web log analysis [Barnum et al. 2003]. Changes to test protocols, including more extensive user debriefings and more active or less passive experimenter intervention can also increase the problem yield (albeit with concerns about reliability). We intend further user testing to be asymptotic, i.e. we will keep adding users and changing test protocols until we stop finding new problems.

We will thus test more than five users, but we will also make systematic changes to the testing procedures that cannot be 'rushed through'. We have therefore reported a surprising interim result with immediate implications for usability specialists: changing report format can improve analyst performance on validity and appropriateness. Establishing the impact on thoroughness requires further work as stated. Only tentative conclusions can currently be drawn here.

We will also further develop the report format to improve analyst competence and resource elicitation, and will explore analyst interviews and group discussions for eliciting analyst use of discovery and analysis resources.

8 Conclusions

Improved evaluation performance occurs when analysts are required to explicitly report and rationalize their use of heuristics, and of discovery method and confirmation/elimination knowledge resources. A report format that demands more reflection appears to enhance usability inspection, resulting in fewer false positives and more appropriate heuristic usage. Neither of these claims appears to be undermined by differences between the current and earlier study. This suggests that approaches derived from the DARe model can significantly improve HCI methods that have stagnated for a decade.

UIMs can clearly be improved. However, even with the current report format, analysts continue to fail to find all problems and still generate false positives. There is room for improvement in discovery methods and analysis resources. Through focusing on method extensions, such as analyst education to improve competence, it becomes possible to fix the analyst with a fixed method.

The evolution of the DARe model shows the value of constant improvement in research protocols and instruments, with each iteration initially exposing and then extending its validity and applicability. At the same time, generic and specific improvements to inspection methods are developed. This theory driven approach shows the effective and valuable coupling of research and practice in HCI where pragmatic practice based approaches have failed to deliver method improvements.

References

Barnum, C., Bevan, N., Cockton, G., Nielsen, G., Spool, J., & Wixon, D. [2003], The 'Magic Number 5': Is It Enough for Web Testing?, *in* G. Cockton & P. Korhonen (eds.), *CHI'03 Extended Abstracts of the Conference on Human Factors in Computing Systems*, ACM Press, pp.698–9.

Cockton, G. & Lavery, D. [1999], A Framework for Usability Problem Extraction, *in* A. Sasse & C. Johnson (eds.), *Human–Computer Interaction — INTERACT '99: Proceedings of the Seventh IFIP Conference on Human–Computer Interaction*, Vol. 1, IOS Press, pp.347–55.

Cockton, G. & Woolrych, A. [2001], Understanding Inspection Methods: Lessons from an Assessment of Heuristic Evaluation, *in* A. Blandford, J. Vanderdonckt & P. Gray (eds.), *People and Computers XV: Interaction without Frontiers (Joint Proceedings of HCI2001 and IHM2001)*, Springer-Verlag, pp.171–92.

Cockton, G., Lavery, D. & Woolrych, A. [2003], Inspection-based Methods, *in* J. A. Jacko & A. Sears (eds.), *The Human–Computer Interaction Handbook*, Lawrence Erlbaum Associates, Chapter 57, pp.1118–38.

Connell, I. W. & Hammond, N. V. [1999], Comparing Usability Evaluation Principles with Heuristics: Problem Instances vs. Problem Types, *in* A. Sasse & C. Johnson (eds.), *Human–Computer Interaction — INTERACT '99: Proceedings of the Seventh IFIP Conference on Human–Computer Interaction*, Vol. 1, IOS Press, pp.621–9.

Dumas, J. S. [2003], User-based Evaluations, *in* J. A. Jacko & A. Sears (eds.), *The Human–Computer Interaction Handbook*, Lawrence Erlbaum Associates, Chapter 56, pp.1093–117.

Gray, W. D. & Salzman, M. C. [1998], Damaged Merchandise? A Review of Experiments that Compare Usabilty Evaluation Methods, *Human–Computer Interaction* **13**(3), 203–61.

Hertzum, M. & Jacobsen, N. E. [2001], The Evaluator Effect: A Chilling Fact about Usability Evaluation Methods, *International Journal of Human–Computer Interaction* **13**(4), 421–43.

Instone, K. [1997], Usability Engineering on the Web, *Advancing HTML: Style and Substance* **2**(1). Available at http://www.w3j.com/5/s3.instone.html (last accessed 2003.05.26).

Kieras, D. [2003], Model-based evaluations, *in* J. A. Jacko & A. Sears (eds.), *The Human–Computer Interaction Handbook*, Lawrence Erlbaum Associates, Chapter 58, pp.1139–68.

Kuhn, S. & Muller, M. J. [1993], Participatory Design — Introduction to the Special Section, *Communications of the ACM* **36**(4), 24–8.

Lavery, D., Cockton, G. & Atkinson, M. P. [1996], Heuristic Evaluation: Usability Evaluation Materials, Technical Report TR-1996-15, University of Glasgow. Available at http://www.dcs.gla.ac.uk/publications/reports/1996-15.pdf (last accessed 2003.05.17).

Lavery, D., Cockton, G. & Atkinson, M. P. [1997], Comparison of Evaluation Methods using Structured Usability Problem Reports, *Behaviour & Information Technology* **16**(4-5), 246–66.

Lavery, D. & Cockton, G. [1997], Representing Predicted and Actual Usability Problems, *in* H. Johnson, P. Johnson & E. O'Neill (eds.), *Proceedings of the International Workshop on Representations in Interactive Software Development*, Queen Mary and Westifeld Colelge, University of London, pp.97–108.

Nielsen, J. [1992], Finding Usability Problems Through Heuristic Evaluation, *in* P. Bauersfeld, J. Bennett & G. Lynch (eds.), *Proceedings of the CHI'92 Conference on Human Factors in Computing Systems*, ACM Press, pp.373–80.

Nielsen, J. [1994], Enhancing the Power of Usability Heuristics, *in* B. Adelson, S. Dumais & J. Olson (eds.), *Proceedings of the CHI'94 Conference on Human Factors in Computing Systems: Celebrating Interdependence*, ACM Press, pp.152–8.

Sears, A. [1997], Heuristic Walkthroughs: Finding the Problems Without the Noise, *International Journal of Human–Computer Interaction* **9**(3), 213–34.

Wharton, C., Rieman, J., Lewis, C. & Polson, P. [1994], The Cognitive Walkthrough Method: A Practitioners Guide, *in* J. Nielsen & R. L. Mack (eds.), *Usability Inspection Methods*, John Wiley & Sons, pp.105–40.

Woolrych, A. [2001], Assessing the Scope and Accuracy of the Usability Inspection Method Heuristic Evaluation, MPhil Thesis, School of Computing, Engineering and Technology, University of Sunderland, UK.

Woolrych, A. & Cockton, G. [2001], Why and When Five Test Users aren't Enough, *in* J. Vanderdonckt, A. Blandford & A. Derycke (eds.), *Proceedings of IHM-HCI'2001, Joint AFIHM-BCS Conference on Human–Computer Interaction: Interaction without Frontiers, Volume 2*, Cépaduès-Éditions, pp.105–8.

Woolrych, A. & Cockton, G. [2002], Testing a Conjecture Based on the DR-AR Model of UIM Effectiveness, *in* H. Sharp, P. Chalk, J. LePeuple & J. Rosbottom (eds.), *Proceedings of HCI'02: Volume 2*, British Computer Society, pp.30–3.

Ontological Sketch Models: Highlighting User–System Misfits

Iain Connell, Thomas Green & Ann Blandford

UCL Interaction Centre (UCLIC), University College London,
26 Bedford Way, London WC1H OAP, UK

Email: *{i.connell,a.blandford}@ucl.ac.uk,*
thomas.green@ndirect.co.uk

Ontological Sketch Modelling (OSM) is a novel approach to usability evaluation that concentrates on both the user's conceptual models of the domain and 'working practices', and the conceptual models built into a device or a work-system. Analysing the degree of fit between these models can reveal potential problems in learning and use that are not revealed by existing HCI approaches. We show how OSM can identify such potential misfits between user and system. We also describe how an OSM analysis can be edited, conventionalized and viewed in tabular form, thereby allowing automatic highlighting of user-system misfits. Illustrative examples are a typical drawing application and a digital music library.

Keywords: ontological sketch modelling, usability evaluation, conceptual models, misfits, drawing application, digital music library.

1 Background to OSM

Ontological Sketch Modelling (OSM) is a novel approach to usability evaluation that concentrates on both the user's conceptual models of the domain and 'working practices' (that is: how the device fits in with the way the user works), and the conceptual models built into a device or a work-system. Analysing the degree of fit between these models can reveal potential problems in learning and use that are not revealed by existing HCI approaches. Essentially, OSM aims not just to say whether a device might be easy to use, but whether the device does something that makes sense to the user. OSM is also exceptional among HCI evaluation methods in that the same approach can apply either to individual devices or to a whole work system: our investigations have ranged from digital watches to the London Ambulance Service dispatch system [Blandford et al. 2002].

Devices and systems can exhibit substantial mismatches between the user's preferred conceptualization and that which is imposed. For example, users of a video link may be compelled by the system to define the Quality of Service in terms of bandwidth, while they think of it in terms of frame rate or image resolution. Similarly, the user of a drawing program (see below) may think in terms of representations of domain objects (e.g. "this part of the drawing shows the whale's tail") while the program supports only the manipulation of device objects (e.g. curves, text boxes). We call these mismatches 'misfits'.

Central to OSM's approach is the simultaneous representation, *in the same language*, of the user's conceptualization of the domain and the conceptualization that is built into the system or device. (Note that for brevity we may find ourselves referring to either 'the system' or 'the device'; in each case, we mean the whole gamut.) Misfits cannot be revealed by any approach to HCI that focuses solely on either the user or the device: both must be considered. Traditional task-centred user-modelling for HCI has had some very effective results, but in our view it cannot reveal misfits because it does not explicitly consider how the user's conceptual model relates to the model imposed by the device.

Application of OSM to several full-scale examples, two of which are described below, has shown that effective and useful insights can be readily obtained. We have also demonstrated that non-experts can be quickly taught the technique to a standard that is reasonably effective [Blandford & Green 1997].

In an OSM analysis the analyst describes first the visible entities and attributes that are linked within the device or system; then the entities contained in the user's conceptual model; and lastly those entities embodied within the device that are not part of the user's conceptualization, but which users need to be aware of in order to use the device effectively. The resulting entities may be private to the *device* (the user cannot alter them), or they may be private to the *user* (the device does not represent them), or they may be *shared* (accessible to both the device and the user). All communication between the two worlds of device and user takes place through the shared entities. If the user-private entities do not fit well onto the shared entities, the device will have usability problems. If the device-private entities are difficult to discover or understand, the user is likely to have difficulty learning to work with them.

The OSM notation is informal and intentionally sketchy. However, we have developed an OSM editor (illustrated below) which enforces a consistent format and terminology. The editor output data can be displayed in whatever manner is convenient; at present we use a stylized tabular format that is simple but revealing. In this paper we show how such a format may be used to reveal user-system misfits. A certain amount of algorithmic analysis is also possible, but we anticipate that the main effectiveness of the approach will lie in the insights gained by codifying and reflecting upon conceptual models and device features.

OSM's emphasis on conceptual modelling has roots in such work as Payne's 'task-entity analysis' [Payne 1993], which demonstrated how users' conceptual models of the time-management domain were ill-served by the electronic diaries then available; and in Moran's ETIT analysis [Moran 1983], which mapped 'external' domain tasks onto 'internal' device tasks. These studies, though ground-breaking, demonstrated only what could be achieved when the analyst was an expert in applied cognitive science. To be practically useful to non-experts, a methodology needed to be developed. Attempts at methodologies which have influenced OSM include the framework of 'cognitive dimensions' (CDs) developed by Green [1989] and others [Blackwell et al. 2001], some of which can be interpreted as misfits; "Entity-Relationship Models for Information Artefacts" (ERMIA) developed by Green & Benyon [1996]; and "Programmable User Models" (PUMs) [Young et al. 1989; Blandford & Young 1996].

Broadly speaking we would argue that none of these methodologies achieved the right blend. CDs have been taken up by some practitioners but for some purposes are under-defined, while ERMIA and PUMs are too detailed and too difficult. In contrast, we claim that OSM is novel in that encourages its users to scrutinize and reflect on all parts of the system without forcing them to employ detailed and time-consuming new notations.

2   The Structure of an OSM

An OSM is not a formal model, in the fullest sense of that word, but it is highly conventionalized in structure. The central feature of the model is a list of *entities*. For each entity there is a statement of how it can be created and deleted (if possible), and — more importantly — whether or not the entity is explicitly known to the user, whether or not it is represented at the user-system interface, and whether or not it is represented within the system. These elaborations are illustrated below.

Each entity potentially has a set of *attributes*. For each attribute there is a similar statement of how its value can be set and changed, how far it is known to the user, and how far it is represented at the interface and in the system.

The methods for creating and deleting entities, and for setting and changing attributes, are *actions*. Each action can be moded and/or disguised (i.e. available but hard to find).

The model also contains *relationships* of several types. First, an entity can *consist-of* other entities: this term covers many different types of possible relationship, which it would be counter-productive to distinguish in detail. There are two forms of 'constraint' relationship: one attribute's value can constrain another either as a *device-constraint*, present whether the user likes it or not, or as a *goal-constraint*, a state of affairs that is important to the user but is not necessarily imposed by the device. For example, it is a device constraint that all of a drawing must lie within the bounds of the drawing space; it is a potential goal constraint that certain parts of a drawing should be aligned neatly (if the constraint is violated the resulting drawing might not make proper sense, but the device will permit it). Lastly, it is necessary to note that changing one attribute may change another — e.g. changing page margins in a word processor may change the number of pages needed for a given document.

The examples illustrated below feature entities and attributes rather than actions. Unabridged versions of the analyses from which they are derived may be obtained from the OSM Web site[1].

---

[1] http://www.uclic.ucl.ac.uk/annb/OSM.html

An OSM model can be displayed in any convenient form. In fact, we are still searching for the best visualization technique for such a structure. At present we export the model into XML format and translate that into a stylized hypertext table. As will be demonstrated, this allows for the tabulation of the model in concise form; it also provides opportunity for the automatic highlighting of likely user-system misfits.

3   Procedure

In its current form an OSM analysis consists of the following stages:

1. The analyst gets to know the system and the users and constructs a paper-based analysis. This sets out in tabular form the main device and user entities and attributes, plus actions and relationships. A table of user-interface-system dependencies is also constructed.

2. The analysis is then conventionalized as an OSM model, preferably by setting it out in our OSMosis editor (available from the OSM Web site). The conventionalized model can be displayed in tabular format, preferably in hypertext, and if necessary can be revised. User-system misfits are highlighted automatically.

3. The conventionalized model can also be converted to Prolog assertions to allow algorithmic analysis of further types of misfits. (This will not be illustrated here.)

3.1   Initial Analysis

The first stage of the initial (paper-based) analysis is to identify in tabular form the core entities, attributes, actions and relationships. We group entities and attributes into device and user. Actions are typically described in terms of interaction processes. Some relationships may arise immediately out of the initial device-user considerations (our first example, the drawing application, being a case in point).

In the second stage, for each entity and attribute so far described, we delineate the differences between the device/domain (system) and user concepts, and the ways in which these are mediated via the interface.

At these initial stages the analyst must rely on a certain amount of craft knowledge, depending on familiarity with the device and/or domain. For a simple device such as a drawing application the main device entities and attributes may be revealed by inspection and exploration alone. More complex systems such as digital libraries may require input from designers and domain specialists, as well as resort to manuals and help files. In order to elicit users' conceptual entities, techniques such as structured interviewing or verbal protocol analysis can be used, perhaps allied to observation. The second analysis illustrated in this paper made use of interviews with musicians (see Blandford et al. [2002] for an account of the interviewing and inquiry methods used in a study of dispatch methods at London Ambulance Service).

The first stage is heavily iterative, requiring frequent re-visiting of concepts and relationships. It is also likely that return will be made to these putative results after the conventionalizing stage, for example in order to enforce consistency with the edited and tabulated version.

3.2 Conventionalizing and Viewing the Model

The paper-based analysis is likely to include too much detail in some parts, along with gaps in others. It is also likely to contain inconsistencies and omissions. By conventionalizing the model many of these problems can be eliminated, at the inevitable cost of omitting much free-form detail. Our experience indicates that a strict method of conventionalizing is essential; otherwise, despite our best intentions, we have found ourselves cheating. Thus we transcribe the initial analysis into our OSM editor, OSMosis. We then export the result in XML format and translate it into HTML using an XSLT processor. The resulting structure can be viewed in various formats, among them the stylized tables illustrated below.

Since the quantity of the input to the conventionalized model is not restricted, the amount of detail to be included depends partly on the purposes for which the model is being made. However, a tool like OSMosis does confine the analyst to a certain degree of formalism. The examples below show how fairly extensive paper analyses (six pages, for even the drawing application) can be reduced to a more manageable quantity and viewed in shorthand format.

Inspection of the model can highlight the potential user-system misfits which have been revealed by the initial analysis, particularly the delineation of the device/domain, interface and user dependencies. This in turn can feed back into the paper analysis and the initial model. The misfit-highlighting process has been automated and is illustrated for the examples below.

3.3 Algorithmic Analysis

Finally, algorithmic analysis can reveal further misfits. These have mostly been derived from Green's cognitive dimensions framework [Green 1989]. For example, in that framework *viscosity* denotes resistance to change: a change that the user conceptualizes as a single operation turns out to require multiple actions (*repetition* viscosity); alternatively, an action may turn out to require several cleaning-up operations to restore internal consistency (*knock-on* viscosity).

It is relatively easy to convert the conventionalized OSM model into Prolog assertions and scrutinize the model for examples of viscosity and other such misfits. Details will not be given here because to date this has formed only a minor part of our analyses.

4 Example Analyses

As illustrations of the OSM analysis process, we present two representative examples. The first, a drawing application, will be familiar to most readers. In this application most of the key activities take place in the system; the challenges for the user are to understand the tools that are available and how to manipulate the display objects. The second example is an Internet-based digital library. This is an application where the user's understanding and requirements reside largely 'in the head', and need to be expressed in a form suitable for accessing system information. As noted above, we

Entity	Type	Create by	Delete by	Notes
Drawing Object	Shared	Select palette tool and insert in drawing space	Select object and delete	To create an object the appropriate tool must first be selected from the palette

Attributes	Instances	Set by	Change by
Configuration (object type)	Straight line, Rectangle, Oval, Polygon, Free line	Select tool from palette	Select a different palette tool
Size		Select tool	Select grab handles and drag
Shape	As per object type	Select tool	Cannot generally be changed
Fill colour	As shown on colour palette	Select from colour palette	Re-select
Orientation	Horizontal, vertical	Object defaults	Use 'rotate' tool
Grouped	Grouped, not grouped	Select several objects & group	Ungroup

Entity	Type	Create by	Delete by	Notes
Drawing	User	Add, manipulate and combine drawing objects	Select and delete	A drawing consists of drawing objects which can be combined together

Attributes	Instances	Set by	Change by
Size		Within drawing space	Expand and reduce
Shape		Combine drawing objects	Re-combine drawing objects
Orientation	Horizontal, vertical	As for drawing objects	

Figure 1: A shared device entity (Drawing Object) and a user entity (Drawing), plus attributes of each entity, for a drawing application. See text for description.

have completed analyses of both smaller and larger systems; for example, Blandford et al. [2002] report on the application of OSM to a multi-person work system.

For reasons of space, we focus on entities, attributes and relationships and omit the details of the OSM editor (as well as the Notes transferred from the paper tables). The complete analyses are available from the OSM Web site.

4.1   Drawing Application

Common features of typical desktop drawing applications are a drawing space, a set of drawing tools (e.g. palette, tool bar(s), panels), and the means to change and combine created drawing objects. In OSM terms, the drawing objects are entities whose attributes can be manipulated and changed using the appropriate tools.

4.1.1   Initial Analysis

The first main device entity is the Drawing Object out of which drawings are realized. This is a *shared* entity, meaning that it is part of both the user's conceptualization and the device's representation. See Figure 1. The object has several attributes, the first of which is its configuration or object type (straight line, rectangle, oval, polygon, free line). Drawing objects are created by selecting the appropriate tool from the palette or tool bar (etc.) and inserting the object into the drawing space; once created, an object can be changed by manipulating its size, shape, fill colour (etc.) attributes. Some of these changes can be made 'directly' (e.g. by dragging the object's grab handles), some 'indirectly' (e.g. via dialogue boxes initiated from

Relationship	Actor	Type	Acted On	Notes
Define_object	Palette tool	Constrained_ by_device	Drawing Object	The drawing object to be created depends on the palette tool which is first selected
Define_actions	Drawing Object	Constrained_ by_device	Palette tool	Some actions which can be performed on a drawing object are defined by the object type
Consists_of	Drawing	Consists_of	Drawing objects	

Figure 2: Two device-constraint relationships and a consists-of relationship for a drawing application. See text for description.

Entities & Attributes	User	Interface	System
Drawing	Explicit	Direct	Absent
Orientation	Explicit	Direct	Present
Shape	Explicit	Direct	Present
Size	Implicit	Direct	Present
Drawing object	Implicit	Direct	Present
Configuration	Implicit	Disguised	Present
Fill colour	Explicit	Direct	Present
Grouped	Absent	Hidden	Present
Orientation	Explicit	Direct	Present
Shape	Explicit	Direct	Present
Size	Explicit	Direct	Present

Figure 3: Part of a User-Interface-System table (showing entities Drawing and Drawing Object) for a drawing application. See text for description.

menu options), and some only by means of certain palette or tool bar selections (e.g. by switching between 'drawing' and 'text' cursors).

In relation to the latter, we find that there are device constraints (in the OSM editor jargon, 'constrained_by_device' relationships) between the currently selected tool and the drawing object: not only does the tool dictate the drawing object to be created, but certain attributes of a drawing object can be changed only by particular tools. See Figure 2. In addition, the main user entity, a Drawing, can comprise only the drawing objects which the palette allows us to create (though drawing objects can be grouped together). We denote this as a 'consists_of' relationship (Figure 2).

For each of the entities and attributes so far described we now set out the main components of the dependencies between the user, interface and system. See Figure 3.

In the current OSM configuration, we judge the user's conceptualization of each component (entity or attribute) as being Explicit, Implicit, or Absent, and the system's as either Present or Absent. If a component is explicit or implicit to the user but absent from the system, we record that as a definite user-system misfit. Similarly, if a component is present in the system (domain or device) but absent from the user's model, that also represents a misfit.

At the interface, an entity or attribute is judged to be one of the following: Direct, Disguised, Delayed, Hidden, Undiscoverable or Absent. Currently we interpret these terms as follows:

Direct   Represented and easily interpreted by the user.

Disguised   Represented, but hard to interpret.

Delayed   Represented, but not available to the user until some time later in the interaction.

Hidden   Represented, but the user has to perform an explicit action to reveal the state of the entity or attribute.

Undiscoverable   Represented only to the user who has good system knowledge; unlikely to be discovered by most users.

Absent   Not represented at the interface.

In general, if an interface component is disguised or delayed, this may represent a misfit, depending on the other two (user or system) components; if, however, it is deemed to be hidden, undiscoverable or absent, we record that as a misfit independently of the other components.

In this example, Figure 3 shows that both drawings and drawing objects have been judged to be directly represented at the interface and part of the user's explicit or implicit conceptual model. However, some drawing object attributes are deemed to be either disguised or hidden at the interface, and the user's drawing itself is absent from the system model. In particular, the 'Grouped' attribute is shown as both absent from the user's conceptual model and hidden at the interface. This will be highlighted as a serious misfit when the OSM model is conventionalized. See the next section.

4.1.2   Conventionalizing and Viewing the Model

We now transcribe the essential elements of the paper-based analysis into the OSM editor, OSMosis. Figure 4 shows sample editor content, for the entity 'Drawing_object' and the attribute 'Grouped' (featured in Figures 1 & 3). The leftmost dialogue box shows the full entity-action-attribute-relationship listing; the middle dialogue box the six attributes of the highlighted entity (illustrated in Figures 1 & 3); and the rightmost box the system-interface-user dependencies, plus 'set by' and 'change by' actions, for the highlighted attribute.

Once thus transcribed we can export the model in XML and view it in a stylized hypertext table, as partially illustrated (minus the Actions and without any transcribed Notes) in Figure 5. For reasons of legibility, this and the corresponding table from Section 4.2.2 (Figure 8) have been reproduced from the resulting HTML output: see the OSM Web site for the originals.

Misfits are flagged against the 'User Interface System' table just described. In this example the only serious misfit (denoted **) relates to the attribute 'Grouped', others being recorded as either less serious (denoted *) or merely potential misfits (denoted ?? or ?). (The user-interface-system table is also colour-coded to enhance visual interpretation.)

In this first example analysis, then, the main source of user-interface-system misfits has been attributed to the inferred absence of a system concept for a drawing,

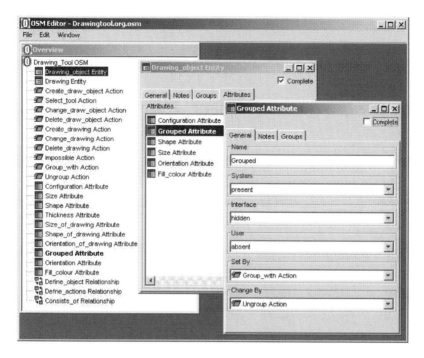

Figure 4: OSMosis editor with sample content for a drawing application. See text for description.

the strong relationship between drawing objects and palette tools, and the absent-hidden-present nature of drawing object grouping.

The second example which follows illustrates how a different set of misfits may be focused more on the user's expectations of how system information should be organized, in this case in an online digital library.

4.2 New Zealand Digital Music Library

The New Zealand Digital Music Library[2] is part of the New Zealand Digital Library (NZDL). It holds a large number of digitized melodies which can be retrieved over the Internet and played back on the client computer. Melody files may be browsed or searched. Searching may be by title ('text query') or by tune matching ('music query'), the latter including sung or played inputs. We summarize the results of an OSM analysis (full version available from the OSM Web site) carried out on the Music Library in the form in which it existed between October 2001 and January 2002. (Since then, partly as a result of this and related analyses [e.g. Blandford & Stelmaszewska 2002], the interface has been revised.)

4.2.1 Initial Analysis

The NZDL Music Library consists of several sub-collections, each of which contains indexed melody files. A Melody File is thus the main device entity, whose attributes

[2] http://www.nzdl.org/fast-cgi-bin/music/musiclibrary

OSM Model of: Drawing_Tool

Notes

Relationships

Name	Actor	Type	Acted_on	Notes
Define_object	Palette_ tool	constrained _by_device	Drawing_ object	
Define_actions	Drawing_ object	constrained _by_device	Palette_ tool	
Consists_of	Drawing	consists_of	Drawing_ object	

Entities

Relns: actor in upright, acted-on in *italics*.
User:Interface:System : blue=OK, dark grey=dodgy, black=bad, green=not sure yet.

Name	Create/ set	Delete/ change	Relns.	User	Interface	System	
Drawing	Change_ drawing	Delete_ drawing	Consists_of	explicit	direct	absent	*
Orientation	Create_ draw_obj	Change_ draw_obj		explicit	direct	present	
Shape	Create_ draw_obj	Change_ draw_obj		explicit	direct	present	
Size	Create_ draw_obj	Change_ draw_obj		implicit	direct	present	?
Drawing_ object	Create_ draw_obj	Delete_ draw_obj	Define_actions *Define_object* Consists_of	implicit	direct	present	?
Configuration	Create_ draw_obj	Select_ tool		implicit	disguised	present	??
Fill_colour	Create_ draw_obj	Change_ draw_obj		explicit	direct	present	
Grouped	Group_with	Ungroup		absent	hidden	present	**
Orientation	Create_ draw_obj	Change_ draw_obj		explicit	direct	present	
Shape	Create_ draw_obj	Change_ draw_obj		explicit	direct	present	
Size	Create_ draw_obj	Change_ draw_obj		implicit	direct	present	?

Figure 5: Part of a stylized hypertext table (tabulated model) for a drawing application, reproduced from the original on the OSM Web site. Potential misfits are flagged with asterisks and question marks, according to seriousness. See text for explanation.

Entity	Type	Create by	Delete by	Notes
Melody File	Device	Impossible for end user. (NZDL: retrieve from external source or create from score)	Impossible for end user. (NZDL: Remove from sub-collection)	Sub-collections consist of melody files held in different formats.

Attributes	Instances	Set by	Change by
How indexed	Title, alphanumeric	Impossible for end user. (Done by NZDL)	Impossible for end user. (Done by NZDL)
Name	Many and various		
No. of components	3 to 5		
Playback format	MIDI0, MIDI1, AIFF, etc.		
Size	Various		
Type of components	Melody, score, title, lyrics, etc.		

Figure 6: NZDL Music Library: Entities and attributes for the device entity Melody File. See text for description.

Entity	Type	Create by	Delete by	Notes
Tune	User	Recall	Forget	In order to make a match with a sub-collection melody file the user must first recall the tune

Attributes	Instances	Set by	Change by
Melody, pitch, notes, spaces, tempo, harmony, rhythm, tonality	(Requires specialised musical knowledge)	Play, sing or otherwise transcribe a recalled tune	Play, sing or transcribe differently

Figure 7: NZDL Music Library: Entities and descriptor attributes for the user entity Tune. See text for description.

include file name and file size. Each sub-collection's melody files have particular component types and playback formats. Neither a Melody File nor its attributes may created, deleted or changed by end users. See Figure 6.

In order to retrieve a melody file from a sub-collection by tune matching, the user must input (that is, sing or play) the tune into the client computer. That version of the melody is then matched against the stored data using a proprietary conversion system named Meldex [McNab et al. 1997]. Successful tune matching thus requires that the stored version of the tune be compatible with the converted version, which in turn requires that the sung or played input be in suitable form.

However, musicians' conceptual models of both tunes and melody file searching may be more complex. Figure 7 shows some potential descriptors (attributes) of a 'tune' derived from interviews carried out with musicians of varying IT and music information retrieval experience. Besides the melody itself, these include harmony, pitch, tempo, rhythm and tonality. (The same interviewees also offered a variety of additional criteria on which they might expect to perform 'text' searches, such as composer, year, period, artist.) Thus we judged there to be some potential misfits between the tune-matching requirements of the Music Library and those of its likely users. These are recorded in the User-Interface-System table using the same conventions as described for the drawing application. When conventionalized, they are highlighted (flagged) in the stylized hypertext table, as illustrated in the next section.

4.2.2 Conventionalizing and Viewing the Model

The result of conventionalizing and viewing the Music Library tune matching model is partially illustrated (minus Actions and Notes) in Figure 8. Again, for legibility this table has been reproduced from the original on the OSM Web site.

In this more complex and extensive example we have identified, amongst others:

- Two serious misfits (flagged **), namely those related to playback format and melody file size (both absent-hidden-present).

- System concepts deemed absent from the user's model (indexing, number, and type of melody file components), flagged *?.

- Implicit user concepts for a tune other than melody itself, such as harmony, pitch, rhythm, tempo, tonality, which were judged to be absent from the system model of the tune matching process (flagged *??).

(The latter may, however, be revealed in the scores of retrieved melodies once displayed and/or played back on the user's computer.)

In this second example the main sources of misfits were attributed to the contrast between system melody file concepts which may be absent from the user's conception and hidden at the interface (absent-hidden-present, denoted **), and user concepts for a tune which may be both delayed at the interface (until retrieved and played back) and absent from the system model for tune matching (implicit-delayed-absent, denoted *??).

5 Conclusions

OSM presents an evaluation methodology which appears to guide non-expert analysts successfully towards an understanding of how far a device or a system matches or falls short of a typical user's conceptualization of that domain. By its deliberately sketchy nature, it avoids drowning the analyst in detail, but it can be made almost as detailed, or as broad-brush, as desired.

The scope of OSM analysis is restricted to conceptual misfits. It has little to say about other issues, such as the rendering of the system image, the choice of communicative language (cf. heuristic evaluation, Nielsen [1994]) or speed of operation (cf. the keystroke level model, Card et al. [1983]). Conversely, those methods may have little or nothing to say about conceptual misfits.

Inferences about misfits between the system and the user's conceptualization may be revealed both by the tabular format and by algorithmic analysis. Experience to date (illustrated by the examples presented in this paper) suggests that much is revealed by the former process, for it encourages the analyst to question assumptions about the fit between system and user. The algorithmic analysis, in contrast, is only effective when a reasonable amount of detail has been made available.

OSM model of: NZDL_Music_Library

Notes

Relationships

Name	Actor	Type	Acted_on	Notes
Contains	Sub_ Collection	consists_of	Melody_file	
Defined_by	Sub_ Collection	constrained _by_goal	type_sub_ collections	
Described_by	Melody_file	constrained _by_device	Playback_ format	

Entities

Relns: actor in upright, acted-on in *italics*.
User:Interface:System : blue=OK, dark grey=dodgy, black=bad, green=not sure yet.

Name	Create/ set	Delete/ change	Relns.	User	Interface	System	
Melody_ file	record_ melody	remove_ melody	Described_ by *Contains*	implicit	delayed	present	??
How_ indexed	set	set		absent	delayed	present	*?
Name_of_ melody_file	add_ melody	remove_ melody		implicit	delayed	present	??
Num_of_ components	add_ melody	remove_ melody		absent	delayed	present	*?
Playback_ format	select	select	*Described_ by*	absent	hidden	present	**
Size_of_ melody_file	add_ melody	remove_ melody		absent	hidden	present	**
Type_of_ components	default	default		absent	disguised	present	*?
SubCollection	impossible	impossible	Contains Defined_by	explicit	direct	present	
Name_of_ subcollection	add_ subcolln.	delete_ subcolln.		explicit	direct	present	
No_of_ melodies	add_ melody	remove_ melody		absent	delayed	present	*?
Tune	recall	forget		explicit	delayed	absent	*?
Harmony	recall	forget		implicit	delayed	absent	*??
Melody	recall	forget		implicit	delayed	present	??
Notes	recall	forget		implicit	delayed	absent	*??
Pitch	recall	forget		implicit	delayed	absent	*??
Rhythm	recall	forget		implicit	delayed	absent	*??
Spaces	recall	forget		implicit	delayed	absent	*??
Tempo	recall	forget		implicit	delayed	absent	*??
Tonality	recall	forget		implicit	delayed	absent	*??

Figure 8: Part of a stylized hypertext table for the NZDL Music Library, reproduced from the original on the OSM Web site. Potential misfits are flagged with asterisks and question marks, according to seriousness. See text for explanation.

At present, our main concern is with relationships. Typically, analysts can readily unearth entities: user entities may be uncovered through the knowledge elicitation techniques outlined above, while system entities are quickly found by inspection. Attributes also appear to be speedily unearthed. But relationships can be easily missed, for they are neither externalized on the interface nor likely to be immediately grasped by the analyst. Unfortunately, it is often the degree to which a system helps its users to meet goal constraints that determines how useful it is. Much, therefore, hangs on the analyst's success during the first stage, that of constructing the paper-based model and eliciting relevant knowledge.

How does OSM relate to other approaches? Of the non-modelling approaches to usability evaluation, perhaps the nearest comparison is with Cognitive Walkthrough (CW) [Polson et al. 1992]. CW was intended to guide non-expert analysts towards a cognitive analysis by considering novice-user usability issues. Both CW and OSM require the analyst to make decisions about the potential user's knowledge, but their focus is different: CW considers each individual action step required to achieve a stated goal, but has nothing to offer about structural relationships. In our experience, CW does a good job of highlighting potential difficulties in learning to use a device, but has almost nothing to say about whether that device fits the user's conceptualization, and therefore, in our view, nothing to say about whether the device is useful. OSM is almost exactly complementary in its approach. Current work is exploring the ways in which OSM and CW differ in their potential to identify misfits associated with everyday systems such as ticket vending machines. It is hoped that this will also demonstrate measurable differences between the two methods. Other OSM analyses, for example of the NZDL Music Library summarized in Section 4.2.1, have generated recommendations for changes to existing systems.

After applying OSM to several full-scale systems, two of which are illustrated here, we are confident that the technique has real-life potential for the illumination of a range of applications including both analogue tools (e.g. a fob watch) and digitally-based applications (e.g. desktop tools, online diaries, ticket vending machines, digital libraries) as well as work practice studies (e.g. ambulance dispatch, health care IT support). OSM goes well beyond the confines of the laboratory, and future work is directed at further testing its scope and the practicalities of incorporating the approach into design practice.

OSM does not purport to supplant the analyst's judgement: in many cases, the analyst will have to decide whether or not an action is easy to find, and will always have to decide how much detail to include. It is hard to imagine that any approach could totally remove the need for judgement; however, we persist in the belief that even inexperienced analysts know what questions they are trying to answer.

Acknowledgements

We are grateful for the information about the NZDL Music Library provided by David Bainbridge of Waikato University. The OSM editor was developed by Owen Green. The work reported in this paper has been supported by EPSRC grant number GR/R39108.

References

Blackwell, A. F., Britton, C., Cox, A., Green, T. R. G., Gurr, C. A., Kadoda, G. F., Kutar, M., Loomes, M., Nehaniv, C. L., Petre, M., Roast, C., Roes, C., Wong, A. & Young, R. M. [2001], Cognitive Dimensions of Notations: Design Tools for Cognitive Technology, *in* M. Beynon, C. L. Nehaniv & K. Dautenhahn (eds.), *Cognitive Technology: Instruments of Mind – Proceedings of the 4th International Conference (CT 2001)*, Vol. 2117 of *Lecture Notes in Artifical Intelligence*, Springer-Verlag, pp.325–41.

Blandford, A. E. & Green, T. R. G. [1997], OSM: An Ontology-based Approach to Usability Evaluation, *in* E. O'Neill (ed.), *Proceedings of Workshop on Representations*, Queen Mary & Westfield College, pp.82–91.

Blandford, A. E. & Stelmaszewska, H. [2002], Usability of Musical Digital Libraries: a Multimodal Analysis, *in* M. Fingerhut (ed.), *Proceedings of the 3rd International Conference on Musical Information Retriveal (ISMIR 2002)*, IRCAM, pp.231–7.

Blandford, A. E., Wong, B. L. W., Connell, I. W. & Green, T. R. G. [2002], Multiple Viewpoints on Computer Supported Team Work: A Case Study on Ambulance Dispatch, *in* X. Faulkner, J. Finlay & F. Dètienne (eds.), *People and Computers XVI (Proceedings of HCI'02)*, Springer-Verlag, pp.139–56.

Blandford, A. & Young, R. M. [1996], Specifying User Knowledge for the Design of Interactive Systems, *Software Engineering Journal* **11**(6), 323–33.

Card, S. K., Moran, T. P. & Newell, A. [1983], *The Psychology of Human–Computer Interaction*, Lawrence Erlbaum Associates.

Green, T. R. G. [1989], Cognitive Dimensions of Notations, *in* A. Sutcliffe & L. Macaulay (eds.), *People and Computers V (Proceedings of HCI'89)*, Cambridge University Press, pp.443–60.

Green, T. R. G. & Benyon, D. R. [1996], The Skull Beneath the Skin; Entity-relationship Modelling of Information Artefacts, *International Journal of Human–Computer Interaction* **44**(6), 801–28.

McNab, R. J., Smith, L. A., Bainbridge, D. & Witten, I. H. [1997], The New Zealand Digital Library MELody inDEX, *D-Lib Magazine* **3**(5). Access the paper at http://www.dlib.org/dlib/may97/meldex/05witten.html (last accessed 2003.06.08).

Moran, T. P. [1983], Getting Into a System: External-internal Task Mapping Analysis, *in* A. Janda (ed.), *Proceedings of the CHI'83 Conference on Human Factors in Computing Systems*, ACM Press, pp.45–9.

Nielsen, J. [1994], Heuristic Evaluation, *in* J. Nielsen & R. L. Mack (eds.), *Usability Inspection Methods*, John Wiley & Sons, pp.25–62.

Payne, S. J. [1993], Understanding Calendar Use, *Human–Computer Interaction* **8**(2), 83–100.

Polson, P., Lewis, C., Rieman, J. & Wharton, C. [1992], Cognitive Walkthroughs: A Method for Theory-based Evaluation of User Interfaces, *International Journal of Man–Machine Studies* **36**(5), 741–73.

Young, R. M., Green, T. & Simon, T. [1989], Programmable User Models for Predictive Evaluation of Interface Design, *in* K. Bice & C. H. Lewis (eds.), *Proceedings of the CHI'89 Conference on Human Factors in Computing Systems: Wings for the Mind*, ACM Press, pp.15–9.

Interaction Techniques: Looking, Listening, Pointing, Stroking

Improving the Acquisition of Small Targets

Andy Cockburn & Andrew Firth

Human–Computer Interaction Lab, Department of Computer Science, University of Canterbury, Christchurch, New Zealand

Tel: *+64 3 364 2987*

Fax: *+64 3 364 2569*

Email: *andy@cosc.canterbury.ac.nz,*
andrew.firth@alliedtelesyn.co.nz

This paper describes the design and comparative evaluation of three methods that aid the acquisition of small targets. The first method, called 'bubble targets', increases the effective width of the target as the pointer approaches. The second method uses a form of 'stickiness' to restrict movement as the pointer passes over an object. In the third method, called 'goal-crossing', the user simultaneously presses two mouse buttons before passing the pointer over the item. Goal-crossing overcomes the need for the user to decelerate the mouse when acquiring the target. Two evaluations were conducted, with the first (n = 37) based on the acquisition of abstract targets for Fitts' Law modelling, and the second based on an ecologically oriented window resizing task (n = 11). Both showed that goal-crossing allowed the fastest target acquisition, but that it produced high error rates and was unpopular with participants. The 'bubble' and 'sticky' techniques also allowed faster target acquisition than the traditional approach, and users were enthusiastic about them. Fitts' Law accurately modelled all techniques. Implications of the results for general user interface design are briefly discussed.

Keywords: target acquisition, Fitts' Law, expanding targets, sticky icons, goal-crossing.

1 Introduction

As the resolution of computer displays increases, designers of graphical user interfaces can increasingly rely on accurate and precise depiction of small user interface components. It is now common to find direct manipulation interface controls such as window borders, drop-down menus, and margin-markers that are smaller than 10 pixels (= 2mm on typical displays) on one or both dimensions. Although small components may be readily discernible (by those with normal eyesight), acquiring them with a mouse-driven cursor can be slow and frustrating. Making interface components larger decreases the acquisition time but reduces the number of items that can be placed in the display and adversely affects visual design.

Recently three separate schemes have been proposed for reducing target acquisition time without demanding increased screen space: expanding targets, sticky icons, and goal-crossing. McGuffin & Balakrishnan [2002] showed that expanding targets, which enlarge as the cursor moves towards them, improve performance even when the expansion begins very late in the overall movement towards a target. Sticky icons effectively 'grab' the cursor as it moves over them [Worden et al. 1997]. Large movements 'snap' away from the icon, but small movements remain inside the item. Worden et al.'s evaluation suggested that sticky icons were particularly effective for older users when targeting small items. Goal-crossing interfaces [Accot & Zhai 1997, 2002] allow items to be selected by passing the cursor over the target area. They improve selection times because users do not need to decelerate and stop the cursor over the item. Details of these studies, and other related work, are provided in Section 2.

This paper describes the design and comparative evaluation of variants of these three schemes for aiding mouse-driven selection of small targets. The evaluation focuses on three factors: the comparative efficiency of the techniques, the degree to which Fitts' Law models their use, and the subjective preferences for the schemes. Although we expect our results to support those of related prior studies, direct comparison of the methods has not been possible due to differences in experimental methods. In particular, subjective preferences for the methods have not previously been compared.

Two separate evaluations were conducted. The first used an abstract selection task to generate data independent of any particular usage scenario. The second is more ecologically oriented, using a realistic window-resizing task to investigate the limitations of each technique in a more natural setting.

The following section presents related work on modelling and enhancing target acquisition in graphical user interfaces. Section 3 then describes the three targeting interfaces evaluated. Section 4 presents the method and results of the first evaluation based on abstract target acquisition tasks, and Section 5 details the window resizing evaluation. Results and further work are discussed in Section 6, and Section 7 concludes the paper.

2 Related Work

2.1 Fitts' Law

Fitts' Law [1954] is commonly used to predict the time to move a mouse pointer from one location to another. Using the 'Shannon formulation' of Fitts' Law [MacKenzie 1992], cursor movement time, MT increases linearly with the 'Index of Difficulty' (IoD), which relies on the logarithm of the distance moved (the amplitude), A, over the width of the target, W. The two constants, a and b, are determined experimentally and depend on cognition and motor preparation time, and on hand-eye coordination, respectively. Fitts' Law also provides a measure of human processing of movement tasks, called the 'Index of Performance' (*IoP*) or 'bandwidth' (measured in 'bits/second') which is calculated from the reciprocal of the constant *b*:

$$MT = a + b \times IoD$$

where:

$$IoD = \log_2 \left(\frac{A}{W} + 1 \right)$$

Also:

$$IoP = \frac{1}{b}$$

Fitts' law was originally proposed for one-dimensional motion tasks. For movements in two dimensions, the target width *W* is normally measured using the smallest value of the width and height dimensions [MacKenzie & Buxton 1992].

2.2 Expanding Targets

One approach to easing acquisition of small targets is to enlarge targets when they are needed. The commercial MacOS X Dock[1] demonstrates the technique, providing an icon panel in which the icons expand as the cursor approaches. Unfortunately, the MacOS X implementation can frustrate targeting because the expansion causes the icons to move if the cursor approaches the panel from a non-perpendicular angle. This problem is eased if expanded icons overlap one another [McGuffin & Balakrishnan 2002] or if the expansion only takes effect when the cursor velocity decreases on final target approach [Gutwin 2002].

McGuffin & Balakrishnan [2002] closely examined the degree to which Fitts' Law modelled targeting expanding targets in one-dimensional tasks. They found that Fitts' Law accurately models performance, and that movement time is primarily governed by the final expanded target size. This result held even when the targets began expanding after most (90%) of the movement towards the target was complete. McGuffin & Balakrishnan's study examined selection of a single object with no surrounding objects, so the influence of distraction due to neighbour-object motion was not examined.

2.3 Sticky Targets

Another approach to aiding target acquisition uses a metaphor based on gravity, magnetism, or stickiness. Worden et al. [1997] implemented 'Sticky Icons' by decreasing the mouse control-display gain [MacKenzie & Riddersma 1994] when the cursor enters the icon (control-display gain determines the mapping between physical mouse movement and resultant cursor movement). In this way, the user must move the mouse further to escape the boundary of the icon, effectively making the icon larger without using extra screen space. Worden et al.'s evaluation showed Sticky Icons to be efficient for selecting small targets.

---

[1] http://www.apple.com/macosx/theater/dock.html

Langdon et al. [2000] performed an evaluation of a similar 'force feedback' concept. Users were required to select the inner circle of a pair of concentric circles, either using or not using force feedback. In the force feedback condition, when the cursor entered the outer circle, a 'force' warped the pointer toward the inner one. The force feedback condition was 30% to 50% faster than the normal condition. The utility of this technique is limited because of the undesirable impact on selecting near-neighbour interface components. A scrollbar, for example, would be difficult to use if the pointer continually warped toward the window border.

2.4 Goal-crossing Targets

With goal-crossing [Accot & Zhai 1997, 2002] the user selects an item by passing the pointer over the target area with some modifier key pressed. The motion is fluid and rapid in comparison to the normal selection process of moving the cursor, decelerating on approach to the target, stopping on the target, and finally clicking. Their studies were based on input using a stylus rather than a mouse.

Accot & Zhai [1997] found that selection through goal-crossing conforms to Fitts' Law, but differs from pointing techniques in the value of W, which is effectively infinite because there is no need to stop the cursor within the target's border. Rather than using a 'Smallest-of' model (see Section 2.1) for width, goal-crossing moves toward a 'Largest-of' model. For elongated interface controls such as window borders, the 'Largest-of' model is many magnitudes larger than 'Smallest-of'.

MacKenzie [1992] described a 'Stoke-through' technique similar to goal-crossing, where an icon is selected by depressing the mouse beside the icon, followed by a dragging motion over the icon, finishing with a button release on the other side. This technique was shown to be 40% faster than a standard point and select approach.

The main difference between moving the mouse for pointing tasks and for goal-crossing is that the mouse buttons are depressed, resulting in a dragging state. MacKenzie [1991] found that dragging times are slower than pointing times, and concluded that this was caused by interference from the additional task of holding down a mouse button. Thus, the Fitts' law values of a and b are increased for goal-crossing, but they would need to increase considerably to counteract the additional efficiency arising from a higher effective width value W.

3   Three Targeting Interfaces

The purpose of our evaluation is to directly compare the efficiency and subjective preferences for sticky, goal-crossing and expanding techniques in acquiring small targets. This section describes the three techniques evaluated.

All three interfaces, and the control 'normal' setting, were implemented in Tcl/Tk for Experiment 1 and Java Swing for Experiment 2. The experiments were run on a 1.4GHz AMD Athlon computer running the Linux operating system, with a 19″ display of 1600×1200 pixels. Control-display gain was set to a constant ratio of approximately 1:1.6 in both experiments. Input was provided through a three-button Logitech mouse.

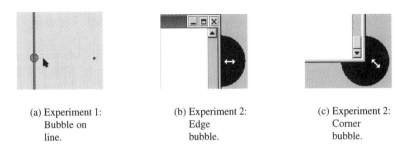

(a) Experiment 1:
Bubble on
line.

(b) Experiment 2:
Edge
bubble.

(c) Experiment 2:
Corner
bubble.

Figure 1: Bubble targets used in Experiments 1 and 2. The target line or edge expands.

3.1 Bubble Targets Implementation

Based on expanding targets, bubble targets increase their effective size as the cursor approaches. In Experiment 1 (Figure 1a) the bubble appeared as a circle centred on the x-axis of the line and on the y-axis of the cursor location. In Experiment 2, the bubble appeared on the outside edge (Figure 1b) or corner (Figure 1c) of the target window.

Two design decisions with bubble targets involve trade-offs between visual distraction and the timing and size of the bubble display. McGuffin & Balakrishnan [2002] showed that expanding targets remain efficient even when the expansion starts very late in the movement towards the target. This means that the bubbles need not be displayed until the cursor is very close to the target, reducing visual distraction. In our implementations, bubbles were only displayed when the cursor came within 15 pixels (Experiment 1) and 50 pixels (Experiment 2) of the targeted item. Similarly, larger bubbles are theoretically faster, but they are likely to increase visual distraction. Experiment 1 used a circular bubble with a 10 pixel radius, and Experiment 2 used a radius of 40 pixels.

3.2 Sticky Targets Implementation

To provide a sense of 'stickiness', cursor motion must be constrained while within a sticky target. The primary design decision is in calibrating the level of 'stickiness' so that it aids targeting while not interfering with pointing elsewhere, including passing the cursor over the top of a sticky item.

We implemented sticky targets differently in Experiments 1 and 2, but the resultant interaction was similar in both implementations. In Experiment 1 we used the Tcl/Tk motion event bindings to determine whether the pointer had moved sufficiently far to 'snap out' of a sticky target. When inside a sticky target, each time the movement event was registered (at most, once every 20ms on our machine), the software would calculate whether the cursor had moved more than a threshold distance (20 pixels) since the last motion event. If not, the cursor would warp back to the centre of the item. The cursor snapped out of the item once the threshold was exceeded. The resultant effect was that the cursor would stay motionless in the middle of the target when the mouse is moved slowly, but a slight acceleration would snap out of the target. Calibrating a threshold level that provided a seemingly subtle and natural behaviour was straightforward.

In Experiment 2, like Worden et al. [1997], we implemented sticky targets by reducing the mouse control-display gain to approximately 10% (1:0.16) of its original value when inside a sticky target. The interaction difference of this implementation to Experiment 1's is that continual slow motion within a sticky target will eventually leave the target's boundary.

The primary theoretical disadvantage of sticky targets stems from the risk of the cursor being 'grabbed' en-route to another target. One way to reduce this problem is to implement stickiness on only one axis. In Experiment 2, for example, where the tasks involved window resizing, the sticky effect was implemented across the window border, but not along it. Consequently, vertical window edges were horizontally sticky, and horizontal edges were vertically sticky. Beyond this, we have found that small sticky targets are surprisingly effective in coincidentally discriminating between ballistic motion to a different target (when stickiness is not desirable) and the decelerated motion of final acquisition (when it is). The reason is that when the cursor passes rapidly over an interface component, the motion is often too rapid for the window system's event model to trigger an event on the underlying widget. The resultant effect, from our anecdotal experience, is a very natural effect that the cursor snaps onto targeted items, but passes over un-targeted ones without disruption.

3.3   Goal-crossing Targets Implementation

In our implementations, goal-crossing selection was achieved by dragging the cursor over a target while holding down the left and right mouse buttons. In Experiment 1, acquiring the target caused the cursor to lock onto the stationary target (by warping) until either mouse button was released. In the window resizing tasks of Experiment 2, the target window border followed the cursor, continually resizing the window border, until either mouse buttons was released. Two simultaneous mouse buttons were used because dragging tasks with one mouse button are commonly used by applications.

Theoretically, goal-crossing should allow the fastest target acquisition of the three techniques because the user does not have to decelerate the cursor on target approach. However, we wanted to inspect subjective preferences for a technique that we believed felt awkward with the mouse due to the unusual rapidly dragging action.

4   Experiment 1: Abstract Task

The first experiment compared the three methods and the traditional method in an abstract one-dimensional task similar to that used by Accot & Zhai [2002]. The experimental interface consisted of a 6 pixel diameter dot placed some distance from the 6 pixel wide grey target line in the middle of the window (Figure 1a). Participants clicked on the dot to start each task and then acquired the line as quickly as possible. Software logged the time between clicking the dot and acquiring the target. Acquiring the target involved clicking on the line (for normal and sticky

Method	Line of best fit (MT =)			r^2	IoP (bits s^{-1})
Normal	74	+	152×IoD	0.96	6.59
Bubble	-115	+	149×IoD	0.97	6.70
Sticky	153	+	132×IoD	0.94	7.55
Goal	-282	+	121×IoD	0.81	8.26

Table 1: Linear regression equations, r^2 values and Indices of Performance for the four techniques.

targets), clicking on the line or expanded bubble (for bubble targets), or goal-crossing the line with the left-mouse button held down. Software also logged all missed clicks and all mouse movement.

All participants used all four interfaces, with the order of exposure randomized to control learning effects. Five training selections and thirty-five logged selections were used per interface, with the same randomly determined distances to the left and right of the target line reused with each interface. The amplitudes between the starting circle and the line were between 10 and 390 pixels.

After using each interface the participants were asked to respond to the questions "Selecting the line was physically demanding (high effort)" and "Selecting the line was efficient (fast)" using five point Likert scales, from one (disagree) to five (agree). After completing the tasks with all of the interfaces, they were asked to rank the four methods, from their favourite to their least preferred, and to provide any additional comments.

Thirty-seven undergraduate Computer Science students took part in the experiment. They were rewarded with a $5 shopping voucher. Participants were encouraged to rest and flex their wrists between tasks.

4.1 Data Analysis

The experimental data is inspected in two ways. First, regression analysis is used to determine whether Fitts' Law holds for each of the techniques. 'Bandwidth' measures (Section 2.1) are also calculated from the regression analysis to determine the psychophysical throughput of each method. Second, a 4×4 repeated-measures analysis of variance (ANOVA) is conducted for factors 'interface type' and 'distance'. The factor 'distance' allows us to inspect whether any of the techniques favoured short or long distances. Its four levels are 'short' (10–100 pixels), 'low-medium' (101–200 pixels), 'high-medium' (201–300 pixels) and 'high' (301–390 pixels). Error rates are also inspected.

4.2 Results

4.2.1 Conformity to Fitts' Law

In calculating the Index of Difficulty of each task, we used the visible thickness of line target, which was constant at 6-pixels. It is important to note, however, that the three new selection schemes are designed to increase the actual target size, through expansion, stickiness or goal-crossing, reducing the *IoD*.

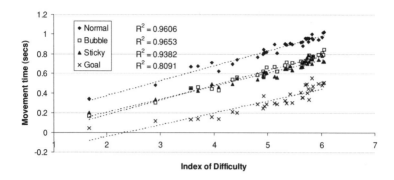

Figure 2: Movement time plotted against Index of Difficulty for the four interfaces. Linear regression lines of best fit are shown.

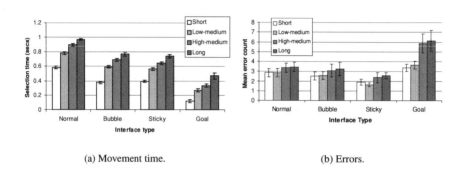

(a) Movement time.   (b) Errors.

Figure 3: Mean movement times and error counts for the four interfaces by distance. Error bars show ±1 standard error around the mean.

Linear regression analysis of the relationship between movement time and *IoD* shows that Fitts' Law accurately models all four methods-lines of best fit are shown in Figure 2. The r^2 values for the four techniques were 0.96, 0.97, 0.94 and 0.81 for the normal, bubble, sticky and goal-crossing techniques (r^2 values exceeding 0.8 are normally deemed to be accurate in experiments involving human participants). The lines of best fit, r^2 values, and Index of Performance measures for the four techniques are shown in Table 1.

4.2.2 Differences Between the Methods

All three of the new target selection techniques were significantly faster than the traditional approach, as shown in Figure 3a. The mean target acquisition times for normal, bubble, sticky and goal-crossing interfaces were 810ms (s.d. 185ms), 607ms (s.d. 186ms), 585ms (s.d. 180ms) and 298ms (s.d. 216ms) respectively, producing a reliable difference $F_{3,108} = 199.8$, $p < 0.001$. In pairwise comparison, a Tukey test produces an Honest Significant difference of 111ms, revealing a reliable difference ($p < 0.05$) between all interface types except bubble and sticky targets, which performed similarly. It is telling that the slowest of the new techniques, bubble targets, reduced targeting time by 25% of the normal method.

There was a reliable interaction between interface type and distance ($F_{9,324} = 2.16$, $p < 0.05$), meaning that performance with at least one interface deteriorated differently to the others as distance increased. One probable explanation is the comparatively high performance deterioration with goal-crossing between high-medium (201–300 pixels) and long (301–390 pixel) amplitudes of motion. We believe this effect is due to the difficulty of maintaining a dragging state over long distances. This explanation is supported by the analysis of errors, reported below.

The number of off-target clicks was also analysed. Any mouse press between selecting the initial dot and clicking the target line was added to the 'missed clicks' total. The mean number of misses across the 35 logged tasks were significantly different ($F_{3,108} = 7.8$, $p < 0.001$) at 10.4 (s.d. 15.7) with the normal method, 7.9 (s.d. 11.9) with bubble targets, 6.1 (s.d. 7.3) with sticky targets, and 16.3 (s.d. 15.7) with goal-crossing, as shown in Figure 3b. The high standard deviations for error counts indicate a non-normal distribution, with many participants making few errors while others made many.

The 'miss' count for goal-crossing is an upper-bound measure because the software logged any mouse press after selecting the initial dot as a miss. With goal-crossing, however, it is legitimate for the user to initiate the task by clicking the dot, but only acquire goal-crossing mode (by pressing both mouse-buttons) on final approach to the target. The fastest goal-crossing users initiated goal crossing mode at the same time as selecting the initial dot, but many users moved most of the distance towards the target before pressing both buttons. Consequently, the high 'error' count for goal-crossing is suspect.

One final measure suggests that goal-crossing became more difficult and error prone than other methods as the distance increased. When analysing errors using the same two-factor ANOVA as that used for movement time, there is a marginal interaction between interface type and distance: $F_{9,324} = 1.9$, $p = 0.05$. This interaction is visible in the comparatively large step between goal-crossing errors in the short to low-medium distances vs. the high-medium and long distances. The participants' comments support the explanation that this is due to the difficulty of maintaining two-button dragging states over long distances. Possibly, with more experience users would learn to only initiate the goal-crossing mode when finally approaching the target.

4.2.3 Subjective Preferences

The participants indicated that targeting with all of the methods demanded relatively low effort. Responses to question one "Selecting the target was physically demanding (high effort)" ranged from low values with bubble and sticky targets (both means 2.5, s.d. 1.1) through goal-crossing (3.0, s.d. 1.5) to the most demanding normal interface (3.1, s.d. 1.3). Although these ratings do not produce a reliable difference (Friedman $\chi^2 = 6.5$, $p = 0.09$), the participants' comments reflected the trend in the ratings. For example, one participant commented: "Goal-crossing is

Method	Preference Ranking			
	1st	2nd	3rd	4th
Normal	4	6	12	15
Bubble	8	12	13	4
Sticky	17	12	6	2
Goal	8	7	6	16

Table 2: Preference rankings for the four interface types.

more physically demanding because holding down the mouse buttons locks up your wrist more making it harder to scroll around with the mouse, reducing fine control and increasing fatigue."

Interestingly, despite the substantially faster performance with goal-crossing, the participants rated it relatively poorly for efficiency. Mean responses to Question 2 "Selecting the line was efficient (fast)" for the bubble, sticky, goal-crossing and normal interfaces were 3.8 (s.d. 1.2), 3.9 (s.d. 0.9), 3.4 (s.d. 1.6) and 2.6 (s.d. 1.1) respectively, producing a reliable difference: Friedman $\chi^2 = 23.8$, $p < 0.01$.

The overall rankings of the four techniques show a strong preference for the sticky technique, as shown in Table 2. Forty-six percent of the participants ranked sticky targets first, and a further 32% ranked it second. Goal-crossing, in contrast, was ranked first by 22% of the participants, and last by 43%.

Bubble targets were consistently in the middle rankings. Negative comments about bubble targets concerned the visual distraction that they caused and the fact that they encouraged the participants to become sloppy in their targeting. For example, one participant commented: "I became over-confident and sometimes missed even the bubble." and another stated: "I wonder if my times were actually worse with bubbles because I changed my attitude. I didn't worry about accuracy because the target was so big, so I often overshot."

4.3   Summary

The results support prior work showing that Fitts' Law accurately models all four techniques. Although goal-crossing allowed extremely rapid performance, the subjective responses, comments, and error rates suggest that the users found it awkward and clumsy. It must be stressed that this finding applies only to mouse-driven goal-crossing, and does not apply to stylus input methods.

Sticky targets were extremely popular, rated first or second favourite by 78% of participants. They also performed well, with mean selection times 28% faster than the normal method, and with 41% fewer target misses.

5   Experiment 2: Window Resizing Evaluation

The second experiment examines how the four techniques compare in a more ecologically oriented task. The aim is to explore the design decisions necessary to deploy the methods in support of real tasks, and to validate the results of the abstract tasks in Experiment 1.

5.1   Window Resizing

Resizing windows is a common action in graphical desktop environments — Gaylin [1986] found that it comprised 2% of all windows commands and 12.4% of commands when a user logs onto a computer. Despite the frequency of window resizing, the traditional method requires a high level of precision in acquiring and dragging the window border (normally only a few pixels wide). Some window management systems, such as Sawfish[2], allow customizable key-bindings to remove the need to acquire the window border, but this approach suffers the disadvantages that the user must customize and memorize the key binding, and that the key bindings can clash with those used by application software.

5.2   Interface Modifications

The bubble and goal-crossing methods were modified for the resizing task, based on the design decisions that we felt would be necessary to create commercially viable implementations.

Bubbles only appeared on the outside window edges (see Figures 1b & c). This change would be necessary in commercial deployment to avoid targeting collisions between bubbles and interface controls such as scrollbars that are close to the window edge. Also, to reduce visual distraction, the bubbles only appear when the cursor is inside the window. Consequently, when resizing a window that the cursor is initially outside, the user would have to sweep the cursor inside the window, then move outwards towards its edge. The radius of the part-bubble was 40 pixels, and the bubbles appeared when the cursor was less than 50 pixels from the window edge.

Like bubble borders, goal-crossing mode could only be initiated from inside the window being resized. This meant that when the cursor was initially outside the target window, the user would have to sweep the cursor inside the window to acquire goal-crossing mode, and then move outwards across the border with mouse buttons one and three held down. We felt that this design decision would be necessary in a commercial implementation to avoid problems associated with passing the cursor over other windows in the display. If goal-crossing mode could be acquired from outside a window boundary, then the user would need to carefully coordinate the timing of their mouse button presses to ensure that windows lying between the initial cursor location and the target window were not mistakenly resized.

5.3   Method

Five window-resizing tasks were carried out with each of the four interfaces. The window borders used to resize the windows were 6 pixels wide, and the corners extended 25 pixels along the border. The tasks differed by whether the window was being enlarged or diminished, whether a side border or corner was used, and whether the cursor started inside or outside the window (see Table 3). The different resize directions, borders used and cursor locations were included to illuminate differences between the techniques-they were not intended to be independent experimental factors. Each task consisted of five subtasks that varied the distance the pointer

---

[2]http://sawmill.sourceforge.net

Task	Resize	Border used	Cursor location
1	Enlarge	Right	Inside window
2	Diminish	Right	Inside window
3	Enlarge	Bottom-right corner	Inside window
4	Enlarge	Left	Outside window
5	Diminish	Left	Outside window

Table 3: Window resizing tasks used in Experiment 2.

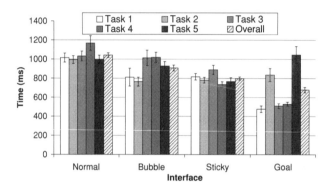

Figure 4: Mean movement times for the four interfaces by task. Error bars show ±1 standard error around the mean.

started from the border. The interface order was randomly assigned to each participant to control learning effects.

Tasks were initiated by clicking on a red dot positioned 20, 50, 100, 200 or 500 pixels from the target border. The participants then acquired and dragged the window border into a large blue-coloured region that was 50 pixels from the border in the resizing direction. The software automatically logged task times. Participants were invited to comment on the interfaces between tasks.

Eleven participants took part in the experiment. All were Computer Science graduate students.

5.4   Results

Timing data from the experiment was analysed in a $4 \times 5 \times 5$ repeated measures analysis of variance (ANOVA). The three factors (all within subjects) were Interface type (normal, bubble, sticky and goal-crossing), Task (one to five, as shown in Table 3), and Distance (20, 50, 100, 200 and 500 pixels).

The results support those of Experiment 1. Across the 1100 subtasks, the mean window resizing time was relatively fast at 855ms, with a standard deviation of 438ms. ANOVA revealed a significant main effect for Interface type ($F_{3,30} = 27.0$, $p < 0.01$), with goal-crossing fastest (678ms, s.d. 460ms), and progressively slower through sticky borders (797ms, s.d. 274ms), bubble borders (907ms, s.d. 502ms), and normal borders (1041ms, s.d. 398ms). Figure 4 shows the mean task times for each of the interfaces across the five tasks.

As expected, there were significant main effects for factors Task ($F_{4,40} = 4.5$, $p < 0.01$) and Distance ($F_{4,40} = 44.8$, $p < 0.01$). Mean task times increased through Tasks one (mean 779ms, s.d. 465ms) to five (mean 933ms, s.d. 441ms). The increasingly complex movements required to complete the tasks explain this increase (discussed below). Similarly, mean subtask times increased as the distance increased: from a mean of 689ms (s.d. 348ms) at 20 pixels to 1101ms (s.d. 522ms) at 500 pixels.

There was an interesting interaction between Task and Interface type ($F_{12,120} = 7.0$, $p < 0.01$), visible in Figure 4. Unlike the other interfaces, goal-crossing performance was dramatically different between tasks that involved window enlarging (one, three and four) and shrinking (two and five). This effect is explained by the need to change mouse direction while holding down the mouse button when goal-crossing. In task two, the cursor begins inside the window, so the user must issue the crossing action rightwards over the right hand window border before changing direction to drag the border leftwards. The advantage of goal-crossing in avoiding deceleration is reduced, and its performance is similar to the other interfaces. In Task five, which involves decreasing the window size starting outside the target window, goal-crossing performs even more poorly. Again, this is explained by the mouse direction changes required while holding the mouse button down. The user must first move inside the window, press and hold the mouse button while sweeping outward to acquire the border, and then change direction for a second time to shrink the window. Interestingly, goal crossing remained efficient in Task 4, even through a direction change is required. We suspect that the reason for this is that the mouse button is not held down while changing direction because users move the cursor into the window before changing direction, pressing the mouse button, and sweeping outward over the border.

5.5 Comments

Many of the participants were surprised by how poorly they performed with the normal interface. One stated: "You don't realize how slow the normal technique is until you try some of these other methods."

Although seven of the participants stated that they liked the rapid speed of goal-crossing, several noted that the high speed was at the cost of accuracy. When goal-crossing, most participants made rapid sweeping motions with the mouse, moving the cursor much further than the minimum movements required. The experimental tasks promoted this rapid and crude movement because the participants were informed that the timing stopped when the window border entered the target blue-coloured region. The experiment fails to indicate whether goal-crossing would remain as efficient if specific window sizes were required.

6 Discussion and Further Work

Although the results show that goal-crossing is a highly efficient method of mouse-driven target acquisition, the participants' subjective preferences indicate that it should be used with caution in mouse driven graphical user interfaces. In general, users felt a lack of control with goal-crossing due to the in accuracy of rapid dragging. It is highly likely that this negative perception only applies to mouse-driven input and would not be observed with the more dexterous input available with a stylus. However, stylus input devices remain specialist hardware that is unusual on everyday desktop computers.

Bubble targets resulted in improved performance when compared to the normal method, but many participants stated that they found the appearance of the bubbles distracting. The bubbles also induced a 'sloppy' targeting behaviour in some participants who, anticipating the appearance of the bubble, targeted the region around the target rather than the target itself. This behaviour adversely affected their effectiveness due to hunting effects. In the window-resizing tasks of Experiment 2, the hunting effect was exacerbated because the bubbles only appeared on the outside edge of the window that the cursor was inside. Consequently, having overshot the bubble, it would disappear, and would only reappear once the cursor had re-entered the window. Due to the risks of visual distraction and of encouraging hunting, we recommend that expanding targets be used with caution.

Sticky targets were efficient and popular. Participants liked the fact that they created no visual distraction, yet simplified targeting. Interestingly, we did not observe a sticky target learning effect equivalent to that with bubbles, where the participants became more 'sloppy' in anticipation of eased targeting. We suspect this is explained by the absence of the bubble's affordance — the participants would decelerate towards the small target as normal, but the stickiness caused the cursor to snap to the line, reducing overshooting.

Despite the efficiency and popularity of the sticky method, it should still be used with caution, and further research is necessary to determine how closely sticky components can be placed without causing interference between targets. By 'interference', we mean situations where the cursor unintentionally locks onto a sticky target nearby another sticky component. The user would have to 'snap' the cursor away from the item, with the consequent risk of overshooting the target.

We intend to further investigate how sticky targeting can be enhanced through feedback in other modalities. Brewster et al. [1994], for example, showed that scrollbar use was enhanced through the addition of auditory feedback. Similarly, Fraser & Gutwin [2000] show that in visually stressed situations, redundant visual and auditory feedback reduced targeting time. Oakley et al. [2001] examined how haptic feedback affected simple user interface controls, finding that it did not reliably influence task time, but significantly reduced the number of errors.

We also intend to investigate how targeting aids such as these can be used to assist users who have visual or motor-coordination impediments.

7 Conclusions

It is increasingly common for graphical user interfaces to contain direct manipulation controls that measure only a few pixels on one or both dimensions. Acquiring small targets using a mouse demands a high level of precision and can be frustratingly error-prone and slow.

This paper described the design, implementation and evaluation of three alternative schemes to aid the mouse-driven acquisition of small targets. Bubble targets increase in size when the cursor is close. Sticky targets either alter the mouse control-display gain or warp the cursor once the target boundary is crossed to produce a sense of 'stickiness'. Goal-crossing targets are acquired by sweeping the cursor over the item while holding down a modifier key or mouse button. Although all three techniques are based on prior research, the methods have not previously been evaluated in direct comparison.

Measurements in an abstract targeting task confirmed that Fitts' Law accurately models all three techniques, and that they all reduced the normal target acquisition time by at least 25%. Although goal-crossing was extremely rapid, many of the participants felt it was impractical with a mouse due to a lack of accuracy. Sticky targets were popular due to their natural behaviour and their absence of visual distraction. Performance measures and subjective preferences in a more ecologically oriented window-resizing task confirmed the results and preferences of the abstract task.

The results are promising, and future work will focus on identifying the factors affecting the commercial deployment of sticky interface components. We also wish to investigate how these techniques can be used to aid those with visual and motor-coordination impairments.

References

Accot, J. & Zhai, S. [1997], Beyond Fitts' Law: Models for Trajectory-based HCI Tasks, *in* S. Pemberton (ed.), *Proceedings of the CHI'97 Conference on Human Factors in Computing Systems*, ACM Press, pp.295–302.

Accot, J. & Zhai, S. [2002], More than Dotting the i's — Foundations for Crossing-based Interfaces, *in* D. Wixon (ed.), *Proceedings of CHI'02 Conference on Human Factors in Computing Systems: Changing our World, Changing Ourselves*, CHI Letters **4**(1), ACM Press, pp.73–80.

Brewster, S. A., Wright, P. C. & Edwards, A. [1994], The Design and Evaluation of an Auditory-enhanced Scrollbar, *in* B. Adelson, S. Dumais & J. Olson (eds.), *Proceedings of the CHI'94 Conference on Human Factors in Computing Systems: Celebrating Interdependence*, ACM Press, pp.173–9.

Fitts, P. M. [1954], The Information Capacity of the Human Motor System in Controlling Amplitude of Movement, *British Journal of Educational Psychology* **47**(6), 381–91.

Fraser, J. & Gutwin, C. [2000], The Effects of Feedback on Targeting Performance in Visually Stressed Conditions, *in* S. Fels & P. Poulin (eds.), *Proceedings of Graphics Interface Conference*, Morgan-Kaufmann, pp.19–26.

Gaylin, K. [1986], How are Windows Used? Some Notes on Creating an Empirically-Based Windowing Benchmark Task, *in* M. Mantei & P. Orbeton (eds.), *Proceedings of the CHI'86 Conference on Human Factors in Computing Systems*, ACM Press, pp.96–100.

Gutwin, C. [2002], Improving Focus Targeting in Interactive Fisheye Views, *in* D. Wixon (ed.), *Proceedings of CHI'02 Conference on Human Factors in Computing Systems: Changing our World, Changing Ourselves*, CHI Letters **4**(1), ACM Press, pp.267–74.

Langdon, P., Keates, S., Clarkson, P. & Robinson, P. [2000], Using Haptic Feedback to Enhance Computer Interaction for Motion-Impaired Users, *in* P. Sharkey, A. Cesarani, L. Pugnetti & A. Rizzo (eds.), *Proceedings of 3rd International Conference on Disability, Virtual Reality and Associated Technologies (ICDVRAT 2000)*, Reading University, pp.25–32.

MacKenzie, I. [1991], Fitts' Law as a Performance Model in Human–Computer Interaction, PhD thesis, University of Toronto.

MacKenzie, I. A. [1992], Movement Time Prediction in Human–Computer Interfaces, *in* N. Jaffe (ed.), *Proceedings of Graphics Interface '92*, Canadian Information Processing Society, pp.140–50.

MacKenzie, I. & Buxton, W. [1992], Extending Fitts' Law to Two-Dimensional Tasks, *in* P. Bauersfeld, J. Bennett & G. Lynch (eds.), *Proceedings of the CHI'92 Conference on Human Factors in Computing Systems*, ACM Press, pp.219–26.

MacKenzie, I. & Riddersma, S. [1994], Effects of Output Display and Control-Display Gain on Human Performance in Interactive Systems, *Behaviour & Information Technology* **13**(5), 328–37.

McGuffin, M. & Balakrishnan, R. [2002], Acquisition of Expanding Targets, *in* D. Wixon (ed.), *Proceedings of CHI'02 Conference on Human Factors in Computing Systems: Changing our World, Changing Ourselves*, *CHI Letters* **4**(1), ACM Press, pp.57–64.

Oakley, I., Brewster, S. A. & Gray, P. D. [2001], Solving Multi-target Haptic Problems in Menu Interaction, *in* M. M. Tremaine (ed.), *CHI'01 Extended Abstracts of the Conference on Human Factors in Computing Systems*, ACM Press, pp.357–8.

Worden, A., Walker, N., Bharat, K. & Hudson, S. [1997], Making Computers Easier for Older Adults to Use: Area Cursors and Sticky Icons, *in* S. Pemberton (ed.), *Proceedings of the CHI'97 Conference on Human Factors in Computing Systems*, ACM Press, pp.266–71.

A Directional Stroke Recognition Technique for Mobile Interaction in a Pervasive Computing World

Vassilis Kostakos & Eamonn O'Neill

Department of Computer Science, University of Bath, Bath BA2 7AY, UK

Tel: *+44 1225 384432 / 383216*

Email: *{vk, eamonn}@cs.bath.ac.uk*

This paper presents a common gestural interface to mobile and pervasive computing devices. We report our development of a novel technique for recognizing input strokes on a range of mobile and pervasive devices, ranging from small devices with low processing capabilities and limited input area to computers with wall-sized displays and an input area as large as can be accommodated by motion-sensing technologies such as cameras. Recent work has included implementing and testing our stroke recognition technique and associated object-tracking by camera. Ongoing and future work includes optimizing our stroke recognition and camera-based object-tracking techniques, developing input based on human body tracking and running extended usability evaluations.

Keywords: stroke recognition, gestural interfaces, pervasive computing, ubiquitous computing, mobile interaction.

1 Introduction

One of the most exciting developments in current HCI is the shift in focus from computing on the desktop to computing in the wider world. Computational power and the interfaces to that power are moving rapidly into our streets, our vehicles, our buildings and our pockets. The combination of mobile/wearable computing and pervasive/ubiquitous computing is generating great expectations.

We face, however, many challenges in designing human interaction with mobile and pervasive technologies. In particular, the input and output devices and methods of using them that work (at least some of the time!) with desk-bound computers are often inappropriate for interaction on the street.

To take a simple example, a keyboard does not transfer well from the office to the street. Simplistic solutions seen with several current mobile and wearable devices, such as making the keyboard much smaller, create their own usability problems. Similarly, usability problems are introduced by taking an interface designed for desktop monitors, such as a desktop operating system's graphical front-end, and putting it, with minimal changes, on a Pocket PC with a tiny display area and very different input devices.

Physically shrinking everything including the input and output devices does not create a usable mobile computer. Instead, we need radical changes in our interaction techniques, comparable to the sea-change in the 1980s from command line to graphical user interfaces. As with that development, the breakthrough we need in interaction techniques will most likely come not from relatively minor adjustments to existing interface hardware and software but from a less predictable mixture of inspiration and experimentation. For example, Brewster and colleagues have investigated overcoming the limitations of tiny screens on mobile devices by utilizing sound and gesture to augment or to replace conventional mobile device interfaces [Brewster 2002; Brewster et al. 2003].

2   Searching for New Interaction Techniques

In our current research, we assume that there will be an increasing convergence between mobile/wearable computing and pervasive computing. The latter, being built into the environment, for example in a shop or library or on a bus, can have very large processing and data storage power and (at least in the fixed location examples) very fast, high bandwidth connections to other distributed resources. In addition, input and output devices can take many different forms, from traditional keyboards and monitors to huge displays and touch screens.

In contrast, and notwithstanding continuing improvements in hardware and communications technologies, mobile and wearable computers are likely to continue to suffer from relatively weaker data storage, processing power and network connectivity.

As the technologies mature, we must learn to play to the strengths of each form. For many applications, the user may want to use, say, the wall display in the shop with the high bandwidth connection rather than the tiny display on her PDA with its relatively poor connectivity. For other applications, the user may prefer to take advantage of the characteristics of her mobile device. Indeed, some applications may be most usable through simultaneous use of a combination of pervasive and mobile computing power.

A persistent problem with the usability of mobile computing has been the conflation of the physical characteristics of the device with the characteristics of the interface between the user and the computing functionality which the device delivers. For example, as mobile and wearable devices become ever smaller, their display areas, which typically serve as both input and output devices, become ever smaller and less usable. The legitimate desire to make mobile and wearable devices more mobile and easier to wear through miniaturization will render these devices less and less usable so long as the interface and its associated interaction techniques continue to be conflated with the physical characteristics of the device itself.

In attempting to resolve this dilemma, we are exploring ways of decoupling the interaction techniques from the devices. In the context of converging mobile and pervasive technologies, this means developing interaction techniques that will work with devices ranging from the smallest wearable computer or smart ring to a wall-sized display driven by a powerful fixed-location computer in a shop or street. In this paper, we focus on our work to develop an input technique that will satisfy these criteria.

3   Stroke Recognition for Mobile and Pervasive Interaction

Given the inadequacies of traditional desktop input techniques, i.e. mouse and keyboard, in a pervasive computing environment and, even more so, with mobile and wearable computing, there has been considerable research investigating alternative techniques. Prominent amongst these is gesture or stroke based input [Pirhonen et al. 2002]. This has formed the basis for many of the input techniques used with PDAs, whether in the form of touchscreen strokes to perform commands or in the form of alphabets, such as Graffiti on the Palm range of PDAs.

Moreover, stroke recognition predates PDAs by quite a while. One of the first applications to use some sort of stroke recognition was Sutherland's Sketchpad [Sutherland 1963]. The idea of mouse strokes as gestures dates back to the 1970s and pie menus [Callahan et al. 1998]. Since then, numerous applications have used similar techniques for allowing users to perform complex actions using an input device. For instance, design programs like [Zhao 1993] allow users to perform actions on objects by performing mouse or pen strokes on the object. Recently, Web browsing applications, like Opera[1] and Mozilla[2], have incorporated similar capabilities. Guimbretiere et al. [2001] show how FlowMenu [Guimbretiere & Winograd 2000] may be used with large wall displays. FlowMenu is very similar to pie menus. Unless the FlowMenu has been displayed, any pen stroke is interpreted as simple mouse input, using a simple down-move-up event model.

There is a number of current open source projects which involve the development of stroke recognition, including Mozilla, Libstroke[3], XScribble[4], and WayV[5].

The latter is a library created for recognizing characters as well as strokes. It is based on a technique called point density analysis which uses matrix mathematics. In its latest version it has included a second 'backup' method for recognizing strokes, which implements a form of directional recognition. This method imposes an $n \times n$ matrix on the stroke and assigns every stroke point to a cell in the matrix. By comparing the relative position of two boxes which contain consecutive stroke

---

[1] http://www.opera.com/features/mouse/
[2] http://optimoz.mozdev.org/gestures/
[3] http://www.etla.net/libstroke/libstroke.pdf
[4] http://www.handhelds.org/projects/xscribble.html
[5] http://www.stressbunny.com/wayv/

points, a sequence of directions is produced, and is used to assist the point density analysis algorithm in the recognition of the stroke.

The Mozilla browser uses a simpler technique. Each point of the gesture is compared to the previous one, and one of four directions is generated (U, D, L, R), while discarding consecutive U's, D's etc. Then, the sequence is compared against a table of stroke signatures, and if no exact match is found, then only the last 2 and then the last 3 elements of the direction signature are used. If that fails, then the signature is processed for diagonals, simply by replacing consecutive L's and D's by '1' (for diagonally left-down), R's and D's by '3', L's and U's by '7', and R's and U's by '9'. Then, this modified signature is checked against a table for matches.

Learning techniques have been applied to stroke recognition, with some success. For instance, Boukreev[6] has implemented stroke recognition using neural networks. This technique involves recording the path of the stroke, smoothing it to base points, translating it to the sines and cosines of the points' angles, and then passing these values to a neural network. The neural network will try to recognize the stroke, and in the process of doing so, will actually improve its recognizing capability.

Its range of uses over the past three decades illustrates a key characteristic of stroke recognition as an input technique: it is not tightly bound to a particular device. Our aim in this research is to exploit this characteristic to develop an input technique that can be used seamlessly across the wide range of devices in a mobile-populated, pervasive computing world.

The diverse characteristics of such devices, and potential future devices, impose key requirements on such an interaction technique. At one end of the scale, the user may wish to interact with a device as limited in processing power and surface area as a smart ring or credit card, perhaps using a stylus to make the gestures. At the other end of the scale, the user may wish to interact with a wall-size display, perhaps using the smart ring itself, or indeed using just the user's hand, to make the gestures in the air. Igarashi et al. [2000] present a framework for using wall-sized displays using pen input. They describe how defining different application behaviours can provide a means of dealing with input strokes in different ways.

The work reported here presents a technique for recognizing input strokes which can be used successfully on devices with very low processing capabilities and very limited space for the input area. The technique is based on the user's denoting a direction rather than an actual shape and has the twin benefits of computational efficiency and a very small input area requirement. We have demonstrated the technique with mouse input on a desktop computer, stylus and touchscreen input on a wearable computer and hand movement input using real-time video capture.

4   Directional Stroke Recognition

We have developed a technique for directional stroke recognition. As its name implies, this is a technique for recognizing strokes based solely on their direction. Other characteristics of a stroke are not used. For instance, the position of a stroke is of no importance, nor are the relative positions of several strokes.

---

[6]http://www.generation5.org/aisolutions/gestureapp.shtml

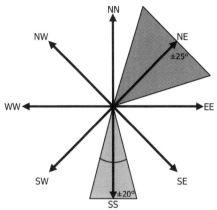

For consistency purposes, every direction is represented by a two letter combination. Therefore, North, East, South, and West are represented as NN, EE, SS, and WW respectively.

Figure 1: Calculating the direction of a line.

4.1   Stroke Recognition

The first step of our stroke recognition method is to collect the input data. Typically, the data for a stroke performed by the user is a set of coordinates. Our method regards the input stroke as an ordered set of lines. Each line consists of a 'fromPoint' and a 'toPoint'. Using these two coordinates, we can calculate the direction of each line as shown in Figure 1.

Humans tend to be more accurate at drawing vertical and horizontal lines than diagonals [Pirhonen et al. 2002], especially when on the move. Therefore, by adjusting the relative angle for acceptance, e.g. a variation of 25° for diagonals and 20° for other strokes, we may accommodate inaccuracy in stroke direction.

At this stage we have a stream of 'directions', for example: "SS, SS, SS, SS, WW, WW, WW, WW, NW, NW, NW". The next step is to remove noise from this stream. This is achieved by setting a threshold as a percentage of the length of the whole stroke. This threshold is applied by removing any sequence of identical directions that does not reach the threshold. So, for example, for a threshold value of 10% and a stroke recorded as a stream of 40 directions, any contiguous sequence of fewer than 4 identical directions would be removed.

It is worth noting that this method performs very badly when given a stroke which resembles a curve. Because a curve is a sequence of lines which continuously changes direction, our method would calculate that the whole curve is noise, and thus would not be able to recognize it.

Having removed the noise, we then reduce adjacent appearances of a given direction to just one occurrence. At this point, we are left with a 'signature' that looks, for example, like "SS, WW, NW". Using the signature that we have derived from the stroke, we can execute predefined operations. Some sample strokes along with their signatures are shown in Figure 2.

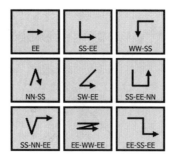

Note that strokes like NN-SS and EE-WW-EE do not need to form an angle, but are shown like this for illustration purposes.

Figure 2: Some strokes and their signatures.

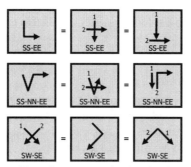

For any possible stroke, users may decide to break up the stroke into any number of sub-strokes, and then perform each sub-stroke independently, regardless of its relative position to the rest of the sub-strokes.

Figure 3: Different strokes with identical signatures.

4.2   Multi-stroke Gestures

The next development of our method was to recognize gestures that consist of more than one stroke. In order to allow users to perform multi-stroke gestures, the GUI has to allow for a short 'timeout' period, in which the user is able to stop drawing a stroke and start drawing a new stroke. For example, in the case of pen input, the user would be able to draw a stroke, lift the pen, and within the timeout period start drawing a new stroke. In this case, a special symbol may be used in the input stream to denote that the pen was lifted.

Having allowed for gestures consisting of more than one stroke, we have introduced an interesting characteristic. Now, different gestures may map to the same signature. Thus, a signature and, in turn, an operation can have more than one way of being accessed. For example, a stroke that looks like L and a gesture that looks like a cross may have the same signature, as shown in Figure 3.

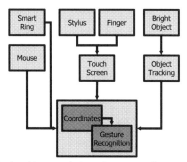

Any method and input technique that can produce a meaningful set of coordinates may be used with our stroke recognition technique.

Figure 4: Stroke recognition used with various techniques.

This sort of flexibility is beneficial when users may be working with multiple devices, each with different form factors and characteristics. In the case where screen size is limited, users may choose to decompose a gesture as finely as they wish, even into separate single-line strokes. The single-line strokes may be performed on top of each other, thus requiring less space on the screen. On the other hand, users with enough space may choose to perform one long composite stroke in order to save time.

It may be argued that the number of possible operations is limited when many gestures are mapped to the same signature. Although this is true, we believe that in many cases the flexibility provided by our method outweighs the need for a plethora of different operations. The optimum solution is probably to allow the user to choose between different gestures mapping to the same or different signatures, perhaps according to the visual similarity of gestures as described in [Long et al. 2000]. Rubine [1991], for example, demonstrates an approach to training a system for various gestures. This is a focus of our ongoing work.

5 Real-time Video Capture of Hand Movements as Input

In principle, our stroke recognition method deals with pure coordinates and nothing more. Therefore, any input technique could work with our stroke recognition method, as long as there is a meaningful way of deriving a set of coordinates from the input technique. This supports our aim of developing a flexible interaction technique that can be used across multiple devices and platforms (Figure 4). For example, in the converging world of mobile and pervasive computing, our user may at one moment wish to interact with her PDA using a common set of gestures and in the next moment move seamlessly to interacting with the wall display beside her using the same set of gestures. At one moment the PDA provides the interaction area on which the gestures are made using a stylus; in the next moment, the PDA itself becomes the 'stylus' as our user makes the gestures in the air with the PDA while interacting with the wall display. As a proof of principle, we implemented a real-time object tracking technique that we then used along with our stroke recognition algorithm as an input technique.

For our prototype we implemented an algorithm that performs real-time object tracking on live input from a Web camera. The user can select a specific object by sampling its colour, and the algorithm tracks this object in order to generate a series of coordinates that describe the position of the object on the screen or, to be precise, the position of the object relative to the camera's view. We then pass these generated coordinates to our stroke recognition algorithm, which then proceeds with the recognition of the strokes.

Due to the characteristics of our stroke recognition method, the coordinates may be supplied at any rate. So long as this rate is kept steady, the stroke recognition is very successful. Thus, despite the fact that our object tracking algorithm is not optimal, it still provides us with a useful prototype.

Object recognition is performed using HSL (Hue – Saturation – Luminosity) sampling. The object to be tracked is described in terms of HSL based on its colour. We then apply a varying threshold of approximately 5% to the live video input, which results in certain pixels being identified as belonging to the object. We then perform a second pass in order to identify which region has the highest density of object pixels, and from this we derive the object's centre. These coordinates are then passed on to the stroke recognition algorithm.

An issue that we had to address was how to allow for an act corresponding to lifting the stylus from a touch screen. Our initial approach has been that the user can, for example, hide the object within the palm of her hand. This does not limit functionality in terms of stroke recognition — remember that any signature can be performed as one long stroke — and contributes to the similarity of input methods across platforms and devices. A potentially less cumbersome solution to this would be to allow for an 'invisible' light, such as infrared, to be emitted from a small handheld object and to be used by the object-tracking camera. Such an object could be a dedicated input device for interacting with pervasive computing facilities and could emit light when squeezed or held at a certain orientation. Alternatively, and more in line with our general vision of integration across mobile and pervasive devices, a PDA or other device that can provide an input area (e.g. a touchscreen) for gestures could also act as a 'stylus' by emitting infrared on user demand. This would allow for seamless transitions, using a common gesture alphabet, between interacting with a mobile device and interacting with surrounding pervasive computing devices. We are currently developing this functionality as part of our ongoing research.

6 Conclusions and Future Work

We have incorporated the stroke recognition method described here in a test harness application. This has given encouraging results. For testing purposes, the stroke recognition method was implemented as a library in C++, and was used by an application written in Microsoft Visual C++. The testing platforms were:

- A standard desktop PC with conventional mouse input.

- A Xybernaut MA V wearable computer with touchscreen and pen input.

- A PC with 61 inch plasma display and camera picking up hand input.

The results have been very positive. For mouse and pen-based input the recognition rate peaked for a threshold of about 9%. For multi-stroke gestures, a timeout of 800 milliseconds produced the best results. Gestures consisting of up to five single-line strokes were readily recognized. The real-time video capture algorithm also produced encouraging results. We tested the method on both standing users with the camera facing them, and on sitting users with the camera above them facing down to their table. The main problem we faced was the speed at which objects were recognized and coordinates generated. We used a bright yellow tennis ball as our testing object. With the current implementation, the users had to move the tracked object quite slowly, because fast movements were not processed well. On average, for video input of dimensions 320×240 pixels, one frame every 200ms was processed. Although the strokes were recognized, it was frustrating for the users to move their hands at such speeds.

The main bottleneck in the existing implementation is rather naïve processing of the camera input. We have drawn in colleagues with expertise in computer vision in order to optimize this. Our collaboration with them should lead to improvements in usability by removing the current need for relatively slow hand gestures when using camera-based object tracking.

For further improvements at the subsequent stage of stroke recognition, we are developing a mechanism for adjusting the threshold for every sub-stroke, in order to increase the recognition rate. This will also allow for more sub-strokes to be recognized.

Our ongoing work includes developing and evaluating a range of applications which use the stroke recognition method. Usability evaluation issues include the question of mapping multiple gestures to one or more signatures. Further work will evaluate alternative strategies for this mapping, including user-definable strategies.

The stroke recognition method is usable on small devices with limited processing capabilities and small input areas. Typical current PDAs stand at the upper end of this scale. The method is of potential value for even smaller devices, such as rings, buttons and smart cards, for example. Moving in the opposite direction in scale, the method can also be applied to live graphic input and on wall-sized display areas. As we have demonstrated, a user may hold an object or even attach it to her fingers as, for example, a ring, in order to perform strokes in the air, on a table or on an interactive surface [cf. Rekimoto 2002].

Any other way of providing a set of coordinates can also be used with our stroke recognition method. To expand the range of input options in a pervasive computing environment, we are exploring the generation of coordinates by users' hand gestures without an object acting as a 'stylus'. To this end, we are beginning research with colleagues in sports science to develop alternative input methods using body tracking technologies. Thus, our stroke recognition method has great potential value in exploring and developing common interaction techniques that will allow us successfully to take the human-computer interface out into our streets and wider lives.

References

Brewster, S. A. [2002], Overcoming the Lack of Screen Space on Mobile Computers, *Personal and Ubiquitous Computing* **6**(3), 188–205.

Brewster, S. A., Lumsden, J., Bell, M., Hall, M. & Tasker, S. [2003], Multi-modal "Eyes Free" Interaction Techniques for Wearable Devices, *in* G. Cockton & P. Korhonen (eds.), *Proceedings of CHI'03 Conference on Human Factors in Computing Systems, CHI Letters* **5**(1), ACM Press, pp.473–80.

Callahan, J., Hopkins, D., Weiser, M. & Shneiderman, B. [1998], An Empirical Comparison of Pie vs. Linear Menus, *in* M. E. Atwood, C.-M. Karat, A. Lund, J. Coutaz & J. Karat (eds.), *Proceedings of the CHI'98 Conference on Human Factors in Computing Systems*, ACM Press, pp.95–100.

Guimbretiere, F. & Winograd, T. [2000], FlowMenu: Combining Command, Text and Data Entry, *in* M. Ackerman & K. Edwards (eds.), *Proceedings of the 13th Annual ACM Symposium on User Interface Software and Technology, UIST2000, CHI Letters* **2**(2), ACM Press, pp.213–7.

Guimbretiere, F., Stone, M. & Winograd, T. [2001], Fluid Interaction with High-resolution Wall-size Displays, *in* J. Marks & E. Mynatt (eds.), *Proceedings of the 14th Annual ACM Symposium on User Interface Software and Technology, UIST2001, CHI Letters* **3**(2), ACM Press, pp.21–30.

Igarashi, T., Edwards, W. K., LaMarca, A. & Mynatt, E. D. [2000], An Architecture for Pen-based Interaction on Electronic Whiteboards, *in* S. Levialdi, V. di Gesu & L. Tarantino (eds.), *Proceedings of the Working Conference on Advanced Visual Interfaces*, ACM Press, pp.68–75.

Long, A. C., Landay, J. A., Rowe, L. A. & Michiels, J. [2000], Visual Similarity of Pen Gestures, *in* T. Turner & G. Szwillus (eds.), *Proceedings of the CHI'00 Conference on Human Factors in Computing Systems, CHI Letters* **2**(1), ACM Press, pp.360–7.

Pirhonen, A., Brewster, S. & Holguin, C. [2002], Gestural and Audio Metaphors as a Means of Control for Mobile Devices, *in* D. Wixon (ed.), *Proceedings of CHI'02 Conference on Human Factors in Computing Systems: Changing our World, Changing Ourselves, CHI Letters* **4**(1), ACM Press, pp.291–8.

Rekimoto, J. [2002], SmartSkin: An Infrastructure for Freehand Manipulation on Interactive Surfaces, *in* D. Wixon (ed.), *Proceedings of CHI'02 Conference on Human Factors in Computing Systems: Changing our World, Changing Ourselves, CHI Letters* **4**(1), ACM Press, pp.113–20.

Rubine, D. [1991], Specifying Gestures by Example, *in* J. J. Thomas (ed.), *Proceedings of the Conference on Computer Graphics and Interactive Techniques*, ACM Press, pp.329–37.

Sutherland, I. [1963], Sketchpad: A Man–Machine Graphical Communication System, *in Proceedings of the Spring Joint Computer Conference*, IFIP, pp.329–46.

Zhao, R. [1993], Incremental Recognition in Gesture-based and Syntax-directed Diagram Editors, *in* S. Ashlund, K. Mullet, A. Henderson, E. Hollnagel & T. White (eds.), *Proceedings of INTERCHI'93*, ACM Press/IOS Press, pp.95–100.

Look or Listen: Discovering Effective Techniques for Accessing Speech Data

Steve Whittaker & Julia Hirschberg

Department of Information Studies, University of Sheffield, Regent Court, 211 Portobello Street, Sheffield S1 4DP, UK

Tel: *+44 114 222 6340*

Fax: *+44 114 278 0300*

Email: *s.whittaker@shef.ac.uk*

Commercial interfaces for accessing digital speech data are based on 'tape recorder' metaphors. However, such interfaces make it highly laborious to access complex speech data. The absence of effective interfaces is a major obstacle to exploiting the increasing number of speech archives now available online. More novel research interfaces provide potentially more effective access by presenting *visual* or *textual* indices into the underlying speech data. The current experimental study evaluates the utility of these newer techniques compared with a 'tape recorder' interface. We compare:

1. **High-level Visual Overviews showing the distribution and density of user query terms.**
2. **Textual Transcripts generated using state of the art ASR.**
3. **A tape recorder baseline.**

Laboratory tests showed that, contrary to our expectations, high-level visual information proved more useful than textual information, although both perform better than a tape-recorder baseline. Visual overviews enable users to quickly identify relevant regions to be played. In contrast, Textual transcripts can mislead users who try to extract detailed information solely by reading the transcript, without listening to the underlying speech.

Keywords: speech browsing, speech recognition, transcripts, visualization, laboratory study, evaluation, speech-as-data, multimedia access.

1 Introduction

Recently, there have been major increases in the amounts of data stored in digital speech archives. Broadcasting companies have made radio programmes available, public records such as the US Congressional Debates are being archived, and large private archives of audio conferences and voice mail can be cheaply stored for subsequent reference. Furthermore, better tools could exploit other types of speech record, such as recordings of meetings [Arons 1994], or telephone calls [Hindus et al. 1993; Wilcox et al. 1994]. However, these archives are currently under-utilized, in large part due to the absence of effective user-centred techniques for speech access.

Browsing speech is difficult because of limitations in human ability to extract information from sequential media. In contrast, experiments on extracting information from texts show that people do not read these sequentially or in their entirety. Instead they quickly visually scan text, focusing on content as opposed to function words, exploiting structural information (such as headings) and looking for key words to find regions that merit detailed further processing [Askwall 1985; Oakhill & Garnham 1988].

Such a strategy is not possible with speech, which has to be processed sequentially. The absence of explicit speech structure makes it hard to control information processing to proactively focus on important, and ignore irrelevant information. Furthermore, when users try to scan ahead in speech, they often experience difficulties in remembering what they have already listened to. For example, a study of information extraction from a 4-minute corpus of short voice mail messages using a 'tape-recorder' interface showed that users repeatedly replayed material they had already heard [Whittaker et al. 1998b]. This suggests people have problems with remembering both the structure of the message and also the details of what they have just heard. Clearly these access problems will be exacerbated when accessing large databases containing hundreds of hours of speech.

However, a number of recent speech browsing tools potentially overcome these limitations of sequential access. These tools rely on constructing different types of external indices into the speech record. These indices enable users to focus on relevant speech regions for detailed processing, while ignoring less relevant information. Two main types of index have been developed: high-level visual and textual indices. High-level visual representations include information about: speakers [Hindus et al. 1993; Oard 1997; Kazman et al. 1996], emphasis [Arons 1994; Wilcox et al. 1994], or visual events such as key frames in accompanying video [Christel et al. 1998; Drucker et al. 2002; Kazman et al. 1996]. The second technique of constructing textual indices works in the following way: textual indices are derived by applying automatic speech recognition (ASR) to recorded speech. The textual transcript is time-aligned with the corresponding speech. Even though the ASR transcript contains errors where the original speech is mis-recognized, it can still be effective for accessing the underlying speech. Users can read or search the transcript, select relevant regions and play the related speech [Kazman et al. 1996; Whittaker et al. 1999, 2002].

There have been several evaluations of combined textual and high-level visual indices [Kazman et al. 1996; Whittaker et al. 1999, 2002]. These found objective benefits to combining both high-level visual and textual indices when compared with a 'tape-recorder' style interface. Of course, however, the design of these studies makes it hard to determine which type of index — textual or high-level — was more useful in supporting information extraction from speech.

Our study attempts to compare the utility of textual and high-level visual indices, to determine which technique is more useful for accessing speech. As a control, we evaluate each of these against a baseline 'tape-recorder' UI that supports sequential access. Our expectation was that textual indices will be more effective than visual ones, because the information presented in visual interfaces is a *subset* of that provided by textual ones. Contrary to our predictions, we find that high-level visual indices are more effective than automatic textual indices, although both are better than a 'tape-recorder' UI. Both supported browsing better than the tape-recorder interface. We conclude by discussing the design and theory implications of our findings, and provide an explanation for these unexpected results.

2   Overall System

We compare three different types of interfaces for speech browsing in the context of a system that allows querying and retrieval of a large archive of speech 'documents' such as news stories [Garofolo et al. 2000]. Specifically, we contrast the effects on browsing of providing:

- High level visual structural information relevant to a user's query.

- Textual information provided by an ASR generated transcript of the speech.

- A tape recorder player.

Prior research shows that ASR accuracy is an important determinant of speech browsing performance using transcripts [Stark et al. 2000]. Obviously, with perfect ASR transcripts users can extract information directly from the transcripts without needing to play them. And if transcript quality is poor then users have to rely on playing the entire story. In this study, we used state of the art ASR. Our mean word error rate (28%) matched that for this class of data in the latest public evaluation [Garofolo et al. 2000]. Other recent evaluations show that this level of ASR quality is state of the art for other classes of spontaneous speech data, e.g. voice mail and human–human dialogues[1].

To make our experimental comparisons, we built a modular system that allowed us to enable and disable various UI components (see Figure 1). We first describe the overall system and then present the different experimental systems that people used in the three conditions.

2.1   *System Data, Segmentation and Querying*

The system provides access to broadcast news from the NIST/DARPA test set [Garofolo et al. 2000]. This dataset consists of recorded radio and TV news. It is made up of programmes such as current affairs discussions, breaking news and

---

[1] See the Web site at http://www.nist.gov/speech/.

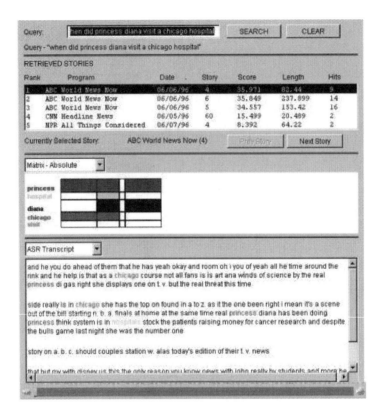

Figure 1: Modular User Interface.

headlines. The stations and programmes include: NPR: All Things Considered, ABC: World News Tonight, CNN: Early Primetime News, NPR Market Place.

Our system first transcribes the speech in order to generate the high level visual and textual representations. To do this, we segment the speech into 'audio paragraphs', using acoustic information, classify the recording conditions for every audio paragraph (narrow-band or other) and apply relevant acoustic and language models to each. Our recognizer uses a standard time-synchronous beam search algorithm operating on a weighted function transducer representing the context-dependency, lexical and language model constraints and statistics of the recognition task. Context-dependent phones are modelled with continuous density, three state, left to right hidden Markov models. State densities are modelled by mixtures of up to 12 diagonal covariance Gaussians over 39-dimensional vectors [Bacchiani et al. 2001].

We concatenate ASR results for each audio paragraph so that for every 'speech document' we have a corresponding (errorful) ASR transcript. As mentioned above word error rates averaged 28% in this experiment. When the speech recognizer makes errors, they are deletions, insertions and substitutions of the recognizer's vocabulary, rather than the types of non-word errors that are generated by OCR. So, if the target speech contains large numbers of words that are not in the recognizer's vocabulary, this leads to multiple word substitution errors. In addition, recognition errors often cascade: the underlying language model explicitly models inter-word relationships, so that one mis-recognition may lead to others. Finally function words tend to be mis-recognized more than content words.

Terms in each transcript are indexed for retrieval by the SMART IR engine [Salton 1971]. When the user types a query ("When did Princess Diana visit a Chicago hospital?") into the Search box at the top of the browser, the system searches the errorful transcripts for relevant documents (see Figure 1). Search results are depicted in the panel immediately below, as a relevance-ranked list of 5 'speech documents', corresponding to the 5 most relevant news stories. The user selects a story by clicking on it.

2.2   Visual Overview

The Visual Overview component is intended to provide high-level visual information about individual 'speech documents'. Users can rapidly scan this to locate potentially relevant audio regions within a story. It displays which query terms appear in each audio paragraph of the story. Each query word is colour-coded, and each audio paragraph is represented by a vertical column in a visual matrix. A similar technique is used for textual documents in [Hearst 1995]. Thus the word 'Chicago' occurs in the first and second audio paragraph and hence in the first and second matrix columns. The width of the matrix columns represents the relative length of each audio paragraph. The occurrences of different query term within a given audio paragraph are shown as blocks within the same column. For example, column 2 in the Overview in Figure 1 indicates that audio paragraph 2 contains instances of each of the words, 'princess', 'Diana', 'Chicago', and 'hospital'. Such co-occurrence of several query terms suggests a potentially highly relevant region within the 'document'.

Users can also examine the distribution of specific query terms by examining colour distributions across audio paragraphs. Most importantly, the visual index can be used to access speech. Users can directly access the speech for any audio paragraph by double clicking on the corresponding column. Selecting a column initiates play from the start of the corresponding audio paragraph. The Overview also supports global comparison between 'speech documents'. Visually comparing Overviews for multiple documents can suggest which have a greater density of query terms and hence contain potentially more relevant regions.

It is important to note that the success of the visualization depends on speech recognition quality. If key terms are incorrectly recognized, they will not be displayed in the Overview.

2.3   Transcript

The ASR Transcript is intended to provide detailed, if sometimes inaccurate, textual information about the contents of a story. It uses the same ASR transcripts that are used to support search. The Transcript panel displays a transcription of the selected story. Because the transcript has been generated automatically, it usually contains

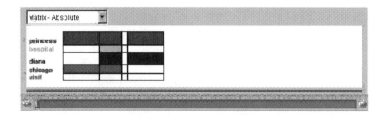

Figure 2: Overview and Player Interface providing high-level visual access.

errors (e.g. in paragraph 2 of the transcript in Figure 1, the first word 'Di' (as in Princess Di) is transcribed as 'side').

Query terms in the Transcript are highlighted and colour-coded, using the same coding scheme used in the Overview (e.g. the words 'Chicago' and 'princess' are highlighted in Figure 1, paragraph 1 of the Transcript). Users can play a given audio paragraph by double-clicking on the corresponding paragraph in the Transcript. Alternatively they can select a paragraph and click on the player to play that paragraph.

The Transcript has several potential functions. First, in regions where it is accurate, users can find relevant information simply by reading – without listening to the audio. Like the Overview, it supports rapidly visual scanning to find relevant regions in the audio. The Transcript also provides local contextual information: users can decide whether to play a particular audio paragraph by reading surrounding paragraphs to determine its likely relevance. Finally, overall Transcript quality can help users assess the likely accuracy of Transcript, search and overview information. For example, bizarre phrases like "story on abc should couples station ...'" (beginning of paragraph 3, Figure 1) indicate the Transcript is inaccurate suggesting to users that they should rely more on the audio rather than the Transcript.

2.4 Player

The player is shown at the bottom of Figure 1. The UI is analogous to a tape-recorder. Like most state of the art commercial speech players, it presents a simple play bar that in this case represents a single story. Users can insert the cursor at any point in the bar to indicate the position to begin playing. Start, fast-forward, rewind and stop operations are available to control play. The buttons shown in the player are context sensitive and change state in response to user's actions. For example the 'play' button on the right hand side of the player becomes a 'stop' button after play is started. The player may be used in isolation, or in combination with the Overview and Transcript once a paragraph or story has been selected.

2.5 The Three Experimental Systems

The goal of this study was to compare the utility of high level visual, textual and tape-recorder components. We therefore modified the modular system in three ways. In one condition, users had access to high-level visual, but no textual information (Figure 2). In the second, they had only textual information from the errorful

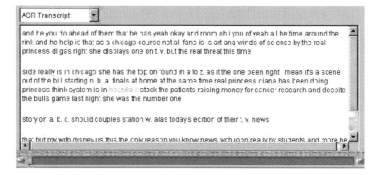

Figure 3: Transcript and Player Interface providing textual access.

Transcript (Figure 3). In both conditions they also had access to the Player. We compared these two experimental conditions with a control condition in which they only had access to the Player. The control represents the current state of the art for browsing tools, and we wanted to determine whether our two experimental UIs outperformed this baseline. In all conditions users were also able to change stories using the Header Panel. This panel was present in all experimental conditions but is not shown in Figures 2 & 3. It can be seen in Figure 1, however.

The current experiment was concerned with browsing and not search. We therefore disabled the search engine, giving users pre-generated queries so that they all accessed consistent sets of documents for each experimental task. We also removed all identifying information from the header panel about the stories (Programme Name, Duration, Relevance Score, Hits), as we did not want this external identifying information to influence users' browsing behaviour in the experiment.

3 Method

3.1 Tasks

We wanted to compare retrieval situations along several different dimensions, including: making global judgements about sets of 'speech documents', and locating specific information from within a 'document'. We therefore compared the three interfaces on the following two tasks that ethnographic studies [Whittaker et al. 1998a] indicated are representative of real-world user tasks with this type of data:

- Relevance Judgements — compare five news stories to determine which is most relevant to a given topic (e.g. "how good was Valujet's safety record prior to the Florida accident?").

- Fact-Finding — extract detailed factual information from a story to answer a specific question (e.g. "who starred in the Broadway musical 'Maggie Flynn'?").

The study was controlled by a sequence of Web pages, one for each task. At the start of each task, we automatically generated the pre-specified query and users were asked to carry out a given task associated with the query, using whichever of the three browser types (Overview, Transcript, Player-only) was presented on the page. So for example, users might be presented with the query: "how good was Valujet's safety record prior to the Florida accident?"), along with the Transcript browser, and a short description of the relevance judgement task, i.e. to identify which of five stories shown in the Header Panel was most relevant to the query. For all tasks, users could potentially access five stories, and our pre-specified queries meant that these were common across all users for a specific task. We attempted as far as possible to normalize story length across the tasks.

3.2   Procedure and Measures

The experimental design was randomized within subjects. Nineteen users (8 women and 11 men, ranging in age from 18–42) took part. Users were volunteers consisting of researchers, administrative staff and marketers at a large corporate research lab. They had no prior knowledge of the project or experimental hypotheses, but all were experienced users of standard PC software. The entire procedure took about an hour and users were given a small food reward for participating. They were first given a self-paced tutorial about how to use the overall system, followed by three trial tasks — with the Transcript, Overview and Player, to familiarize themselves with the technologies and the procedure. This normally took about 10 minutes.

Once users were ready to proceed with the experiment itself, we gave them a total of 12 tasks each (6 relevance and 6 fact finding). For one third of the tasks they used the Overview browser, for one third the Transcript browser and one third the Player only. The order of tasks was fixed, but we randomized the sequence in which different browsers were presented. Our prior studies showed that there is enormous variability between different users' performance and strategy in accessing audio data [Whittaker et al. 1998b, 1999, 2002]. Using a within-subjects experimental design allowed us to control for this variance by directly comparing users with their own baseline performance.

For each question we measured outcome information: time to solution and solution quality (as assessed by two independent judges). To determine solution quality, the judges listened to the relevant programmes in their entirety while reading perfect human generated transcripts of the original recordings that we provided them. They then agreed correct answers to all questions, independently scored users' responses (0–100 for each question) before verbally resolving scoring disagreements.

Previous research has demonstrated that users differ in the amount of time and effort they dedicate to optimize performance on these types of experimental tasks [Whittaker et al. 1999, 2002]. If users are prepared to spend a long time listening to broadcasts they have a much greater chance of success, whatever interface they are using. To control for this, we used a compound success measure in which success scores are normalized in terms of the time the user took to complete the task, i.e. score/(unit time). Our predictions below will focus on normalized success. For the sake of completeness, we will report independent time and quality scores, although we make no explicit predictions about these as independent measures.

We also collected information about the processes by which people answered each task. We logged each browser operation along with information about how much speech (if any) was played for that operation.

We also collected subjective data, by administering a short Web-based post-test questionnaire after each task. We asked users to judge the difficulty of the task they had just completed (on a 5 point Likert scale). If they had used the Transcript or Overview for that task, then we also asked them whether they would prefer to use the Transcript or Browser if they were to do that task again. Because we were interested in browsing strategies and processes, we also encouraged users to 'think aloud' as they carried out the tasks, and we tape-recorded their statements.

3.3 Hypotheses

We made predictions about Outcome, Task Effects, Processes (i.e. playing behaviour) and Subjective Judgements. We first present motivation for our experimental hypotheses, then our results for each hypothesis:

Outcome: Overall we expected users to perform better with the Transcript than the Overview. The Transcript provides richer information than the Overview. Both afford a way to quickly see the distribution of query terms across audio paragraphs, allowing access to relevant areas of underlying speech. However the Transcript also provides additional detailed information. It shows non-query terms that can be used to aid browsing in two ways. If the Transcript is accurate then information can be read directly from it. If the Transcript is inaccurate, these other terms may still provide a finer grained index to access and play relevant regions of the underlying speech. These led us to predict the superiority of the Transcript compared with the Overview.

We also expected both Overview and Transcript to perform better than the Player. The additional information that each provides about the distribution of query hits should provide greater control over what gets played.

Tasks: We also expected task differences. We expected the Transcript to better support Relevance judgements than the Overview, again because it provides richer information. Although the Transcript may contain errors, it should still enable users to determine the gist of a story without playing it. In contrast, the Overview provides only rudimentary information about a story, necessitating playing parts of the story to judge its Relevance. The other task, Fact-finding, requires detailed and accurate analysis of stories. As neither the Overview nor Transcript provides this, we expected performance to be equivalent. We expected both Overview and Transcript to perform better than Player for both tasks, because of the more detailed information each provides.

Amount of Speech Played and Number of Play Operations: We expected more play operations, and more speech to be played overall in the Overview than the Transcript condition. This is because the Transcript should enable people to extract information by reading rather than playing. Even when the Transcript is inaccurate, the additional lexical information it provides should still allow users to determine the overall gist of the story by reading. We therefore also expect Transcripts to reduce both the number of play operations and the amount played more in the Relevance-judgement than the Fact-finding task We expected the smallest number of play operations in the Player condition, because we anticipated that the lack of structural information in the Player would lead users to simply play messages from beginning to end. This uninterrupted play strategy should mean that users have fewer play operations but play more speech overall with the Player, than the Overview and Transcript.

Subjective Judgements: We expected these to be closely related to outcome and play operations, so that the Transcript should be perceived as making tasks easier than the Overview. Both should be judged to make tasks easier than the Player. Overall users should prefer the Transcript to the Overview when asked to choose between these.

4   Results

We tested the predictions using Analysis of Variance (ANOVA). In all analyses, we used the following independent variables: Browser (Transcript vs. Overview vs. Player), and Task (Fact-finding vs. Relevance). The respective dependent variables were: normalized success score, amount of speech played, number of play operations, and perceived task difficulty. The results are shown in Tables 1 & 2. Table 1 shows overall data independent of task, while Table 2 shows task interactions. The results for each hypothesis were as follows:

Outcome differences: We expected people to generate better solutions more quickly with the Transcript than the Overview. Both should be better than the Player.

Our predictions were not confirmed (as Table 1 shows). Overall, we found that there were differences between browsers for the normalized success measure ($F(2,234) = 13.4$, $p < 0.001$). Contrary to our prediction, however, planned comparisons showed that users performed better with the Overview than the Transcript browser ($p < 0.05$). As predicted planned comparisons showed that users performed better with the Overview and Transcript than the Player ($p < 0.001$ and $p < 0.05$ respectively).

Time to solution results were identical ($F(2,234) = 14.3$, $p < 0.001$), with post-hoc differences between Overview and Transcript and between Transcript and Player. However success scores showed a slightly different pattern: browsers were different ($F(2,234) = 6.4$, $p < 0.005$), and Overviews scores were better post hoc than Transcript and Player, but there were no post hoc differences between Transcript and Player.

Task differences: We expected that users would perform better with the Transcript than the Overview in the Relevance-judgement task. We expected equivalent

	Overview	Transcript	Player	Statistical Significance?
Mean Normalized Performance	0.57	0.36	0.24	O > T > P
Mean Time to Solution (s)	227.1	262.3	397.3	O < T < P
Mean Success Score (%)	86.1	76.8	76.6	O > T = P
Mean Amount of Speech Played (s)	123.9	37.6	237.8	T < O < P
Mean # of Play Operations	15.3	11.0	7.23	O = T > P
Mean Perceived Task Difficulty (1=very hard, 5=very easy)	3.5	3.1	2.6	O = T > P

Table 1: Effects of Browser on Outcome, Process and Subjective Measures.

performance between browsers for the Fact-finding task. We expected that both would be better than the Player for both tasks.

There was an interaction between task and browser ($F(2,234) = 6.5$, $p < 0.005$). Again, however, as Table 2 shows, our comparisons between Overview and Transcript contradicted the Task hypothesis. Planned comparisons showed that users did not perform better with the Transcript for Relevance judgement tasks ($p > 0.05$). Instead users performed better with the Overview for Fact-finding tasks ($p < 0.05$). As predicted, planned comparisons showed that Overview and Transcript performed better than Player for each task (all $p < 0.05$), except when the Transcript was used for Fact-finding ($p > 0.05$).

Amount of Speech Played and Number of Play Operations: The Transcript should enable users to play less speech and use fewer play operations overall than the Overview browser. We also expected Transcripts to reduce the amount played and number of play operations more than the Overview for the Relevance-judgement task. There should be no differences for the Fact-finding task. Both Overview and Transcript should have more total play operations than the Player, and less overall speech played.

Table 1 shows our predictions were confirmed about the effects of the browsers on the amount of speech people played. People played different amounts of speech with the different browsers ($F(2,234) = 42.7$, $p < 0.001$). Planned comparisons showed as predicted, that users played less speech when using the Transcript than the Overview ($p < 0.001$). Both Transcript and Overview had less playing than the Player (both $p < 0.001$).

There was an expected interaction between browser and task ($F(2,234) = 3.7$, $p < 0.05$). As predicted (and as shown in Table 2), users played considerably

	Relevance Judgement			Fact finding		
	Overview	Transcript	Player	Overview	Transcript	Player
Mean Normalized Performance	0.29	0.29	0.18	0.84	0.42	0.31
Mean Amount of Speech Played (s)	193.4	045.1	295.8	054.4	030.0	179.7
Mean # of Play Operations	21.9	12.1	8.08	08.6	09.8	06.4
Mean Perceived Task Difficulty (5=very easy, 1=very hard)	2.90	2.90	2.33	4.10	3.20	2.80

Table 2: Effects of Task on Performance with Transcript, Overview and Player Browsers.

more speech using the Overview than Transcript for the Relevance-judgement task ($p < 0.001$). Planned comparisons between Overview and Transcript showed no differences between the amounts of speech users played on the Fact-finding task ($p > 0.05$).

Play Operations: The hypotheses are also partially confirmed for play operations. Table 1 shows there were different numbers of operations between the three browsers ($F(2,234) = 9.4$, $p < 0.001$). Contrary to predictions, however, planned comparisons show there were no differences between the Overview and Transcript ($p > 0.05$). Consistent with our predictions that there were fewer operations using the Player than either Overview or Transcript (both $p < 0.01$).

Table 2 shows there was an expected interaction between browser and task for play operations ($F(2,234) = 5.31$, $p < 0.01$). Planned comparisons between Overview and Transcript showed no differences between the number of play operations in the Fact-finding task ($p > 0.05$). As predicted, users had considerably more play operations with the Overview than Transcript for the Relevance-judgement task ($p < 0.001$).

Subjective judgements: We expected users to perceive tasks to be easier when using the Transcript compared with the Overview browser. When given a choice between the two browsers, we also expected them to express a preference for the Transcript browser. We expected tasks to be perceived as harder when using the Player, than both Overview and Transcript.

There were overall perceived differences between the browsers in their effects on task difficulty ($F(2,234) = 7.5$, $p < 0.001$). Contrary to our predictions, however, planned comparisons showed there were no overall differences between the Overview and Transcript browsers ($p > 0.05$). However when we asked users which of the two browsers they would choose for the task they had just completed, they chose the Overview 71% of the time. This is significant on a one-sample t

test ($t(155) = 3.5$, $p < 0.001$). As we predicted both Overview and Transcript were judged to make browsing tasks easier than the Player (both $p < 0.005$).

User comments: Our objective findings suggest that the Overview was useful for directing play operations for both tasks. User comments are consistent with this:

> "I used the Overview to direct my playing to regions where I thought there would be important information."

In contrast, users reported problems with the Transcript in the Fact-finding task, when they tried to access particular facts directly from the Transcript. For example one user tried to scan the Transcript for a specific word:

> "I thought that I could find the word 'found' in the Transcript, but it was like trying to find a needle in a haystack, because [the Transcript] was so bad."

5   Conclusions

What are the implications of this work? First we confirm previous studies showing the utility of ASR generated textual indices for speech browsing when compared with commercial UIs [Whittaker et al. 1999, 2002]. Our data show that Transcripts were more effective than the Player; they reduce the amount of speech users played – allowing users to identify specific regions of speech for detailed processing, or read information directly from Transcripts. However there are limitations to Transcripts that we discuss below. We also found good evidence for the utility of another interface technique, namely Overviews. Again these reduced the amount of speech that users played, by allowing them to focus on relevant regions.

Contrary to our expectations, however, high-level visual information provided by Overviews proved more useful than Transcripts. This is a significant result because it disconfirms our initial hypothesis, motivated by our belief that Transcripts provided more information than Overviews. Why then did users perform better with Overviews than Transcripts? One significant clue is offered by the fact that users played much more speech with Overviews. It seems that users may have relied too much on the errorful Transcripts, by trying to extract information from them directly by reading. Alternatively they may have spent too much time trying to decipher the meaning of the transcripts in order to better direct their playing.

The notion that transcripts can sometimes be misleading is consistent with the task data. We found that Overviews were better than Transcripts for fact-finding. Indeed Transcripts were no better than the Player for this task. Users played much more speech when using the Overview and Player than the Transcript for this task. This offers strong support for the view that users were sometimes misled into trying to extract detailed information directly — by reading errorful Transcripts. In contrast, people used the Overview to focus on important regions of speech, which they then played to extract information. On the Relevance Judgement task, there were no differences between the browsers. Both were better than the Player for this task. This indicates that Transcripts are reasonably effective for gisting information.

Here, users spent much more time playing speech with the Overview than with the Transcript, even though overall performance was equivalent in both tasks. This suggests that the costs that Overview users incurred in having to access more speech were balanced by the effort needed to gist information from poor Transcripts.

Of course, as we noted earlier, our findings about Transcripts are dependent on the quality of the actual Transcript. Perfect transcripts would enable users to reliably answer all questions by reading without having to play any of the underlying story. And other research confirms that transcript quality has a large effect on speech browsing [Stark et al. 2000]. However the data we report is for currently state of the art levels of ASR [Garofolo et al. 2000]. It also seems that ASR performance levels will not improve drastically in the next few years[2], making our findings important for the design of speech browsing systems in the near future.

We now turn to the design implications of our study. Our findings about the utility of Overviews suggest future research should focus on the development of novel visual representations of speech data. We also partially confirm earlier research in showing benefits for textual indices. However, our findings also suggest that users may spend time trying to directly decipher poor quality transcripts when they might be better employed playing the speech associated with these. What then might we do to preserve the demonstrated benefits of Transcripts, while preventing these maladaptive behaviours? One possibility is that we might use ASR confidence scores to present visual information about the quality of a Transcript, e.g. by greying out regions of the Transcript, where the ASR had low recognition confidence. This would signal to users when they can trust the transcript, and hence read information from it directly, and when they need to switch strategies and play the speech associated with it. Further research might be directed at other automatic methods for determining transcript quality, and hence indicating to users when the transcript can be read directly.

Finally, our unexpected and counterintuitive results, together with other observations of task-specificity, suggest that we need to combine the development of new techniques for speech access and browsing, with careful empirical work evaluating these effects.

Acknowledgements

Thanks to the users for donating their time to do the experiment.

References

Arons, B. [1994], Interactively Skimming Speech, PhD thesis, MIT Media Lab.

Askwall, S. [1985], Computer Supported Reading vs. Reading Text on Paper: A Comparison of Two Reading Situations, *International Journal of Man–Machine Studies* **22**(3), 425–39.

Bacchiani, M., Hirschberg, J., Rosenberg, A., Whittaker, S., Hindle, D., Isenhour, P., Jones, M., Stark, L. & Zamchick, G. [2001], SCANMail: Audio Navigation in the Voicemail Domain, *in* S. Young (ed.), *Proceedings of the Workshop on Human Language Technology*, IEEE Computer Society Press, pp.105–11.

---

[2]See the Web site at http://www.nist.gov/speech/.

Christel, M. G., Smith, M. A., Taylor, C. R. & Winkler, D. B. [1998], Evolving Video Skims into Useful Multimedia Abstractions, *in* M. E. Atwood, C.-M. Karat, A. Lund, J. Coutaz & J. Karat (eds.), *Proceedings of the CHI'98 Conference on Human Factors in Computing Systems*, ACM Press, pp.171–8.

Drucker, S. M., Glatzer, A., Mar, S. D. & Wong, C. [2002], Consumer Level Browsing and Skipping of Digital Video Content, *in* D. Wixon (ed.), *Proceedings of CHI'02 Conference on Human Factors in Computing Systems: Changing our World, Changing Ourselves*, *CHI Letters* **4**(1), ACM Press, pp.219–26.

Garofolo, J., Lard, J. & Voorhees, E. [2000], TREC-9 Spoken Document Retrieval Track, http://www.nist.gov/speech/tests/sdr/sdr2000/sdr2000.htm (last accessed 2003.05.26).

Hearst, M. A. [1995], TileBars: Visualisation of Term Distribution Information in Full Text Information Access, *in* I. Katz, R. Mack, L. Marks, M. B. Rosson & J. Nielsen (eds.), *Proceedings of the CHI'95 Conference on Human Factors in Computing Systems*, ACM Press, pp.59–66.

Hindus, D., Schmandt, C. & Horner, C. [1993], Capturing, Structuring and Representing Ubiquitous Audio, *ACM Transactions on Office Information Systems* **11**(3), 34–51.

Kazman, R., Al-Halimi, R., Hunt, W. & Mantei, M. [1996], Four Paradigms for Indexing Videoconferences, *IEEE Multimedia* **3**(1), 63–73.

Oakhill, J. & Garnham, A. [1988], *Becoming a Skilled Reader*, Blackwell.

Oard, D. [1997], Speech Based Information Retrieval for Digital Libraries, *in* M. Maybury (ed.), *Proceedings of AAAI Spring Symposium On Cross Language Text and Speech*, AAAI Press, pp.34–42.

Salton, G. [1971], *The SMART Retrieval System*, Prentice–Hall.

Stark, L., Whittaker, S. & Hirschberg, J. [2000], ASR Satisficing: The Effects of ASR Accuracy on Speech Retrieval, *in* A. Black (ed.), *Proceedings of International Conference on Spoken Language Processing*, IEEE Publications, pp.34–8.

Whittaker, S., Hirschberg, J., Amento, B., Stark, L., Bacchiani, M., Isenhour, P., Stead, L., G., Z. & Rosenberg, A. [2002], SCANMail: A Voicemail Interface That Makes Speech Browsable, Readable and Searchable, *in* D. Wixon (ed.), *Proceedings of CHI'02 Conference on Human Factors in Computing Systems: Changing our World, Changing Ourselves*, *CHI Letters* **4**(1), ACM Press, pp.275–82.

Whittaker, S., Hirschberg, J., Choi, J., Hindle, D., Pereira, F. & Singhal, A. [1999], SCAN: Designing and Evaluating User Interfaces to Support Retrieval from Speech Archives, *in* F. Gey, M. Hearst & R. Tong (eds.), *SIGIR'99 Proceedings of the 22nd Annual International ACM SIGIR Conference on Research and Development in Information Retrieval*, ACM Press, pp.26–33.

Whittaker, S., Hirschberg, J. & Nakatani, C. [1998a], All Talk and All Action: Strategies for Managing Voicemail Messages, *in* C.-M. Karat & A. Lund (eds.), *CHI'98 Conference Summary of the Conference on Human Factors in Computing Systems*, ACM Press, pp.249–50.

Whittaker, S., Hirschberg, J. & Nakatani, C. [1998b], Play It Again: A Study of the Factors Underlying Speech Browsing Behaviour, *in* C.-M. Karat & A. Lund (eds.), *CHI'98 Conference Summary of the Conference on Human Factors in Computing Systems*, ACM Press, pp.247–8.

Wilcox, L., Chen, F., D., K. & Balasubramanian, V. [1994], Segmentation of Speech Using Speaker Identification, *in* S. Isard (ed.), *Proceedings of International Conference on Computer Speech and Signal Processing*, IEEE Publications, pp.234–8.

E-commerce

Social and Cultural Obstacles to the (B2C) E-Commerce Experience

Liisa Dawson, Shailey Minocha & Marian Petre

Department of Maths and Computing, The Open University, Walton Hall, Milton Keynes MK7 6AA, UK

Tel: *+44 1908 858806*

Email: *{L.H.Dawson, S.Minocha, M.Petre}@open.ac.uk*

Not only is creating value and generating a total customer experience important for e-commerce in order to *attract* customers — with increasing competition in the marketplace, it is becoming increasingly difficult to *retain* customers. This paper addresses a perspective on how e-commerce environments can provide value to the customers to build long-term relationships and reduce customer defections. The paper presents findings of a 'naturalistic' user-observation study that investigated barriers that can prevent customers from achieving a satisfactory experience with an e-commerce environment. The data from this study suggests that there are patterns or themes of social, cultural and organizational obstacles that influence customer's perception of value and experience with an e-commerce environment.

The paper integrates these 'themes of obstacles' into a conceptual framework for evaluating the service quality of e-commerce environments. This framework is intended to help organizations identify the obstacles that mar a customer's experience. Conversely, organizations will be able to identify the Customer Relationship Management (CRM) strategies or heuristics that can enhance the quality of the e-commerce experience as perceived by the customers.

The paper argues that an organization whose Web site is usable in HCI terms (that satisfies the Web Design heuristics / e-commerce guidelines) might not always generate a valuable customer experience. It is important that along with usability heuristics, CRM strategies are integrated into the design of the e-commerce environment for developing robust, long-term, online customer–organization relationships, and consequently, customer retention.

Keywords: e-commerce, usability, total customer experience, obstacles, SERVQUAL, service quality, customer relationship management (CRM).

1 Introduction

Despite the recent collapse of many dot-coms, Business to Consumer (B2C) e-commerce has grown. In November 2002 alone, UK shoppers spent more than £1billion on the Internet. Spending was double the previous year's, with 43% of homes online in the UK and many accessing the Internet from work. Spending is expected to rise[1]: in the UK, online sales make up 4% of the total retail sales; in the US, B2C e-commerce is predicted to reach $269billion by 2005.

In the expanding space that is the Internet, companies need first to ensure that they distinguish themselves from their competitors, but also to ensure that their click-through rates are optimized. Statistics show that 67% of transactions on the Web are never completed [Cohen 1999].

Only 36% of customers are satisfied by electronic transactions, and this bad experience tends to drive customers to other channels [Chatham 2002]. Of the transactions that are not completed, 53% of abandoned transactions require a phone call or off-line action. This has a knock on effect, as call centre costs rise due to increased call volumes — with a reported rate of increase in volume of up to 65% as Internet use increases [Millard 2001].

In the Human–Computer Interaction (HCI) literature, research into the success or failure of (B2C) e-commerce sites has focused primarily on the usability of the core Web site [e.g. Nielsen et al. 2001; Spool et al. 1999; Vividence 2002]. Central to this has been how design criteria such as ease of navigation, optimal response time, and appropriate content can be managed to create usable customer-focused e-commerce sites. Research in HCI / Usability concerning e-commerce has largely been concerned with identifying heuristics or guidelines for designing 'usable' Web sites.

A growing body of research is now beginning to address the problems of designing e-commerce sites that suit the cultural needs of local users. In our recent work on cross-cultural usability [Smith et al. 2001; French et al. 2002], we have proposed a framework of cultural 'attractors' which when embedded into e-commerce sites will help to match the culture of the intended local audience. Examples of these attractors are colours and colour combinations, use of culturally specific symbols and iconography, linguistic cues, religious iconography and charity giving, and focusing on locally significant brand identities.

On the other hand, some researchers have been concerned about the internationalization of e-commerce environments, that is, designing for the global market. Becker & Mottay [2001] discuss that many dot-com failures have happened because of lack of corporate vision in addressing global aspects of online marketing. They argue that cultural diversity and sensitivity must be considered in order to ensure that the e-shopping experience is the same for every customer regardless of

---

[1]BBC Business News, December 2002, http://news.bbc.co.uk/1/hi/business/2574627.stm

locality. They state that the strategic goals of an organization should be customer-driven rather than being driven by short-term financial gains or time-to-market. Becker & Mottay [2001] propose the use of a Web-based usability assessment model that promotes customer satisfaction and online experience as an integral part of an e-business development process. Some of the usability factors in this model are page layout, navigation, design consistency, reliability, security, information content, and cultural sensitivity in contrast to the 'local needs' approach. Cultural sensitivity involves avoidance of country- (or culture-) centric elements such as colours, icons, terminology, animations, images, etc. when designing for a global market.

Another way in which HCI has approached the design and evaluation of e-commerce environments has been to explore the notion of the quality of customer experience. Zhang & von Dran [2001] have proposed a framework of quality factors of Web sites that address customers' perceptions and quality expectations from an e-commerce environment. Their quality model aims to:

> "systematically examine the features commonly used in Web site design." [Zhang & von Dran 2001, p.13]

Their categories of quality factors for Web design include security, privacy, information representation, cognitive outcomes, information content, visual appearance, navigation, credibility, etc. Based upon evidence generated from empirical studies of six domains in e-business (Finance, e-commerce, Education, Government, Entertainment, and Medicine / Health), the authors have suggested that customers do not regard all quality factors to be equally important and that the rankings of quality factors differ from one Web domain to another.

Even though Zhang & von Dran's considerations of customers' perceptions and behaviours in e-commerce environments have extended the existing HCI studies of e-commerce into the marketing discipline, it is evident from the relationship marketing literature [e.g. Payne et al. 1995; Christopher et al. 1991] that such a uni-dimensional focus on Web design features and usability of an e-commerce site ignores the broader service delivery system within which the virtual customer-organization interaction occurs. In developing robust long-term customer-organization relationships it is the operation of this service delivery system, which is critical, irrespective of whether the customer interaction occurs off-line or online.

The question then is how can the Customer Relationship Management (CRM) strategies, be engineered into e-commerce environments? Against this backdrop, the aim of the research reported here has been to identify factors — in addition to usability problems — which might make a customer dissatisfied with one or more aspects of his experience with an e-commerce environment. This is part of a larger research programme which aims to determine how service quality and hence CRM strategies can be incorporated into the design of e-commerce operations so as to engender customer retention, trust, and loyalty. This larger research project embodies a cross-disciplinary approach integrating relationship marketing and HCI.

In order to examine why customers may be prevented or discouraged from returning to a Web site, the study reported here focused on negative experiences encountered by e-commerce customers. This paper discusses, in the first instance, the methodology employed in this study. It then presents a flavour of the findings in a 'catalogue of obstacles'. Finally it compares the catalogue of obstacles to two current frameworks in the marketing literature: a model of Web site design features presented by Zhang & von Dran [2001], and e-SERVQUAL [Zeithaml et al. 2002], which aims to identify a customer's perception of service quality of an e-commerce environment.

2 Service Quality and Customer Loyalty

An *e-commerce* environment implies not only the front-end of the e-commerce, which is the Web-based retail site, but also the back-office systems such as the security of credit card handling, delivery of products / services, post-sales support and contact with staff. In an e-commerce environment, the users are *customers*. A customer is willing to do business with an e-commerce environment only if he gets *value* from his exchange with it.

2.1 The Total Customer Experience

The *Total Customer Experience* (TCE) encompasses all stages of a customer's interaction with an e-commerce environment. The three stages of a customer's interaction with an e-commerce environment constitute a *service encounter* [Gabbott & Hogg 1998]: a pre-encounter stage; an encounter with the e-shopping site; and finally a post-encounter (or post-transaction) The TCE is the customer's holistic experience over all the three stages of this service encounter. The breadth of the TCE highlights that it is not only the physical design of the Web site — the retail front-end of the organization and its usability, or the price of the product / service, but the entire purchase (and after care) experience that influences customer satisfaction and perception of value.

Value from a customer perspective may be defined in terms of satisfaction with, and perceived quality of, the service received in the course of the TCE. Creating value and generating a positive TCE is important for e-commerce environments in order to acquire and retain customers. E-commerce environments need to see that they *continuously* provide value to the customers in order to build up customer loyalty, and reduce customer defections. The emphasis, therefore, is shifting from *customer acquisition* to *customer retention*.

Customer loyalty, in general, increases profit and growth in many ways — so much so that by increasing the percentage of loyal customers by as little as 5% the profitability can be increased by as much as 30% to 85%, depending upon the industry [Reichheld & Sasser 1990], a ratio estimated to be even higher on the Web [Reichheld & Schefter 2000]. Customer retention has never been more critical in financial services. According to Tower Group, a 5% decrease in customer defections results in an increase in profitability of 25% (or even more). The reason for this is that loyal customers are typically willing to pay a higher price and are more tolerant when something goes wrong. They are easier to satisfy as the vendor can learn more about the customers' expectations [Reichheld & Sasser 1990]. Indeed the success of some well-known e-commerce sites (e.g. eBay, Amazon) can be attributed in part of their ability to maintain a high degree of customer loyalty.

Relationship marketing [Payne et al. 1995] involves getting close to customers in order to better identify and satisfy their needs. In recent years, CRM has emerged as a broad heading for some approaches and techniques of maintaining and enhancing customer loyalty [Minocha 2000b; Dyche 2002].

CRM or Relationship Marketing is a set of business strategies designed to add value to customer interactions by providing service quality that exceeds the customers' expectations. To date conceptualization of CRM has been anchored in conventional (i.e. off-line) marketplaces. The critical issue for investigation in our research programme is whether such conceptual frameworks remain valid within online marketplaces.

2.2 Service Quality and e-CRM

The essence of service quality is the ability to deliver what the customer needs and expects. *Service Quality* is the customer's subjective assessment that the service received during the TCE is the service expected. If the service quality of the customer's TCE exceeds expectations, the customer will be willing to come back and do future business with the vendor. Conversely, customers who experience low service quality will be more inclined to defect to other vendors because they are not getting what they expect.

Research indeed shows that in many traditional companies, perceived service quality influences customer loyalty strongly and directly. Service quality, as we have seen earlier, is also crucial to online organizations. As e-commerce proliferates, the most experienced and effective e-tailers are recognizing that the key determinants of success or failure are not merely Web presence or low price but rather the delivery of service quality. A customer assesses the service quality of his TCE on the basis of all the cues and encounters that occur before, during, and after the transaction with an e-commerce environment.

To encourage repeat purchases and build customer loyalty, the managers of e-commerce environments, therefore, need to address the following questions: What do customers really desire from their online shopping experiences? What are their expectations? What attributes are most important in their judgements of service quality, satisfaction and loyalty? What is good service on the Web? What actions can be taken to deliver service quality? What are the underlying dimensions or heuristics of superior service quality of the service encounter? What are the social and cultural obstacles to service quality in an e-commerce environment?

This paper argues that, in addition to the Usability / HCI criteria, which are anyway important to make the customer's interaction with the Web site a satisfying one, it is imperative that CRM heuristics are also integrated into the design of the e-commerce environment for development of robust long-term online customer-organization relationships, and customer retention.

The specific focus of the reported research is on (B2C) e-commerce services, given the complexity of such services and the conventional emphasis on relationship development. The outcomes of the paper will, however, be applicable to other forms of e-business such as Business to Business (B2B) relationships.

3   Exploring What Hinders a Customer's TCE

In the standard ISO-9241 Part 11, *Usability* has been defined as the extent to which a product (computer system) can be used by specified users to achieve a specified goal with effectiveness, efficiency and satisfaction in a specified context of use. In this definition, it is the specified (target) users' satisfaction that has been emphasized. But for the success of an e-commerce environment, it is imperative to aim for customers' loyalty rather than just satisfaction. Satisfaction along with trust, are antecedents for customer loyalty. As a result, the usability guidelines, heuristics or principles that exist in the literature for designing and evaluating user interface designs of computer systems are useful, but they are not enough to generate a positive TCE in an e-commerce environment.

A usability problem or defect has been defined as:

> "aspects of user interface that may cause the resulting system to have reduced usability for the end-user." [Nielsen & Mack 1994, p.3]

It has also been defined as:

> "a characteristic of a product that makes it difficult or unpleasant for users to achieve their goals." [Kahn & Prail 1994, p.169]

The traditional notions of usability (and therefore, usability problems) tend to be inherently limiting and miss out social, organizational, personal and cultural factors that influence a customer's TCE. Examples of such factors are customer's motivation, emotional state, use of existing 'mental models' or references of shopping, personal preferences of online interactions, cues on the Web site that diminish trustworthiness, etc.

The aim of the research reported in this paper has been to identify factors, in addition to usability problems, which hinder a customer's TCE, that is, factors that might make a customer unsatisfied with one or more aspects of the TCE with an organization's e-commerce environment. We have called these factors *obstacles*.

3.1   Obstacles to a Positive TCE

We define obstacles as those aspects of an e-commerce environment, which makes it unpleasant, onerous, inefficient, or impossible for the customer to achieve a positive TCE. These are situations when customer's experiences with an e-commerce environment fall below his expectations. Obstacles could be:

- usability problems with the site such as use of ambiguous terminology, or use of flashy features that look good but only work for those customers with high-speed Internet access; or

- situations that could adversely influence, or even erode the customer-organization relationship. Examples of such obstacles are hidden costs, such as shipping costs, taxes or tariffs, return information, or pop-surveys that appear at inopportune moments.

Obstacles can often cause breakdowns in the customer-organization relationship. A breakdown is a 'deal breaker', for example, when the customer abandons shopping on a site and moves to a competitor site, or when the customer may not want to return for a repeat purchase or visit. Examples of breakdowns and the obstacles that cause them are presented below:

- A break in the smooth course of a customer's interaction with the *front-end of the e-commerce environment*, that is with the Web site. Here, the obstacles are the usability problems with the site such as animations or images that cause computers to crash, or a customer not being able to find a product / service because of ineffective search mechanisms, or a mismatch of cultural requirements and expectations.

- A break in the customers' interactions *with other aspects of the e-commerce environment* such as pre-sales support, security in credit card handling, delivery of products / services. Examples of obstacles causing such breakdowns include asking a customer to register before the customer has decided to shop on the Web site, automatic newsletter registration after a purchase from which it is difficult to unsubscribe, or unsupportive customer services.

The framework of obstacles to the TCE that we have derived is discussed in the next section.

3.2   User Observation Study

The aim of the study reported here was to identify 'obstacles' (pauses, deviations, breakdowns) in interactions with e-commerce, and thereby to expose factors — particularly those in addition to usability problems — that might impair a TCE. To do so it was necessary to observe customers embarking upon genuine interactions with e-commerce.   Only *in situ* observations of authentic interactions would encompass the customer's complete interaction environment (physical, social, and psychological) and hence have the potential to expose factors not predicted — or possibly not attended to — by existing research. Consequently, we decided against more controlled task-based observation approaches such as user-observations, hierarchical task analysis and GOMS (goal, operation methods and selection rules) [Preece et al. 2002] as these might 'design away' the very factors on which the study focused.

3.3   Methodology

The strength of this approach was that the observations were opportunistic and user-directed. Given the need for genuine interactions in authentic contexts, they were carried out in the customer's own environment during tasks that were customer-motivated and potentially committing the customer's own resources. This allowed us to observe tasks in their full, realistic context, including personal, task and technical aspects.

Two researchers observed ten adult users over a period of one and a half months. Eight out of the ten users were female and two were male. Eight out of the ten users

User 1 / MP/2-Dec/1:30pm	PO-E 1o
1. Events leading up to an obstacle.	MP wanted to order a soft copy of an online book from their Web site. On ordering it she reached a window that said "now please call us to confirm your order!" They were in the US.
2. Obstacle situation.	Having to use the telephone to complete an online transaction!
3. Obstacle.	Illogical disjunction between communication channels.
4a. How did the obstacle affect the customer?	MP was shocked by the mismatch between communication channels. MP has not called yet.
4b. What did the customer do in response?	MP was quite put out by this and it stopped her from continuing at that point. She felt that a Web site that had an Web-based book should be able to support online transactions.
5. How did the sociological account conclude?	It hasn't yet.
6. Did the obstacle result in a breakdown (from the business perspective)?	Yes.
7. Requirements and design solutions.	Only use other channels if it is really required. Or, inform the customer with some justification for the inconvenience.

Table 1: Template of an Obstacle index card.

were academics; one was a project engineer and one was a sales representative in the manufacturing industry. The group was culturally diverse including six nationalities and four non-native English speakers. However, all of the participants had been living in the UK for five years or over. All were already Internet and e-commerce users. Whilst we recognized that the group may not be representative of the broadest, multi-cultural e-commerce user population, the aim of this study was to identify factors that prevented a positive TCE, and for this initial demonstration, it was sufficient to have a group selected on a pragmatic basis. Future work will attempt to identify appropriate demographic variables for group selection and to extend the work reported here.

During the study, on an average each user interacted with 10 Web sites. The observed tasks included browsing, to comparing products, searching for information and shopping. The users used their own machines, ensuring access to their personal Internet links, shortcuts, e-mail, telephone, and so on. For a number of the users, the fact that they were in their natural settings helped them to achieve their goals.

Each observation session lasted between 40 and 90 minutes and involved as little interaction with the user as possible. The observers took extensive notes in addition to making a video record of the screen and an audio record of the user's utterances. Users were encouraged to comment about what they were doing throughout the task. Directly after each session, the observers carried out a debriefing interview with the user in order to address any questions or queries that had arisen during the session. Additionally, this enabled the user to draw on past experiences, preferences and expectations in order to support the discussion and clarify intentions and actions.

3.4 Data analysis

Data analysis was inductive. With the support of the video and the audio recordings, the observation notes were transcribed creating a detailed and descriptive account of each session. The notes were then scrutinized, and any suggestion of an obstacle occurring was highlighted. Typically, each session uncovered between 10 and 15 obstacles. Each obstacle was then captured on an index card (see Table 1) using a unique identifier; coding to indicate the user number, their initials, the date and time of the observation session; and a description under headings adapted from critical incident and causal analysis techniques [Bitner & Booms 1990; Minocha 2000a]. Hence, each obstacle was captured in its context.

Recording each obstacle in the same way facilitated comparisons and judgements about the types of obstacles that were occurring and helped to keep the growing collection of obstacles easy to reference.

In all, 132 obstacle cards were created from the 10 sessions. Each obstacle was then grouped along with similar obstacles in a process similar to that of card sorting [Rugg & McGeorge 1997]. Category and sub-category names were selected, based on the card sort producing a 'catalogue of obstacles' (see Table 2). Categories identified the broad factors that were understood to give rise to the observed 'obstacle occurrences'; sub-categories enumerate the types of obstacles within each category as illustrated by the obstacles recorded on the cards.

3.5 Data Validation

Validation of the emergent 'catalogue of obstacles' was iterative with two coders independently sorting a subset of the obstacle cards using the then-current catalogue. Conflicts between the coders were resolved through discussion, and then a clarified catalogue was used for the next iteration. When the catalogue was judged to be sufficiently operationalized, two independent coders sorted the whole corpus, agreeing on 106 of 132 assignments, hence reaching coder agreement of 80.3%.

3.6 Benefits of the chosen Methodology

The approach taken in this study proved to be successful. The obstacle data elicited through observation of genuine interactions was rich and meaningful and was amenable to this data-indexing process.

The nature of the observations meant that all participants were self-motivated, performing those tasks that they alone had decided to conduct. We had not offered incentives and the users were able to work in a natural way without the binds of time constraints or pressures of achieving set tasks. The data uncovered many aspects of the TCE, enabling the exploration of the pre-shopping experience, interaction with the Web site, cultural and social influences upon the interaction, and the significance of customer services in the TCE.

4 A Flavour of our Findings

Some obstacles that arose were primarily attributable to characteristics of the customer and some to the characteristics of the e-commerce site. Those obstacles that were characteristic of the customer reflected the social, cultural and cognitive

Obstacle type	Sub-Categories: Description of Obstacles
1. Misleading or influential existing references (strong influence / trigger).	Mismatch with other software applications and Web sites. Catalogue mismatch. Store mismatch (generic / same brand store to Web site). Combination of the above. Excessive extension/insufficient representation of the metaphor.
2. Problematic UI elements (trigger).	Limited / illogical mechanisms for carrying out a search of the Web site. Missing/misleading functionality. Ambiguous (or too technical) UI terminology / Semantics. Mismatch of cultural experiences. Front end UI doesn't match with suggested functionality. Ineffective UI design controls. Uninviting look and feel. Laborious interaction / Cumbersome security entry.
3. Cues that diminish trustworthiness (trigger).	Old, unkempt overall appearance. No logos or links to credible organizations. Furtive default settings / information limited insufficient contact details. Misspelled words / incorrect grammar. Making the information difficult to find.
4. Personal influences that effect the interaction (strong influence).	Personal preferences. Mismatch with users preferred habits of interaction (based on previous experience). Negative emotions of the user: Boredom, uninterested, distracted. Lack of motivation. Convictions, fears, beliefs / Cultural values.
5. None UI Disruptions to task whilst on a Web site.	Laborious/limiting user interaction to suit the back end process of the Web site, rather than the customer needs. Distracting windows (banners, animation, advertising window, etc.) that distract or disrupt cognitive processes.
6. Informational obstructions on the Web site.	Limiting, incomplete, missing or unavailable information. Misleading information. Users expectations about information are not met; for example. The variety of products is limiting or the information about a product is unsatisfactory. Inaccurate information provided by Web site.
7. Navigational Interference of a Web site.	Unexpected/sneaky navigation. Misleading labels or titles of links or Web addresses. Inability to back track. Excessive back-tracking. Not having relevant links on relevant pages.
8. Ineffective access mechanisms.	Web page / search engine — search strings are too broad or too selective. Typing in the wrong address in the address line or search string. Reoccurring search results even after iterative refining of the search.
9. Limitations of users' domain knowledge.	User doesn't know key words to support a successful search. Not having enough domain knowledge to continue within a Web site. Excessive use of domain terminology.
10. Incompatible/problematic s/w and or technology.	Browser-related inconsistencies. Operating system mismatches. Connection problems. Slow connections / downloading time. Being 'timed-out'.
11. The aims of the Web site doesn't support the users intentions.	Intentions of the users' task vs. Web site goal. User expectations of search do not match the goals of the Web site.
12. Asynchronous match between different communication channels.	No integration between digital and analogue customer care i.e. telephone, Web-site, email, etc.
13. Unsupportive customer service.	Ineffective customer services. Additional means of communication is necessary to support Web-based interaction with organization. Unsupportive customer service prior to interaction with the Web site.
14. Unforeseen Informational requirements.	User not having sufficient information to meet the demands of the Web site. Informational requirements that are not identified when transaction takes place. This may effect the follow-up service that the customer has requested.
15. Mismatches with the provided services/products.	Product not meeting the original specification — once it has been delivered.

Table 2: Catalogue of Obstacles and their sub-categories.

diversities of the customers that have great bearing upon the TCE. Such customer characteristics are expectations, preferences, existing shopping references, and the knowledge of both the (application) domain and the e-commerce environment held by the individual customer. Conversely, 'problematic UI elements' and 'informational obstructions' were primarily e-commerce situated obstacles. In addition, some obstacle types reflected the mismatch between customers' goals and the business goals of the organization and its e-commerce environment.

4.1 Customer-Situated Obstacles

The examples of obstacles caused by a customer's personal and cultural attributes and values came under three categories: reference to analogous experiences; personal influences; and limitations of domain knowledge.

4.1.1 References to Analogous Experiences or Existing References

The influence of referring to a previous, analogous experience arose as an obstacle on a number of occasions. For example, the range of products presented by a Web site was often compared to the range of products that were known to be available in a high street store or in a catalogue. If the range did not correspond to the customer's expectations they would be inclined to leave the site. This also concerned the types of functions provided by Web sites. For example, one customer who had bought a present for a friend online, expected to be able to write a personal message to accompany the parcel. This expectation had arisen from experiences with another Web site that did provide this option.

A number of the customers had developed workarounds to resolve obstacles they had experienced in their interactions with the Web. In particular, this involved preparation prior to interacting with an e-commerce site. For example, Laura made sure that she had her credit card to hand prior to logging onto the Internet. She had experienced frustrating instances of being 'timed-out' whilst hunting for her credit card. Having to repeat the data entry process to online forms was considered too much of a burden.

4.1.2 Personal Influences

Category 4 of Table 2 reflected more general influences than those created from referencing analogous experiences. These personal influences are considered to develop over time and act as a personal benchmark against which the interaction with e-commerce environments could be evaluated. This category encompasses a range of cultural concerns, convictions and beliefs. For example, a conviction about supporting local business led one customer to filter his search according to the actual location of the businesses he found on the Internet. Another popular example was a concern about shipping that made customers very sceptical about buying products online. Buying from the US was viewed as a particular hazard with little confidence in products arriving unharmed. Furthermore, if the products were inappropriate it would be expensive and very inconvenient to return the products.

Issues about privacy and data protection also emerged. For example, one user had received a confirmation letter by post following an online credit card application. She was asked to confirm that all of the information that she had provided was accurate and up to date. However, due to problems with the Web site interaction while making the online application, she was not sure which of her data the company had retained. Consequently, she did not feel that she was able to make this confirmation. Her TCE was severely hampered. Additionally, some customers were so concerned about the security in online environments that they had credit cards, which they used only when buying products online.

4.1.3   Limited Domain Knowledge

Another set of customer oriented obstacles reflected a lack of domain knowledge. This gave rise to a number of interesting points. On some Web sites, few support mechanisms were available to the customer who had limited domain knowledge. We witnessed a number of customer innovations that had evolved to support the e-commerce experience. For example, Lucy, who wished to find an e-business specializing in certain sports equipment, had obtained some basic information prior to starting her task on the Web. She had asked a friend who was a fitness instructor and was, therefore, knowledgeable about this domain. This provided Lucy with a starting point for her search. Another user, Sheila, requested a mail-order catalogue for the health care equipment she was planning to search and shop for on the Web. This preparation helped Sheila to effectively search, make informed decisions, and shop on the e-commerce environments.

This obstacle type illustrated two important concerns for e-commerce environments: First, a Web site should consider the information requirements of customers who are not necessarily domain experts. Some support in understanding terminology and jargon; finding specialist products, etc., would be a valuable asset. Second, the importance of understanding the TCE was evident. These obstacles, in particular, had illustrated the problems that can occur prior to conducting business with an e-tailer, as well as the preparations that customers make before reaching an e-commerce environment.

4.2   E-Commerce-Situated Obstacles

In addition to the customer-situated obstacles, there existed a wide set of obstacles that were primarily concerned with the e-commerce end of the TCE. Many of these obstacles overlapped with the HCI, usability and service quality literature: issues of user interface and usability, quality of service and trust were clearly important.

4.2.1   Usability Obstacles

Category 2 (Table 2) reflected the sorts of hindrances caused by the user interface (UI), for example, an instruction to use a 'submit' button when no such button existed. Users also encountered cumbersome data entry for inputting personal information and radio buttons that were very difficult to see and, therefore, use. One particular UI obstacle involved a site that enabled the user to search for business by trade and in local areas. The idea was that the mouse would be held over the name of the county and a list of possible businesses would appear. However, as soon as the mouse was moved off the county name the list disappeared. This was problematic as some of the lists that appeared were so long that they had scroll-down mechanisms in order to move through the list. As soon as the user tried to go to scroll, and thereby taking the mouse off the county name, the list disappeared.

4.2.2 Trustworthiness

While issues with the UI were important there were also other obstacles to the TCE. Trust and the level of trustworthiness that a Web site exhibited proved to be a recurring obstacle. For example, if a site had seals of approval, links to other credible organizations, and evidence that it was updated regularly, the site was more likely to increase the feeling of trustworthiness. Particular obstacles occurred when default settings were difficult to find or conflicted with the aims of the user. One instance of this involved a low cost airline Web site. The customer did not want the Web site to maintain her personal details; however, the default setting was set to retain this information. The radio button, to alter this setting was very small and at the very bottom of the page. The customer immediately felt that this was dishonest and furtive of the Web site and her judgement of the site's trustworthiness was diminished.

4.2.3 Interaction Obstacles

A number of categories derived from the user observations reflected issues with the site interaction. For example, many navigational obstacles arose, which are presented in Category 7, such as misleading labels of links, or inability to back track, or requiring excessive backtracking. Even problems with the speed of downloading and software or hardware incompatibilities were seen to hinder the value of the TCE (see Category 10).

An important obstacle type involved those hindrances caused by the information presented on the Web site and whether it was inaccurate, misleading, missing, or incomplete (Category 6). Where information was insufficient or technically challenging, the customer struggled to build an understanding of either the services, products or both that were on offer. Such obstacles seemed most likely to prevent a valuable TCE from being achieved.

4.3 Summary of Section 4

Although it has only been possible to illustrate a small selection of the obstacles derived from the data, it is hoped that the selected examples provide a flavour of the richness and quality of the data. From the data it has been possible to build a 'catalogue of obstacles', a framework for considering both interface-related and personal factors affecting customer satisfaction.

In the following section, the catalogue of obstacles that was presented in Table 2 is compared to two published frameworks in the marketing literature: e-SERVQUAL [Zeithaml et al. 2002], and Zhang & von Dran's [2001] categories of Web site design features.

5 Comparing our Results

In their paper Zeithaml et al. [2002] present the e-SERVQUAL framework for measuring e-service quality in online markets. e-SERVQUAL has evolved from SERVQUAL [Parasuraman et al. 1985], which offers a set of generic dimensions of service quality that customers use to assess the quality of service in traditional off-line marketplaces. The e-SERVQUAL framework, that focuses on the online marketplace, consists of seven dimensions: *Privacy; Efficiency; Fulfilment; Reliability; Responsiveness; Contact* and *Compensation.* Notably, the latter three dimensions are considered only when a customer experiences a problem or when a question arises with some aspect of the service being provided.

If the dimensions of e-SERVQUAL are compared to the obstacles catalogue presented in Table 2, it is clear that these dimensions occur at a higher level to the obstacle categories. The dimension 'efficiency' taken from e-SERVQUAL, would subsume obstacle categories 6, 7 and 8 which concern informational obstructions navigational interference and access mechanisms respectively. This relationship is made clear in the first two columns of Table 3. Additionally, the dimensions of e-SERVQUAL clearly map on to only one half of the categories illustrated in the obstacles catalogue. These concern primarily elements of the interaction and also the 'back end' service provision. In addition e-SERVQUAL has identified the dimension *compensation* as being a factor of promoting quality of service. This has not been identified in the obstacles catalogue as it did not arise from the observations.

Whilst e-SERVQUAL proposes the dimensions of service quality in the online marketplaces, Zhang & von Dran's model comprises of Web site design features and are concerned only with the customer's interaction with the Web site — the front-end of e-business. These factors reflect the other half of the obstacles catalogue, which are primarily concerned with the user interface. Zhang & von Dran's framework additionally identifies the feature *enjoyment* as being a feature of Web site design. Interestingly this has not emerged from our study as it focused on those negative elements of the e-commerce experience.

By examining the relationships between the Obstacles Catalogue, e-SERVQUAL and Zhang's Web site design features, as shown in Table 3, it is clear that the user observation study has helped to identify a wide range of obstacles that can cause a negative TCE. The 'catalogue of obstacles' incorporates the majority of those dimensions exhibited in both e-SERVQUAL and Zhang & von Dran's, In addition, it clearly indicates that obstacles are not only situated at the e-commerce end, but are also central to the customer. This latter group of obstacles situated at the customer end include motivation of the user, the emotional state of the user, cultural and personal influences, and social expectations. Various obstacles can combine to contribute to a negative TCE.

6 Conclusion

The reported observation study has identified a range of obstacles that hinder a customer's TCE. Overall customer satisfaction and customer's perception of value and service quality is a function of *both* usability and CRM factors. If an e-commerce environment has a high usability rating but is not able to provide assurances of security, or does not respond to customer queries promptly and with empathy and courtesy, the customers will not have a satisfying experience. Thus, a balance of usability and conformance to e-CRM heuristics is essential.

Identifying negative factors in an e-commerce experience, and then sorting these obstacles into a conceptual framework for evaluating the service quality of e-commerce environments has driven the development of the 'catalogue of obstacles'. Equally, the framework could be used by Web designers and e-businesses to anticipate the obstacles that might mar a customer's experience and to identify the

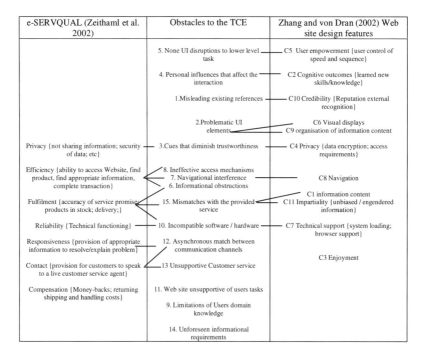

e-SERVQUAL (Zeithaml et al. 2002)	Obstacles to the TCE	Zhang and von Dran (2002) Web site design features
	5. None UI disruptions to lower level task	C5 User empowerment {user control of speed and sequence}
	4. Personal influences that affect the interaction	C2 Cognitive outcomes {learned new skills/knowledge}
	1.Misleading existing references	C10 Credibility {Reputation external recognition}
	2.Problematic UI elements	C6 Visual displays C9 organisation of information content
Privacy {not sharing information; security of data; etc}	3.Cues that diminish trustworthiness	C4 Privacy {data encryption; access requirements}
Efficiency {ability to access Website, find product, find appropriate information, complete transaction}	8. Ineffective access mechanisms 7. Navigational interference 6. Informational obstructions	C8 Navigation
Fulfilment {accuracy of service promise; products in stock; delivery;}	15. Mismatches with the provided service	C1 information content C11 Impartiality {unbiased / engendered information}
Reliability {Technical functioning}	10. Incompatible software / hardware	C7 Technical support {system loading; browser support}
Responsiveness {provision of appropriate information to resolve/explain problem}	12. Asynchronous match between communication channels	
Contact {provision for customers to speak to a live customer service agent}	13 Unsupportive Customer service	C3 Enjoyment
Compensation {Money-backs; returning shipping and handling costs}	11. Web site unsupportive of users tasks	
	9. Limitations of Users domain knowledge	
	14. Unforeseen informational requirements	

Table 3: Comparing Obstacles to e-SERVQUAL and Zhang & von Dran's model.

CRM heuristics that will help to enhance the customer's perception of quality — and hence to create a more effective e-commerce environment designed to minimize obstacles.

The catalogue of obstacles presented in this paper provides:

- Awareness of the need to provide continuous value to the customer in order to build up customer loyalty and retention.

- Categories and sub-categories of obstacles that influence the value of the TCE which can lead to breakdowns.

- Support in the identification of CRM heuristics or strategies that will help to enhance customers' perception of quality within an e-commerce environment.

In the studies to follow, we intend to explore further the boundaries of the TCE. This will help us to extend the catalogue of obstacles and contribute to our evolving understanding of the TCE. Only by taking the opportunities to watch real customers carrying out motivated and complete interactions with e-commerce sites can we begin to understand those elusive social and cultural obstacles that make or break the TCE. E-commerce is a rapidly evolving marketplace, which must look beyond the usability of its Web sites and concentrate upon providing service quality that encourages customer retention.

Acknowledgements

This research programme in CRM and Service Quality was first initiated in 2001 as part of a Shailey Minocha's BT Research Fellowship, and was supported by BTexact (2001–2). It is currently being supported by the EPSRC Grant No GR/R60867/01. We are grateful to all the participants who gave time to contribute to this study. We thank Gordon Rugg of Keele University, Dave Roberts of IBM, UK and Ann Blandford of UCL for their comments and advice on the earlier drafts of this paper.

References

Becker, S. A. & Mottay, F. E. [2001], A Global Perspective on Web Site Usability, *IEEE Software* **18**(1), 54–61.

Bitner, M. J. & Booms, B. H. [1990], The Service Encounter: Diagnosing Favorable and Unfavorable Incidents, *Journal of Marketing* **54**(January), 71–85.

Chatham, B. [2002], Exposing Customer Experience Flaws, Technical Report, Forrester Research.

Christopher, M., Payne, A. & Ballantyne, D. [1991], *Relationship Marketing*, Butterworth–Heinemann.

Cohen, J. [1999], The Grinch Cometh, Neteffect.

Dyche, J. [2002], *The CRM handbook: A Business Guide to Customer Relationship Management*, Addison–Wesley.

French, T., Minocha, S. & Smith, A. [2002], eFinance Localisation: An informal analysis of Specific eCulture Attractors in Selected Indian and Taiwanese Sites, *in* J. Coronado, D. Day & B. Hall (eds.), *Proceedings of Fourth International Workshop on Internalisation of Products and Systems*, pp.9–21. Available at http://www.optimum-web.co.uk/iwips/ (last accessed 2003.05.27).

Gabbott, M. & Hogg, G. [1998], *Consumers and Services*, John Wiley & Sons.

Kahn, M. J. & Prail, A. [1994], Formal Usability Inspections, *in* Nielsen & Mack [1994], pp.141–71.

Millard, N. J. [2001], Creating the Customer Experience: Holistic Interaction from Website to Call Centre and Beyond, *in* M. J. Smith & G. Salvendy (eds.), *Proceedings of the 9th International Conference on Human–Computer Interaction (HCI International '01)*, Vol. 2, Lawrence Erlbaum Associates, pp.134–6.

Minocha, S. [2000a], Causal Analysis: A Technique to Explore Breakdowns in Usage Scenarios, *in* S. Turner & P. Turner (eds.), *Proceedings of HCI'2000: Volume 2*, British Computer Society.

Minocha, S. [2000b], Design of E-Business Sites for Effective Customer Relationship Management, *in* C. Paris, N. Ozkan, S. Howard & S. Lu (eds.), *Proceedings of Australian Conference on Computer–Human Interaction OzCHI 2000*, IEEE Computer Society Press, pp.68–9.

Nielsen, J. & Mack, R. L. (eds.) [1994], *Usability Inspection Methods*, John Wiley & Sons.

Nielsen, J., Molich, R., Snyder, C. & Farrell, S. [2001], *E-Commerce User Experience*, Nielsen Norman Group.

Parasuraman, A., Zeithaml, V. A. & Berry, L. L. [1985], A Conceptual Model of Service Quality and Its Implications for Future Research, *Journal of Marketing* **49**(Fall), 41–50.

Payne, A., Christopher, M., Clark, M. & Peck, H. [1995], *Relationship Marketing for Competitive Advantage: Winning and Keeping Customers*, Butterworth–Heinemann.

Preece, J., Rogers, Y. & Sharp, H. (eds.) [2002], *Interaction Design: Beyond Human– Computer Interaction*, John Wiley & Sons.

Reichheld, F. F. & Sasser, W. E. J. [1990], Zero Defections: Quality comes to Services, *Harvard Business Review* **68**(5), 2–9.

Reichheld, F. F. & Schefter, P. [2000], E-Loyalty: Your Secret Weapon on the Web, *Harvard Business Review* **78**(4), 105–13.

Rugg, G. & McGeorge, P. [1997], The Sorting Techniques: A Tutorial Paper on Card Sorts, Picture Sorts and Item Sorts, *Expert Systems* **14**(2), 80–93.

Smith, A., Minocha, S. & French, T. [2001], The importance of usability to Asian software development: User needs and practical Problems, Paper presented at a breakout session at the Third International Workshop on Internationalisation of Products and Systems, Open University, UK.

Spool, J. M., Scanlon, T., Schroeder, W., Synder, C. & DeAngelo, T. [1999], *Web Site Usability: A Designer's Guide*, Morgan-Kaufmann.

Vividence [2002], Stop Losing Customers on the Web, Vividence White Paper published via http://www.vividence.com/ (access requires registration).

Zeithaml, V. A., Parasuraman, A. & Malhotra, A. [2002], Service Quality Delivery through Web sites: A Critical Review of Extant Knowledge, *Journal of the Academy of Marketing Science* **30**(4), 362–75.

Zhang, P. & von Dran, G. M. [2001], User Expectations and Rankings of Quality Factors in Different Web Site Domains, *International Journal of Electronic Commerce* **6**(2), 9–33.

Trust at First Sight? A Test of Users' Ability to Identify Trustworthy E-commerce Sites

Jens Riegelsberger, M Angela Sasse & John D McCarthy

Department of Computer Science, University College London, Gower Street, London WC1E 6BT, UK

Tel: *+44 20 7679 3643*

Fax: *+44 20 7387 1397*

Email: *{j.riegelsberger, a.sasse, j.mccarthy}@cs.ucl.ac.uk*

Consumer trust in e-commerce is a key concern in current HCI research. In this paper, we report a study that investigated (1) if users can correctly identify trustworthy vendors based on cues they perceive in the interface. A further aim was to test (2) if users' judgement can be influenced by the introduction of an affective element — an employee photo. Since such elements have been reported to have negative effects on usability, we also checked for (3) effects of the photo on users' visual gaze pattern and task performance when interacting with the sites. At first sight of a page, users' ability to identify trustworthy vendors was not better than chance. Only after detailed exploration could users reach correct trust decisions. A photo only had an effect on participants' first impression of a vendor. We did not find effects of the photo on task performance.

Keywords: e-commerce, Web design, consumer trust, surface cues, interpersonal cues, eye tracking, affective trust, decision-making, photos.

1 Introduction

There is wide agreement that e-commerce currently suffers from a lack of consumer trust [Brynjolfsson & Smith 2000; Einwiller 2001; Egger 2002]. However, there is little knowledge about what individual online vendors can do to overcome this 'lack of trust' and show that they are professional, reliable and reputable — in short

— trustworthy. For traditional shops, the situation is different: Most consumers have a high level of generalized trust, based on previous experience, institutional frameworks, and branding. In most situations, they will not consider fundamental problems such as being defrauded or not receiving a good at all. Their risk considerations will mainly focus on the quality or pleasantness of the service. With regard to these risks, they can make quick trust assessments based on cues they perceive from the interior, the goods and the sales staff [Einwiller 2001]. In fact, most purchases are routine actions, where individual trust reasoning will be replaced by an *expectation of continuity* [cf. Luhmann 1979]. Not so on the Web: Users perceive many risks and are unsure to what extent they can base trust decisions on the cues they perceive through a vendor's interface (*surface cues*). In our recent qualitative study, some users voiced concerns that "anyone could knock up a trustworthy-looking Web site" [Riegelsberger & Sasse 2001]. Thus, the first aim of this study is to find out (1) *how well shoppers can differentiate trustworthy, i.e. reliable and professional vendors, from untrustworthy ones, based on surface cues.*

Several HCI researchers have looked at how e-commerce vendors can optimize such surface cues [Studio Archetype & Cheskin Research 1999; Shneiderman 2000; Riegelsberger & Sasse 2001; Nielsen Norman Group 2002; Egger 2002]. This study puts one cue from these guidelines on *designing for trust* to the test: the 'friendly face'. We chose this cue of interpersonal interaction because it is commonly used in advertising to convey an emotional atmosphere and engender trust. Photos of employees, virtual shopping assistants, or live text-based assistance can also be seen on several e-commerce sites now. Not surprisingly, such cues and their effect on online trust have recently received attention in the HCI community (see Section 2.2). Hence, the second aim is to investigate (2) *if the judgement of shoppers can be influenced by adding a photo of an employee to the interface of an existing online vendor.*

However, adding elements whose sole purpose is to communicate trustworthiness might have adverse effects on usability. When an online shopper's primary task is to select a product from a list, additional elements might make search more difficult. Hence, we want to investigate (3) *the effect of an employee photo on visual attention and usability.* To identify fine-grained effects on visual search patterns, we use eye tracking as a method.

The paper starts by introducing work on trust and affective cues in the HCI and marketing literature (Section 2). Based on this we describe how the experimental design (Section 3) addressed the research questions introduced above. In Section 4, we present the results and discuss their implications in Section 5. We finish with substantive (6.1) and methodological conclusions (6.2).

2 Background

2.1 Consumer Trust in E-commerce

Trust has been described as willingness to be vulnerable based on positive expectations about the actions of others [Rousseau et al. 1998; Corritore et al. 2003]. This implies that trust is only required in the presence of *risk* and *uncertainty*. Online shopping carries more risk than off-line shopping because it relies on a complex socio-technical system that stretches interaction over space and time [Brynjolfsson & Smith 2000], a process that is called *dis-embedding* [Giddens 1990]. Dis-embedding also increases users' uncertainty because it decreases the amount of information that is available about the vendor. Professionalism and reliability are examples of *trust-warranting properties* [Bacharach & Gambetta 2001] that might not be readily observable when interacting online. In an earlier study [Riegelsberger & Sasse 2001] we found that online shoppers feel it is more difficult to distinguish trustworthy vendors from untrustworthy ones on the Web than in a traditional shopping context. This may be partly due to a current lack of experience, but also because there are fewer cues available to base their expectations on. Furthermore, the cues that are available in an e-commerce interface are not necessarily firmly linked to trust-warranting properties. The size and state of the physical environment of a traditional vendor allows potential customers to assume that the vendor, is interested in future business. A vast e-commerce site, on the other hand, could just be a fabricated façade — the e-commerce equivalent of a *Potemkin Village*.

2.2 Affective Surface Cues

Apart from appearing competent (*ability*), trustworthiness is commonly communicated by showing that it is in the vendor's own long-term interest to behave as promised (*motivation* [cf. Deutsch 1958]). A good reputation for example signals good past performance and therefore professionalism, but it can also act as a sanctioning mechanism, as a vendor might not want to risk tarnishing it by disappointing or defrauding a customer. Trust based on such considerations is described as *cognitive trust* or *reliance* [Corritore et al. 2003; Lahno 2002] as it relies on assessing the incentive structure under which a vendor is operating. However, human trust-decisions are also based on affective reactions [Corritore et al. 2003; Einwiller 2001; Lahno 2002]. Research on consumer decision-making has established that purchase decisions are often based on immediate affective reactions that are rationalized *post-hoc* [Aaker 1996]. In his seminal paper '*Feeling and Thinking*', Zajonc [1980] posits that the most immediate reaction to any stimulus is along the dimension of *like — dislike*, and that the position on this continuum will influence the subsequent processing of the stimulus. Thus, it is not surprising that advertising these days largely relies on friendly faces and emotional imagery.

In the domain of e-commerce, the majority of studies focused on simple implementations of affective cues in the form of photographs. Fogg et al. [2001] found that photos can increase the credibility of online articles. Steinbrueck et al. [2002] found that an employee photo embedded on the homepage of an online-banking interface increased consumers' perception of trustworthiness. Zachar & Schaumburg [2002], on the other hand, could not find an effect on trustworthiness for an animated assistant. Trustworthiness and credibility in these studies were measured with questionnaires and rating scales. In a study based on qualitative interviews [Riegelsberger & Sasse 2002], we found a wide range of reactions, including very negative ones, to the different photos we tested. Our most recent study showed that photo effects depend on photo site interactions [Riegelsberger et al. 2003]. Table 1 gives an overview on the studies to date.

Authors	Description	Measurements	Results
Fogg et al. [2001]	Investigated how credibility of online articles varied in the presence of a photo.	Web survey with rating scales.	Photos increased credibility of articles.
Riegelsberger & Sasse [2001]	Embedded photos of editors, founder, customers and assistants in a mock-up of online retailer Amazon.de.	Focused Interviews, qualitative analysis.	Wide range of reactions, depending on photo implementation and user type.
Steinbrueck et al. [2002]	Compared mock-up of an online-bank with and without an employee photo.	E-Commerce trust questionnaire [Kammerer 2000].	Photo significantly improved trust perception.
Zachar & Schaumburg [2002]	Researched the effect of an animated assistant on trust in a mock-up of an e-commerce site.	Trust questionnaire by [Kammerer 2000].	No effect of animated assistant.
Riegelsberger et al. [2003]	Effect of 8 different photos of employees across 12 different vendor sites.	Decisions taken under financial risk.	Photo effects depend on site variables.

Table 1: Recent studies on the effect of affective cues on consumer trust in e-commerce.

Due to the great range in reactions to different implementations in these studies, we include two different photos in this study. These were selected based on results in a pre-study (see Section 3.1).

2.3   Effects on Visual Attention

Besides prompting immediate affective reactions, interpersonal cues such as photos of faces are also known to attract visual attention [Kroeber-Riel 1996]. While this effect is desired in advertising (where the advertiser has to compete with other stimuli for the recipient's attention), it might be counterproductive in the design of e-commerce systems. A user who cannot concentrate on his or her task due to too many affective stimuli being present might well decide to abandon a vendor's interface — not because of a lack of trust, but due to lack of usability. For trust-building surface cues to be successful in winning customers, it is important that they are perceived, but without interfering with the users' main task.

However, there is evidence that the findings from classic media do not directly translate to interactive media. The Poynter Project [Lewenstein et al. 2000] found that readers of online news largely focus on headlines and text and ignore photos and graphical information. Similarly, Benway's [1998] notion of *banner blindness* holds that Web users have learnt to ignore graphical and animated elements, as they consider them as non-functional advertisements. Pagendarm & Schaumburg [2001] compared an 'aimless browsing' task and a search task. They found that recall and recognition for peripheral elements was higher in the browsing task. They take this as an indication that task type might mediate the effects of peripheral elements, and

Vendor 1 (V1)	Vendor 2 (V2)	Vendor 3 (V3)
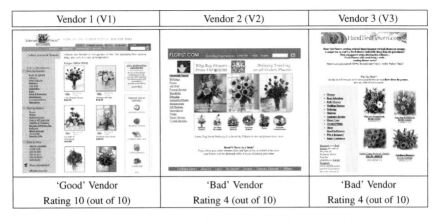		
'Good' Vendor	'Bad' Vendor	'Bad' Vendor
Rating 10 (out of 10)	Rating 4 (out of 10)	Rating 4 (out of 10)

Table 2: Vendors and their performance ratings (10 'good' / 1 'bad').

could also explain the differences in findings between classic and interactive media. A reader of a magazine might not be as task-focused as a user of a highly interactive online news site. While it is not clear that affective visual cues attract attention in e-commerce systems, many Web usability specialists recommend minimizing the use of non-functional elements [Nielsen 2000; Krug 2000]. This advice is supported by the very negative reactions of some users in our earlier study [Riegelsberger & Sasse 2001], who claimed that photos "clutter the page" and thus made it difficult to find the functional elements they were looking for. In this study, we investigate this claim by comparing versions of the vendors' homepages, with and without photos embedded. Furthermore, with reference to Pagendarm & Schaumburg [2001], we compare two task types ('get an impression of the page' vs. search task; see Section 3.3).

3 The Study

3.1 Material

Flower delivery sites were used as material for this study. This domain poses a high non-monetary risk, such as embarrassment, if the service is not on time or the products are of lower than expected quality. Furthermore, quality cannot be assured by branded goods from trusted manufacturers, as is the case for buying electronics or computer hardware online.

For each vendor in the study, we had quality of service ratings that had been taken from the reputation sharing services Bizrate[1] and Epinions[2]. These services rate online vendors based on post-order performance, handling of privacy and security, and customer satisfaction. Thus, these ratings are indicators for the presence of trust-warranting properties (see Section 2.1) that ensure shoppers against vendor-related risks that are present in e-commerce. As Bizrate and Epinions use different

[1] http://www.bizrate.com
[2] http://www.epinions.com

#	Measure	Range	Description
M1	Preference	1 (bottom-ranked) 3 (top-ranked)	'Where would you feel most comfortable buying from?'
M2	Evaluation	1 ('bad') 10 ('good')	Rating of vendor on a scale from 1 ('bad') to 10 ('good') based on expected level of service and reliability.
M3	Estimate	1 ('bad') 10 ('good')	After a short explanation, participants estimated quality of service ratings as given by Bizrate and Epinions.
M4	Investment	0–100 Pence	Participants invested in vendors they expected to be 'good' vendors. Investments in a 'good' vendor earned them the amount they risked on top of their pay. Incorrect ones lead to a loss of the investment.

Table 3: Overview on measures used.

scales, we converted the ratings to a scale from 1 (poor rating) to 10 (best rating). On this scale, two of the sites were rated 4 and one site was rated 10 (see Table 2). As shorthand, we refer to the poorly rated vendors as 'bad' vendors and to the highly rated one as the 'good' vendor.

We mirrored the homepages and the first layer of the sites. This allowed us to vary the appearance of the homepage according to the experimental condition, while participants could at the same time explore the sites in depth. Information such as privacy, returns and shipping policy was accessible on all sites.

Two photos — one at a time — were embedded on the vendors' homepages. The photos had been selected based on the results of the study reported in Riegelsberger et al. [2003], in which 8 candidate stock photos were embedded on the three sites used in this study. We chose the photo that resulted in the highest ratings given to the sites, and the photo that resulted in the lowest ratings (averaging across the sites). The best-performing photo showed a young professional woman, the poorly performing one showed a man in his late fifties wearing a headset.

3.2 Measures

3.2.1 Preference & Risk-Taking

To date, research on trust in e-commerce has largely relied on qualitative interviews or questionnaires. However, eliciting trust responses through questionnaires and verbal accounts is limited by consumers' desire to appear as rational decision-makers. Hence, rather than asking people for several aspects of their trust reasoning — and possibly prompting factors that participants might not have considered in their everyday decision-making — we asked for simple decisions, some of them taken under financial risk. Table 3 gives an overview on the measures we used; below we introduce them in more detail.

For the preference measure (M1), we asked participants to rank the vendors they looked at in terms of shopping likelihood (assuming that prices are the same). This measure is of highest relevance for online vendors and it is also one users find easy to

Measure	Description
Scanpath	Total length of saccades (eye-movements) across the screen.
Backtracking	Backtracking occurs, if the angle between two subsequent saccades is acute (<90°). It signifies a reversal in the direction of gaze.
Fixations in Region	Constant gaze of at least 100ms with a regional deviation of less than 7mm.
Binary Attraction	Whether a particular participant fixated a region of interest.

Table 4: Overview on eye tracking measures taken.

make. To allow for a finer graduation of their responses, we also asked participants to rate the vendors' expected quality of service (M2) on a scale of 1 to 10. We used the simple anchors '*good*' and '*bad*'; as this reflects the way we think about simple, everyday decisions [Zajonc 1980]. Both measures were elicited twice: Initially after the first view of the homepage, and then again after the participants had explored the sites in more depth (see Section 3.3). This allowed for analysing the data for the stability of first impressions.

Glaeser et al. [2000] maintain that trust is best operationalized by having participants make decisions under risk. Such measures put more pressure on participants to distinguish 'good' vendors from 'bad' ones. We used two measures with financial incentives: Participants estimates of vendors' quality of service ratings (M3) and participants' willingness to risk parts of their participation pay on vendors (M4). These measures and their conceptual background are introduced in detail in Riegelsberger et al. [2003]; below we give a short overview: For measure M3, we explained to the participants that we had performance ratings for the vendors and asked them to guess the actual ratings on a scale from 1 to 10. To motivate the participants to estimate as accurately as possible, we added £3 to their base pay and deducted from this according to the squared error of their estimate. Measure M4 gave the participants the chance to invest up to £1 per vendor. Investment in the 'good' vendor was paid on top of their participation pay; investments in 'bad' vendors were deducted from their participation pay. As participants did not know the ratio of 'good' to 'bad' vendors, their investment could potentially impact their final pay in a range of £6. As our sample consisted mainly of students (for which these amounts have a high utility), this range created considerable risk. Measure M4 is based on the understanding of trust as 'willingness to be vulnerable': A participant who invests in a vendor exposes herself to risk for the chance to achieve a gain. We took these financial incentive measures only after the preference measures (M1 & M2) had been taken twice. By doing so we sought to avoid skewing the preference measures by introducing the financial incentives between the two measurements of preference.

3.2.2 Eye Tracking

To identify potential effects of the photos on users' gaze pattern and on usability, we used the LC Eyegaze eye tracking system. It allowed us to record a participant's location of gaze on the screen with a frequency of 50Hz. The LC Eyegaze system

#	Material	Task		Measurement	
T1	Screenshot of homepages	Just get an impression of the page. Decide which vendor you would be most comfortable buying from.	No Risk	Preference (M1) Evaluation (M2)	Eye Track
T2	Functional copies of vendors' sites	Now you can explore the sites in more depth. You have 2 minutes per vendor.	No Risk	Preference (M1) Evaluation (M2)	
			Risk	Estimate (M3) Investment (M4)	
(search tasks on other sites)					
T3	Screenshot of homepages	Find where you would go to order a bouquet of roses.			Eye Track

Table 5: Overview on experimental tasks.

is a remote tracking system that does not require the participant's head to stay in a fixed position. As a result, however, when participants change their body posture too quickly or move out of the tracking field, data is lost. We excluded participants whose gaze was tracked less than 90% of the time. We defined the area where the photo was embedded as a *region of interest*. The tracking software[3] allowed us to calculate time spent looking at this region of interest, as well as the number of fixations and revisits to the region. Time spent in a region might not be a good measure to describe patterns of visual attention, as (a) there are great individual differences in processing speed and (b) due to differences in processing times of different types of visual content of a region. Thus, in this study we use a *binary attraction* measure. It states whether a particular participant fixated a region during a measurement period. Apart from region-specific measures, we also calculated the aggregate measures *scanpath-length* and number of *backtracks*. These measures are thought to be indicators for poor usability [Goldberg & Kotval 1998]. Table 4 gives an overview on all measures we calculated from the raw data stream.

3.2.3 Procedure and Tasks

When participants arrived at the lab, we briefed them about the study; then they completed questionnaires eliciting demographic data and information on their use of the Internet. The study consisted of three tasks (T1–T3, see Table 5). In Tasks T1 and T2 participants were asked to form an impression of the vendors. Both tasks were followed by eliciting their ratings and decisions (M1–M4, see Table 5).

In Task T1 the participants' exploration was limited to the vendors' homepages. In Task T2 they could explore the sites in more detail. Finally, Task T3 was a visual search task on the vendors' homepages. We recorded eye tracking data for T1 and T3. As the eye tracking system only allowed for displaying static pages, we could not record gaze data during the free browsing task (T2). For each

---

[3]EyeBrowse is Open Source software developed as part of the HIGHERVIEW research project. Please contact John D McCarthy (j.mccarthy@cs.ucl.ac.uk) for further information.

Preference (M1)

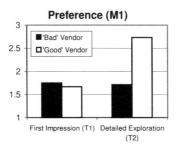

Figure 1: Preference measure (3 best, 1 worst). Difference significant for detailed exploration (T2; $U(23,16) = 52$, $p < 0.001$).

Evaluation (M2)

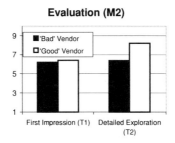

Figure 2: Evaluation measure (10 good, 1 bad). Difference significant for detailed exploration (T2; $t(37) = -3.6$, $p = 0.001$).

vendor's homepage, we created 3 versions in our experimental system: the original version, one with a 'trustworthy' photo, and one with a 'less trustworthy' photo (see Section 3.1). Each participant saw all three vendors, one with the trustworthy photo, one with the less trustworthy photo and one without any photo added. We had three different conditions, which — between them — gave us measurements for each vendor with each photo and no photo. Presentation order was counterbalanced.

4 Results

4.1 Participants

We had 39 participants (22 male, 17 female, average age 23 years). Most participants were students. 31 out of 39 spend two hours or more per day on the Internet and 30 of them had shopped online before. As such our participants are not representative of the current Internet user population, rather they represent the more experienced users we might expect in the future when consumers are collectively more Internet literate.

4.2 Telling 'Good' from 'Bad' Vendors

The first question of this study was whether users can tell 'good' from 'bad' vendors — where a 'good' vendor is understood to be one that is professional,

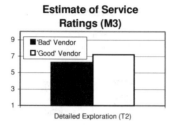

Figure 3: Difference for the financial incentive estimate measure (10 good, 1 bad; T2; $t(37) = -1.95$, $p = 0.06$).

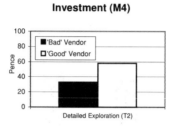

Figure 4: Significant difference in investment in vendor. (T2; $t(34.7) = 0.001$; using Levene's correction.)

reliable, and offers high level of privacy protection and security (see Section 3.1). Hence, we analysed the participants' responses in the baseline condition — without any photos added. We found that — purely based on a first impression (T1) — participants could not tell the poorly performing vendors from the 'good' ones (see Figures 1 & 2). However, based on a detailed exploration (T2), they rated the 'bad' vendors significantly worse than the 'good' vendor. This also holds for the investment measure (M4, see Figure 4), in which participants could risk parts of their participation pay. The difference is less pronounced for the estimate measure (M3, see Figure 3).

The difference between first impression and detailed evaluation can be illuminated further by looking at the number of participants who correctly ranked the 'good' vendor highest (see Table 6). Based on their first impression, only 5 out of 16 participants who saw the 'good' vendor in the baseline condition rated it highest. As there were 3 vendors in the study, this is no better than chance. After a detailed exploration, this number rose to 13, a result significantly better than chance (p=0.0001). This result also holds under financial risk (M4): 13 out of 16 participants risked parts of their participation pay with the 'good' vendor.

4.3 Effects of Photos on Trust and Preferences

On the 'good' vendor's site (V1), photos biased first impressions (T1), but there was no significant effect on the 'bad' vendors' sites (see Figure 5). However, this positive

	Incorrect	Correct
First Impression (T1)	11	5
Detailed evaluation (T2)	3	13

Table 6: Correct best ranks (M1) for the best vendor based on first impression vs. detailed evaluation (expected count > 5 for all cells, $\chi^2 = 8.13$, $p = 0.006$).

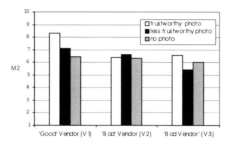

Evaluation (M2) for First Impressions (T1)

Figure 5: Effects of photo on first impression evaluation (Measure M2 1, bad – 10, good). Differences are significant for vendor 1 ($F(2,36) = 4.76$, $p = 0.015$).

bias on the 'good' vendor's site was not strong enough to significantly increase the number of correct decisions based on first impressions. Analysing the data for the participants' detailed evaluation (T2) we could not find any effect of the photos.

4.4   Eye Tracking and Task Performance

After removing participants with insufficient tracking accuracy, we had measurements for 25 participants for the impression task (T1). Participants did not significantly differ in the time they spent looking at the vendors' homepages, nor did the presence of a photo have an impact on the time spent looking at the pages. Comparing the two photos does also not yield a significant difference: Participants looked as long at the 'trustworthy' photo as they did at the 'less trustworthy'. The photos were fixated by the majority of participants: 21 out of 25 fixated the less trustworthy photo and 24 out of 25 fixated trustworthy one.

For the search task (T3) we had valid measurements for 29 participants. The presence or type of photo had no significant effect on the time it took participants to find their search target. Similarly, there was no significant difference in the time they spent looking at either the 'trustworthy' or 'less trustworthy' photo. However, comparing the binary attraction of the photos in the impression task (T1) and in the search task (T3) we found a difference (see Tables 7 & 8): While nearly all of the participants looked at both photos in the impression task, only one third looked at them in the search task.

'Trustworthy' Photo		
	Not fixated	Fixated
Impression task (T1)	16%	84%
Search task (T3)	62%	38%

Table 7: Percentage of participants who fixated the 'trustworthy' photo (expected count > 5 for all cells, $\chi^2 = 11.8$, $p = 0.001$).

'Less Trustworthy' Photo		
	Not fixated	Fixated
Impression task (T1)	4%	96%
Search task (T3)	76%	24%

Table 8: Percentage of participants who fixated the 'less trustworthy' photo (expected count > 5 for all cells, $\chi^2 = 28.4$, $p < 0.001$).

5   Discussion

5.1   Telling 'Good' from 'Bad' Vendors

We found that users can tell 'good' from 'bad' vendors based on an inspection of surface cues. This result is particularly convincing as we did not elicit users' trust perceptions or attitudes, but their actual preferences. Furthermore, two trust measures (M3, M4) were taken under financial risk, lending additional credibility to the findings. Our results are encouraging for the development of trust in e-commerce: Based only on information given in the vendors' interface, users could tell 'good' vendors from 'bad' ones. This suggests that surface cues are linked to trust-warranting properties, and that the surface cues are perceived and correctly decoded by users. Thus, as users collectively learn how to tell 'good' online vendors from 'bad' ones, general trust in the market place can be expected to grow: They see that they are capable of making correct trust-decisions and can thus iteratively risk more.

However, these encouraging results hold only for in-depth exploration (T2). Based on a quick glance of the home pages, our participants did not do better than chance when trying to tell 'good' from 'bad'. There are several factors that may explain this finding: First, users — even our highly Internet-literate ones — have not accumulated as much experience with online shopping as they have with traditional shopping. Consequently, the processing of cues and subsequent decision-making are not as well trained and thus take longer. If this is the case, this problem is likely to diminish with time and experience. However, we might also face a persistent problem: The link between trust-warranting properties (such as professionalism and reliability) and cues may remain weaker on the Web than in the real world. The more important cues (i.e. those that are firmly linked to trust-warranting properties) may not lie in the spatial design of the homepage (the source of our participants' first impressions), but in the interaction experience across the whole site; i.e. how the information is structured, how easy it is to find relevant policies, and how extensive the site is.

5.2 Effects of Photos on Trust and Preferences

We found that adding a photo to the homepages had an effect on participants' first impression (T1) of one out of the three vendors only. In that respect, our results support the earlier studies on affective cues in e-commerce by Steinbrueck et al. [2002]. As the positive effect was only observed on the 'good' vendor's site, the result opposes findings from our previous study [Riegelsberger et al. 2003], where — averaging across 12 sites and 8 photos — we found that photos had the most uniform positive impact on poorly performing sites. In that study, however, participants could instantly explore the site beyond the homepage and we did not split the measurement into first impression and in-depth evaluation.

The lack of effect for the in-depth exploration (T2) in the present study suggests that the effect of interpersonal cues depends on the depth of users' processing of these cues. This could also explain the contradicting results of previous studies (see Section 2.2). Affective cues might only influence users with low involvement [Petty & Cacioppo 1986] that don't go beyond the home page for their trust assessment.

The findings further support the notion introduced above that valid cues for trustworthiness are not to be found as much in home page layout and content but more in site structure and cognitive trust elements such as security and privacy policies. Users in this study were specifically asked to explore the sites in depth after their initial assessment and did better at telling 'good' from 'bad' vendors than users in the previous study [Riegelsberger et al. 2003]. Clearly, such a focus on in-depth exploration might not be found in field settings, where users might take decisions quickly.

5.3 Eye Tracking and Task Performance

As in our previous eye tracking study [Riegelsberger et al. 2002], in which we compared a page with a photo to one with a text box of the same size, we could not find any effects of photos on task performance in this study. Hence, photographs might not have an effect on task performance, but they might decrease user satisfaction, as users struggle to keep performance high.

An interesting result is the difference in the binary attraction measure between the impression task (T1) and the search task (T3). This effect could be due to repeated exposure. We previously found that participants in two successive goal-focused tasks ignored non-functional elements the second time they did a task on the same page [Riegelsberger et al. 2002]. In this study, however, several minutes passed between the two tasks, during which participants also completed search tasks on other pages. Thus, these results support Pagendarm & Schaumburg's [2001] notion that a higher level of goal-direction in a task will lead users to be less susceptible to peripheral stimuli such as banner ads or photos.

6 Conclusions

6.1 Substantive Conclusions

With reference to the title of this paper, the clear answer is: *don't trust at first sight.* Users' first assessments of trustworthiness were not accurate and could be skewed by a simple intervention — the addition of a stock photo. Revisiting the aims of this study in detail, our substantive conclusions are as follows: (1) Surface cues are linked to vendors' trust-warranting attributes and (2) users are able to perceive them; i.e. they are able to reach correct decisions about a vendor's trustworthiness based on cues present in the interface. However, (3) they are only able to do so after a detailed exploration of the interface.

With regard to photos as an example of affective surface cues that are supposed to build trust, we found an effect only on first impressions of the 'good' vendor's site (4). We could not find effects of photos on the correctness of users' trust-decisions, nor were the photo-effects consistent across different vendors. We could not find an effect of the presence of a photo on task performance. However, we found (5) that the photos attracted less attention in the search task than in the impression task.

Online vendors looking to increase consumer trust have to decide whether to invest in an impeccable e-commerce interface, or in other means such as classic advertising, or third party assurance mechanisms. Our results emphasize the significance of the interface as a communicator of trustworthiness. With regard to introducing affective trust cues, our recommendation is to be cautious — we only found effects based on first impressions, and those disappeared after participants could explore the sites in depth.

For researchers, the findings from this study encourage further investigation of surface cues, as they allow users to reach correct trust-decisions. The first question to address is which cues allow for a correct trust assessment. These are not necessarily those that are listed in designer's guidelines, as many of those cues might also be used by 'bad' vendors who want to appear trustworthy. On the contrary, it is desirable to find cues that cannot be easily included in a guideline on designing for trust. Identifying cues that cannot be easily mimicked could help to educate users about how to reach correct online trust-decisions, rather than only providing guidelines for vendors that are seeking to look trustworthy. Identifying cues that are hard to forge, and educating users about them, is likely to increase general trust in the whole market place.

6.2 Methodological Conclusions

In this study, we introduced several methodological innovations. First, we used existing vendors' sites whose level of service — based on reputation ratings — was known to us. This allowed us to compare participants' preferences and ratings to actual performance data. We could establish the correctness of participants' decision. A second advantage of this approach is that we could reward correct trust-decisions. We thus induced financial risk in our participants' decision-making, lending further credibility to the results (see Section 3.2). Finally, tests for trust were combined with a check for potential negative impacts on usability, the traditional core interest of the field of HCI. While this multidimensional approach surely can be further refined (see future work), we believe that it points in the right direction, as HCI has to combine an evaluation of classic usability criteria such as task performance with elements of user experience such as trust.

6.3   Future Work

The immediate questions that arise from this study need to be addressed: Trust based on first impressions should also be tested with a measure that induces risk (such as M4) to see whether the effects of photos hold for this stricter measure. Also, the discrepancy between user satisfaction ("photos distract") and constant task performance needs to be further investigated, possibly using physiological measures to determine whether users have to work harder to keep task performance constant [Wilson & Sasse 2000]. Finally, the effect of task-type (impression vs. search task) needs to be tested in a study that counterbalances the order of the tasks. On a more general level, as said above, rather than identifying cues that can persuade users into trusting, research should be focused on identifying cues that enable users to reach correct trust-decisions.

Acknowledgements

This study was conducted as part of the HIGHERVIEW project, funded by BT. Jens Riegelsberger is funded by a BT studentship (WEB 164414/CT501045).

References

Aaker, D. A. [1996], *Building Strong Brands*, Free Press.

Bacharach, M. & Gambetta, D. [2001], Trust as Type Detection, *in* C. Castelfranchi & Y. Tan (eds.), *Trust and Deception in Virtual Societies*, Kluwer, pp.1–26.

Benway, J. P. [1998], The Irony of Attention Grabbing on the World Wide Web, *in Proceedings of the Human Factors and Ergonomics Society 42nd Annual Meeting*, Human Factors and Ergonomics Society, pp.463–7.

Brynjolfsson, E. & Smith, M. [2000], Frictionless Commerce? A Comparison of Internet and Conventional Retailers, *Management Science* **46**(4), 563–85.

Corritore, C. L., Kracher, B. & Wiedenbeck, S. [2003], On-line Trust: Concepts, Evolving Themes, A Model, *International Journal of Human–Computer Studies* **58**(6), 737–758.

Deutsch, M. [1958], Trust and Suspicion, *Journal of Conflict Resolution* **2**(4), 265–79.

Egger, F. N. [2002], Consumer Trust in E-Commerce: From Psychology to Interaction Design, *in* J. E. J. Prins, P. M. A. Ribbers, H. C. A. van Tilborg, A. F. L. Veth & J. G. L. van der Wees (eds.), *Trust in Electronic Commerce: The Role of Trust from a Legal, an Organizational and a Technical Point of View*, Kluwer, pp.11–43.

Einwiller, S. [2001], The Significance of Reputation and Brand for Creating Trust in the Different Stages of a Relationship between an Online Vendor and Its Customers, *in* M. Schoop & R. Walczuch (eds.), *Proceedings of the 8th Research Symposium on Emerging Electronic Markets (RSEEM2001)*. Available at http://www-i5.informatik.rwth-aachen.de/conf/rseem2001/papers/einwiller.pdf (last accessed 2003.05.26).

Fogg, B. J., Marshall, J., Kameda, T., Solomon, J., Rangnekar, A., Boyd, J. & Brown, B. [2001], Web Credibility Research: A Method for Online Experiments and Early Study Results, *in* M. M. Tremaine (ed.), *CHI'01 Extended Abstracts of the Conference on Human Factors in Computing Systems*, ACM Press, pp.295–6.

Giddens, A. [1990], *The Consequences of Modernity*, Stanford University Press.

Glaeser, E. L., Laibson, D., Scheinkman, J. A. & Soutter, C. L. [2000], Measuring Trust, *Quarterly Journal of Economics* **115**(3), 811–46.

Goldberg, J. H. & Kotval, X. P. [1998], Eye Movement-based Evaluation of the Computer Interface, *in* S. K. Kumar (ed.), *Advances in Occupational Ergonomics and Safety*, IOS Press, pp.529–32.

Kammerer, M. [2000], Die Bestimmung von Vertrauen in Internetangebote, Lizensiatsarbeit, Der Philosophischen Fakultät der Universität Zürich.

Kroeber-Riel, W. [1996], *Bildkommunikation: Imagerysysteme für die Werbung*, Vahlen.

Krug, S. [2000], *Don't Make Me Think: A Common Sense Approach to Web Usability*, New Rider Publishing.

Lahno, B. [2002], Institutional Trust: A Less Demanding Form of Trust?, http://www.uni-duisburg.de/FB1/PHILO/index/Lahno-Trust.htm (last accessed 2003.05.26).   Revista Latinoamericana de Estudios Avanzados (RELEA). 16.

Lewenstein, M., Edwards, G., Tatr, D. & DeVigal, A. [2000], The Stanford Poynter Project, http://www.poynter.org/eyetrack2000/ (last accessed 2003.05.26).

Luhmann, N. [1979], *Trust and Power*, John Wiley & Sons.

Nielsen, J. [2000], *Designing Web Usability*, New Riders.

Nielsen Norman Group [2002], E-commerce User Experience: Design Guidelines for Trust and Credibility, http://www.nngroup.com/reports/ecommerce/trust.html (last accessed 2003.05.26).

Pagendarm, M. & Schaumburg, H. [2001], Why are Users Banner-blind? The Impact of Navigation Style on the Perception of Web Banners, *Journal of Digital Information* **2**(1). http://jodi.ecs.soton.ac.uk/Articles/v02/i01/Pagendarm/ (last accessed 2003.05.26).

Petty, R. E. & Cacioppo, J. T. [1986], *Communication and Persuasion: Central and Peripheral Routes to Attitude Change*, Springer-Verlag.

Riegelsberger, J. & Sasse, M. A. [2001], Trustbuilders and Trustbusters: The Role of Trust Cues in Interfaces to E-commerce Applications, *in* B. Schmid, K. Stanoevska-Slabeva & V. Tschammer (eds.), *Proceedings of E-commerce, E-business, and E-government*, Kluwer, pp.17–30.

Riegelsberger, J. & Sasse, M. A. [2002], Face It — Photos don't Make a Web Site Trustworthy, *in* L. Terveen & D. Wixon (eds.), *CHI'02 Extended Abstracts of the Conference on Human Factors in Computing Systems*, ACM Press, pp.742–3.

Riegelsberger, J., Sasse, M. A. & McCarthy, J. D. [2002], Eye-catcher or Blind Spot? The Effect of Photographs of Faces on E-commerce Sites, *in* J. L. Monteiro, P. M. C. Swatman & L. V. Tavares (eds.), *Proceedings of the 2nd IFIP Conference on E-commerce, E-business, E-government (i3e)*, Kluwer, pp.383–98.

Riegelsberger, J., Sasse, M. A. & McCarthy, J. D. [2003], Shiny Happy People Building Trust? Photos on E-commerce Web Sites and Consumer Trust, *in* G. Cockton & P. Korhonen (eds.), *Proceedings of CHI'03 Conference on Human Factors in Computing Systems, CHI Letters* **5**(1), ACM Press, pp.121–8.

Rousseau, D. M., Sitkin, S. B., Burt, R. S. & Camerer, C. [1998], Not So Different After All: A Cross-discipline View of Trust, *Academy of Management Review* **23**(3), 393–404.

Shneiderman, B. [2000], Designing Trust into Online Experiences, *Communications of the ACM* **43**(12), 57–9.

Steinbrueck, U., Schaumburg, H., Duda, S. & Krueger, T. [2002], A Picture Says More Than a Thousand Words — Photographs as Trust Builders in E-commerce Websites, *in* L. Terveen & D. Wixon (eds.), *CHI'02 Extended Abstracts of the Conference on Human Factors in Computing Systems*, ACM Press, pp.748–9.

Studio Archetype & Cheskin Research [1999], eCommerce Trust Study, Studio Archetype has been taken over by Sapient. http://www.studioarchetype.com/cheskin where the report was accessible is no longer accessible.

Wilson, G. M. & Sasse, M. A. [2000], Do Users Always Know What's Good For Them? Utilising Physiological Responses to Assess Media Quality, *in* S. McDonald, Y. Waern & G. Cockton (eds.), *People and Computers XIV (Proceedings of HCI'2000)*, Springer-Verlag, pp.327–39.

Zachar, T. & Schaumburg, H. [2002], Einfluss von Anthropomorphen Agenten auf das Vertrauen von Ecommerce Usern, *in* E. van der Meer, H. Hagendorf, R. Beyer, F. Krüger, A. Nuthmann & S. Schulz (eds.), *43. Kongress der Deutschen Gesellschaft für Psychologie*, Pabst Science, p.149.

Zajonc, R. B. [1980], Feeling and Thinking: Preferences Need No Inferences, *American Psychologist* **35**(2), 151–75.

'On the Move': Mobile Interaction

MovieLens Unplugged: Experiences with a Recommender System on Four Mobile Devices

Bradley N. Miller, Istvan Albert, Shyong K Lam, Joseph A Konstan & John Riedl

GroupLens Research Group, University of Minnesota, Minneapolis, MN 55446, USA

Email: *{bmiller, ialbert, lam, konstan, riedl}@cs.umn.edu*

Recommender systems have changed the way people shop online. Recommender systems on wireless mobile devices may have the same impact on the way people shop in stores. There are several important challenges that interface designers must overcome on mobile devices: Providing sufficient value to attract prospective wireless users, handling occasionally connected devices, privacy and security, and surmounting the physical limitations of the devices. We present our experience with the implementation of a wireless movie recommender system on a cellphone browser, an AvantGo channel, a wireless PDA, and a voice-only phone interface. These interfaces help MovieLens users select movies to rent, buy, or see while away from their computer. The results of a nine month field study show that although wireless has still not arrived for the majority of users, mobile recommender systems have the potential to provide value to their users today.

Keywords: collaborative filtering, mobile devices.

1 Introduction

Shoppers today face a bewildering array of choices, whether they are shopping online, or at a store. To help shoppers cope with all of these choices, online merchants have deployed *recommender systems* that guide people toward products they are more likely to find interesting [Konstan et al. 1997; Schafer et al. 1999; Sarwar et al. 2001]. Many of these online recommender systems work by suggesting products that complement products you have purchased in the past. Others suggest products that complement those you have in your shopping cart at checkout time. If you have ever bought a book at Amazon.com, or rented a movie from Netflix you have probably used a recommender system. The problem is that online recommender systems don't help you when you are browsing the aisles of your favourite bricks and mortar store.

Imagine that you have just come to the end of the new release aisle at your local video store. Nothing along the way caught your attention and the rows and rows of older videos look too daunting to even start wandering through. What do you do? Do you leave the store empty handed? No, instead you pull out your cellphone and start up its wireless browser. Through the wireless browser you access the MovieLens Unplugged service that recommends videos you might be interested in. One of the highest recommended videos is just what you had in mind so you find it and rent it for the night.

There are many possible ways that the above scenario could play out. For example, the recommender system might be a Web site that you access with a wireless PDA, or perhaps you downloaded a set of recommendation pages to your PDA through a service like AvantGo. Another possibility is that you access the recommendations through a voice-enabled site using a regular cellphone. In this paper we describe the results of real world user experiences with a movie recommender system interface for each of the devices mentioned above.

The key to making a mobile recommender system really useful for people is in the interface. While there has been an enormous amount of research on creating better recommender algorithms [Herlocker et al. 1999; Breese et al. 1998; Sarwar et al. 2000, 2001], relatively little has been done on recommender interfaces. The contributions of this paper are as follows:

- Design and implementation experiences in fielding a recommender system on four mobile devices.

- The design of a recommendation system infrastructure that supports a single recommendation engine with multiple front ends.

- A comparison of user experiences across four mobile devices and a regular browser interface.

- Rules of thumb for future builders of recommender system interfaces on mobile devices, based on our experience.

The rest of the paper proceeds as follows. In Section 2, we will review the relevant literature on recommender systems in e-commerce, mobile computing, and interfaces for recommender systems. Next, we present the requirements that drove the design for MovieLens Unplugged. In Section 4 we present our high level architecture and design for the system, and provide a comparison of the interfaces. In Section 5 we outline the details of two field studies we performed. Finally, we give the detailed results of the field studies and rules of thumb for future builders of wireless recommender interfaces.

2 Related Work

Over the past eight years, recommender systems have been deployed across many domains. The GroupLens recommender system helped users wade through articles in Usenet news [Konstan et al. 1997]. Ringo allowed users to get music recommendations online and connect with other music fans [Shardanand & Maes 1995]. Fab, and other systems like it have helped users find Web pages, news articles, and other documents online [Balabanović & Shoham 1997; Claypool et al. 1999; Melville et al. 2002]. Our work builds on and extends our movie recommendation research service (http://movielens.umn.edu).

Perhaps the most widely known, if controversial, study of wireless device usage is Ramsay & Nielsen [2000]. In this field study of 20 cellphone users in the UK, the authors concluded that WAP (Wireless Access Protocol) was not ready for prime-time. In fact only 15% of the users they surveyed said that they would be likely to make a purchase of a Web enabled cellphone within a year. Looking out three years 45% of their users thought they would have a Web enabled cellphone. Another, more recent, account of wireless device usage is the study by Grinter & Eldridge [2001] in which they examine the use of instant text messaging on cellphones by teenagers. They find that teenagers use text messaging for many social purposes, and find it to be quick, easy, and cheap. Swearingen & Sinha [2002] compare several online recommender systems for music and provide five key ideas for recommender system designers to strive for as they build systems. The key ideas are: inspire trust in the system, make the system logic transparent, provide details about the recommended object including pictures and community ratings, and allow users to refine their recommendations by including or excluding items at the genre level.

Work on small device interfaces has been split along solving two key problems: making efficient browsers for small devices, and user interface problems. For example, Buyukkokten et al. [2000] designed and implemented a new browser for the Palm platform. Buchanan et al. [2001] look at general usability problems on wireless browsers and other small screen devices. They propose four guidelines for WAP usability: direct, simple access; keep navigation to a minimum; reduce vertical scrolling; and reduce keystrokes. We build upon and extend the ideas from both groups in the design of MLU.

Finally, our work intersects with agent systems research. For example, the MAGNET [Collins et al. 1998] and Kasbah systems [Chavez & Maes 1996] examine architectures for agents that match buyers and sellers in a commerce environment. One of the first systems to extend these architectures into the mobile area was Zacharia et al. [1998]. In this study, Zacharia et al. look at the design of an agent system that enables comparative shopping at the point of sale. We extend some of their ideas into the area of recommender systems.

3 MLU Requirements

In this section we present the requirements for the design of the MLU interface. The requirements were driven by a task analysis for two scenarios, as well as the results of a survey of MovieLens users to learn more about their wireless usage habits.

Device	Own	Day	Wk	Mon	Sporadic
Cellphone	72%	71%	21%	7%	1%
Web phone	14%	33%	25%	8%	34%
PDA	41%	75%	15%	5%	5%
Wireless PDA	7%				100%

Table 1: Ownership and usage statistics for MovieLens users.

The key set of requirements for MLU can be broken down into the following categories: Video and theatre use cases, Multiple delivery platforms Occasionally connected operation, Small screen operation, Data input, and Privacy and Security.

3.1   Use Case Scenarios

As part of our survey, we asked users if they would find movie recommendations on a wireless device useful. 90% of the users surveyed said that they would. When asked about specific instances where they would find recommendations useful 83% said that they would like to have recommendations while renting a video, 33% said they would like recommendations while they were at the theatre, and 15% said they would like recommendations while shopping to purchase videos. These responses lead directly to two use cases: renting a video and going to a movie in a theatre.

Both use cases describe activities that a person does while he is away from his desktop computer. In order to focus our implementation on functionality that supports the scenarios, we make the assumption that MLU is a companion to the MovieLens service. Other functionality, such as registration and configuration, is available only on the main MovieLens Web site using a desktop browser. We now define the two scenarios in more detail:

Video: The first scenario is that of selecting a video to rent or buy. In this scenario the user is at the video rental store or at a video retail outlet trying to select a movie. Because both retail and rental stores devote so much shelf space to recently released videos, we provide a feature that presents recommendations of recently released videos to our users. Because many users keep a personal wish list of movies that they want to see on video, we provide them with the ability to view their wish list, with recommendations, from a wireless device.

Theatre: The second scenario is that of deciding which movie currently showing in the theatre to see. For this use scenario, our user may be standing outside the local 'megaplex', at a restaurant, or in a hotel trying to decide which movie to see after dinner. When making a movie decision, users will consider the proximity of the theatre and the times the movies are showing. To support this scenario we allow users to get a list of theatres that are nearby. For each of the nearby theatres we provide a list of recommended movies along with their show times. Finally, we provide a short plot synopsis to help users with their decision.

3.2 Multiple Delivery Platforms

One of our goals for this project was to investigate recommender system interface issues on a broad range of devices. Getting users online in a wireless environment is a classic chicken and egg problem. Users are not ready to spend money for wireless devices until they feel they are getting a good value. Meanwhile content providers are not ready to invest in providing the content until there are enough users. To understand the magnitude of the challenge we were up against with MovieLens users we conducted our own survey to find out what kind of devices our users own, and how they use them. We found that the vast majority of our users owned a cellphone but very few owned devices that provide them wireless Internet access. Table 1 shows the percentage of users that own each device and how frequently each device is used.

We asked users who did not own or use a wireless device for accessing information on the Web why they did not. 82% of the users said that they did not because the price was too high or they did not get enough value from the service. 14% of the users said that their reason was that the interface was too difficult to use, and 4% had no answer. In free form responses to the same question the following answers were typical:

> *I don't believe there's sufficient practical value in it yet to justify the cost and poor design of those devices. The field is immature, and its better to wait until the technology is ready.*

> *Its just not that important to me to be able to access the Internet when I'm out and about.*

Even though our own survey showed that few users owned some of the devices we were interested in, we forged ahead to build interfaces for all four devices anyway. In particular some of our early adopters owned all of the devices and we were interested in comparing their experiences across the board. Each of these interfaces must be able to communicate a set of recommendations to the user on whichever device she is using.

3.3 Occasionally Connected Operation

Our survey showed that nearly half of our users owned PDAs, but few of them were equipped for wireless communication. One popular service that allows users to access information on their PDA even though they are disconnected from the network is AvantGo. AvantGo is a service that allows users to synchronize Web pages to their PDA at the same time they synchronize their calendars, contacts, and email. Such devices are often called occasionally connected. An occasionally connected device is one in which a user usually interacts with data that has been downloaded or synchronized to the device.

Designing an interface for an occasionally connected mobile device is challenging in two primary ways. First, a user must remember that his data is only as current as the last time he synchronized. For a movie recommendation application theatres typically only change their schedules weekly. However, many of our users assumed that theatre schedules change daily and therefore they were reluctant to trust the show time information we provided. Second, a user must remember that when a device is not connected to the network the response to form-based input is delayed until after the next time he synchronizes. This delay makes interactive features, like search, frustrating and confusing for some users. The requirement for interface designers is to provide good cues to remind the user of these limitations.

3.4   Small Screen Operation

Small screen sizes present challenges for recommender systems designers because they severely limit the amount of information you can present to the user. Our requirement for a cellphone browser was that the information had to be formatted for a screen that was only fifteen columns by five rows of text. Many movie titles by themselves are more than 15 characters long. In a recommender application you must give the user several choices, along with a recommendation for each choice. The requirement for our interface is that we provide a maximum amount of useful information in the space provided.

In a voice-only system the screen size is effectively zero which puts the additional burden on the user to remember what recommendations she has been offered.

3.5   Data Input

It is no secret that data input is difficult on a small cellphone keypad. Even entering the URL to get to a service on a cellphone browser can be a daunting task. For this reason, many wireless applications are read only, with user input limited to scrolling through content, or selecting a link. For recommender systems, data input is more important because they rely on getting user feedback in order to improve. Our requirement was to limit data input to menu selection and scrolling.

3.6   Privacy and Security

Ackerman et al. [1999] surveyed Internet users about their concerns around privacy. They found that the following four factors were key determinants in a user's decision to share data online:

1. Whether or not the site shares the information with another company or organization.

2. Whether the information is used in an identifiable way.

3. The kind of information collected.

4. The purpose for which the information is collected.

Our requirement is simply to provide the same level of privacy that we do in our MovieLens system.

4   MLU Design and Implementation

The main functionality available on the MovieLens Web site as well as our MLU devices can be summarized as follows:

	Recs	Show times	Synopsis	Saw	Wish list	Search	Rate	IMDB	Groups
Video	req		opt		req	opt		opt	
Theatre	req	req	opt					opt	
Voice	✗	✗							
WAP browser	✗	✗	✗		View				
AvantGo II	✗	✗	✗		View				
AvantGo I	✗	✗	✗	✗	View/add	✗	✗		
Wireless PDA	✗	✗	✗	✗	View/add	✗	✗		
Full Browser	✗		✗	✗	View/add	✗	✗	✗	✗

Table 2: Feature comparison across all platforms.

Recommendations: Provide recommendations for movies showing in the theatre, new release DVDs and new release videos.

Show times: Provide recommendations and show times for movies showing in theatres near you.

Synopsis: Provide a short summary of the movie's storyline.

Saw: Allow users to indicate that they have seen a movie. If the user indicates that they have seen a movie, it will no longer appear on his recommendation lists. The user will also be able to view the movies that they have seen but not rated.

Wish list: Allow users to add a movie to a list of movies they would like to see later. The user can also view the set of movies currently on the list.

Search: Allow the user to filter recommendations according to simple search criteria such as genre or year of release.

Rate: Allow users to rate movies on a scale from one to five.

IMDB: Provide a link to the Internet Movie Database. This link allows the user easy access to reviews, and other information about the movie.

Groups: Provide recommendations for a group of people.

Table 2 shows a comparison of the features that we were able to implement on the different devices and which of those features support the video and theatre use cases. The first two lines of the table show the features that were required (req) or optional (opt) for the video and theatre use cases. The rest of the table provides a comparison of the features we implemented on the various devices.

For some devices, we were able to go beyond the abstract interface and implement additional features. For example the Wireless PDA interface supports: search, rate, and saw. We initially provided this same functionality for AvantGo (see the AvantGo I) line but further analysis showed that these features were confusing for users with the AvantGo client. We'll discuss the confusion in detail in Section 6.

We will now look in detail at the interface implementation for each device, by examining the steps required to complete the theatre scenario. The following script is typical for an interaction in which the user, 'Bill', wants to find a movie showing in a theatre near him using the voice interface.

Bill dials 1-800-555-TELL

At the menu prompt Bill continues to dial 1-74356 per the instructions on the MovieLens Web site.

MLU: Welcome to MovieLens Please enter or say your pin number

Bill: Says pin number

MLU: You are now logged in to the MovieLens voice interface, Hello. Hello Bill. For new releases press 1 or say 'new' For DVD releases press 2 or say 'dvd' For video release press 3 or say 'video' For theatres press 4 or say 'theatre' For help press 0 or say 'help' To quit at any time say 'goodbye'

Bill: theatre

MLU: now playing around zip code fifty five thousand four hundred forty six. To skip to the next theatre say 'next'. Theatre Mann Plymouth 12 plays the following movies. Eight mile, four stars, plays at twelve ten, two twenty five, two thirty, four fifty, four fifty five... Fam-Fe-Taal, four stars, plays at twelve twenty five, two forty five, ...

The above dialogue illustrates some important issues with the voice only interface. First, we provide our voice users with a PIN number to replace their user name and password. Since we have no way to remember voice only users we decided that a simple PIN number was much easier than entering or trying to say their user name, which in most cases is an email address and password. Because the zip code is represented as a five digit number the VoiceXML translator speaks it as fifty five thousand four hundred forty six. Some words are difficult to translate into speech. For example the movie pronounced as fam-fe-taal is really *Femme Fatale*. The pronunciation is so far off as to leave the user totally mystified as to what movie was just recommended. Meanwhile, the system continues to speak other recommendations unaware of the user's confusion.

We now look at how you would get a similar set of recommendations for movies showing in theatres, using a PDA and either the AvantGo service or a wireless Web connection. The interface for these two is identical for this scenario.

The user brings up the MLU home page through the AvantGo or wireless browser client installed on her PDA. The MLU home page is shown on a Palm in Figure 4a. The user must enter her MovieLens user name and password the first time she accesses MLU, after that a cookie is stored on her device or the AvantGo gateway. Once a cookie is established no more logins are necessary. Tapping on the 'My Theatres' link brings the user to a list of theatres along with movies and show times. The movies are sorted by recommendation within each theatre. Tapping on the movie title will show the user a short synopsis of the movie.

(a) Main Menu.

(b) Movies, show times.

Figure 1: Palm pages.

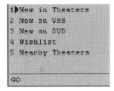

(a) MLU main
menu.

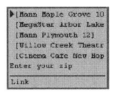

(b) Theatre
selection.

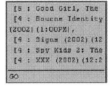

(c) Rating, show
time.

Figure 2: Cellphone browser interface.

Finally, we look at the cellphone browser interface for getting a list of movies showing in theatres. The main steps are shown in Figure 4.

The user must get to the MLU home page either by painstakingly typing in the URL for MLU or by accessing it through their bookmarks. Figure 4a shows the MLU homepage as seen on a Nokia phone simulator. The user can position the cursor over 'Nearby Theatres' and press the go soft-key or can simply press the 5 button to get to a list of theatres. Figure 4b shows a list of theatres that are close to the zip code 55446. At the bottom of the list the user has the option to enter a new zip code to get a different list of theatres.

Selecting a specific theatre displays the list of movies showing at that theatre along with recommendations and current show times. Figure 4c shows what this list looks like through the cellphone browser interface. The recommendation is on the left, followed by the movie title, and then the list of show times. Selecting a movie displays its synopsis.

5   Design Investigation

We used two methods to investigate the designs reported in the previous section: a Field Test, and a Virtual Lab Test. Here we describe each method briefly; in the following section we analyse the results of the two investigations:

Field Test: The first method we used to evaluate the user interface was with a long term field test. In November 2001 we launched an AvantGo channel for MovieLens to test our design for a wireless interface. Since then we have had 180 people use MLU on their PDAs. We set up the field trial as a service to MovieLens users without any obligation on their part to provide feedback. We recruited users to be a part of this field test by putting a graphical link on the MovieLens home page advertising the service.

Over the course of the AvantGo field test we have collected data on usage patterns through the use of log files which allow us to monitor the features of the AvantGo interface people use most frequently. In addition we recently e-mailed a survey to all of our AvantGo users to find out about their experience. To date, more than 21% of the users have responded to the survey.

Virtual Lab Test: The second way we investigated the interface design was through a virtual lab test. In our virtual lab test we asked users to perform the two tasks defined in the video and theatre scenarios. After completing the two tasks using one or more of the four interfaces, the participants were asked to respond to a survey on their experience. Although this study is more informal than a lab study in which we could have observed users doing the tasks, it allowed us to include geographically dispersed users, and enabled them to perform the tasks in a natural setting.

To recruit users willing to try the video and theatre scenarios we offered a survey to a random sample of MovieLens users. In this survey we asked users about any wireless devices they owned and their usage habits. We then asked them if they would volunteer to try the tasks on one or more of the interfaces. From this pool of volunteers 10 users tried out a wireless PDA, 11 users tried the voice interface, 6 users tried the cellphone browser, and 11 tried AvantGo. This relatively small number of users is consistent with the findings of the Nielsen and Ramsay report on the adoption of wireless.

6   Analysis of the User Experience

In this section we will discuss what we learned from our field and virtual lab tests in more detail. Because we received the most feedback from users of the AvantGo system we will focus more deeply on the issues around occasionally connected devices than some of the others. This section is loosely organized around the requirements we defined in Section 3. We discuss the specific aspects of our design that help overcome the challenges imposed by the requirement, the user response to the design, and provide rules of thumb for future builders of wireless recommender systems.

6.1 General Observations

We learned early on that most MovieLens users don't believe there is sufficient value in wireless services to justify the cost and effort required to get online. So we focused on finding ways to make it easy for them to find and use our service. For AvantGo users we provided them with a one click link to add the AvantGo channel to their PDA. For cellphone browser users we provided instructions for adding the MLU URL to their Yahoo mobile bookmark page. Since Yahoo is listed as a portal by most wireless providers, users can get to a personalized 'my yahoo' page without needing to log in each time. The bookmark page allows users to maintain a list of wireless sites they visit using a standard keyboard and browser. This approach can save users the trouble of entering in a URL on their phone keypad. For our voice only users we created a separate numeric PIN for them to use in place of their regular user name and password.

6.1.1 User Experience

When we asked our users to volunteer for the virtual lab test and gave them their choice of interface devices, 34% of our volunteers chose AvantGo on their PDA, 31% chose the voice interface over a phone, 21% chose a Web enabled cellphone, and 14% chose to use a wireless PDA. Given that many users think that wireless Web access is too expensive it is not surprising that the majority of the users chose the option with the lowest cost and commitment.

Because we ran the field test on AvantGo for over nine months we were able to learn about the long-term impact on the usage of the MovieLens Web site for users that also had access through a wireless interface. We tracked the average number of Web site visits per week both before and after a user signed up for MLU. We found that visits to the Web site dropped by an average of 1/2 visit per user per week after users signed up for MLU.

The fact that users visit the Web site less is very encouraging for the success of MLU, but somewhat surprising given that users repeatedly stated their preference for the Web site. We asked our users directly whether they preferred MLU or a desktop browser interface to MovieLens better. Most users said they preferred the desktop for reasons similar to this user:

> *Desktop. I need to find additional information on film to weigh the value of a recommendation. Read up on IMDB about it, look for reviews, etc.*

However, many users still found value in the portability and convenience of MovieLens unplugged like these users:

> *MLU — Much more convenient (video store, in front of the Tivo, etc.)*

> *In my attempt to find a recommended movie, I will now hand my PDA to the Video Store Clerk, so he can check his inventory and see if he has any of the obscure movies that are recommended. I am now known as the "Guy with the List".*

6.1.2 Rules of Thumb

Use WAP push technology: Openwave has been spearheading the development of new technology that would allow a Web site to push a link or a page

(a) Iteration one on a Pocket PC.	(b) Iteration two on a Pocket PC.

Figure 3: MovieLens Unplugged DVD recommendations.

of content directly to a user's phone. This would greatly reduce the cellphone user's need to type in tedious URLs, and allow recommender sites to directly push new recommendations to the phone as they become available. For example a user might set up MovieLens to send them movie recommendations for the coming weekend every Friday afternoon. (http://demo.openwave.com/pdf/wappush_tech_overview.pdf).

Take advantage of location awareness: Location awareness is a great feature for wireless recommendation systems. Location awareness is often talked about, but is difficult if not impossible for developers to use on today's generation of phones. Today we must approximate location awareness by using techniques like configuring a zip code. Imagine the benefits of being able to get recommendations for movies in a nearby theatre, or meals at a restaurant, if the system already knew where you are.

6.2   Occasionally Connected Devices

6.2.1   Our Approach

Our design for an *occasionally connected device* centres around the AvantGo service. There are two key design challenges for the *occasionally connected device*: how interactive to make the channel, and how much data to synchronize.

To look at the challenges associated with making an AvantGo channel interactive, we field-tested two iterations of the design. In the first iteration we made the interface very interactive. In the second iteration we removed nearly all of the interactive features. Figure 3 show the difference between iteration one and two. We note that all of the interactive functionality shown in Figure 3a was retained in the wireless interface.

The two figures show that the ability to add an item to your wish list or mark a movie as already seen was removed. The reason these features were removed

feature	1x	2x	5x	10x	more
search	67	15	4	0	0
rate	33	17	19	10	7
wish list	24	10	19	5	7
change zip	40	10	12	2	1

Table 3: Summary of interactive feature usage by users for AvantGo channel.

is that the user did not get meaningful feedback about their action until after the next time they synchronized. In fact the feedback they got was quite confusing. For example if a user were to tap on the wish list check-box for the movie "wild strawberrys" in Figure 3a, then scroll to the bottom of the screen and tap submit, the user would see a dialogue box that said "Your submission has been recorded and will be sent during the next synchronization". When the dialogue box was dismissed the user would see that the screen was restored to its initial state with the check-box cleared. The lag time in processing a request also made the search function very confusing. tapping on the search link would bring up the list of recommended movies corresponding to the results of the search that the user entered *before* their most recent synchronization.

We chose to make our synchronization fairly shallow, both to avoid using lots of memory on the PDA, and to keep the interaction with the PDA simple. One outcome of this decision is that users only have access to a limited number of recommendations. A second outcome is that we do not synchronize links that are external to the MovieLens domain. As a result, AvantGo users do not have access to reviews and other information about the movie from sites like the Internet Movie Database (IMDB).

6.2.2 User Experience

In the early part of the first field study we monitored the usage of the interactive features of the AvantGo Channel. What we learned was that most users tried the interactive functions at least once, but very few used them more than once. Table 3 shows the frequency with which users tried to use the interactive features of the MovieLens channel. For example, the table shows that although 67 users tried the search function once, only five users used it five or more times.

A second question we investigated with respect to *occasionally connected devices* was whether there were times when users could not accomplish their chosen task because they were offline. The responses from our users were fairly evenly split. Some users could accomplish all of their tasks without any additional online information. Other users missed the ability to search interactively. Still others found the unavailability of outside reviews to support recommendations to be an obstacle. A final point of confusion for many users of the AvantGo channel is summed up by the following user:

> The "My Theatres" section would be more useful if it was downloadable through a wireless connection, rather than through syncing. I have a

Palm VII, and can download directly to my Palm from other Web sites that are compatible. After I leave work on Friday, the movie times in the "My Theatres" section get stale...

What users don't understand is that most movie theatres change their schedules only once a week. Other recommendation applications may need more timely access to supporting information, but movies change relatively slowly compared to device synchronization.

6.2.3   Rules of Thumb

Choose the correct data to synchronize: Users clearly indicated that they need other data such as a movie synopsis or third party movie review to support the recommendations. The AvantGo channel interface makes it possible for the designer to subscribe to an external source for this data and reformat it for a small device.

Limit false interactions: Because of the lag between data entry and synchronization it is best to limit data input to areas where users clearly understand that a time lag is OK before that data gets to the online system.

Maximize available interactions: One alternative for a recommender system designers to consider is to create a dedicated client that is fully interactive, and only needs to have a database of information downloaded periodically. For example rather than synchronizing a set of HTML pages through AvantGo, a user might synchronize an XML file of recommendations. In fact, recommendations and titles for the entire database of 5400 movies in the MovieLens database would take less than 200KB of memory even without using compression on the text. This would allow users to have the entire database at their fingertips and be fully searchable by title.

6.3   Physical Limitations

As we saw in the preceding section data input on an occasionally connected device could cause lots of user confusion. In this section we will look at the challenges for data input as well as screen size challenges for other wireless devices.

6.3.1   User Experience

Users did not specifically complain about the amount of information available on their screens, however they all said that they would like to be able to request another screen of recommendations if they didn't find something that they liked on the first screen. This problem could be overcome quite easily by adding a 'show more' link to the page. Several users told us that they had problems understanding the synthesized voice, and navigating in the voice interface:

... voice synthesizer didn't do a great job with the movie titles. On several, I couldn't quite make out what title had been quoted. And wrong syllable accents lead to funny results. Who is Lorentz of Arabia?!

It was annoying how many times I had to repeat myself, and it was difficult to navigate, even when punching in the digits.

6.3.2 Rules of Thumb

Limit input: Automatic command completion has been a part of Emacs and Unix shell interfaces for years, but now some mobile devices have incorporated this feature that looks at the first few letters you have entered for a word and then tries to guess what word your are spelling. In a limited vocabulary application like recommending or searching for movie titles this technology could be very effective.

Use multimodal interface techniques: As voice recognition improves, multimodal interfaces that use both voice and gestures for input may help make highly interactive applications possible [Oviatt & Cohen 2000]. In particular the limited vocabulary required to provide spoken commands to a recommendation system could be augmented by a gesture based system for selecting particular movies or theatres. As PDA's and cellphones become more powerful we expect this will make interaction on small devices more tolerable.

Use mixed initiative interfaces: At the present time, the voice interface recommender system steers the dialogue; a mixed initiative interface would allow the user more control [Ramakrishnan et al. 2002]. For example a future voiced based recommender system could have the following features: Pause the recommendation stream; Back up in the list to hear a recommendation or show times again; Save a movie to a temporary list of 'interesting movies'; Save a movie to a wish list; Tell the system that you have already seen a movie.

Some of the items mentioned above could have been implemented in the current version of the system, however the current generation of tools makes implementation very challenging.

7 Conclusion

In this paper we have examined the challenges associated with building a recommender system for four wireless interfaces: A PDA using the AvantGo service, a Web enabled cellphone browser, a voice interface over phone, and a wireless PDA. We have presented our solutions to these challenges for the MovieLens Unplugged recommendation system, a companion service to the MovieLens Web site.

At this time it appears that there are still many obstacles that keep users from purchasing wireless services. Users mention expense and lack of value received as their primary reasons for not signing up for wireless mobile access. Although the AvantGo service provides an excellent and inexpensive alternative to having access to information while offline, the delayed feedback on input is a significant obstacle to creating highly interactive applications. In addition the limitations of devices like cellphones force designers to find creative ways to reduce the amount of data entry, and maximize the use of screen space.

Our research does show that recommender systems can be valuable services on mobile devices. Users value having the recommendations with them at the point-of-decision. Further, the recommendations can help solve some of the problems of small device interfaces, by selecting the most valuable information to present in the limited available screen real estate.

References

Ackerman, M. S., Cranor, L. F. & Reagle, J. [1999], Privacy in E-Commerce: Examining User Scenarios and Privacy Preferences, *in* S. Feldman & M. Wellman (eds.), *Proceedings of the First ACM Conference on Electronic Commerce*, ACM Press, pp.1–8.

Balabanović, M. & Shoham, Y. [1997], Content-based Collaborative Recommendation, *Communications of the ACM* **40**(3), 66–72.

Breese, J. S., Heckerman, D. & Kadie, C. [1998], Empirical Analysis of Predictive Algorithms for Collaborative Filtering, *in* G. F. Cooper & S. Moral (eds.), *Proceedings of the 14th Conference on Uncertainty in Artificial Intelligence (UAI-98)*, Morgan-Kaufmann, pp.43–52.

Buchanan, G., Farrant, S., Jones, M., Thimbleby, H. W., Marsden, G. & Pazzani, M. J. [2001], Improving Mobile Internet Usability, *in* V. Y. Shen, N. Saito, M. R. Lyu & M. E. Zurko (eds.), *Proceedings of the Tenth International World Wide Web Conference (WWW10)*, ACM Press, pp.673–80. See also http://www10.org/.

Buyukkokten, O., Molina, H. G., Paepcke, A. & Winograd, T. [2000], Power Browser: Efficient Web Browsing for PDAs, *in* T. Turner & G. Szwillus (eds.), *Proceedings of the CHI'00 Conference on Human Factors in Computing Systems*, *CHI Letters* **2**(1), ACM Press, pp.430–7.

Chavez, A. & Maes, P. [1996], Kasbah: An Agent Marketplace for Buying and Selling Goods, *in Proceedings of the First International Conference on the Practical Application of Intelligent Agents and Multi-Agent Technology (PAAM'96)*, Practical Application Company, pp.75–90.

Claypool, M., Gokhale, A., Miranda, T., Murnikov, P., Netes, D. & Sartin, M. [1999], Combining Content-based and Collaborative Filters in an Online Newspaper, *in* I. Soboroff, C. K. Nicholas & M. J. Pazzani (eds.), *Proceedings of ACM SIGIR Workshop on Recommender Systems: Algorithms and Evaluation*, ACM Press.

Collins, J., Tsvetovat, M., Mobasher, B. & Gini, M. [1998], Magnet: A Multi-agent Contracting System for Plan Execution, *in Proceedings of the Workshop on Artificial Intelligence and Manufacturing: State of the Art and State of Practice*, AAAI Press, pp.63–8.

Grinter, R. & Eldridge, M. [2001], y do tngrs luv 2 txt msg?, *in* W. Prinz, M. Jarke, Y. Rogers, K. Schmidt & V. Wulf (eds.), *Proceedings of ECSCW'01, the 7th European Conference on Computer-supported Cooperative Work*, Kluwer, pp.219–38.

Herlocker, J., Konstan, J., Borchers, A. & Riedl, J. [1999], An Algorithmic Framework for Performing Collaborative Filtering, *in* F. Gey, M. Hearst & R. Tong (eds.), *SIGIR'99 Proceedings of the 22nd Annual International ACM SIGIR Conference on Research and Development in Information Retrieval*, ACM Press, pp.230–7.

Konstan, J. A., Miller, B. N., Maltz, D., Herlocker, J. L., Gordon, L. R. & Riedl, J. [1997], GroupLens: Applying Collaborative Filtering to Usenet News, *Communications of the ACM* **40**(3), 77–87. Special Issue on Recommendation Systems.

Melville, P., Mooney, R. J. & Nagarajan, R. [2002], Content-boosted Collaborative Filtering for Improved Recommendations, *in Proceedings of the Eighteenth National Conference on Artificial Intelligence (AAAI-02)*, AAAI Press, pp.187–92.

Oviatt, S. L. & Cohen, P. R. [2000], Multimodal Interfaces That Process What Comes Naturally, *Communications of the ACM* **43**(3), 45–53.

Ramakrishnan, N., Capra, R. & Perez-Quinones, M. A. [2002], Mixed-Initiative Interaction = Mixed Computation, *in* P. Thiemann (ed.), *Proceedings of the 2002 ACM Symposium on Partial Evaluation and Semantics-based Program Manipulation*, ACM Press, pp.119–30.

Ramsay, M. & Nielsen, J. [2000], WAP Usability Deja Vu: 1994 All Over Again, Technical Report, Neilsen Norman Group.

Sarwar, B., Karypis, G., Konstan, J. & Reidl, J. [2001], Item-based Collaborative Filtering Recommendation Algorithms, *in* V. Y. Shen, N. Saito, M. R. Lyu & M. E. Zurko (eds.), *Proceedings of the Tenth International World Wide Web Conference (WWW10)*, ACM Press, pp.285–95. See also http://www10.org/.

Sarwar, B., Karypis, G., Konstan, J. & Riedl, J. [2000], Analysis of REcommender Algorithms for E-Commerce, *in* A. Jhingran, J. M. Mason & D. Tygar (eds.), *Proceedings of the 2nd ACM Conference on Electronic Commerce*, ACM Press, pp.158–67.

Schafer, J. B., Konstan, J. & Riedl, J. [1999], Recommender Systems in E-Commerce, *in* S. Feldman & M. Wellman (eds.), *Proceedings of the First ACM Conference on Electronic Commerce*, ACM Press, pp.158–66.

Shardanand, U. & Maes, P. [1995], Social Information Filtering: Algorithms for Automating 'Word of Mouth', *in* I. Katz, R. Mack, L. Marks, M. B. Rosson & J. Nielsen (eds.), *Proceedings of the CHI'95 Conference on Human Factors in Computing Systems*, ACM Press, pp.210–7.

Swearingen, K. & Sinha, R. [2002], Interaction Design for Recommender Systems, *in Proceedings of the Symposium on Designing Interactive Systems: Processes, Practices, Methods and Techniques (DIS'02)*, ACM Press.

Zacharia, G., Moukas, A., Guttman, R. & Maes, P. [1998], An Agent System for Comparative Shopping at the Point of Sale, *in* B. S.-S. Jean-Yves Roger & P. T. Kidd (eds.), *Technologies for the Information Society: Developments and Opportunities*, IOS Press.

Effective Web Searching on Mobile Devices

Kerry Rodden, Natasa Milic-Frayling[†], Ralph Sommerer[†] & Alan Blackwell[‡]

Instrata Ltd, 62 Kingston Street, Cambridge CB1 2NU, UK
Email: *kerry@instrata.co.uk*

[†] *Microsoft Research Ltd, 7 J J Thomson Avenue, Cambridge CB3 0FB, UK*
Email: *{natasamf, som}@microsoft.com*

[‡]*University of Cambridge Computer Laboratory, 15 J J Thomson Avenue, Cambridge CB3 0FD, UK*
Email: *Alan.Blackwell@cl.cam.ac.uk*

Web pages with complex layout do not display well on small screens, and require extensive amounts of scrolling, both horizontally and vertically. This quickly leads to disorientation within the page. In order to make optimum use of the small displays on mobile devices for Web browsing and searching, it is necessary to enforce both overview and detail concerns of page viewing. However, this typically requires two different visual renderings. SmartView provides an overview in the form of a zoomed out image of the page, with outlines segmenting it into detail regions; the user can select any of these regions in order to view it separately from the rest of the page. The content in the selected region is reformatted to fit the display, reducing any scrolling to a single direction. SearchMobil extends this approach with the aim of providing support for searching: pages retrieved by a search engine are displayed in an overview that is annotated to show the locations of search terms. We carried out a user study to compare SearchMobil's page representation to the one currently used in Pocket Internet Explorer, with a special emphasis on exploring the impact of page structure and query term selection on its effectiveness.

Keywords: PDA, handheld, mobile devices, World Wide Web, searching, browsing, overview plus detail, page viewer, evaluation.

Figure 1: A Web page with complex design, as seen on a Pocket PC. Only a small area can be shown in detail, and the overview (the rest of the page) only becomes visible through scrolling.

1 Introduction

Mobile devices (such as PDAs and smart phones) have small screens. Yet most HTML pages are designed with the assumption that they will be displayed on a standard desktop screen, meaning that they can be difficult to view on a mobile device (e.g. Figure 1). Ideally, Web authors could use a generic document description format that would allow flexible and adaptive layout of document content on various devices. Such a format does not yet exist, however, so authors must create different versions of a page to suit particular target devices (e.g. using Wireless Markup Language), or Web browsers on mobile devices must be capable of dynamically modifying page appearance.

1.1 Overview Plus Detail

Generic solutions to the problem of viewing large amounts of information in a small area are known as *overview plus detail* displays [Card et al. 1999]. These enable the user to focus on a selected region, while maintaining a representation of his or her context within the whole, and allowing navigation to other regions of it. Such displays have diagrammatic properties that intentionally obscure or distort some part of the content in order to make the relationship between overview and detail explicit [Carpendale et al. 1997]. Every such visual representation emphasizes some aspects of the structure or content while obscuring others [Green et al. 1991; Petre et al. 1998]. The overview and detail might be displayed simultaneously in different parts of the screen, or separately.

A very simple example of an overview plus detail mechanism is the scrollbar, which is used most widely on mobile devices at present. However, the right trade-off between readability of the content and the amount of horizontal and vertical scrolling required to view a page is very difficult to achieve. Restricted view and need for extensive scrolling has been linked to impoverished performance in information seeking tasks on small devices in comparison to devices with standard screen size [Jones et al. 1999, 2002].

When viewing Web content on a mobile device, there are three common situations in which overview plus detail concerns can arise:

- The detail region is a portion of a Web page, and the structure of the page provides the overview for navigation within the page.

- The detail region is a page within a site, and the structure of the site provides the overview for navigation to other pages.

- The detail region is a page in a set of search results (of varying potential relevance) that have been returned from a search engine, and the overview is the set itself.

In this paper, we concentrate on the first and third of these situations.

1.2 Evaluation of Mobile Web Browsers

Given the wide range of possible Web page layouts and Web activities, representations of overview plus detail are always more suited to some combinations of these than they are to others. This makes the evaluation of novel Web browsers rather difficult. One option is to run an evaluation exercise in which the browser is evaluated only with respect to pages and tasks that are known in advance to meet the assumptions of the browser designers. This type of study is relatively common; the reported results may be impressive, but they are not informative about the wider applicability of the new representation.

An alternative is to explicitly recognize that all representational decisions will improve performance on some tasks while reducing performance on others. The ideal design is one in which relatively large improvements on some kinds of task are balanced by relatively small decrements elsewhere. But to establish that this is the case, it is necessary to explicitly evaluate new browsers with tasks or structures where the representation strategy is expected to fare poorly, as well as with those where it is expected to perform well. This is what we have done in this project, and we present it here as a case study and recommendation for other teams developing browser technologies.

2 System Description

SmartView [Milic-Frayling & Sommerer 2002a,b] is a prototype application that takes a novel approach to the problem of displaying Web pages on mobile devices. It partitions a document into a number of regions, by analysing the layout structure of the underlying HTML. These regions are indicated to the user by superimposed lines on a thumbnail overview of the document, from which he or she can then select a region and read its content in a detailed view.

Figure 2: SmartView — overview of the page layout, with logical regions outlined in green (left), and direct access to the detail regions of the page (right).

SearchMobil extends this approach to support the user in looking for a particular piece of information on the page, by annotating the regions to indicate how well they match given search terms, facilitating relevance assessment.

We describe both of these applications in more detail, and then present a user study that focuses on the effectiveness of SearchMobil's page annotations, exploring the impact of different document structures (as discussed in the previous section).

2.1   SmartView

SmartView analyses the structure of an HTML page in order to segment the page into meaningfully separate detail regions, and present an overview of the structure in thumbnail form. HTML does not explicitly describe conventional layout features such as the multiple columns, sidebars, etc., that are commonly used in Web page designs. Web authors usually resort to HTML tables with fixed column widths and small blank images to express page structure. This results in rigid, inflexible, fixed-size Web page layouts that require a certain minimal amount of screen space and cannot be re-flowed to preserve the logical structure when viewed on smaller screens, such as those of mobile devices.

Figure 1 depicts the front page of a news site, showing the portion of the page that can be seen using Internet Explorer on a Pocket PC. Note that the link bar on the left occupies more than half of the screen width of the Pocket PC, and that the scroll bars indicate that an extensive amount of both vertical and horizontal scrolling is required to see other parts of the page. Also, the main text body of the page (in the central column) is too wide to fit on the screen, thus requiring horizontal scrolling to read the text. Such overview and detail restrictions are inappropriate for most reading.

In SmartView, we discover the logical structure of the page, so that it can be presented to the user in an overview. This involves analysing layout features such as the table format used to define the position of page elements. The page overview is

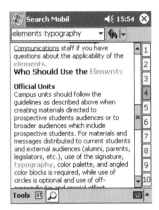

Figure 3: SearchMobil, showing the results from a search for 'elements typography', where the user is currently viewing result 4. The overview (on the left) shows the logical segments of the page, annotated with the number of term hits; the region with most hits is outlined in red instead of green. The detailed view (on the right) shows a selected segment, with the query terms highlighted.

displayed with superimposed outlines indicating the segments (Figure 2, left). The user can navigate to a specific detail region by tapping on one of the outlined areas with the stylus. The corresponding segment is then extracted and presented in the browser window, re-flowed to accommodate the narrow screen of the mobile device (Figure 2, right). These individual text units can be presented as meaningful detail regions, because they are usually HTML fragments with a simple structure.

Currently, the page structure analysis and thumbnail creation are implemented as a proxy service. However, it would also be possible to perform both locally on the device.

Most previous research into Web browsing on mobile devices has focused on integrating overview and detail information into a single screen, using text-based summary representations of the page content [Buyukkokten et al. 2001; Trevor et al. 2001]. While there are many benefits of this approach, we believe that there is a value in delivering the content of a page as originally designed by the author, and maintaining an overview that gives a consistent look-and-feel of the pages across different devices. The more recent system of Chen et al. [2003] presents a page overview that is split into sections, but greatly changes the page's original appearance by shading the sections in different pastel colours to differentiate them.

2.2   SearchMobil

SearchMobil is intended to support the user in looking for information matching a requirement, in particular when he or she has submitted a query to a Web search engine, and is browsing through the results. It does this in two ways:

- While the search engine produces a ranking according to its estimate of which documents in the result set are most relevant to the query, SearchMobil provides an indication of which *part* of a particular document is most relevant to the posed query. It enhances SmartView by adding annotations to assist users in judging the relevance of each page region to the requirement, enabling them to quickly direct their attention to the most promising parts of a document. In the overview of a page, small squares are placed in each region to indicate the number of query term hits it contains, and the region with most hits is outlined in red instead of green (Figure 3, left). In the detailed view of a selected region, the query terms are highlighted (Figure 3, right), as in previous systems for supporting document reading [Graham 1999] or Web browsing [Milic-Frayling & Sommerer 2001] on desktop computers; these terms will often mark important contextual locations within the page. These enhancements are facilitated by local or proxy-based processing of the documents retrieved by the search engine.

- The set of the top ten result pages is automatically downloaded, and is itself presented in an overview plus detail form: a tabbed 'booklet', as shown in Figure 3. The tabs along the right-hand side of the page provide an overview indicator that shares the screen with the current detail region, thereby allowing direct access to each search result. When the user taps on one of the tabs, he or she is presented with the annotated overview of that document. The user can also choose to be taken directly from the booklet view to the best scoring logical unit on the given page, instead of the overview.

The SearchMobil interface also provides a local search facility, so that the user can carry out a refined search over the set of documents returned by the search engine. If a document matches the local search, the colour of its corresponding tab in the booklet is changed to red. This facility may be helpful if the user's requirement is initially vague, but becomes more specific as he or she reads through some of the results.

3   User Study

In order to test our hypothesis that query-specific overview and detail views of a page (like those in SearchMobil) would be helpful to users, we carried out a user study to compare them to Pocket Internet Explorer's default presentation. As we have already discussed, certain user tasks and page or site structures are likely to emphasize the benefits of particular rendering and navigation strategies for overview plus detail.

Studies of Web usage have found that there is a wide range of different types of activity; Sellen et al. [2002], for example, identified six main categories, of which those related to Web searching were 'finding' (looking for something specific and well-defined) and 'information gathering' (researching a topic, e.g. to compare alternatives and make a decision). As in previous studies of Web browsing on mobile devices [Buyukkokten et al. 2001; de Bruijn et al. 2002; Jones et al. 1999], we opted for a finding task (locating the answer to a set question), as this offers more control to the experimenter than an open-ended information gathering task. To further reduce variability, we also chose to use a single Web page per task.

As we mentioned in Section 1.2, unlike previous researchers we deliberately chose some tasks that did not suit our prototype system, as well as some that did, in order to explore the advantages and disadvantages of our overview plus detail strategy. We hoped to find that the improvement in performance with the favourable tasks was greater than the decrement with the unfavourable tasks.

When carrying out a 'finding' task using a search engine, the user must enter some query terms, which form only a partial representation of his or her actual requirement. When looking at a retrieved page that contains relevant information, the user must be able to identify and locate it on the page, and so the effectiveness and efficiency of this process depends on the positioning and prominence of the relevant information. Techniques such as query term highlighting can be helpful here, but their usefulness depends on how close (both in terms of representation and location) the user's query is to the information that satisfies his or her actual requirement. The same applies to the highlights on SearchMobil's page overview, and its indication of the region containing most hits; for these to be helpful, the query terms and the relevant information need to co-occur within the same layout element of the page. This observation was essential to our experiment design.

Based on the structure of the Web page containing the answer to the question, and the particular search terms used, we split the tasks into three groups:

Type X: Where the answer page can be divided up into sections by SearchMobil, and where the correct answer is in the section that is outlined in red in the overview (i.e. marked as most relevant, according to the search terms used). We expected SearchMobil to perform better than Pocket IE in these tasks.

Type Y: Where the answer page has only a single section. We expected that SearchMobil would perform slightly worse than Pocket IE in these tasks, because the overview adds no additional information to the detail view.

Type Z: Where the answer page can be divided up into sections by SearchMobil, and where the correct answer is *not* in the section that is outlined in red in the overview. One situation where this can arise is when the user has entered search terms that are more general than his or her actual requirement. For example, the goal of task Z2 is to find the postal address of the charity 'Shelter', but the search term is simply 'shelter', and thus in the SearchMobil overview (shown in the bottom right of Figure 4), the main part of the page is marked as most relevant, not the sidebar on the left that contains the address. We felt that because the participants were being directed to a section that did not contain the correct answer, SearchMobil would probably perform slightly worse.

The 12 questions we used are listed in Table 1; they were drawn from TREC-9 and TREC-10 [Voorhees 2001], and are based on logs of Web search engine usage. We selected the search terms ourselves and submitted them to Google, and the answer pages were all taken from the top ten results for those terms. We favoured questions where it was unlikely that the participants would already know the answer, and adapted some of the questions to make them more suited to a UK audience. We favoured pages where the answer was stated unambiguously, without requiring interpretation by the participants.

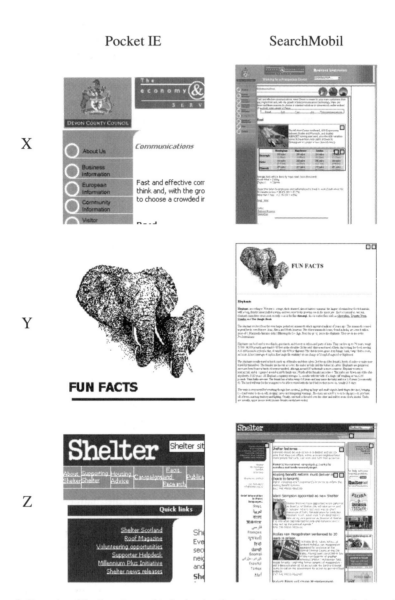

Figure 4: Examples of the three types of task, showing the portion of the answer page that was visible without scrolling, for both types of browser. In the SearchMobil overviews, the recommended region is outlined in red, with two yellow squares in the top right corner.

Question and search terms	ID
How many hexagons and pentagons are there on a football?	X1
hexagons pentagons football	
How tall is the Sears Tower, in feet?	X2
sears tower height	
In which year did Hawaii become a state of the USA?	X3
hawaii became state	
Who is credited with inventing the paper clip?	X4
paper clip invented	
What is the salary of a UK member of parliament?	X5
uk mp salary	
How many miles is it from London to Plymouth?	X6
miles london plymouth	
How much was a third-class ticket for the ship 'Titanic'?	Y1
titanic ticket cost	
Which polymer is used to make bulletproof vests?	Y2
polymer bulletproof	
How long is the average elephant pregnancy?	Y3
elephant pregnancy	
What is the telephone number of the University of Sussex?	Z1
university sussex	
What is the postal address of the charity 'Shelter'?	Z2
shelter	
Which metal has the highest melting point?	Z3
metal highest melting point	

Table 1: The questions (and their associated search terms) used in the experiment.

After pilot studies, we decided to modify the indication of search term hits on the page overview. The region with most hits contains two yellow squares, and other regions with hits contain one yellow square (instead of using one yellow square per hit). We also chose to place them in the top right of the region instead of the top left, as this made them less likely to obscure any text at the top of the region. The change can be seen by comparing the overviews in Figures 3 & 4.

3.1 Method

3.1.1 Participants

We used 24 participants, all with normal or corrected-to-normal vision (self-reported). 16 were male and 8 female, and they ranged in age from 20 to 42. As in the previous studies by others, all of our participants had a computing background (the majority were undergraduate students in computer science), and all considered themselves to be experienced Web users.

3.1.2 Materials

The participants used a Compaq iPAQ 3760, running Microsoft Pocket PC. The answer pages were all cached on the iPAQ, so no network connection was required, and the experimental timings could not be affected by network performance. We generated a question page for each task, which presented the question in a hyperlink to the answer page, with the original search terms given in italics below it (as in Table 1). We also generated an additional page for each participant, which contained one hyperlink to each of the question pages, in a random order. We used a stopwatch to record the time taken to find the answer to each question.

3.1.3 Design

As previously discussed, we chose 6 tasks where we expected SearchMobil to perform better than Pocket IE (Type X), and 6 where we expected it to perform worse (3 of Type Y, and 3 of Type Z). Because of this anticipated interaction between task and interface type, we used a between-subjects design (half of the participants used Pocket Internet Explorer alone, and half of them used Pocket IE with the SearchMobil overview of the answer page). All participants did the same 12 tasks, which were presented in a different random order for each participant.

3.1.4 Procedure

After reading the instructions and filling in an initial questionnaire, the participants were shown how to use the Web browser on the Pocket PC, and were walked through an initial practice question. The participants who were assigned the SearchMobil view were given an explanation of its features and were shown how to use it. Then, all of the participants did two more practice questions on their own. The first practice task was of Type X, the second of Type Y, and the third of Type Z.

In each task, the participants were attempting to locate the answer to a factual question, on a single Web page. Participants started each task from their own index page, following a link to the question page, which they could look at for as long as they wanted. Then, when they were ready, they clicked on the link to the page containing the answer, and said 'Go', prompting the experimenter to start the stopwatch. When they had found the answer on the page, they said 'Stop', and timing stopped.

They were told to imagine that they had already done a Web search to try to answer the question (using the query terms shown on each question page, as in Table 1), and that the given page was one of the results of the search. They were also told that the answer was always present on the given page, and that even if they knew the answer already, they still had to locate it on the page.

If they were unable to locate the answer within 2 minutes, the experimenter asked them to stop looking, and they moved on to the next question. In the instructions, they were asked not to rush through the task, despite the time limit, and to work at their normal Web browsing speed, making sure that they had found the right answer before saying 'Stop'.

When they had done all 12 tasks, they filled in a post-experiment questionnaire, containing both closed and open questions.

3.2 Results and Discussion

The dependent variable was *time*, the time taken between the participant saying 'Go' and 'Stop'. Like most timing data, the distribution of this variable was positively skewed (with a long tail to the right), and we therefore applied a log transform

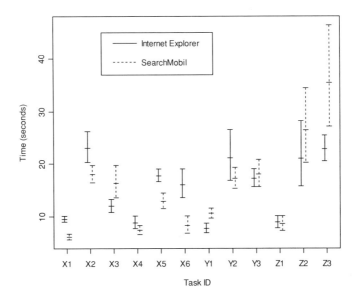

Figure 5: The inverse log mean time for each combination of task and browser, ±1 standard error of the mean.

to it (as is standard) to make the distribution more normal, before carrying out further analysis. In three cases, the participant had not found the answer within the time limit, and these were regarded as missing data. We chose the statistical package S-Plus for data analysis, and used its linear regression features to construct a linear model. The response variable was log(*time*), and the predictor (independent) variables were: *trial* (the sequence number of the trial, from 1 to 12), *task* (the ID of the task, with 12 levels), *browser* (either IE or SearchMobil), and *participant* (12 levels for each browser, as the design was between-subjects). We also included the interaction between task and browser.

Then, we used the Analysis of Variance (ANOVA) function to extract results from the fitted model. We found that there was no main effect of browser type ($F(1,238) = 1.26$, $p = 0.23$); overall, there was very little difference between the two browsers, with a raw mean of 17.87 seconds for Pocket IE and 18.13 seconds for SearchMobil (the inverse log mean was 14.37 seconds and 13.36 seconds respectively).

As we expected, however, there was a significant difference in performance between tasks ($F(11,238) = 25.0$, $p < 0.001$), and also a significant interaction between browser and task ($F(11,238) = 3.83$, $p < 0.001$). These differences are enumerated in Table 2, and illustrated in Figure 5; in the following sections we analyse them in more detail.

Looking at the questionnaire results, for the statement "It was easy for me to find the answers to the questions", participants using IE gave a median agreement score

	X1	X2	X3	X4	X5	X6	Y1	Y2	Y3	Z1	Z2	Z3
IE	9.67	25.2	12.7	9.67	18.3	18.1	8.25	29.3	18.3	9.58	31.2	24.3
SM	6.42	18.8	19.7	7.92	13.9	11.2	11.1	18.8	20.2	9.83	36.1	47.6

Table 2: Raw mean completion times (in seconds) for each combination of task and browser.

Figure 6: The SearchMobil overviews of the answer pages for tasks X3 (left) and Z3 (right), showing only the portion that was visible without vertical scrolling. Again, the recommended region is outlined in red, with two yellow squares in the top right corner.

of 3 (on a scale of 0–6, where 6 is 'strongly agree'), while those using SearchMobil gave a median score of 5. This difference was significant ($p < 0.05$) in a Wilcoxon rank-sum test.

Participant 21 (Pocket IE), on what made a search easier or more difficult:
> Having to scroll left to right as well as top to bottom made it more difficult. Easiest with just top to bottom scrolling. [It was] difficult to get an idea of the structure of the document.

For the statement "I thought the Web browsing software was useful", the medians were 4.5 and 5 respectively, but this difference was not significant ($p = 0.25$).

3.2.1   Type X

As we expected, SearchMobil generally outperformed Pocket Internet Explorer for these tasks (where the answer to the question was in the section marked as most relevant). Task X3 is the only exception; Figure 6 shows that in the SearchMobil view of task X3's answer page, only a small part of the most relevant section was visible (at the bottom of the screen) without vertical scrolling. Many of the participants did not see it and clicked on the top section instead.

3.2.2   Type Y

We expected that SearchMobil would perform slightly worse than Pocket IE for these tasks, because the answer page was simply a single long document (which SearchMobil could not divide into sections). This was generally true, although in the case of task Y2 (where the answer was quite far down the page), it seems that SearchMobil's term highlighting helped participants to find the answer more quickly. In pages of this type, the user should probably be taken straight to a suitable detail view, instead of navigating via an intermediate overview. In the future, as an alternative visualization of page structure, such documents could be segmented at the paragraph level.

3.2.3 Type Z

Again, we expected that SearchMobil would perform worse than Pocket IE for these tasks. Task Z1 was relatively easy in both browsers, because the page was small, and although in the SearchMobil view the answer was not in the red-outlined section, there were only three other sections to check, all of which contained very little text.

Task Z2 (whose answer page is shown at the bottom of Figure 4) had a lot of variability in performance in both browsers. With Pocket IE the answer was just below the portion of the page that was initially visible, and so those participants who chose to scroll down first found the answer immediately, but those participants who scrolled to the right first tended to have to look around the whole page before finding the answer. With SearchMobil, some participants guessed from the overview display that the red-outlined section would not contain the answer, and clicked on the correct detail region immediately, while others went to the red-outlined section first, spending some time looking through it before returning to the overview display and trying again. In the questionnaire, many participants commented on the fact that they had made use of their knowledge of Web page design conventions when looking for certain types of information.

Participant 18 (SearchMobil), describing his search strategy:
> Addresses and the like usually located at edge of page, so look there first for those. Other content, check main body of page, top to bottom, if information not found, try another part of the page. Very easy to move around the document and focus in on particular sections. Having an overview, with a little practice, allows you to guess where the content you want may be fairly well — especially for addresses etc.

There was a lot of variability in performance with task Z3, but only in the SearchMobil view, shown on the right of Figure 6. The answer page contains a table with three columns and five rows, and the answer is in the cell at the bottom left of the table, but the information indicating this is in the cell to its right (as outlined in red in the SearchMobil view). The participants using SearchMobil therefore had to notice that the page was a table, and infer the location of the correct answer, after looking at the red-outlined section. Some did this immediately, and therefore answered very quickly, while others were puzzled and spent a lot of time clicking on all of the other sections — this accounts for both the poor performance and high variability.

Participant 14 (SearchMobil), describing his search strategy:
> If the search words were quite specific, look carefully in the box highest recommended. If they weren't, look there first but then back out quickly to the overall format and guess where they would place that information.

Participant 20 (SearchMobil):
> Occasionally it would fragment the page too much so that a lot of repeated zoom ins and zoom outs were needed to find data.

4 Further Work

In selecting tasks for this experiment, it was much easier to find those of Type X than of Type Y, and finding tasks of Type Z was especially difficult. We take this as informal evidence that the SearchMobil strategy is appropriate to the relative frequencies of these different page types, but we plan to carry out a more formal survey of Web pages in order to investigate this further.

We also intend to carry out more user studies, to test SearchMobil's booklet interface, and investigate the trade-offs of alternative designs for presenting an overview of a set of search results on a mobile device (as in the work of Woodruff et al. [2001] in the desktop context). For example, in this study the participants always knew that the answer was present on the given page; in more realistic search tasks, the user has to continually make judgements about the likelihood that a particular page will yield useful information, and it would be very interesting to see how well the different interfaces support this activity.

As well as one-off queries, SearchMobil could also annotate pages based on a predefined set of topics of interest to the user [Graham 1999], or a more implicit indication of the user's evolving interest, based on his or her browsing path (as discussed by Lieberman [1997] and others).

As an alternative to the yellow squares, search terms could be enlarged on the overview, as in Popout Prism [Suh et al. 2002]; these would have the advantage of providing the user with readable text before he or she has selected a region, but the disadvantage of distorting the page's appearance.

5 Conclusions

In order to make optimum use of the small displays on mobile devices for Web searching, it is necessary to separate overview and detail concerns of the search task into different visual renderings. We have discussed three designs that achieve this in different ways. SmartView uses a compressed overview visualization to facilitate navigation to structurally significant regions of a page. SearchMobil annotates that overview to show the location of search terms of interest. The SearchMobil booklet view presents the overview of a set of retrieved pages in a cache, ordered according to relevance. As with all overview plus detail visualizations, these solutions suit some tasks and information structures better than others. Our evaluation has confirmed this dependency, and highlights the kind of tasks that SmartView and SearchMobil can facilitate.

References

Buyukkokten, O., Garcia-Molina, H. & Paepcke, A. [2001], Accordion Summarization for End-game Browsing on PDAs and Cellular Phones, *in* J. A. Jacko & A. Sears (eds.), *Proceedings of CHI'01 Conference on Human Factors in Computing Systems*, *CHI Letters* **3**(1), ACM Press, pp.213–20.

Card, S. K., Mackinlay, J. D. & Shneiderman, B. (eds.) [1999], *Readings in Information Visualization: Using Vision to Think*, Morgan-Kaufmann.

Carpendale, M. S. T., Cowperthwaite, D. J. & Fracchia, F. D. [1997], Extending Distortion Viewing Techniques from 2D to 3D Data, *IEEE Computer Graphics and Applications* **17**(4), 42–51.

Chen, Y., Ma, W.-Y. & Zhang, H. [2003], Detecting Web Page Structure for Adaptive Viewing on Small Form Factor Devices, *in* G. Hencsey, B. White, L. Kovács & S. Lawrence (eds.), *Proceedings of the Twelfth International World Wide Web Conference (WWW2003)*, ACM Press, pp.225–33. Also available as a Technical Report from Microsoft Research, MSR-TR-2002-120.

de Bruijn, O., Spence, R. & Chong, M. Y. [2002], RSVP Browser: Web Browsing on Small Screen Devices, *Personal and Ubiquitous Computing* **6**(4), 245–52.

Graham, J. [1999], The Reader's Helper: A Personalized Document Reading Environment, *in* M. G. Williams & M. W. Altom (eds.), *Proceedings of the CHI'99 Conference on Human Factors in Computing Systems: The CHI is the Limit*, ACM Press, pp.481–8.

Green, T. R. G., Petre, M. & Bellamy, R. K. E. [1991], Comprehensibility of Visual and Textual Programs: A Test of Superlativism Against the 'Match–Mismatch' Conjecture, *in* J. Koenemann-Belliveau, T. Moher & S. P. Robertson (eds.), *Empirical Studies of Programmers: 4th Workshop*, Ablex, pp.121–46.

Jones, M., Buchanan, G. & Thimbleby, H. [2002], Sorting Out Searching on Small Screen Devices, *in* F. Paternò (ed.), *Human Computer Interaction with Mobile Devices: Mobile HCI 2002*, Vol. 2411 of *Lecture Notes in Computer Science*, Springer-Verlag, pp.81–94.

Jones, M., Marsden, G., Mohd-Nasir, N. & Boone, K. [1999], Improving Web Interaction on Small Displays, *Computer Networks* **31**(11–6), 1129–37. Proceedings of the Eighth International World Wide Web Conference.

Lieberman, H. [1997], Autonomous Interface Agents, *in* S. Pemberton (ed.), *Proceedings of the CHI'97 Conference on Human Factors in Computing Systems*, ACM Press, pp.67–74.

Milic-Frayling, N. & Sommerer, R. [2001], MS Read: Context Sensitive Document Analysis in the WWW Environment, Technical Report MSR-TR-2001-63, Microsoft Research.

Milic-Frayling, N. & Sommerer, R. [2002a], SmartView: Enhanced Document Viewer for Mobile Devices, Technical Report MSR-TR-2002-114, Microsoft Research.

Milic-Frayling, N. & Sommerer, R. [2002b], SmartView: Flexible Viewing of Web Page Contents, Poster paper presented at the Eleventh International World Wide Web Conference (WWW2002). Available at http://www2002.org/CDROM/poster/172/index.html (last accessed 2003.05.26).

Petre, M., Blackwell, A. F. & Green, T. R. G. [1998], Cognitive questions in software visualisation, *in* J. Stasko, J. Domingue, M. Brown & B. Price (eds.), *Software Visualization: Programming as a Multi-Media Experience*, MIT Press, pp.453–80.

Sellen, A. J., Murphy, R. & Shaw, K. L. [2002], How Knowledge Workers use the Web, *in* D. Wixon (ed.), *Proceedings of CHI'02 Conference on Human Factors in Computing Systems: Changing our World, Changing Ourselves, CHI Letters* **4**(1), ACM Press, pp.227–34.

Suh, B., Woodruff, A., Rosenholtz, R. & Glass, A. [2002], Popout Prism: Adding Perceptual Principles to Overview+Detail Document Interfaces, *in* D. Wixon (ed.), *Proceedings of CHI'02 Conference on Human Factors in Computing Systems: Changing our World, Changing Ourselves, CHI Letters* **4**(1), ACM Press, pp.251–8.

Trevor, J., Hilbert, D. M., Schilit, B. N. & Koh, T. K. [2001], From Desktop to Phonetop: A UI for Web Interaction on Very Small Devices, *in* J. Marks & E. Mynatt (eds.), *Proceedings of the 14th Annual ACM Symposium on User Interface Software and Technology, UIST2001, CHI Letters* **3**(2), ACM Press, pp.121–30.

Voorhees, E. [2001], Overview of the TREC 2001 Question Answering Track, *in* E. M. Voorhees & D. K. Harman (eds.), *Proceedings of TREC 2001*, NIST, pp.42–51.

Woodruff, A., Faulring, A., Rosenholtz, R., Morrison, J. & Pirolli, P. [2001], Using Thumbnails to Search the Web, *in* J. A. Jacko & A. Sears (eds.), *Proceedings of CHI'01 Conference on Human Factors in Computing Systems, CHI Letters* **3**(1), ACM Press, pp.198–205.

M-RSVP: Mobile Web Browsing on a PDA

Oscar de Bruijn & Chieh Hao Tong

Department of Computation, UMIST, PO Box 88, Manchester M60 1QD, UK

Tel: *+44 161 200 5829*

Email: *o.debruijn@co.umist.ac.uk*

The main challenge in making mobile Web access a desirable option for users of handheld devices lies in the provision of effective user-experiences during Web browsing. We propose M-RSVP as an end-to-end solution for mobile handheld Web navigation. M-RSVP aims to provide users with a rich set of navigational information accessible through a set of simple and natural interactions on a range of handheld devices. In this paper we describe how the RSVP model of Web browsing has been implemented into the RSVP-Browser for PDAs. We further describe how Web content has been adapted to be browsed using the RSVP-Browser. We argue that the adaptation of content for display on the mobile devices calls for a flexible device-independent specification format for Web content. An evaluation study is described in which users were asked to use either the RSVP-Browser or Microsoft Pocket Internet Explorer. It was found that the unfamiliarity of the RSVP-Browser initially caused some problems, but with little experience the RSVP-Browser allowed at least as efficient browsing as Pocket Internet Explorer. A questionnaire given after users performed their browsing tasks revealed some of the particular strengths and weaknesses of the RSVP-Browser. Suggestions for further work and implications for Web browsing on small screen devices are discussed.

Keywords: Web browsing, mobile Internet, mobile devices, small-screen browsers, content specification, content adaptation, interaction design, navigation, usability evaluation.

1 Introduction

The use of mobile communication devices and hand-held PDAs is increasing dramatically. A hand-held device with a browser and wireless modem allows

Figure 1: A typical Web page from the AvantGo server as presented by Microsoft Pocket Internet Explorer on a PDA.

---

connection to the Internet anytime and anywhere. The use of these mobile devices, including other Internet-connected portable devices, such as Web-enabled mobile phones, all point to one important design challenge; to provide effective user-experiences while browsing the Web using devices that inherently have very small display areas.

Currently, Web pages most suitable for viewing on PDA's are those that have been transformed (most of the time this is done manually) on the server's side to fit on a small screen. Transformation is necessary because most browsers render unaltered Web pages in a way that requires users of small-screen devices to scroll substantial amounts horizontally and vertically in order to view the whole page. However, as a consequence of the transformation much of the graphical information present in the original page is generally omitted from the reduced version. What is left is usually not more than a list of textual links (see Figure 1). Thus, it seems that when we want to display Web pages on small screen devices we have a choice between the amount of graphical information being displayed and the amount of scrolling required.

This situation is less than satisfactory. Indeed, it is now well known that *information scent* is a major determinant of Web page usability [Card et al. 2001; Chi et al. 2001], and both the need for scrolling and a lack of graphical elements from Web pages for display on small screens may significantly disrupt the scent of the information that the user is looking for. According to [Spence 2002], the scent of information is determined by the availability of cues that encode where one can go, how much effort it takes to get there and what would be found once there. Web pages may be displayed on small screen devices in such a way that many of these cues are unavailable to the user. When scrolling is required some of these cues may be outside the visible area, and only by scrolling to the right area of the page can the appropriate scent be picked up. This makes Web browsing into a laborious activity, which is made even more difficult because cues towards what one might find outside the visible area of the page are generally not available and most of the time scrolling will have to be done 'blind'.

By reducing the amount of graphical information in a Web page the quality of the remaining navigational cues may equally be insufficient for users to find easily what they are looking for. Pages that have been transformed to be displayed on small screen devices often contain lists of textual links (see Figure 1), sometimes accompanied by a brief textual summary of the target page. The scent of a page linked via a textual hyperlink is determined, amongst other things, by the number of words included in that hyperlink, in the sense that a long phrase is generally a more effective cue than a short phrase [e.g. Kaasten et al. 2002]. Brief textual descriptions or summaries provide additional cues, but at the cost of leaving less of the display area for the presentation of other links and increasing the need for scrolling. Moreover, the graphical information that is normally present in Web pages, such as pictures or icons, is often used by Web designers to provide additional navigational cues.

The realization that graphical information may enhance the efficiency of navigating Web pages has led a number of researchers to examine the benefit of using thumbnail images to represent hyperlinks in the form of size-reduced copies of the target page [Woodruff et al. 2001; Cockburn et al. 1999; Ayers & Stasko 1995; Kaasten et al. 2002]. For example, Woodruff et al. [2001] investigated the usefulness of thumbnails in helping users to recognize the significance of pages returned by a search engine. They demonstrated that thumbnails provide powerful navigational cues, especially if certain distinctive features of the target pages are highlighted in the thumbnail. However, impressive work by Kaasten et al. [2002] investigated the trade-off that exists between a thumbnail's usability and its size, which shows that the size at which thumbnails are truly useful may be such that a significant proportion of the screen area will have to be dedicated to displaying these thumbnails. Therefore, at first glance, it appears that thumbnails are incompatible with applications designed for handheld devices, which already have a severely restricted display area.

The RSVP-Browser was designed to overcome the problems posed by the small screen area proffered by handheld devices [de Bruijn et al. 2002]. Its browsing model revolves around Rapid Serial Visual Presentation (RSVP) of information, which is a method of visualization that, when used on small screens, allows users to view substantial amounts of graphical information without introducing the need to scroll spatially [de Bruijn & Spence 2000]. Using a trade-off between space and time, RSVP is electronically similar to the activity of riffling the pages of a book to get an idea of 'what's there'. With RSVP, the presentation capacity of small screens may be enhanced by making use of the inherent property of the visual system to process and recognize graphical information within a fraction of a second, allowing a substantial amount of graphical information to be assessed by the user within an acceptable length of time and with a minimum of effort [de Bruijn & Spence 2000; Spence 2002].

2 Related Work

A number of additional techniques for visualizing information on small screen devices have been developed and applied to Web browsing. Some browsers aim to avoid the problem of excessive scrolling by dividing the page up into chunks and using focus+context techniques to display the chunks [i.e. the Zoom Browser of Holmquist [1997], and WEST developed by Björk et al. [1999]. Other browsers use a different approach, however, in which the traversal of links is separated from the assessment of content. For example, the Power Browser [Buyukkokten et al. 2000] presents links as a hierarchical structure that users can expand or contract in order to find the page they are looking for. Only once users click on the link to the page they are looking for will any content be displayed. WAP browsing [WAP Forum 2001] follows a similar structure, in which users navigate through a number of link menus before arriving at the content they were looking for. However, the way in which the links are displayed in the Power Browser allows for much more effortless links traversal compared to the WAP Browsers made available by mobile phone manufacturers.

The RSVP-Browser relies similarly on the separation of link traversal and content assessment, but it offers the additional advantage that links can be presented in the form of graphical previews rather than just brief textual descriptions. Before, describing the implementation of the RSVP-Browser and the results of the evaluation, we take the opportunity, therefore, to address an important issue associated with handheld Web browsing, namely the adaptation of Web content to accommodate the limitations typically associated with handheld devices, such as the small screen area. As explained in the Introduction to this paper, content that is designed for viewing on desktop monitors will somehow need to be adapted for presentation in the RSVP-Browser. We therefore like to draw attention to a proposal for specifying content in a format that is device-independent and allows for the easy aggregation of content for display on small screens as well as on standard size desktop monitors.

2.1   *RSVP-Browser Content and Link Previews*

The proliferation of Internet terminal devices in recent years has created a problem for providers of content, in that they can no longer anticipate the capabilities of the devices on which their content may be accessed. As we discussed before in this paper, in order to avoid unacceptable amounts of scrolling on the part of the user, a Web page designed to be viewed on a desktop monitor is unlikely to be effectively understood when viewed on a handheld device, since the severely limited size of the display would require an unacceptable amount of scrolling on the part of the viewer. A number of techniques have been suggested to ameliorate this problem, most of which are aimed at customizing the original Web content for displaying on small displays [Trevor et al. 2001]. In order to allow content servers to automatically customize content to suit a range scenarios involving different devices, network conditions and users, a number of efforts have been launched aimed at providing the necessary device, network and user descriptions.

Navigation with both WAP and Power Browsers relies entirely on textual links. In contrast, navigation with the RSVP-Browser relies on graphical link previews, which can be riffled rapidly. However, all three browsers rely on a hierarchical page structure, in which users have to drill down to find the content they are looking for. Furthermore, a hierarchy of pages is also a popular structure for Web sites designed to be viewed on a standard size screen. For example, Figure 2 shows a screen shot of the start page of a typical news site (http://www.itn.co.uk) designed to be displayed

Figure 2: Content and layout of a typical News Web site a displayed by Windows IE.

Figure 3: Examples of the link preview (left) and page view (right) modes of a news story in the RSVP-Browser.

on a desktop monitor. The majority of the screen is filled with a display of news headlines each consisting of a short headline text, a summary of the story content and an illustrative image. On the left hand side of the screen is a menu with a choice of news categories such as 'Britain News' and 'Sports News'. When visitors to the page select a news category, a new selection of stories appears on the right of the screen in the same format of headline, summary and picture. Underneath the summary is a hyperlink that readers can select if they want to read the entire story. Many news sites on the Web follow exactly the same format, which suggests that for this type of content a hierarchical site structure is the favourite solution.

The content from a news site such as that shown in Figure 2 is easily adapted for presentation in the RSVP-Browser. For example, the headline news item at the top of the page displayed in Figure 2 is adapted to create the link preview (left) and content page (right) shown in Figure 3.

Two related developments aim to provide the means by which Web based content can be automatically transformed for mobile access on small display devices. These are the User Agent Profile (UAProf) included in the WAP2 standard [WAP Forum 2001] and the CC/PP (Composite Capabilities/Personal Preferences) specification developed by the Klyne et al. [2002]. UAProf and CC/PP provide mechanisms for describing the capabilities of clients and the preferences of users to application servers. This information permits servers to adapt their content accordingly. However, one particularly severe drawback to this approach is that providers of content will have to decide how to match content to the particular *composition* of capabilities represented by each type of terminal. Even though it may be possible to rely to some extent on knowing how to adapt content to suit individual capabilities, the requirements imposed by the composition of capabilities within a particular Internet terminal are unlikely to be successfully predicted by considering each of these capabilities in isolation. Thus, when the task of adapting content to suit different types of Internet terminals is left to the providers of this content, it seems likely that for many types of terminals the content will not be optimally configured. In the next sections we describe an alternative way in which content can be made accessible to the full range of potential Internet terminals.

2.2   Content Negotiation

In contrast to the approaches taken by the WAP Forum and W3C to ameliorate the problem of adapting content in which the server decides what content would be suitable to send, we propose that the *user agent* should be able to decide which content can and cannot be accessed, and how it should be displayed. Such a solution would remove from creators of content the burden of anticipating all possible significantly different Internet terminal profiles. It would also give device manufacturers and software developers more freedom to develop non-standard devices and browsers.

As part of an end-to-end solution for mobile Web browsing, we set out, therefore, developing the means by which providers can describe the content in a way that allows the user agent to decide what should or should not be received. The idea underlying this solution is similar to that underlying MPEG-4's multiplexing [M4IF 2002], in which the user agent can negotiate with the server about which streams to send. However, automated negotiation is possible only if the user agent is able to understand the structure of the available content. For this purpose it is necessary to annotate Web content with meta-information about the function of each bit of content. For example, images are often used to illustrate text, in which case meta-information about this relation between two or more bits of content should be provided to the user agent. Currently, the MPEG-7 standard is under development aiming to provide such a framework for content description meta-data [Martínez 2002]. It is, however, not clear at this stage whether this standard will be able to support a user-centric negotiation between server and user agents. In particular,

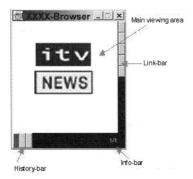

Figure 4: The Pocket PC screen showing the RSVP-Browser layout while the browser is in page mode.

based on our experiences with the RSVP-Browser, we suggest that descriptions of Web content take into account the hierarchical nature of navigation on both small screen devices and standard desktop monitors by providing a hierarchical content description format.

3   The RSVP-Browser Interaction Model

As explained in the previous section, the RSVP-Browser operates in two different modes, separating the activities of link traversal (preview-mode) and content assessment (page-mode). Figure 4 shows a picture of the RSVP-Browser in page-mode together with a labelling of the main screen areas. In page-mode the content of a Web page is displayed in the main viewing area. Each page may consist of a number of separate screens, which can be viewed sequentially. In order to explore the pages that the current page links to, the browser needs to be put in preview-mode, which allows the user to explore the links through the presentation of link previews. Each button in the Link-bar represents a link. In preview-mode, the main viewing area is used for the display of link previews. Browsing of link previews can be done either manually using the buttons in the Link-bar, or by initiating RSVP of the link previews (see Section 2). The History-bar displays a button for each of the previously visited pages in the browsing history. The Info-bar provides information about what is shown in the main viewing area. In page mode this bar shows the position of the currently visible screen in the total sequence of screens that make up the selected page. In preview mode, the bar shows the position of the currently displayed link preview in the sequence of links.

Most available PDAs have buttons that can be used by the hand holding the device. Currently, such buttons are employed only to a limited extent as almost all user input is stylus based. We decided to take advantage of these buttons to explore the possibility of single-handed user interaction with the RSVP Browser. Most of the browser's functionality can be accessed using the four-directional pad near the bottom of the iPAQ. The use of such buttons for navigation avoids some of the

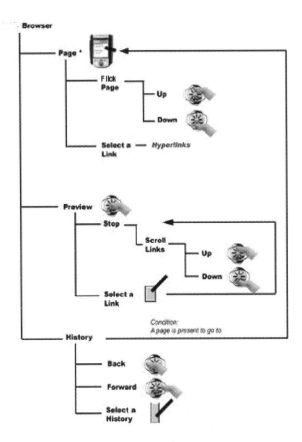

Figure 5: Lean Cuisine+ notation [Philips 1995] of the browser's interaction model.

problems associated with stylus-based interaction, such as needing to have two hands available and requiring considerable accuracy in touching the screen. Furthermore, by limiting most user input to the iPAQ's pad we were forced to limit user interaction to include only the most basic operations. The pad offers five distinct input events by pressing on the upper, lower, left, right or centre parts of the pad. An additional input event is offered by tapping a finger anywhere on the iPAQ's screen provided it is inside the area of the RSVP-Browser window.

Web browsing can be characterized by three questions that users may typically ask. These are, 'Where am I', 'Where can I go' and 'Where have I been'. These questions correspond respectively to the 'Page', 'Preview' and 'History' menemes that form part of the Lean Cuisine+ notation [Philips 1995] of the interaction model shown in Figure 5. A meneme is an individual selectable representation of an object, operation, state or value. The fact that each of these three menemes occur on the same level underneath the RSVP-Browser means that they are continually selectable while the browser is operating. This allows the user to continually switch from one browsing mode to another. When viewing a page, the user can flick through the screens by pressing up or down on the four-direction pad, allowing them to assess the relevance of the content on display. Users can determine where they can go next by clicking the centre of the pad and thereby starting the RSVP of link previews. Link previews appear rapidly one after the other in the viewing area until the user presses the centre of the pad again to stop the RSVP. One or more presses up can subsequently be applied to go back to the desired link in case of an overshoot during the RSVP. A link preview can also be selected by tapping the stylus on a link button in the link bar. To view the page represented by the link preview the user taps a finger or the stylus anywhere in the main viewing area of the browser. Following a link in this way is the only interaction that cannot be achieved using the pad. However, because of the size of the sensitive area, it is easy to select the page using a finger tap even when the user is not looking at the screen. Users can access previously visited pages by choosing left ('Back') or right ('Forward') on the pad. When the history function is accessed, the browser automatically returns to page mode.

4 Evaluation of the RSVP-Browser

A previous paper by the first author presents the results of a comparison in the efficiency of browsing using RSVP of link previews and a WAP browser as implemented on a Nokia mobile phone [de Bruijn et al. 2002]. That comparison showed that browsing using RSVP of link previews is at least as efficient as browsing using textual link menus, albeit not as intuitive. Its lack of intuitiveness is not surprising, however, considering the unfamiliarity of most users with RSVP compared to menu driven browsing.

This previous study into the efficiency of RSVP browsing provided a useful evaluation of the RSVP browsing model against the benchmark of the WAP browsing model. However, PC simulations of both browsers were used in the evaluation, and the study, therefore, failed to capture the importance of the limited interaction mechanisms offered by typical handheld devices, which may have been achieved if real implementations had been used. In this section, we describe an experiment in which we studied people's actions when they were using either the RSVP-Browser or Pocket Internet Explorer (Pocket IE) on a Compaq iPAQ PDA to retrieve information from a set of news items. Pocket IE was used in the evaluation because it is the standard Web browser for devices running Pocket Windows, and it can therefore be considered a benchmark for Web browsing on Pocket PCs. Thus we were able to explore the RSVP interaction model within the constraints of an existing handheld device and test it against the benchmark offered by an existing and familiar browser operating under the same constraints.

4.1 Method

30 students from Imperial College took part in the experiment, whose names were all entered into a £25 prize draw as reward for their participation. Half of the participants (Ps) were randomly assigned to use the RSVP-Browser while the other half used Pocket IE None of the participants had any prior experience with the

browser type they were required to use, although all of them had extensive experience with Microsoft IE for Windows and some of them had used a Pocket PC before.

Content and link previews for the RSVP-Browser were prepared in advance from the ITV news Web site (http://www.itv.co.uk). ITV News is also available through the AvantGo[1] mobile Internet service (see Figure 1). Thus it was possible to access the same news content on both browsers. ITN News has five main news categories, namely 'Britain News', 'Entertainment News', 'World News', 'Business News', and 'Sports News'. A set of 24 questions and answers was prepared based on the news items in these five categories. The wording of the questions matched that of the news items in which the answer had to be found. The questions were typed and put on cards. All the questions required the discovery of a single fact. For example, a participant could be given a question such as "The cross-border train link between Belfast and Dublin has been closed after several explosions were heard near the line. Has the cause of these explosions been identified?" The answer to this question was "No".

All the Ps were tested individually using either the RSVP-Browser or Pocket IE to find the answers to eight questions. Three groups of ten Ps were formed and different sets of eight questions were assigned to each group. Half the Ps in each group then used the RSVP-Browser to find the answers and half used Pocket IE. Ps were instructed to find the answers to the questions on the browser regardless of whether they knew the answer already. The answer to the first question (Task 1) had to be found before Ps had received any instructions as to how to use the browser they had to use. Then, during the search for answers to Questions 2–6 (Tasks 2–6), Ps were allowed to ask the experimenter for instructions on how to operate the browser. The answers to Questions 7 and 8 (Tasks 7–8) had to be found again without any assistance. Ps had to find the answer to each question before being allowed to read the next question. While they interacted with the iPAQ the users' hands and the iPAQ's screen was captured on video. This video footage was subsequently reviewed and the interactions were scored and timed using a separate timer.

After finding the answers to the eight questions, Ps were asked about their subjective experience of the browser used by answering a number of questions in a questionnaire. Each of the questions had to be answered using a five-point scale. For example, the question "Did you find it easy to retrieve the answers to the questions" could be answered by selecting one of the following five alternatives; 'Very easy', 'Easy', 'Indifferent', 'Difficult', or 'Very difficult'. In general, the scales ranged from a positive to a negative opinion. Some questions concerned only the Ps who used the RSVP-Browser, but the majority of questions had to be answered by both groups of Ps.

4.2 Evaluation Variables

The independent variables in the experiment were browser-type (RSVP-Browser or Pocket IE), the question's serial position (Questions 1–8), and question-set (three different sets of questions). The dependent variables were the ratings obtained from the questionnaire, plus a number of performance measures derived from the users'

---

[1] http://avantgo.com/frontdoor/index.html

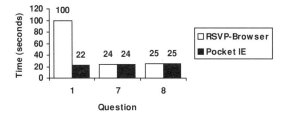

Figure 6: The average times (rounded to the nearest second) needed to answer Questions 1, 7 and 8 for Ps using the RSVP-Browser compared to Pocket IE.

interactions captured on video. We scored the performance on each question by measuring the time to find the correct answer (Time), and the number of unnecessary steps taken to find the answer normalized with respect to the minimum steps required (Steps).

4.3   Results

Analyses of Variance (ANOVA) were performed on the dependent variables Time, Steps and Clicks using a 2×3 factorial design of browser type by question set for Questions 1, 7 and 8 during which Ps were not allowed to ask questions and did not receive instructions. Mauchley's tests of sphericity were performed and Greenhouse-Geisser adjustments applied where necessary.

4.3.1   Time

The means of the time taken to find the answers to Questions 1, 7 and 8 using either the RSVP-Brower or Pocket IE are shown in Figure 6. A significant effect of browser-type was found on the time required by the participants to complete Question 1 $(F(1,24) = 0.517, \text{MSE} = 45732.24, p < 0.001)$ with the mean search times for Ps using the RSVP-Browser almost 5 times greater than those for Ps using Pocket IE There was no significant effect of question set $(F(2,24) = 1.79, \text{MSE} = 2636.15, p > 0.05)$, nor was there an interaction between browser type and question set $(F(2,24) = 0.517, p > 0.05)$. However, by the time Ps reached Questions 7 and 8 there were no effects of browser type, nor any interactions between browser type and question set $(Fs(1,24) < 1)$.

4.3.2   Steps

The mean number of extra steps made while finding the answers to Questions 1, 7 and 8 are shown in Figure 7. Ps using the RSVP-Browser took more unnecessary steps than those using Pocket IE to find the answer to Question 1 $(F(1,24) = 9.49, \text{MSE} = 13.20, p < 0.05)$. This difference between browsers was evident for all three questions sets $(F(2,24) < 1)$, even though it appeared that finding the answer to Question 1 of Set 3 required more extra steps compared to the same question in Sets 1 and 2 (M1 = 0.83, M2 = 0.34, and M3 = 1.83; $F(2,24) = 4.13, \text{MSE} = 5.73, p < 0.05$). When Ps reached Question 7, however, the initial advantage of Pocket IE had more than disappeared, as Ps using the RSVP-Browser needed slightly fewer extra steps to

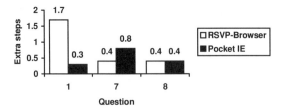

Figure 7: The mean number of extra (unnecessary) steps taken by Ps in finding the answers to Questions 1, 7 and 8 using either the RSVP-Browser or Pocket IE.

find the answer to this question ($F(1,24) = 14.00$, MSE = 1.23, $p < 0.05$). Further analysis revealed that this slight advantage for the RSVP-Browser in answering this question was entirely due to a significant number of extra steps needed to answer Question 7 from Set 1 using Pocket IE ($F(2,24) = 18.98$, MSE = 1.67, $p < 0.05$). The information needed to answer this question could be found at the start of the story. Some Ps missed this information, however, and scrolled all the way to the end of the story and back to the top again. This extra scrolling requires more step in Pocket IE than in the RSVP-Browser. Nevertheless, these extra steps did not lead Ps using Pocket IE to take more time to find the answer to this question (see Figure 6).

4.3.3 Results of Questionnaire

On average, both the RSVP-Browser and Pocket IE attracted very similar ratings on most questions. However, more Ps who used the RSVP-Browser said they found it either difficult or very difficult to find out how to navigate using the PDA's controls compared to Ps who used Pocket IE On the other hand, more Ps who used the RSVP-Browser were either confident or very confident they knew all the functions of the browser compared to Ps who used Pocket IE The questions that specifically targeted the RSVP-Browser also revealed some useful information. For example, it turned out that the fixed rate we had chosen for the presentation of link previews was perceived by 2 Ps to be too fast and by 9 others to be fast. Furthermore, 4 Ps said they found it either difficult or very difficult to select their desired choice at the given speed of presentation. Nevertheless, the same speed caused apparently no problems selecting their choice for 9 Ps, who said they found it easy. 11 out of 15 Ps found it helpful to have pictures associated with the link options, while the remaining 4 were indifferent.

4.4 Discussion of the Findings

Both the performance measures and the subjective ratings seem to indicate that the unfamiliarity with the concept underlying the RSVP-Browser initially put it at a disadvantage compared to Pocket IE. That is, it appears that the Pocket IE interaction model conforms more closely to what people expect from interacting with a PDA. Nevertheless, when Ps were given time to experience using the RSVP-Browser with or without help from the experimenter, this initial disadvantage completely disappeared, and a number of advantages of the RSVP-Browser over Pocket IE became apparent. Indeed, it seems that breaking stories up into separate pages in the

RSVP-Browser may significantly reduce the effort required for scrolling through text documents. Moreover, the simplicity of the interaction model underlying the RSVP-Browser ensured that very little training was required to make users feel confident that they knew all the options the RSVP-Browser had to offer.

5   Overall Discussion and Directions of Future Work

In this paper we have argued in favour of the using M-RSVP technology as an end-to-end solution for Web browsing on PDAs and the wireless Internet. In particular, we have shown that the RSVP-Browser component of this technology offers a viable alternative to the standard Web browser for Pocket PCs, i.e. Pocket IE. We are currently working on an improved version of the RSVP-Browser taking into account the results of the evaluation and the feedback from the users. In particular, we will introduce into the interaction model a control for the speed at which link previews are presented. There are a number of reasons why such a variable presentation rate may improve the usability of the browser. Firstly, the user feedback suggested that each user has a preferred presentation rate that may be different from other users. Secondly, the preferred presentation rate may vary depending on the nature of the material that is being browsed. In our evaluation we used content from a news site, which is perhaps not representative of Web content in general. In particular, it may not always be so easy to select relevant content on the basis of a link preview.

Much of this research is still under development, and much further research, implementation and evaluation will be necessary. However, we feel that the position taken in this paper with regard to the device-independence of Web content remains underrepresented in recent developments in mobile Internet technology, especially in the organizations responsible for the development of Web standards such as the W3C and the WAP Forum. Yet, some of the most innovative solutions to mobile Internet browsing are particularly compatible with our approach of letting the user agent decide what and how much should be accessed based on a hierarchical description of content [e.g. Björk et al. 1999; Buyukkokten et al. 2000; Trevor et al. 2001]. We feel therefore that the development of a hierarchical content description language may represent an important step towards truly device independent information access. We are currently in the process of extending and implementing our own hierarchical content description schema. By testing the schema in a realistic server-client architecture we will be able to investigate the practicality and scalability of content negotiation. Knowing those limits will then allow us to focus our development efforts more effectively in an attempt to define a workable format for the device-independent Web as represented by M-RSVP.

References

Ayers, E. & Stasko, J. [1995], Using Graphical History in Browsing the World Wide Web, *in* I. Goldstein & A. Vezza (eds.), *Proceedings of the 4th International World Wide Web Conference*. Available at http://www.w3.org/Conferences/WWW4/Papers2/270/ (last accessed 2003.05.26).

Björk, S., Holmquist, L. E., Redström, J., Bretan, I., Danielsson, R., Karlgren, J. & Franzén, K. [1999], WEST: A Web Browser for Small Terminals, *in* B. Vander Zanden & J. Marks (eds.), *Proceedings of the 12th Annual ACM Symposium on User Interface Software and Technology, UIST'99, CHI Letters* **1**(1), ACM Press, pp.187–96.

Buyukkokten, O., Molina, H. G., Paepcke, A. & Winograd, T. [2000], Power Browser: Efficient Web Browsing for PDAs, *in* T. Turner & G. Szwillus (eds.), *Proceedings of the CHI'00 Conference on Human Factors in Computing Systems, CHI Letters* **2**(1), ACM Press, pp.430–7.

Card, S. K., Pirolli, P., Van Der Wege, M., Morrison, J. B., Reeder, R. W., Schraedley, P. K. & Boshart, J. [2001], Information Scent as a Driver of Web Behavior Graphs: Results of a Protocol Analysis Method for Web Usability, *in* J. A. Jacko & A. Sears (eds.), *Proceedings of CHI'01 Conference on Human Factors in Computing Systems, CHI Letters* **3**(1), ACM Press, pp.498–505.

Chi, E. H., Pirolli, P., Chen, K. & Pitkow, J. [2001], Using Information Scent to Model User Information Needs and Actions on the Web, *in* J. A. Jacko & A. Sears (eds.), *Proceedings of CHI'01 Conference on Human Factors in Computing Systems, CHI Letters* **3**(1), ACM Press, pp.490–7.

Cockburn, A., Greenberg, S., McKenzie, B., Smith, M. & Kaasten, S. [1999], WebView: A Graphical Aid for Revisiting Web Pages, *in* J. Scott (ed.), *Proceedings of OzCHI'99 The Ninth Australian Conference on Computer–Human Interaction*, IEEE Computer Society Press, pp.15–22.

de Bruijn, O. & Spence, R. [2000], Rapid Serial Visual Presentation: A Space–Time Trade-off in Information Presentation, *in* V. Di Gesù, S. Levialdi & L. Tarantino (eds.), *Proceedings of the Conference on Advanced Visual Interface (AVI2000)*, ACM Press, pp.189–92.

de Bruijn, O., Spence, R. & Chong, M. Y. [2002], RSVP Browser: Web Browsing on Small Screen Devices, *Personal and Ubiquitous Computing* **6**(4), 245–52.

Holmquist, L. E. [1997], Focus+Context Visualization with Flip Zooming and the Zoom Browser, *in* S. Pemberton (ed.), *Proceedings of the CHI'97 Conference on Human Factors in Computing Systems*, ACM Press, pp.263–4.

Kaasten, S., Greenberg, S. & Edwards, C. [2002], How People Recognize Previously Seen Web Pages from Titles, URLs and Thumbnails, *in* X. Faulkner, J. Finlay & F. Dètienne (eds.), *People and Computers XVI (Proceedings of HCI'02)*, Springer-Verlag, pp.247–66.

Klyne, G., Reynolds, F., Woodrow, C., Ohto, H., Hjelm, J., Butler, M. H. & Tran, L. [2002], Composite Capabilities/Preference Profiles (CC/PP): Structure and Vocabularies, http://www.w3.org/TR/CCPP-struct-vocab/ (last accessed 2003.05.26). W3C.

M4IF [2002], MPEG-4 — The Media Standard: The Landscape of Advanced Media Coding, Technical Report, MPEG-4 Industry Forum. Available at http://www.m4if.org/public/documents/vault/m4-out-20027.pdf (last accessed 2003.05.26).

Martínez, J. M. [2002], MPEG-7 Overview, Technical Report ISO/IEC JTC1/SC29/WG11 N4980, International Organization for Standardization.

Philips, C. [1995], Lean Cuisine+: An Executable Graphical Notation for Describing Direct Manipulation Interfaces, *IwC* **7**(1), 49–71.

Spence, R. [2002], Sensitivity Encoding to Support Information Space Navigation, *Information Visualization* **1**(2), 120–9.

Trevor, J., Hilbert, D. M., Schilit, B. N. & Koh, T. K. [2001], From Desktop to Phonetop: A UI for Web Interaction on Very Small Devices, *in* J. Marks & E. Mynatt (eds.), *Proceedings of the 14th Annual ACM Symposium on User Interface Software and Technology, UIST2001, CHI Letters* **3**(2), ACM Press, pp.121–30.

WAP Forum [2001], Wireless Application Protocol WAP 2.0 Technical White Paper, August 2001 version. http://www.wapforum.org/what/WAPWhite_Paper1.pdf (last accessed 2003.05.26) is the latest version.

Woodruff, A., Faulring, A., Rosenholtz, R., Morrison, J. & Pirolli, P. [2001], Using Thumbnails to Search the Web, *in* J. A. Jacko & A. Sears (eds.), *Proceedings of CHI'01 Conference on Human Factors in Computing Systems, CHI Letters* **3**(1), ACM Press, pp.198–205.

Accessibility

Fancy Graphics Can Deter Older Users: A Comparison of Two Interfaces for Exploring Healthy Lifestyle Options

Patricia Wright, Steve Belt & Chris John[†]

School of Psychology, Cardiff University, Cardiff CF10 3YG, UK
Tel: *+44 29 2087 4730*
Fax: *+44 29 2087 6604*
Email: *{wrightp1, belts}@cardiff.ac.uk*
URL: *www.cf.ac.uk/psych/home/wrightp1*

[†] *Computeach International, Jews Lane, Dudley, West Midlands DY3 2AH, UK*
Email: *multichris@yahoo.co.uk*

With the aim of encouraging younger and older people to explore the health implications of changes to lifestyle (e.g. diet, exercise, smoking), two alternative interfaces having identical functionality were compared, using a within-participant design, to see if a graphical interface resulted in more exploration than interacting with numeric tables. The consequences of lifestyle changes were shown as the risk of two major illnesses, coronary heart disease and stroke. When 'advising' hypothetical patients, the amount of lifestyle exploration done by 16 younger adults (mean age 28 years) was similar for the tables and the graphic interface. Using tables, older adults (n = 16, mean age 68 years) explored as much as the younger group but they explored significantly less when using the graphic interface. Both age groups spent less time with the tables but only the older group significantly preferred them. Among the younger group there was no preference consensus but the data suggested sex differences, with younger males tending to prefer the graphic interface. These patterns of data suggest that, in health related decision-making tasks, graphical interfaces can be unsuitable for older people.

Keywords: risk communication, graphical interface, older people, decision aids, decision explorers, health, lifestyle, bar graphs.

1   Introduction

It is a Government priority to reduce deaths from coronary heart disease which is a major source of premature death [Nation 1999]. Health promotion programmes such as Heartbeat Wales have been among the responses to this urgent need [Tudor-Smith et al. 1998]. The Government is also committed to enhancing the shared decision-making approach in which there is a more equal partnership between patients and professionals in taking decisions about health care options [Kendall 2001; Coulter 1999; Elwyn 2001]. A contribution to both these objectives can be made by interactive computer-based tools that help patients understand how a variety of factors influence their risk of having a serious illness, such as coronary heart disease (CHD) or stroke in the next ten years. To facilitate patient-centred approaches to decision-making about health risks [Little et al. 2001], decision support tools need to encourage patients to explore how their personal risk of serious illness can be reduced by changing the levels of some, or all, of the contributory lifestyle factors [Edwards & Elwyn 2001]. This enables people to explore the trade-offs among the available options for modifying lifestyle in the light of their personal values about alternative courses of action. The importance of providing people with customized rather than general advice has been emphasized in recent reviews [Strecher 1999] and elsewhere [Greenhalgh 2001].

Many of the factors contributing to heart disease are well established [DoH 1998]. Nevertheless, encouraging people to reduce their risk of serious illness has not met with great success [Ebrahim & Davey Smith 2000; Tang et al. 1998]. Advice from a health care professional about giving up smoking or taking more exercise yields only 2% more patients taking the advice than would modify their behaviour in a control group [Thorogood et al. 2000]. A systematic review concluded that many lifestyle interventions based on general practice showed promise but none produced large changes [Kendall 2001; Ashenden et al. 1997], partly because people underestimated their personal risk [Samsa et al. 1997] and saw lifestyle factors differently from the epidemiologically based index of risk [Marteau et al. 1995].

It can be particularly difficult for people to understand how their overall level of risk is influenced by specific aspects of lifestyle. Cardiovascular disorders have several contributing lifestyle factors which dynamically interact — e.g. the amount of risk reduction from taking more exercise depends on whether smoking continues. This makes it difficult for clinicians to customize risk levels for patients. Expressing risks of illness as percentages in isolation has little meaning for many people [Bottorf et al. 1998; Cohn et al. 1995], including some health care professionals [Cranney & Walley 1996; Edwards et al. 1998]. Advising patients to modify all lifestyle factors may seem a counsel of perfection, whereas allowing patients to explore the consequences of decisions about specific factors may let them tailor a pattern of behavioural changes to their own personal circumstances. Hence the suggestion that interactive multimedia offer potential "for vastly improved efficacy in communicating risk" [Strecher et al. 1999].

This emphasis on exploration by patients distinguishes the decision aids in this paper from many others that have been discussed in the literature. The traditional approach to decision aids has been for the user, whether patient or clinician, to enter the information requested by the computer and then await the recommended decision [Edwards & Elwyn 1999]. Such decision aids function as *decision advisers*. From the perspective of patient participation in shared decision-making, decision advisers can seem paternalistic and leave the patient with no opportunity to introduce other factors that the computer did not want to consider, or weight the factors for personal relevance. The present focus on decision explorers seeks to meet this need for greater patient involvement.

Another category of decision aid, and one intended for use by patients, presents information in expository form, much as a leaflet would, even if a video or computer screen is used as the presentation medium [Murray et al. 2001a,b]. This category of decision aid might be termed a *decision resource*. Examples of decision resources include medical reference sources such as http://www.nhsdirect.nhs.uk/index.asp and Dipex [Herxheimer et al. 2000] which is a database of patient experiences made available on the World Wide Web for access from home or local library. The advantage of the computer over a printed leaflet in being an information resource for decision-making lies in the richness of the information modality, which may include speech, animated graphics and video. Computers can help patients access the information they personally want, in the order they want it. Although patients have considerable flexibility in how they use decision resources, these aids are similar to decision advisers in that they do not help patients compute trade-offs or examine compromise solutions. Yet computers could facilitate understanding of these dynamic features of decision-making [Ahlberg & Shneiderman 1994]. When documents, either printed or electronic, are used to support decision making it can be important to ensure that the interface adequately meets the needs of specific subgroups of users such as older people [Wright 2000].

A third category of decision aid, and the focus of the present study, offers no recommendations but shows people the expected consequences for their future health of modifying lifestyle factors such as smoking, diet and exercise. Decision aids of this kind will be referred to as *decision explorers* because they help people explore the outcomes of deciding among the courses of action open to them. Decision explorers have in common three underlying assumptions that:

- There is no single 'correct' answer for any individual, rather decisions about the actions to be taken need to fit the individual's circumstances and values.

- Reducing the overall level of risk of serious illnesses such as CHD and stroke is beneficial for people.

- Encouraging people to actively participate in making decisions about what for them are appropriate changes to their lifestyle, will enhance patients' commitment to changing these factors and so reduce their risk of future serious illness.

Such decision aids have been used jointly by consultant and patient with success [Hingorani & Vallance 1999]. The present study seeks to develop an interface that could be used by patients alone, and asks whether the characteristics of such an interface would differ for younger and older users.

The decision explorers will show how a person's risk of CHD and stroke in the next ten years compares with the national average risk for people the same age and sex as the patient. One explorer will do this using numbers in simplified tables to convey the relevant risks, the other will use bar graphs to give the same information. Similarly the changes to lifestyle factors will be done either through clicking up/down arrows to alter the number displayed (e.g. for hours of exercise per week) or by interacting with a graphical gauge giving colour cues and 'smiley face' feedback on the levels chosen (see Materials). It was hypothesized that the graphical interface, which was designed to have a 'game-playing' feel to it, would be found more attractive and would encourage greater exploration of the effects of combined lifestyle changes. This would have implications for the appropriate interface to be used when evaluating a decision explorer in a clinical context.

The intention was that the explorers would be usable by patients with almost no assistance from clinical staff. Therefore one of the goals of the study was to assess whether the online guidance provided, in the form of animated demonstrations and textual help, was adequate to achieve this and whether the interfaces might differ in the amount of support needed.

2 Method

2.1 Design

A within-participants design was used, with the order of using the graphic and tables decision explorers counterbalanced across participants. Performance measures included the amount of exploration undertaken, as reflected in the number of lifestyle changes made, and the time spent using each interface. In addition, during structured interviews, participants rated the ease of using each interface and reported their preference for one of the two interfaces.

2.2 Participants

32 paid adult volunteers took part, 16 male and 16 female. Half comprised a younger group, mean 27.6 years, range 20–40, and half comprised an older group mean 68.6 years, range 61–75.

2.3 Materials

The functionality of both decision explorers was identical. So too was the three-part syntax of the interaction: participants selected a lifestyle factor, adjusted its level and noted the consequences this had for ten year risk of CHD and stroke. Nevertheless, the two decision explorers displayed information in very different visual formats. An example of the graphic decision explorer, with the lifestyle factor *Exercise* highlighted, is shown in Figure 1. The bar graphs show the patient's current levels of risk for CHD and stroke, together with the national average risk for people the same age and sex as the patient. For a discussion of the design history of this interface, together with coloured illustrations of it and its predecessors, see Wright et al. [2003]. The risk levels shown were based on the Framingham equations [Dawber 1980]. As participants made decisions about changing the contributing lifestyle factors, the lengths of the bars moved to reflect the implications of this

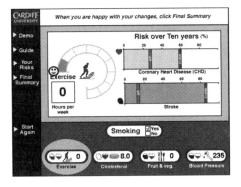

Figure 1: The graphic interface for exploring lifestyle changes.

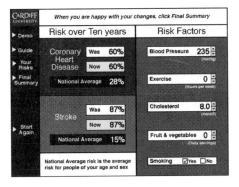

Figure 2: The interactive numeric tables for exploring lifestyle changes.

decision. The software logged which lifestyle factors were adjusted and the levels chosen by participants.

In the tables explorer (see Figure 2) changes to the lifestyle factors were made by clicking arrows on the right of the numeric value. When this produced a change in the ten year risk of either CHD or stroke, radiating circles flashed briefly around the new risk level, shown on the left of the screen, to draw the participant's attention to it.

For both decision explorers there was a multimedia, animated demonstration with spoken explanation in a human, male voice of how the explorer could be used. Participants could replay this demonstration at any time by clicking the *Demo* button on the left of the screen. The same information could be viewed as silent annotated screen shots by clicking *Guide*. Other available functions included the option to reset all lifestyle factors and start the decision exploration again, or to move onto the next patient after clicking *Final Summary*. Clicking *Your Risks* showed a summary of the patient's prospective risk levels for the current lifestyle settings (see Figure 3).

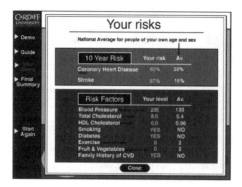

Figure 3: The summary given of lifestyle changes and their combined effects.

2.4 Procedure

The *Demo* button was clicked to show participants how to use the decision explorer. They were then given details of a hypothetical patient whose risk levels of CHD and stroke were far above the national average, and these details were entered into the computer by the experimenter. Participants were asked to use the decision explorer to advise the patient on a pattern of realistic changes to the lifestyle factors that would result in an appreciable reduction in risk of CHD and stroke. Participants were free to take as long as they wished before asking for the next patient and the researcher noted the time taken. Three hypothetical patients were 'advised' and then in a short, structured interview participants rated various features of the interface they had been using on a 7-point scale. After this they were shown the other decision explorer and the *Demo* button was clicked for an explanation of how to use it. Three new hypothetical patients were advised, followed by a structured interview similar to the first. In addition participants were asked which of the explorers they would prefer to use if they had to advise one more patient. The six patient scenarios were done in the same order by all participants.

3 Results

3.1 Ease of Use

Both decision explorers could be used by everyone and did not differ in the ratings for ease of use given after advising three patients (on a 7-point scale where 7 = very easy to use, tables explorer = 6.13, graphic explorer = 6.09). Each explorer received many ratings of 6 or 7 (tables = 25 (78%), graphic = 24 (75%)). Nevertheless, as Table 1 shows, more time was taken with the graphic explorer than the tables (Older group $t(14) = 3.36$, $p < 0.001$; Younger group $t(14) = 3.84$, $p < 0.001$). As would be expected, the older participants took more time on every patient than the younger group (Binomial test $N = 6$, $x = 0$, $p < 0.05$). Less expected was the finding that the men took longer than the women on every patient (Binomial test $N = 6$, $x = 0$, $p < 0.05$) but in this study, time is an ambiguous measure which might reflect either more exploration or more confusion.

Participants	Tables Explorer		Graphic Explorer	
	Mean	S.D.	Mean	S.D.
Older Male	2.75	0.55	4.04	1.51
Older Female	2.56	0.67	3.49	1.02
Older Mean	2.66	0.61	3.77	1.27
Younger Male	1.54	0.27	2.06	0.52
Younger Female	1.60	0.56	2.56	0.76
Younger Mean	1.57	0.42	2.31	0.64

Table 1: Mean times (mins) to advise a patient with each decision explorer.

	Graphic Explorer	Tables Explorer	Mean
Older	3.29	3.75	3.52
Younger	4.19	4.10	4.15
Mean	3.74	3.93	

Table 2: The mean number of modifications to four lifestyle factors for each patient.

3.2 Amount of Exploration

There were four lifestyle factors that could be incrementally adjusted, and one (smoking) that was a binary decision. Everyone in the older group advised at least one patient with each explorer not to smoke, whereas only 9 of the younger group did ($\chi^2(1) = 12.11$, $p < 0.001$). Table 2 summarizes the number of other lifestyle factors that were modified. These figures reflect the number of visits to a lifestyle factor when that visit resulted in some change being made. They do not reflect the amount of change made during a single visit. When using the tables young and old did not differ in the amount of exploration ($t(30) = 0.7$, n.s.) but for the graphic interface significantly more exploration was done by the younger than the older participants ($t(30) = 3.06$, $p < 0.01$).

An indication of the adequacy of the decisions being made is given by the amount of overall risk reduction achieved. Table 3 summarizes the final level of risk achieved for the hypothetical patients. For both CHD and stroke the levels were lower when participants used the graphic explorer than when they used the tables. While lower risk would seem to be a good outcome, if it is achieved through unrealistic settings of the lifestyle factors this could be spurious.

Table 4 summarizes how much the different lifestyle factors were changed to achieve the overall reductions in risk of CHD and stroke. The national average figures, pooled across all patient ages, are also included in Table 4 to assist interpretation. Two points stand out in this summary. One is that the largest difference between the decision explorers was related to changes in blood pressure, which was displayed as the top risk factor in the tables explorer. The other point is that the levels of exercise and diet chosen by participants were more than twice the national average, which may raise questions about the practicality of this 'advice'.

	10 year risk of CHD		10 year risk of Stroke	
	Graphic	Tables	Graphic	Tables
Older	7.77	8.85	4.67	5.02
Younger	7.67	9.73	4.81	5.94
Mean	7.62	8.89	4.74	5.46

Table 3: Level of 10 year risk to which the scenario patient's risk was reduced.

Lifestyle factors	Graphic	Tables	National
	Explorer	Explorer	Mean
Exercise (hours per week)	5.2	4.7	2.0
Diet (daily fruit & veg)	4.3	4.4	2.0
Blood pressure (mm Hg)	143	169	130
Cholesterol (mm ol/l)	4.9	5.2	5.4
N advising a patient to give up smoking (max 16)	16	9	N/A

Table 4: The mean final settings for each lifestyle factor.

3.3 *Preference*

Although participants had rated both interfaces as very easy to use, only the younger participants were as likely to choose the tables explorer as the graphic explorer when asked which they would want to use to advise another patient (see Table 5 where the mean ratings are from a 7-point scale, so 4 is the indifference point). Among the older group there was a significant preference for choosing the tables interface, with only three people opting for the graphic explorer. It may be worth noting that among the younger group, of the seven people preferring the graphic explorer five were male and only one male had a strong preference for the tables (mean rating by young males = 4.63) whereas five of the women in this younger group had a strong preference for the tables (mean rating by young females = 2.88). This difference between the sexes is not statistically significant at the usual cautionary level set for avoiding type one errors ($t(30) = 1.77$, $p < 0.1$) but in applied work it can sometimes be appropriate to relax this level in order to reduce the chance of type two errors (i.e. missing differences that genuinely exist). No such sex differences were observed within the older group (mean ratings male = 2.38, female = 2.88).

4 Discussion

These data confirm that with appropriate online support members of the public are able to use a variety of computer-based decision explorers without needing professional assistance. The time and preference data give no support to there being advantages in having a graphic display but caution is needed in interpreting these findings. The preference could well change in the context of a clinical evaluation by real patients where the data had to be related to personal circumstances because

	Explorer chosen for next patient		Mean rating	p
	Prefer graphic	Prefer tables	(low = Prefer tables)	
Older	3	13	2.63	0.02
Younger	7	8	3.75	n.s.

Table 5: Summary of choices between the two explorers.

suggesting that someone else take five hours exercise a week is much easier than finding the time to do this oneself. So the profile of lifestyle changes apparent in the present data may well differ from those created by real patients in a clinical context. But the aim of the study was to gauge whether the style of the interface mattered, in particular whether it influenced exploration, and the answer is unambiguously affirmative.

The data have shown that a graphic interface can reduce the amount of exploration undertaken by older people. This cannot be due to a reluctance to explore and modify lifestyle factors since the younger and older groups did not differ in the amount of exploration done with the tables explorer. The reluctance to explore as much with the graphic explorer was echoed in the preferences expressed when invited to choose between the explorers to advise another patient. So the question arises as to whether this conclusion is generalizable to other graphic interfaces or whether there was something poor or unfortunate about this particular graphical interface. The display had been through a number of design iterations [Wright et al. 2003] but it remains possible that further improvements could be made. For example, several participants commented that they would have preferred the bar charts to have been vertical rather than horizontal. An interactive aid used co-operatively by consultant and patient that used vertical bars was found very successful [Hingorani & Vallance 1999]. Accommodating two vertical bar charts within the present configuration of the graphic display would entail major redesign of the display, and it seems unlikely that re-orienting the bar graphs would be sufficient to recoup the time difference noted between the displays when used by both age groups.

The pattern of data makes a strong case for conducting a similar comparison of interactive computer-based decision explorers in a clinical context using the methodology of a randomized controlled trial. In such a study it would be possible to relate the decisions made by patients to their intentions concerning specific lifestyle factors and to their subsequent compliance with those intentions. It would also be possible to determine whether encouraging exploration of lifestyle factors enables patients to achieve what is ultimately a more acceptable solution for themselves, which in turn may facilitate adherence to the decisions taken. The preference data in this study suggested that the preferences of younger males might be out of step with the other three subgroups. This might not matter but for the fact that many interfaces are designed by younger males. So the possibility that their interface preferences may be biased by age and gender is highlighted by the present findings and warrants further exploration.

References

Ahlberg, C. & Shneiderman, B. [1994], Visual Information Seeking: Tight Coupling of Dynamic Query Filters with Starfield Displays, *in* B. Adelson, S. Dumais & J. Olson (eds.), *Proceedings of the CHI'94 Conference on Human Factors in Computing Systems: Celebrating Interdependence*, ACM Press, pp.313–7.

Ashenden, R., Silgay, C. & Weller, D. [1997], A Systematic Review of the Effectiveness of Promoting Lifestyle Change in General Practice, *Family Practitioner* **14**(2), 160–75.

Bottorf, J. L., Ratner, P. A., Johnson, J. L., Lovato, C. Y. & Joab, S. A. [1998], Communicating Cancer Risk Information: The Challenges of Uncertainty, *Patient Education and Counselling* **33**(1), 67–81.

Cohn, L. D., Schydlower, M., Foley, J. & Copeland, R. L. [1995], Adolescents' Misinterpretation of Health Risk Probability Expressions, *Pediatrics* **95**(5), 713–6.

Coulter, A. [1999], Paternalism or Partnership? Patients Have Grown Up — And There's No Going Back, *British Medical Journal* **319**(7212), 719–20.

Cranney, M. & Walley, T. [1996], Same Information, Different Decisions: The Influence of Evidence on the Management of Hypertension in the Elderly, *British Journal of General Practice* **46**(412), 661–3.

Dawber, T. R. [1980], *The Framingham Study, The Epidemiology of Atherosclerotic Disease*, Harvard University Press.

DoH [1998], National Service Framework on Coronary Heart Disease — Emerging Findings Report, Department of Health, Health Service Circular 1998/218 LAC(98)29. Available at http://www.doh.gov.uk/pub/docs/doh/coronary.pdf (last accessed 2003.05.26).

Ebrahim, E. S. & Davey Smith, G. [2000], Multiple Risk Factor Interventions for Primary Prevention of Coronary Heart Disease, *The Cochrane Library* **2000**(4). Update Software/Wiley.

Edwards, A. & Elwyn, G. [1999], The Potential Benefits of Decision Aids in Clinical Medicine, *Journal of the American Medical Association* **282**(8), 779–80.

Edwards, A. & Elwyn, G. (eds.) [2001], *Evidence-based Patient Choice: Inevitable or Impossible*, Oxford University Press.

Edwards, A., Matthews, E., Pill, R. M. & Bloor, M. [1998], Communication About Risk: Diversity Among Primary Care Professionals, *Family Practice* **15**(4), 296–300.

Elwyn, G. [2001], *Shared Decision-making: Patient Involvement in Clinical Practice*, Ponsen and Looije.

Greenhalgh, T. [2001], Multimedia Decision Support: An Alternative Interpretation, *British Medical Journal* **323**(7311), 493.

Herxheimer, A., McPherson, A., Miller, R., Shepperd, S., Yaphe, J. & Ziebland, S. [2000], Database of Patients' Experiences (DIPEx): A Multi-media Approach to Sharing Experiences and Information, *The Lancet* **355**(9214), 1540–3.

Hingorani, A. D. & Vallance, P. [1999], A Simple Computer Program for Guiding Management of Cardiovascular Risk Factors and Prescribing, *British Medical Journal* **318**(7176), 101–5.

Kendall, L. [2001], The Future Patient, Technical Report, Institute for Public Policy Research.

Little, P., Everitt, H., Williamson, I., Warner, G., Moore, M., Gould, C., Ferrier, K. & Payne, S. [2001], Preferences of Patients for Patient-centred Approach to Consultation in Primary Care: Observational Study, *British Medical Journal* **322**(7284), 468–72.

Marteau, T. M., Kinmonth, A. L., Pyke, S. & Thompson, S. G. [1995], Readiness for Lifestyle Advice: Self-assessments of Coronary Risk Prior to Screening in the British Family Heart Study, *British Journal of General Practice* **45**(390), 5–8.

Murray, E., Davis, H., See, T. S., Coulter, A., Gray, A. & Haines, A. [2001a], Randomised Controlled Trial of an Interactive Multimedia Decision Aid on Benign Prostatic Hypertrophy in Primary Care, *British Medical Journal* **323**(7311), 494–6.

Murray, E., Davis, H., See, T. S., Coulter, A., Gray, A. & Haines, A. [2001b], Randomised Controlled Trial of an Interactive Multimedia Decision Aid on Hormone Replacement Therapy in Primary Care, *British Medical Journal* **323**(7311), 490–3.

Nation, S. L. O. H. [1999], White paper presented to parliament by the Secretary of State for Health, CM4386, The Stationery Office. Available at http://www.archive.official-documents.co.uk/document/cm43/4386/4386.htm (last accessed 2003.05.26).

Samsa, G. P., Cohen, S. J., Goldstein, L. B., Bonito, A. J., Duncan, P. W., Enarson, C., DeFreisse, G. H., Horner, R. D. & Matchar, D. B. [1997], Knowledge of Risk among Patients at Increased Risk for Stroke, *Stroke* **28**(5), 916–21.

Strecher, V. J. [1999], Computer Tailored Smoking Cessation Materials: A Review and Discussion, *Patient Education and Counselling* **36**(2), 107–17.

Strecher, V. J., Greenwood, T., Wang, C. & Dumont, D. [1999], Interactive Multimedia and Risk Communication, *JNCI Monographs* **25**, 134–9.

Tang, T. L., Armitage, J. M., Lancaster, T., Silagy, C. A., Fowler, G. H. & Neil, H. A. W. [1998], Systematic Review of Dietary Intervention Trials to Lower Cholesterol in Free-living Subjects, *British Medical Journal* **316**(7139), 1213–20.

Thorogood, M., Hilsdon, M. & Summerbell, C. [2000], Changing Behaviour, *Clinical Evidence* **3**, 16–29.

Tudor-Smith, C., Nutbeam, D., Moore, L. & Catford, J. [1998], Effects of the Heartbeat Wales Programme over Five Years on Behavioural Risks for Cardiovascular Disease: Quasi-experimental Comparison of Results from Wales and a Matched Reference Area, *British Medical Journal* **316**(7134), 818–22.

Wright, P. [2000], Supportive Documentation for Older People, *in* C. Jansen, R. Punselie & P. Westendorp (eds.), *Interface Design and Document Design*, Editions Rodopi, pp.81–100.

Wright, P., John, C. & Belt, S. [2003], Designing a Decision Explorer, *Information Design Journal* **11**(1), 115–23.

Towards VoiceXML Dialogue Design for Older Adults

Mary Zajicek, Richard Wales[†] & Andrew Lee

Department of Computing, School of Technology, Oxford Brookes University, Wheatley Campus, Oxford OX33 1HX, UK

Tel: *+44 1865 484579*

Fax: *+44 1865 484545*

Email: *mzajicek@brookes.ac.uk*

URL: *http://www.brookes.ac.uk/speech*

[†] *Age Concern Oxfordshire, The Clockhouse, Long Ground, Oxford OX4 7FX, UK*

Tel: *+44 1865 717787*

Email: *richardwales@ageconcernoxon.com*

The organization Age Concern has established a network of Age Resource Desks to help older people benefit from Information and Communication Technologies (ICT). This paper uses the experience of the Resource Desk run by Age Concern Oxfordshire, and comments from their clients who experimented with a VoiceXML system to address the challenge of enabling older adults to participate in ICT. Older people often have little knowledge of computing and in addition age associated impairment particularly memory and sight loss make using standard desktop computers difficult. The new solution put forward here uses XML-based technology to provide alternative forms of Web access through VoiceXML which offers Web access over the telephone and a grammar system from which to build dialogues. Although this approach removes the need for older adults to learn how to use a standard desktop computer, the would-be dialogue user is still obliged to learn how to interact with a speech system. This paper focuses on the usability of VoiceXML dialogues for older adults and the challenges of embedding context sensitive help and instructions in dialogues used by older adults.

Keywords: older adults, voice dialogues, speech interactions, VoiceXML, Web accessibility, learning ICT.

1 Introduction

The focus of this paper is a report of experiments carried out at Age Concern Oxfordshire using a VoiceXML[1] system, which enables clients to access the Web from their own homes, over the phone and without the need for a computer. Although telephone access to the Web for older adults promises widening accessibility and inclusion, its effectiveness for this user group depends on the usability of the VoiceXML dialogues themselves.

This paper synthesizes the experience of tutors at Age Concern Oxfordshire of teaching older adults to use ICT, with the results of experimentation on the VoiceXML system described in the following sections.

The challenge of experimentation using older adults as subjects is discussed, where the standard homogeneous groups, employed to test design decisions in the User Centred Design process, are difficult to assemble because of the wide diversity of ability and perspective found in older adults.

This paper gathers together the experience of tutors teaching older adults, and then covers the design of dialogues for a Voice Access Booking System (VABS) and in particular explores ways in which instructions and context sensitive help can be incorporated into the dialogue design to help older adults.

A report of experimentation with the dialogues and the interaction paths taken by clients in the trials follows, which provides useful pointers to underlying principles in voice interaction design for older adults. The authors finally reflect on how these principles can be applied to older adults' use of other interactive electronic products.

1.1 Older Adults and Technology

Older adults form a significant proportion of the population numbering some 9.4 million in the UK [Age Concern 2002], with predictions that there will be more over-65s than under-16s by 2014 [Office of National Statistics 2001]. Additionally almost half of the older population is aged at least seventy five, with even larger relative increases being experienced in people over eighty five.

Ageing can result in a combination of accessibility issues. Declines in sensory, perceptual, motor and cognitive abilities that occur with the normal ageing process have implications for interface design. Many of these are catalogued by Morrow & Leirer [1997], whereas Morris [1994], Czaja [1996], and Hawthorn [2000] have described the different declines in abilities that occur with age and the implications of these for human-computer interface design. However very little research has been carried out into what makes an interface easy to use by older adults.

1.2 Lessons Learnt from ICT Taster Sessions

Tutors at Age Concern Oxfordshire have identified five key factors which come into play when older adults learn how to use ICT, some of which contrast with the

---

[1] http://www.w3.org/TR/voicexml20

experience of younger people, whereas others are simply more extreme examples of the needs of any learners:

- Many older adults cannot remember long instructions if given to them before they attempt a new operation. It is much better to give little hints as they are going along. Zajicek & Morrissey [2001] performed experiments which measured the amount of information retained by learners from long and short messages, and found that older adults retained less information from long messages, and that listening to longer messages interfered with the ability to retain information. Similar experiments carried out with younger people showed that the length of message made no difference to information retention.

- All learners need time to assimilate new information, and some older learners, particularly those with poorer memory, less good vision and low dexterity take longer to adjust to the computer. However passing time is not an issue for many older adults therefore learning can take as long as necessary. The time and diligence which older people can invest in learning new skills are real assets.

- Older adults, like all learners, will benefit from positive reinforcement as they learn how to interact with a computer. Zajicek & Hall [2000] showed that with personal support in the form of a helper who simply answered yes or no to their questions older adults were able to use a Web browser where they had not been able before. At the Age Resource Desk the joy which clients have shown as a result of the support and positive reinforcement given to them has been a great reward for everyone.

- Show and do, or learning by example is a very powerful form of teaching for older adults. This is important as some older adults only learn by watching others and so the level of interaction between them and the tutor is minimal. Showing how to do something is different from giving instructions. Show and do is difficult to arrange when people are using a voice system from home but points to the importance of demonstrating the system while potential users are in the company of trainers and other clients at IT taster sessions or an Age Resource Desk.

- No client will progress in any way unless they are comfortable with the equipment and set up. Time is spent at the Resource Desk setting up machines using the accessibility options to meet the needs of individual clients. This is a challenge for the introduction of VoiceXML technology which is designed to be used by people when alone in their houses.

1.3 Dynamic Diversity in Older Adults

As people grow older, their abilities change. This process includes a decline over time in the cognitive, physical and sensory functions, and each of these will decline at different rates relative to one another for each individual. This pattern of capabilities varies widely between individuals, and as people grow older, this variability increases. In addition, any given individual's capabilities vary in the short term due, for example, to temporary decrease in, or loss of, function due to a variety of causes including illness, blood sugar levels and state of awareness.

This collection of phenomena presents a fundamental problem for the designers of interactive systems, whether they be generic systems for use by all ages, or specific systems to compensate for loss of function. Current software design typically produces an artefact which is static and which has no, or very limited, means of adapting to the changing needs of users as their abilities change. Even the user-centred paradigm looks typically at concerns such as representative user groups, without regard for the fact that the user is not a static entity. Processes in use at present are ineffective in meeting the needs of many user groups, or addressing the dynamic nature of diversity. A method is required for designing for dynamic diversity. Gregor et al. [2002] put forward the case for a User Sensitive Inclusive Design approach which would actively seek out diversity and ensure that test users are recruited who represent the whole range of abilities, and which would promote an awareness when defining user requirements of a system that this diversity exists. This is particularly important when using questionnaires, as described in Section 5, where widely differing perceptions average out to a middle of the road score. In fact an average is probably meaningless when working with older people; the range of different perceptions is the reality.

2   The Voice Access Booking System (VABS)

In this section the focus shifts from reflections on teaching older adults ICT and the challenges of designing systems for this group, to the use of voice dialogues by older adults. The dialogue driven system under discussion, the Voice Access Booking System (VABS) was built for Age Concern Oxfordshire, and was based upon a Web accessible database which holds the bookings for IT taster sessions at the Age Resource Desk. The system allows the user to book a taster session with a reminder call, book a taster session without a reminder call, cancel a taster session and notify the database if they are going to be late.

Using the VABS the session organizer can manage the database of appointments using a standard XML-based graphical interface and during office hours clients can book, cancel or re-schedule a session, which the organizer records on the database. The new feature being reported here is that clients can also phone up the database and make their own bookings using a VoiceXML dialogue which interacts with the database, and importantly the system can also phone clients to remind them of an upcoming appointment.

VoiceXML is a new technology, which is only a couple of years old. It offers the dialogue builder simple building blocks known as form and menu, and a set of grammars. The challenge for the dialogue builder is to use these components to construct a successful dialogue, which older adults will be able to use unaided in their own homes to organize their own taster session appointments. Sample code is shown below:

Sample Voice Output tag:

> <prompt>On which day do you wish to book?</prompt>

Sample User Input capture tag with restricted grammar:

> <grammar type="application/x-gsl"> [monday tuesday wednesday thursday friday] </grammar>

Sample 1st Error Recovery Cycle tag — concise:

> <nomatch count="1">Your day was not recognized. Please say a day from Monday to Friday.</nomatch>

Sample 2nd Error Recovery Cycle tag — becoming more expressive:

> <nomatch count="2">Sorry, <value expr="application. uname"/>, your day was not recognized again. Please say a day from Monday, Tuesday, Wednesday, Thursday, or Friday. </nomatch>

Sample Decision/Binary choice tag:

> <prompt>Do you want a morning or afternoon session? </prompt> <grammar type="application/x-gsl"> [morning afternoon] </grammar>

Sample help tag:

> <help>Sessions are generally available Monday to Friday. Please state only one of these days clearly. <reprompt/></help>

The VABS was built following discussion with Age Concern Oxfordshire and the establishment of the five key factors described in Section 2.1.

3   Usability Issues in Dialogue Design

3.1   The Design of Current Telephone Answering Systems

Current telephone answering systems with which we are all involved every day do not adhere to the principles that make for good design for older adults. They use a hierarchical menu system, which places a high cognitive load on the user, as they are required to work out which option covers the goal that they have in mind. Messages are long and often contain preliminary instructions with many options to choose from.

Error recovery and help when a mistake has been made are frequently non-existent. If a user makes a mistake when choosing options it is difficult to get back to where they were. Clients at Age Concern Oxfordshire frequently mention that they do not like such systems.

3.2   Keep Messages Short

As described in Section 2 a major usability aim is to keep output messages or instructions as short as possible. The nature of the VABS dialogue makes for short messages, as users are questioned as they go through the dialogue rather than presented with lists of options as in a standard hierarchical menu driven system. The messages are courteous but hold at most one item of information or ask for only one item of data. One possible path through the dialogue illustrates this as follows:

VABS	A call reminder can be set on the day prior to your booked session. What time do you want your call?
User	11 o'clock.
VABS	Please confirm that you want a call reminder at 11 o'clock.
User	No.
VABS	Try again to select a call reminder. What time do you want your call?
. . .	. . .

3.3   Embedding Help in Dialogues

The primary challenge for the dialogue designer is to provide context sensitive help and instructions to help the older adult to use the dialogue. As described in Section 2 another major usability aim is to keep output messages as short as possible, and provide positive feedback to users. The use of context sensitive help provides a way to support this aim.

3.3.1   Help Interrupt

When using the dialogue older adults were able at any time to say help and the system would jump to help instructions. Help areas are distributed throughout the dialogue and currently instruction takes the form of explanatory text relating to the current state as follows:

Area 1	This system uses voice recognition to understand your commands that should be spoken clearly. Giving your name helps the system to locate your current sessions and gives you access to more functions. You need to contact the centre during office hours to register your name.
Area 2	This system is designed to offer users the ability to book or cancel a computer taster session. Speak your commands clearly and try to use the words given in the question.
Area 3	Sessions are generally available Monday to Friday. Please state only one of these days clearly.
Area 4	Sessions run from 10.30 to 15.30 every hour. Please say something like 'ten thirty' to see if the session is available.
Area 5	To cancel a session you need to find the day and time of the session and then confirm you wish to cancel it.
Area 6	Guest bookings have to be located by day and time. Please ensure that you only cancel your guest booking.
Area 7	Registered users can tell the centre they are running late. This helps the organization of the taster sessions and your help is appreciated.
Area 8	Registered users may ask to receive a telephoned reminder for a training session the day before the session starts. Every attempt will be made to call at the set time.

3.3.2   Embedded Help/Information

The usability issue is how to let the user know the format of input data, for example that call reminders are possible only on the hour. The diagram in Figure 1 shows the generic dialogue for voice input where error recovery i.e. help information is offered after the mistake has been made and is then given in greater detail after a second mistake has been made.

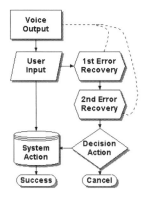

Figure 1: A generic error recovery dialogue.

Help information therefore is embedded in the error recovery loop. The main reason for this is to avoid lengthy introductory messages but also the probability of a user already knowing this information is high since they must be already registered in order to use the service and have probably input data before.

In effect the user is prompted through the dialogue. One client at Age Concern Oxfordshire commented that "the dialogue takes what you have given and then prompts for the gaps".

3.3.3   Use of Defaults

Default input is also used when the user's own data input is unsuccessful. For example the message "Unable to determine a time for a reminder call. Would 7pm be OK?" offers a possible retrieval of the task by offering a default booking time for a call rather than allow the user to leave the dialogue without having completed their task by entering a call reminder time.

This approach contrasts with that of a standard telephone answering system in which users frequently have to start the call all over again if they make an error or forget something.

3.4   Confirmatory Sentences

To make the user feel in control of their interaction confirmatory sentences were used which can be found at several points in Figure **??**, for example. "Please confirm that you want a call reminder at <time>", or "Thank you. You will receive a call at your registered number at <time> the day before your session". Defaults and confirmatory sentences provide positive reinforcement in line with the five key learning factors described in Section 2.1.

4   Evaluation of the VoiceXML System

4.1   The Pre-test Questionnaire

A questionnaire based on a five point Likert scale was used at the start of experimentation to determine user's attitudes to the system. The effects of dynamic diversity described in Section 1.3 comes into play here, as averaging the numerical responses for many questions in the questionnaire would result in a rather bland mid number where the actual responses were decisive and very different. Subjects were encouraged to speak freely around each question and although average scores are not reported here verbal responses are recorded below:

Q1   Access to information about sessions over the telephone will be useful.

      All answers to this were positive.

Q2   Access to my personal information, such as address, over the telephone will be useful.

      Answers were divided for this question. Some users were concerned about who had access to this information.

Q7   Making a booking for a training session over the telephone will be useful.

      All answers were positive, which is encouraging as the whole development focuses on the booking of sessions.

Q8   The ability to make contact out of hours will be useful.

      A range of answers were received for this. Some users are busier than others so appreciate the increased ability to contact the centre, whereas others are happy to make contact during the day.

Q9   A call to remind me about a booked taster session will be useful.

      Mainly positive or neutral answers to this indicate that users are happy to organize themselves although may appreciate a timely reminder on some occasions, probably when they booked the session some time in advance.

Q10   I'd prefer to speak to a human rather than a computer system.

      Most users would rather speak to a human. This is not a reflection on his or her dislike for computer systems but everyone appreciates that a conversation with a human is more involving than a computer system, even though it may be less efficient.

Q11   I would prefer the computer system to have a male/female voice.

      No respondent expressed a preference for either voice. Clients felt that the voice they conversed with didn't matter as long as it was clear.

These responses indicate a positive and open-minded response to the idea of VoiceXML access. Given the negative attitude to standard telephone systems reported above these answers were encouraging.

4.2   Possible Pathways through the Dialogue

4.2.1   Optimum and Worst Task Paths

The set of possible tasks that can be carried out with the system were identified and the optimum and worst potential routes traced. A route includes system output, user input and error cycles. Fatal errors that return the user to the main menu or the operator are denoted by an 'F', one for each potential error.

Table 1. shows the optimum and worst-case number of steps for each VABS task. The figures in the table indicate that the dialogue better supports some tasks than others. Task 9: Guest late, for example is supported to such an extent that the user can carry it out in one step and cannot go wrong. Whereas with Task 8: Registered cancellation, the user could remain in a continuous loop. However Table 2 which

Task	Optimum	Worst
1. Guest Main Menu.	9	18^F
2. Registered Main Menu.	5	14^F
3. Guest booking, yes to call.	6 + 1	$16^{FF}+1$
4. Registered booking, yes to call.	6 + 4	$16^{FF}+9^F$
5. Guest booking, no to call.	6	16^{FF}
6. Registered booking, no to call.	6	16^{FF}
7. Guest cancellation.	7	12^{FFF}
8. Registered cancellation.	1–4	1–∞
9. Guest late.	1	1
10. Registered late.	4	6

Table 1: Optimum, and worst case number of steps for each task.

Task	User1	User2	User3	User4	User5	User6
1. Guest Main Menu.						9
2. Registered Main Menu.	7	5	7	7	5	
3. Guest booking, yes to call.						10 + 1
4. Registered booking, yes to call.	$11+6^F$	11 + 9	13 + 5		13 + 7	
5. Guest booking, no to call.						
6. Registered booking, no to call.				16		
7. Guest cancellation.						12
8. Registered cancellation.		4	4			
9. Guest late.						1
10. Registered late.		5				

Table 2: Number of steps for each user by task.

sets out the actual number of steps taken by test users, shows that the two users who tried Task 8 both carried it out in 4 steps. This demonstrates that the number of possible steps in a dialogue cannot be used alone as a usability measure. The quality and positioning of messages appears to be playing an important part in helping users to avoid the continuous loop situation.

The designer's aim is to reduce the number of potential steps and ultimately make them the same as the optimum path. This is particularly challenging for data entry tasks where input recognition quality is not easy to predict or control.

4.2.2 Users' Paths

The dialogues outlined above were tested with six users at Age Concern Oxfordshire. A PC based version of VABS was used so that factors associated with telephone use would not come into play and dialogue paths alone were under consideration. The user tests were recorded on video camera and the script file from the interaction stored for analysis. Table 2 details the tasks taken by each user and the number of nodes on the route visited to successfully complete the task. This is a useful way of documenting users pathways through the system as it enables easy inspection to see which dialogues are most successful in terms of the number of user steps.

Table 2 shows that only one fatal error was encountered throughout the tests which was due to a misunderstanding by the recognition engine of the desired time for a call reminder. Only one user asked for help and then proceeded to answer the next prompt successfully.

Task 3: Guest booking, yes to call, and Task 4: Registered booking, yes to call, were the most problematic because they rely on voice recognition for data entry. The user paths for those tasks that did not involve data entry were much nearer to the optimum score. Design alternatives for the dialogues supporting Tasks 3 and 4 are put forward in Section 4.4.

4.3   User Feedback

All users expressed dislike for the voice used for speech synthesis which came with BeVOCAL Café, the VoiceXML platform that was used for dialogue implementation. It was American and was purposely set to speak slowly. Despite disliking the voice, users were perfectly able to understand the output. Responses of the users to the system are set out below:

User 1   Expressed dislike for the slow and laborious American voice. Used full sentences when replying to the system or used leaders and trailers around the keywords such as "please ...", "could I ...".

User 2   Originally from America so happier with the accent, also seemed to enjoy better voice recognition. Picked out the use of keywords successfully although had a tendency to use leaders such as "try ..." and "how about ...".

User 3   This user became anxious and was not happy talking to the system because of mis-recognition errors. An experimenter therefore simulated a response to their spoken interaction. The user could appreciate the use of the system out of office hours or on the days when the office is closed.

User 4   Strong dislike for the voice. Became frustrated at the first loop and re-prompt at an error cycle. Not a user of the training sessions anyway and lives so close they would just come around!

User 5   Used the help command on the main menu, although this may have been for exploratory purposes. Became disgruntled at the persistent use of their full name within the prompts, an issue that would be resolved by the use of the underlying database that uses forename and surname separately.

User 6   Enjoyed the challenge of acting as a guest of the system. Listened closely to the voice and completed the booking form quickest of all. Understood that they would just need to pop into the centre to become a registered user.

All users appeared to get quickly frustrated when they encountered an error recovery cycle that failed to explain what they did wrong. The input they gave may have been valid but was not recognized or the input keywords 'Help' and 'Menu' did not convey enough information. This occurred most frequently when booking a session; all but one user gave the time as a particular hour (i.e. 11 o'clock) but the centre runs sessions at half past the hour. Many users that call the centre ask for a morning or afternoon session and the session organizer then allocates them a particular slot.

4.4 Design Improvements

The feedback recorded in Section 5.4 was gathered primarily to look for areas for improvement and therefore by its nature is rather negative. The data in Table 2. however shows that most tasks were completed in near to the optimum number of steps and users were able to use the entire dialogue to complete their tasks. The tasks which require voice input data entry proved to be the most problematic. The next step in dialogue design is to replace these with a 'yes', 'no' type of dialogue proposed by Brownsey et al. [1994], which will in effect perform binary chops on the possible entry data. For example when a time for a reminder call is required instead of being asked to enter the time, the user would be asked "Would you like your reminder call in the morning or afternoon?", as normally occurs when the session organizer sets up the reminder call. If the answer is morning the system would then respond "Before eleven o'clock or after?" The dialogue would continue to halve the search area until a time is found. This new design will be tested against the current data entry structure in future experiments.

5 Conclusions

A first dialogue has been implemented for older adults using VoiceXML demonstrating the potential for the new technology, and providing several lessons.

The ability to set up reminders is a powerful aspect of VoiceXML technology, and can be extended to pre-programmed reminders which place telephone calls to remind an older adult to take some medicine, switch on the heating or remember that a particular person will be visiting. Potentially then a remote carer can populate a database with reminders, which will prompt telephone calls at prearranged times, a useful development for people trying to organize their elderly parents for example.

Principles concerning voice output context sensitive help covered in this paper can be applied equally to interactive electronic products such as interactive TV, and automated machines, where spoken help and instructions could be very useful. As interaction with interactive products become more complex new research questions arise such as, when should help be activated? Should the system learn about a particular user and learn how to help them? Should help kick in when a non-optimal path through the interaction is detected? Should it be set to detect the point when users take a set of wrong paths in their interaction?

As these questions begin to be answered, memory joggers and help systems can play their part in enabling older adults to remain independent for a longer period of time. Older people also often experience difficulty working out how to use interactive gadgets and can be excluded from using many useful products such as automated chair lifts. Spoken help to guide them through their interaction with such products could significantly increase the length of time they are able to live independently.

Acknowledgements

The authors would like to thank the tutors and clients at Age Concern Oxfordshire for their valuable support for the work described above.

References

Age Concern [2002], General Statistics 2001, http://www.ageconcern.org.uk/AgeConcern/ information_428.htm (last accessed 2003.05.26). 0484 Factcard 2001/7,000/02-02.

Brownsey, K., Zajicek, M. & Hewitt, J. [1994], A Structure for User Oriented Dialogues in Computer Aided Telephony, *Interacting with Computers* **6**(4), 433–49.

Czaja, S. [1996], Interface Design for Older Adults, *in* A. F. Ozok & G. Salvendy (eds.), *Advances in Applied Ergonomics*, Elsevier Science, pp.262–6.

Gregor, P., Newell, A. & Zajicek, M. [2002], Designing for Dynamic Diversity — Interfaces for Older People, *in* J. A. Jacko (ed.), *Proceedings of Fifth ACM/SIGRAPH Conference on Assistive Technologies*, ACM Press, pp.151–6.

Hawthorn, D. [2000], Possible Implications of Ageing for Interface Designers, *Interacting with Computers* **12**(5), 507–28.

Morris, J. [1994], User Interface Design for Older Adults, *Interacting with Computers* **6**(4), 373–93.

Morrow, D. & Leirer, V. [1997], Aging, Pilot Performance and Enterprise, *in* A. Fisk & W. Rogers (eds.), *Handbook of Human Factors and the Older Adult*, Academic Press, pp.199–230.

Office of National Statistics [2001], Aging Population: More over 65s then under 16s by 2014, http://www.statistics.gov.uk/cci/nugget.asp?id=287 (last accessed 2003.05.26).

Zajicek, M. & Hall, S. [2000], Solutions for Elderly Visually Impaired People Using the Internet, *in* S. McDonald, Y. Waern & G. Cockton (eds.), *People and Computers XIV (Proceedings of HCI'2000)*, Springer-Verlag, pp.299–307.

Zajicek, M. & Morrissey, W. [2001], Speech Output for Older Visually Impaired Adults, *in* A. Blandford, J. Vanderdonckt & P. Gray (eds.), *People and Computers XV: Interaction without Frontiers (Joint Proceedings of HCI2001 and IHM2001)*, Springer-Verlag, pp.503–13.

WebTouch: An Audio-tactile Browser for Visually Handicapped People

M Macías[†], A Reinoso[‡], J González[†], J L García[‡], J C Díaz[‡] & F Sánchez[†]

[†] *QUERCUS Software Engineering Group and* [‡] *DSP Processing Group, Departamento de Informática, University of Extremadura, Escuela Politécnica. Avda Universidad s/n, 10071 Cáceres, Spain*
Email: *fernando@unex.es*

The Internet offers new possibilities to the access of information, but sometimes the design of Web pages obstructs the contents making them inaccessible to everybody, especially for those people with visual disabilities. The problem has several sides. On the one hand, the inaccessible design of the pages. On the other hand, most of the browsers used to surf the net are thought to be managed by users without visual disabilities. Although there are tools to help in the right design of Web pages or in the interpretation of Web pages for people with visual handicaps, to our knowledge there is not an integrated tool useful for both, the designers and the visually handicapped users. Our research group has developed such a tool called KAI (Kit for the Accessibility to the Internet). KAI is based on two main pillars: a new markup language with accessibility features called Blind Markup Language (BML) and WebTouch, a multimodal browser taking blind people into special consideration. In this paper we focus on WebTouch and its two modalities for surfing the net: voice and tactile skills.

Keywords: Web accessibility, Web browser, speech recognition.

1 Introduction

Since its creation the Internet has offered a new branch of possibilities to the access of information. Through this media, published data are available in the entire world at the same time. But sometimes the design of pages and Web applications are not accessible to everybody. People with disabilities often find difficulties when retrieving information from the net. Some designers and interfaces have replaced the functionality and simplicity with aesthetics and attractiveness; this obstructs the access to the contents, especially for people whose physic disabilities make them unable to enjoy with the design, the blind.

There are tools available to help this kind of users: screen readers such as JAWS[1], hearing browsers [2] and others. But these tools only exploit the hearing skills. Currently, haptic skills are gaining more and more interest in the development of user interfaces for people with disabilities [Sjostrom 2001; Brewster 2001; Challis & Edwards 2000].

Our research group has developed KAI, a Kit for the Accessibility to the Internet for the blind. One of the main components of KAI is WebTouch, a multimodal browser. Multimodal interfaces imply the use of multiple ways of interaction between the user and the computer. WebTouch allows the user to recognize the elements on a Web page by using the sense of touch. The activation of commands and the interaction with the different elements of the Web page is done via voice using an automatic speech recognition system. This multimodality allows the user to form an internal cognitive map of the Web page being visited [Lahav & Mioduser 2001].

In this paper the fundamentals of WebTouch are introduced. The rest of the paper is as follows. In Section 2 the main ideas behind KAI and WebTouch are outlined. Section 3 presents the voice recognition system. Finally conclusions are presented in Section 4.

1.1   KAI

KAI [Macías et al. 2002; González et al. to appear] is an integrated tool with software and hardware components. The main goal of this tool is increasing the accessibility of Web contents to users with visual handicaps, especially the blind.

The architecture of KAI (Figure 1) has two main components: the BML language and the WebTouch browser.

1.2   BML

The Blind Markup Language (BML) has been developed to build accessible Web pages easily. It is derived from XML and quite similar to HTML but including new tags to structure the page better. BML also allows the possibility of assigning different ways of presentation to the different elements of a Web page: textual, graphical, sound and tactile. Web designers can use BML directly or through an editor, which is accessible itself.

A Web designer can write code directly for BML with or without the editor. But, what happens with existing Web pages that are not written in BML? There is another component in KAI that translates existing Web pages from HTML or XHTML into BML by analysing their structure. This process implies several phases: separation of contents and presentation, recovery of inaccessible contents and reorganization of the information using the new tags included in BML. Once the page is coded in BML it can be presented in the WebTouch browser explained below. For other browsers

---

[1]http://www.freedomscientific.com/fs_products/software_jaws.asp.
[2]For example, Home Page Reader, http://www-3.ibm.com/able/hpr.html.

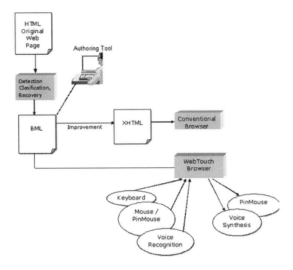

Figure 1: A general overview of KAI.

there is a module in charge of translating the page from BML into XHTML again. The original source code of the Web page has been modified. Now it is more accessible, but its visual presentation is the same.

1.3   WebTouch

WebTouch is a multimodal browser especially developed for blind users. It provides several possibilities of navigation combining audio, voice and tactile skills. It is possible to configure the navigation modality according to users needs. Figure 2 shows a Web page in WebTouch. The different areas of the browser are also outlined.

WebTouch allows one to obtain a tactile representation of the contents of a Web page in the *Representation* area. In this way, visual handicapped users can build a mental map of the contents before surfing. This is an improvement comparing it with other tools such as screen readers. Each element of the page is presented as an icon. Each icon can be recognized by passing a special mouse (PinMouse) over it. PinMouse, also developed in the context of KAI, has two cells of pins like that shown in Figure 3. Whenever the mouse passes over a specific icon then the pins raise up forming a shape. The first cell of PinMouse tells the user the element below the mouse (for example, the presence of a table). The second cell provides additional information regarding accessibility issues, for example, the existence of a summary for the table detected. This helps the user to decide whether continuing surfing or not.

Once the icon has been selected then the user can interact with it using the *Interaction* area. For example, given a text, the user could activate the control for reading it. The user can also use the *Navigation* area to surf the page through the different structures: only tables, only e-mail addresses and so on. This is one of the main advantages of WebTouch: the possibility of selective reading.

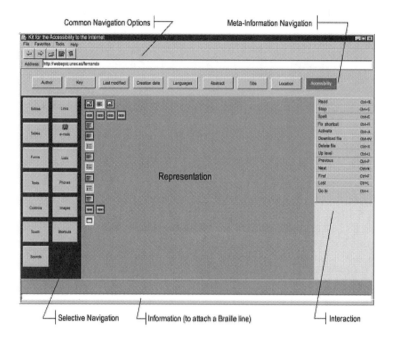

Figure 2: WebTouch interface and working area.

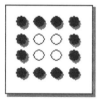

Figure 3: Tactile icon in a pins cell.

Both options and icons are associated with a keyboard combination and a word. So users can interact with the different areas with keyboard, mouse and voice. For this purpose, a speech recognizer has been added to KAI in order to extend the possibilities of navigation. Users can concentrate on a tactile exploration of contents while using their voice to manage the interface.

One of the main objectives in the design of KAI was the final price for the user and the ease of use. The tool is quiet cheap. The user only needs a special mouse and software. The experiments developed up to now demonstrate that the tool is very intuitive for users.

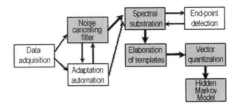

Figure 4: Architecture of Ivory speech recognition system.

2 The Automatic Speech Recognition System

We have considered Ivory [Díaz et al. 2001] as the automatic speech recognition system (ASR). Ivory is a speaker independent ASR methodology for isolated words that is robust to noise. Ivory was originally developed in C for the Texas Instruments TMS320C31 digital signal processor and it is maintained in the current processors of the TMS320C family such as the TMS320C6711. As can be understood, the speaker independence of Ivory makes an important feature for wide use applications such as those related with the World Wide Web. Internally, Ivory is based on a probabilistic model that structures the recognition process in a pipeline of stages that are applied to the voice stream (Figure 4). Each one of these stages is a transformation function.

A feature we have removed from Ivory is the noise robustness. This is due to the environments that it targets, mainly desktop systems, should not need it at all. Thus, the Ivory gets reduced to the four stages that Figure 1 shows. The Java use of Ivory has imposed to define clearly the original interface. Thus, the main functions of the Ivory interface are:

```
void IVORY_spectrum(Channel * spectrum,
    Sample * signal, Energy * energy) ;
void IVORY_template(Template * template,
    Channel * spectrum, Average average[][]) ;
void IVORY_quantization(Centroid * centroid,
    Template * template, int context) ;
void IVORY_parser(Winner * winner, Centroid centroid,
    Energy energy, state_t state, int context) ;
```

The three first stages extract the more significant features of the speech signal. The last one compares these features to the statistical models that have been previously elaborated, the so-called vocabulary of the recognizer. In the case of WebTouch the vocabulary is the set of buttons in the different areas and the different kinds of icons. If the features of the input signal match one of the built-in models, Ivory takes as recognized the word corresponding to that model. The statistical model of each word of the vocabulary is known as the Hidden Markov Model and it has to be previously built. Several samples (observations) of each word are needed. Altogether they form what it is known as the word database, which is later used to construct the set of Hidden Markov Models associated to the vocabulary.

On the interaction with any application, the user usually has available a set of active options or commands. If we define 'work context' as the current state in the handling of the application, the work context comes defined by the set of valid

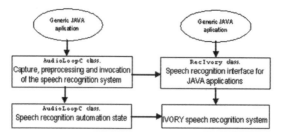

Figure 5: ASR component architecture.

commands. Thus, the work context can be mapped to a given vocabulary, called **active vocabulary**, composed by the set of words used to name such commands. In the case of WebTouch the meaning of a word is different depending on the area being interacted with.

A feature that has been added to Ivory is the work context. An advantage of this focus is that the more reduced the vocabulary, the more precise the recognition task results. The work context has implied to extend the interface of Ivory. Thus, the quantifying stage will use the work context in order to determine the centroids codebook. Similarly, the parsing stage uses the context information to choose the right Markov model.

2.1 The Architecture of the ASR Component

The ASR component consists of two main modules or classes, *AudioLoopC* and *RecIvory*, and a third auxiliary class, *ParserState*, imposed by the work context concept. *AudioLoopC* runs an infinite loop of voice caption and supplies it to the recognizer. *RecIvory* acts as the Java interface to the C functions of Ivory. *ParserState* is used to keep the state of an automaton that manages the voice and silent periods. Figure 5 illustrates the modular design of the component.

It is important to highlight that the execution of the ASR component does not interfere at all with the rest of the application functionalities. This design allows WebTouch to be controlled both by the usual devices such as the mouse, the keyboard and by the human voice.

2.1.1 The AudioLoopC Class

AudioLoopC constitutes the main class of the component. It implements the functionalities of capture and preprocessing of the voice stream and the further invocation of the Ivory pipeline. Likewise, it eventually invokes the method that the user application associates to the recognized word.

The basic task of its constructor is the aperture of an input stream that allows the application to receive the audio data. For portability and efficiency reasons, we have chosen to obtain the stream in a direct way from the general controller of the audio resources of the system, thus avoiding the treatment of specific drivers. This general controller considers the microphone as the standard audio input, which automatically provides the class with a voice stream coming form this device. Once the stream has been obtained, it is opened indicating the audio format of its data and the size of the requested buffer.

AudioLoopC has been designed and implemented in such a way that the whole process of capture, treatment and recognition is executed in the context of an independent thread of control running in concurrency with the rest of the threads or activities launched by WebTouch. The activation of this thread is performed by invoking a method of the *AudioLoopC* class. This method activates the stream and initiates the cycle of capture and recognition. The signal is normalized and fragmented in overlapped windows of 256 samples before being supplied to Ivory.

The current work context is stored in the `context` attribute of the *AudioLoopC* class, which provides methods for reading and writing. When a word is recognized, *AudioLoopC* makes a callback to WebTouch to serve the event.

2.1.2 The RecIvory Class

RecIvory links *AudioLoopC* to the C Ivory interface. It is a class whose methods are declared as natives in order to indicate that its implementation is not done inside the own class and, furthermore, that it has been written in a language different from Java. Each of these methods maps an Ivory function. The instantiation of the class is not necessary because it is just an interface class. For the same reason all its methods are defined as static.

The object code of Ivory is supplied to *RecIvory* loading in memory the dynamic library that results from the compilation of its native routines. This loading process is performed in the class initialization section.

Finally, the class *RecIvory* supplies a mechanism that is independent from the voice capture procedures. This makes it possible for any application to use it in an independent way.

2.2 Using Ivory from Java

Ivory is a DSP application developed in a TMS320C6711 digital signal processor. Code Composer is a C/C++ development environment for these processors. As a result, Ivory is implemented as a C module. The problem posed is using Ivory, a compiled C library, from *RecIvory*, a JAVA class. Fortunately, JAVA helps with the Java Native Interface (JNI). JNI is the Java programming interface to native code. JNI allows Java code, written to run on the JVM, to interoperate with applications and libraries coded in other programming languages, such as C, C++ or assembler. It also allows embedding the JVM in these native applications. This section deals with two issues, the renaming of the Ivory methods and its pointer arguments.

The first problem posed by JNI is that it imposes a renaming of the original Ivory methods. The source file *RecIvory.java* contains the declarations of all the original native methods of Ivory, as well as the load sequence of the resulting library. This file is compiled with the javac tool in order to obtain the *RecIvory.class* file. The javah tool with the -jni option is applied to it to obtain a header file of native methods. As a result we get the header file *RecIvory.h*, with the renamed Ivory methods. Once the native methods have been adapted, we proceed with its compilation. In system such as Solaris a shared library is obtained. In windows systems a dynamic link library is used.

The second problem that this section deals with is the parameter passing to Ivory. Ivory needs to operate upon arrays that contain windows of samples from the voice stream. This means that the access to the elements of an array and its manipulation ability from a native C method is a fundamental issue.

JNI allows specifying if a native method either access to a copy of the array kept by the user Java code or reference directly to it. The real-time requirement of speech processing demands that any interchange between Java and Ivory be performed by reference.

The treatment with matrices deserves a special consideration. Some methods of Ivory receive as argument a matrix of floating point data. Although the declaration and use of this matrix in the Java code does not present any difficulty, the same does not happen on the native side. The procedure of access to the elements of the matrix in the native code come determined by the consideration of it as an array of elements that, in their turn, are collection of data. This view of the matrix is supported by JNI by the general type *jobjectArray*, that allows to declare arrays that contain references to objects instead of data of a primitive type. Thus, the Ivory functions that need the matrix of templates will do it through the corresponding parameter declared of *jobjectArray* type.

2.3 Integration of the ASR System with WebTouch

This section presents the procedure that allows integrating the component in a user application such as WebTouch. In first place, the classes of the component are added to classes belonging to WebTouch. In second place, the main class of WebTouch declares and instances an object of the *AudioLoopC* class, providing the format of the audio stream. Finally, at run-time, WebTouch invokes the method *AudioLoopC*, that activates the thread that starts the activities of voice capture.

Eventually, WebTouch provides Ivory with a new work context, depending on the user actions. This information is supplied through the method that *AudioLoopC* provides with this purpose. When Ivory recognizes a word returns the identifier of the word to *AudioLoopC* that invokes the method of WebTouch associated to the word.

3   Conclusions

KAI, Kit for the Accessibility to the Internet, has a multimodal haptic/voice browser, WebTouch, developed to be used mainly by the blind.

From the haptic point of view, this browser contains a special mouse, PinMouse, which allows the detection of elements of a Web page using the sense of touch. From the voice point of view, the browser allows an interaction using an automatic speech recognition system (ASR). This paper has briefly presented the main ideas behind the ASR system and its integration with WebTouch.

Future works include the possibility of integrating features of initiatives such as Speech Application Language Tags (SALT[3]) in BML. With this, not only the user can interact with the different commands of the browser but also with the page itself.

---

[3]http://www.saltforum.org/

Acknowledgement

This work has been developed with the support of CICYT under project TIC2002–04309-C02–01 and Junta de Extremadura under project 2PR01A023.

References

Brewster, S. [2001], Haptic Interaction, http://www.dcs.gla.ac.uk/~stephen/research/haptics/index.shtml (last accessed 2003.05.26).

Challis, B. P. & Edwards, A. [2000], Design principles for Tactile Interaction, http://www.dcs.gla.ac.uk/~stephen/workshops/haptic/papers/challis.pdf (last accessed 2003.05.26). Proceedings of the Workshop on Haptic Human–Computer Interaction, University of Glasgow.

Díaz, J. C., García, J. L., Rodríguez, J. M., Álvarez, J. F., Espada, P. & Gómez, P. [2001], DIARCA: A Component Approach to Voice Recognition, *in* P. Dalsgaard, B. Lindberg & H. Benner (eds.), *Proceedings of the 7th European Conference on Speech Communication and Technology (Eurospeech 2001)*, Aalborg Universitet, pp.2393–6.

González, J., Macías, M., R., R. & Sánchez, F. [to appear], Accessibility Metrics of Web Pages for Blind End-users, *in* J. M. Cueva, M. González, L. Joyanes, E. Labra & M. P. Paule (eds.), *Proceedings of the International Conference on Web Engineering (ICWE'2003)*, Lecture Notes in Computer Science, Springer-Verlag.

Lahav, O. & Mioduser, D. [2001], Multisensory Virtual Environment for Supporting Blind Persons Adquisition of Spatial Cognitive Mapping: A Case Study, http://muse.tau.ac.il/publications/74.pdf (last accessed 2003.05.26).

Macías, M., González, J. & Sánchez, F. [2002], On Adaptability of Web Sites for Visually Handicapped People, *in* P. De Bra, P. Brusilovsky & R. Conejo (eds.), *Adaptive Hypermedia and Adaptive Web-based Systems: Proceedings of the 2nd International Conference (AH2002)*, Vol. 2347 of *Lecture Notes in Computer Science*, Springer-Verlag, pp.264–73.

Sjostrom, C. [2001], The IT Potential of Haptics. Touch Access for People with Disabilities, Licenciate Thesis, Certec, Lunds Universitet. Available at http://www.certec.lth.se/doc/touchaccess/ (last accessed 2003.05.26).

Two Falls out of Three in the Automated Accessibility Assessment of World Wide Web Sites: A-Prompt vs. Bobby

Dan Diaper & Linzy Worman

School of Design, Engineering & Computing, Bournemouth University, Talbot Campus, Fern Barrow, Poole, Dorset BH12 5BB, UK

Tel: *+44 1202 523172*

Email: *ddiaper@bournemouth.ac.uk*

URL: *http://dec.bournemouth.ac.uk/staff/ddiaper/*

The results of comparing two World Wide Web accessibility assessment tools, Bobby and A-Prompt, is reported. The two tools were applied to a sample of 32 UK university Web site home and search pages. Relating the tools' outputs to the Web Content Accessibility Guidelines, A-Prompt found all the guideline compliance failures that Bobby did at both priority levels 1 and 3 and some more that Bobby did not detect. At priority level 2 there was no agreement between the tools as to the compliance failures they detected.

Keywords: accessibility, Web content accessibility guidelines, assistive technologies, accessibility assessment tools, Bobby, A-Prompt.

1 Introduction

The case for universal accessibility to the World Wide Web is so patent that legislation already exists, e.g. in the USA and UK, or is before various governments, to enforce universal accessibility and, indeed, to punish those who fail to meet legally determined reasonable, minimum accessibility criteria. This, of course, causes great, global confusion, for example, about whether universal accessibility is required legally, in some countries, of all Web sites, or just certain types of them. By the end of 2002, for example, two cases on Web accessibility in different US states have been before the courts and while the cases are reasonably similar, both involve transport company Web sites (Southwest Airlines and the Metropolitan Atlanta Rapid Transit Authority), the legal judgement has gone in opposite directions in the two cases. NB This, of course, is how case law is developed and the legal systems, no doubt, will settle down in a few years time. What is more distressing, except to the cynical, is that anyone should fight against the concept that, ideally, all people should be able to access all of the Web, i.e. universal accessibility.

Universal accessibility is an ideal, of course, and 'nearly' should be inserted in front of both occurrences of 'all' in the definition at the end of the paragraph above. Furthermore, the definition need not be taken to imply that performance won't be different with different Web access mechanisms. Eschewing politically correct terminology, the current focus is on extending Web accessibility to "those with disabilities [Waddell 1999] and those using 'non-standard' Web browsing technology" [Sloan et al. 2002] and, in particular, to cater for Web users who are blind or partially sighted.

There are a lot of assistive technologies [Bergman & Johnson 1995] to help the visually impaired by providing alternative output media such as synthesized speech or Braille. The World Wide Web Consortium's (W3C[1]) Web Accessibility Initiative (WAI) Web site lists about 70 assistive software tools of various types. Many of these assistive technologies rely on Web pages using a standards compliant form of HTML and adhering to accessibility guidelines, notably the Web Content Accessibility Guidelines (WCAGs) produced by the W3C's WAI and, in the USA, Section 508 of the Rehabilitation Act Amendments of 1998. There is considerable overlap between the WCAGs and those derived from Section 508. For example, the Access Board responsible for Section 508 indicates at priority 1 an overlap of 11 check points between the two and 5 that differ; the WCAGs are organized into check points which may be at one of three priority levels, with priority 1 check points being the most important to comply with. There are a total of 66 WCAG checkpoints, with 17 ,29 and 20 at priority levels 1 to 3, respectively. Given that W3C's ambition is to be global, this paper will only concern itself with discussing the WCAGs and not with those associated with the USA centric Section 508 standards.

1.1 Web Content Accessibility Guidelines

Admittedly, not all of the WCAGs and check points are equally clear and the interpretation of some of them requires human craft skill even when assistive technologies are used by Web site developers. We can only agree with Sloan et al. [2002] that:

> "Current accessibility guidelines require developers to fully understand the requirements of each guideline, the reasoning behind that guideline, and the steps to be taken to meet that guideline. Colwell & Petrie [1999] have questioned the effectiveness of the W3C WCAG in successfully helping developers create accessible resources."

Indeed, our suspicions go rather further in that we doubt that even all those involved in the WCAGs development achieve such a comprehensive understanding

---

[1] http://www.w3c.org (last accessed March, 2003).

of all the guidelines as Sloan et al. [2002] say is required, and which we might even question as possible at all with the WCAGs as they are currently expressed. We certainly do not count ourselves amongst such few *cognoscenti* that may exist and we are thus with the vast majority of those concerned and involved with Web design.

To illustrate the sort of difficulty that people, including ourselves, have with understanding and applying the WCAGs' check points, check point 12.2 states "Describe the purpose of frames and how frames relate to each other if it is not obvious by frame titles alone. [Priority 2]". Following the appropriate links on the WAI Web site leads to the relevant part of their document on HTML design (WAI Note 6) which provides a worked example of a newspaper Web site that has three frames described as:

#Navbar — this frame provides links to the major sections of the site: World News, National News, Local News, Technological News, and Entertainment News.

#Story — this frame displays the currently selected story.

#Index — this frame provides links to the day's headline stories within this section.

While these may or may not be good examples of description links such as 'longdesc' in HTML, they self evidently contain nothing about the relationships between the frames as the #Navbar description doesn't mention the 'headline stories' in #Index.

More extremely, we find compliance with WCAG number 14 "Ensure that documents are clear and simple." beyond our own, limited abilities to assure. While there are software tools such as the Clear Language And Design tool (CLAD[2]) which can calculate a reading level to help developers with check points that have some stylistic language requirements, the numerous psychological issues pertaining to different types of document, by different authors, for different readers, in different environments, are such that we believe WCAG 14 is over ambitious on the part of the WAI. We think WCAG 14 should be dropped as part of a desirable simplification of the WCAGs that would make them more understandable and hence usable by a wider range of Web developers. We suggest this because not only are the psychological, stylistic language requirements very complicated and not even agreed upon in theory, but also because the concept of simplicity is not simple and "the world is never as (ahem) simple as that" [Smith et al. 1982, 1987].

For anyone attempting to apply the WCAGs there are two major types of task: 1. finding accessibility problems; and 2. repairing them. While both these task types requires an understanding of the WCAGs, we think the latter is the easier of the two in that finding WCAG compliance failures really does need the accessibility analyst to understand the check points and be able to apply them all, appropriately, to every Web page assessed. This sort of search activity is extremely difficult to master because analysts have no absolute feedback about their own performance, i.e. they

---

[2]http://www.eastendliteracy.on.ca/ClearLanguageAndDesign/start.htm (last accessed April, 2003).

cannot know if they have detected all the possible compliance failures. Obviously different analysts, and the same one on different occasions, may be more or less thorough in their attempts to detect compliance failures. In contrast, most attempts to repair compliance failures are likely to lead to some accessibility improvement, even if the repair is less effective than it could be. We believe that assistive technologies that help Web developers detect possible WCAG compliance failures should provide vital support to help with what, for most people, are very difficult detection orientated tasks.

2   Web Accessibility Assessment

To properly assess a Web site's accessibility is not easy and it must be necessary to adopt an approach like that of Sloan et al.'s [2002], which involved various teams of people and seven different types of method. Even though Sloan et al. are attempting 'discount usability engineering', their method is still far too expensive, in time, money, available expertise, etc., for what are probably the majority of commercial and institutional Web site owners. Our suspicion is that a human expertise shortage is the most serious problem because accessibility is a complex Human–Computer Interaction (HCI) issue that requires a fairly sophisticated understanding of people's psychology, i.e. the "rich, multiple perspectives of human thought and behaviour, which have often taken (psychologists) years to acquire" [Diaper 1989]. We suspect that most Web developers come from a different, technical computing, background and therefore struggle with what are genuinely complex HCI issues. At present, however, no one recommends that Web accessibility assessment tools are used alone, without a human contribution to assessment, but it is just this expertise which we think might be relatively rare amongst Web developers.

To give an example that concerns us, like Sloan et al. [2002], we have found Web sites where the HTML ALT text facility is not merely ignored, but abused. ALT text provides a textual description of non-textual objects, such as images, that assistive technologies for the visually impaired can use, and the WCAG, priority 1, check point 1.1 "Provide a text equivalent for every non-text element" does mean, for the visually impaired, a description of the image and not, for example, as a 'tool tip' and certainly not the same ALT text on every image, e.g. "A picture of this page." as reported by [Sloan et al. 2002].

The WCAG's do allow an option of just using a '*' as a dummy ALT text, but we remain unconvinced that this option is really a good one. For example, we contacted one university Web site developer responsible for their disability pages when we noticed that every image on these pages just contained '*' in the ALT texts. The reply we received was that "The images are of lesser importance." This may not be the institutional position, but illustrates our concern with how real Web developers may operate, in this case using a general excuse for limiting accessibility. Furthermore, users who need ALT text descriptions have to trust the Web developers' judgement that the images are indeed of 'lesser importance'. Perhaps even a legitimate use of '*', if used frequently, indicates a violation of WCAG 14, regarding clarity and simplicity, if pages are cluttered with unimportant images.

Although the WCAGs do try to provide a fairly detailed explanation of what they mean by the term 'equivalent' in check points such as 1.1, this is still a matter of interpretation by Web developers. While the adage that "A picture is worth a thousand words." is hyperbole in that a thousand words is somewhere between two and four typed pages, just how to describe an image in its specific context on a Web page is obviously problematic. A company logo might be a simple thing to put on a home page, but the range of possible ALT texts is vast: at one extreme we might have:

1. "The X company logo."; or

2. we might try and describe the visual appearance of the logo; or

3. at the other extreme, one might try to summarize the corporate identity the logo purports to represent.

Option 2 is a classical, insoluble problem for those who have been blind from birth and thus, while looking a superficially attractive option as a style of ALT text description, is actually the worst case for such blind people as the description will be meaningless. Option 2, however, might be of high utility to the partially sighted and those who have previously enjoyed the sense of vision. Our point here is that to use ALT text wisely requires not only skill, but probably considerable effort on the part of Web developers, if they are to move beyond the tool tip like style of Option 1 and significantly improve accessibility.

Since both Sloan et al. [2002] and our research investigated university Web sites, then obviously we are not suggesting that such institutions have anything but the best intentions about supporting universal accessibility. That both studies do find a considerable number of WCAG compliance failures, including check point 1.1 examples, indicates that there is a genuine problem. Our guess is that when many people are involved in developing a large institution's Web site, then many of them will have little expertise about accessibility issues. We also suspect that Web site development is often poorly co-ordinated and that some things, like accessibility issues, fall between the cracks between different bits of development. One potential problem with Web sites developed by many people is that accessibility assessment tools might indicate someone else's pages are compliant when this isn't really the case, for example, that ALT text place-holders have not been replaced with their intended text.

We strongly support the sort of approach adopted by Sloan et al., and would recommend something like it to any organization really serious about universal accessibility. For the many organizations that are more resource limited and lack sufficient accessibility expertise, then the role of Web accessibility assessment tools becomes increasingly important. Our research is grounded in the real, current world in that we have deliberately chosen to test Web sites which we expect to be of a reasonable quality with regard to accessibility issues. Thus, any WCAG compliance failures that are correctly detected represent real and typical accessibility problems with Web sites. We assume that the tools' developers have already tested their tools on Web pages with contrived compliance failures of all sorts.

The research reported focuses on two Web accessibility assessment tools, Bobby[3] and A-Prompt[4], and compares their relative success. The easy victor is A-Prompt at two of the three WCAGs' priority levels, and with a poor tie at level 2. The reason for choosing to test Bobby is that it is probably the most widely known of all the Web accessibility assessment tools. We chose A-Prompt because it has a similar functionality to Bobby with respect to identifying WCAG compliance failures. An additional reason for choosing these two tools was that they were available free on the Web at the time the research was conducted, in the early months of 2002.

2.1 Bobby

Bobby was first developed in 1996 by the Centre for Applied Special Technology (CAST) before the development of the WCAGs. Since then, CAST has worked closely with the W3C WAI to support the testing of Web sites against the WCAGs. Support for the Section 508 standards was implemented in December 2001. In July 2002, the Watchfire Corporation "acquired Bobby from CAST and has assumed responsibility for the continuing development, marketing and distribution of the technology." (Watchfire Corporation).

Bobby is probably the most widely known of the many Web accessibility assessment tools, which is one reason for choosing it. Web pages that are Bobby and A-Prompt compliant can be publicly badged, which is undoubtedly an incentive to Web site owners who want to appear to be concerned with universal accessibility issues, although compliance, without intelligent, careful, human collaboration with these tools, does not guarantee genuine improvements in accessibility.

Bobby version 3.2 was used in the research described in this paper.

2.2 A-Prompt

While the interface to A-Prompt (Accessibility Prompt) looks different from that of Bobby's, both the history of this software tool and its functionality are similar to Bobby's. A-Prompt was developed by a partnership between the University of Toronto's Adaptive Technology Resource Centre (ATRC) and the Trace Research & Development Centre at the University of Wisconsin. Like Bobby, A-Prompt now tests Web pages against both the WCAGs and Section 508 standards.

A-Prompt version 1.0.5 was used in the research described in this paper.

3   Assessing Two Web Accessibility Assessment Tools

The difficulty with creating Web sites with known accessibility problems with which to test tools such as Bobby and A-Prompt is that this relies on the creativity of the test Web page designer. It is highly unlikely that all of the complex accessibility problems that can arise on real Web pages can be anticipated. We assume that the tools' developers have, at least, already taken this approach during the tools' development. There is thus an argument for testing the tools on real Web sites where complex accessibility problems can arise and thus to test the realistic usefulness of the tools to organizations.

---

[3]http://www.aprompt.ca (last accessed February, 2003).
[4]http://bobby.watchfire.com/bobby (last accessed March, 2003).

There are three styles of approach to assessing accessibility tools on real Web pages. These, in decreasing order of effectiveness and cost, involve comparing a tool against:

1. a full Web site accessibility evaluation;

2. the WCAGs applied manually to a Web site; and

3. other tools.

The first of these would involve comparing a tool's performance to an assessment similar to that of Sloan et al. and, while able to test both how well the WCAGs themselves support accessibility as well as how well assistive tools such as Bobby and A-Prompt perform, this is an expensive approach. The second approach assumes compliance with the WCAGs does improve accessibility and evaluates how well the tools are able to detect compliance failures. The difficulty with this approach is that great expertise is required to manually apply the WCAGs and WCAG experts may not agree on every instance of a potential compliance failure.

The third approach, adopted in the research described, merely requires the application of each tool to the same set of Web pages and a comparison is then made of their relative performance. The virtue of this approach is its cheapness and it is much easier than applying the WCAGs manually to a Web site because, in this third approach, the accessibility analyst has only to consider whether a specific check point, detected by a tool, has not been complied with at a particular locale on a Web page. Against this approach is that there is no independent check of the tools coverage of all the check points, i.e. if two tools are compared and neither detects a compliance failure that is present, then such false negatives will not be detected in the research. On the other hand, this is also a problem with the second approach where, while it is assumed that a WCAG expert will find more compliance failures than the tools to be tested, there can be no guarantee that all potential failures will always be detected by such an expert.

More generally, we believe our comparative approach provides a paradigm example of how assistive technology tools, which purport to have some common functionality, can be usefully assessed. We admit to reaching this opinion post hoc of our experimental analyses and the surprising results we discovered. Similar research, using a larger number of assistive technology tools, is planned and we hope other researchers will be attracted by the efficiency and cheapness of the approach.

3.1 Web Sites Assessed

While we started by examining a range of commercial and government Web sites, we felt that UK universities (and the larger Colleges of Higher Education) provided a good set of Web sites with which to fairly test the two tools. At a high level of generality, the set is relatively homogeneous in that all UK universities have similar, large Web site requirements reflecting each university as a large institution, with many parts to it, with a variety of complex functions and services e.g. Hailes & Hazemi [1998]. The universities have a public duty, made explicit, for example, by the UK Joint Information Systems Committee (JISC[5]), to take into consideration the needs of different types of users. Furthermore, given that one major class of university Web site visitors will be potential students from around the world, then users and their computer platforms are as about divers as it is possible to be.

To ensure the sites we used did indeed reflect some concern for the disabled, from more than 100 university and college Web sites sampled, the 32 sites chosen all had more than three pages on their Web site devoted to disability issues. These Web sites were all HTML based as neither Bobby or A-Prompt claim to cope with more specialized Web design environments. None of the Web pages tested was badged as A-Prompt or Bobby compliant. Restricting ourselves to HTML based sites also facilitated our manual inspection of Web pages.

These university Web sites each contain many hundreds of pages. A Web site's home page is of critical importance [Nielsen 2000] and often determines whether users proceed further into the site. Home pages are thus more likely to have had greater care taken on them than some pages buried deeper in the site. They are also more likely to contain images, tables and other non-text objects, which, for example, should have ALT texts attached to them, than many deeper pages which are often mostly text. Thus the reason for testing home pages is that they provide opportunities for potential WCAG compliance failures to occur and we might expect some attempt to have been made to make such pages as accessible as possible.

All the 32 sites provide a search facility which is either on the home page (in 14 cases) or accessed from the home page (18 cases). Using such search facilities involves rather different tasks from those associated with viewing pages so as to acquire information and thus there are likely to be some different accessibility issues arising from such different tasks. WCAG 13 "Provide clear navigation mechanisms", of course, is particularly relevant, e.g. check point 13.7 "If search functions are provided, enable different types of searches for different skill levels and preferences. [Priority 3]".

3.2   Method

Each Web site's home and search pages were submitted to Bobby and A-Prompt for accessibility assessment and the WCAG check point compliance failures, at each priority level, that each tool detected was recorded.

For the rarer WCAG compliance failures, as well as a sample of the common ones, the source HTML was inspected to test for false positive results, i.e. where a failure is reported that should not have been. Provided the check points are interpreted generously, then false positives did not appear to be a problem with either tool, i.e. we could always see why the tool had reported a compliance failure, even if sometimes we might then decide that it did not require fixing, which is sometimes the appropriate action recommended by the WAI.

We already knew that A-Prompt tests at priority 1 for D-links, which are textual descriptions in addition to HTLM's 'longdesc' ones, and that Bobby does not do so. We have therefore ignored A-Prompt's detection of missing D-links when comparing the two tools.

---

[5]http://www.jisc.ac.uk (last accessed March, 2003)

3.3   Analysis

The possible results of the research are summarized below:

R1   A good result for the tools would be if they performed identically, detecting the same WCAG compliance failures. Such a result would not demonstrate that the tools provided complete coverage of all the WCAGs, but it would give a measure of confidence in that such consistency would mean that the WCAGs were being interpreted in the same manner and that the tools are useful to organizations for detecting real accessibility problems that do occur, even on quality Web sites.

R2   A good result for one tool would be if it detected all of the WCAG compliance failures of the other tool and some more as well. We might not abandon the poorer performing tool because it may be better able to detect compliance failures that were not present in the sampled Web sites, but if only one tool were to be used, then this sort of result would favour choosing the better performing one.

R3   A poorer result for both tools would be where there was little or no overlap between the WCAG compliance failures that each detected. We might not be confident about the tools, even if we elected to always use both tools on Web sites in future, because this sort of result does indicate that both tools are only partially covering the complete set of WCAGs and it is possible that some lack of coverage is shared by both tools and which, of course, comparative tests between them cannot detect.

R4   Both Bobby and A-Prompt will detect some WCAG compliance failures which are present on a Web site, so it is not necessary to consider the truly disastrous outcomes, provided, of course, that the Web sites assessed do contain compliance failures.

There are several possible reasons why the tools might not report the presence of many types of WCAG compliance failure. Perhaps most importantly, many of the check points simply do not apply, for example, because the Web pages assessed don't use moving images, audio or 'new technologies' (Guideline 6) or involve "user control of time-sensitive content changes" (Guideline 7), for example.

The research reported was carried out in the early part of 2002, and while newer versions of both Bobby and A-Prompt will continue to be released, we believe our results are timely and that the issues the results raise will continue to be germane for some time to come.

3.3.1   Statistical Analyses

Non-parametric statistics are used for the usual reasons that such statistics are suitable for relatively small samples because their ordinal counting system basis makes them immune to any effects of skew and kurtosis within the data [Siegel 1956; Miller 1975]. The Wilcoxon Match Pairs Rank Sum Test was used to compare the results from the two tools and to test for differences between sites' home and search pages where these are on different pages. The Mann-Whitney U Test was used to

	Priority 1	Priority 2	Priority 3
Bobby	0.47	3.56	2.05
A-Prompt	1.12	3.12	3.53
Total Different	1.21	6.34	3.75

Table 1: Mean number of WCAG compliance failures, per Web site, detected at priorities 1, 2 and 3 for Bobby, A-Prompt and the number of different compliance failures detected by both tools.

test for differences between home pages that incorporated a search facility (N = 14) to those where search was carried out from other than the home page (N = 18). As the latter involves testing two Web pages, then the sum of the compliance failures detected for both pages was divided by two before comparison with the data from the pages which have search engines on their home pages. All tests were two-tailed as no predictions were made as to which tool might perform better than the other.

3.4   Results

Neither Bobby or A-Prompt differed in the number of WCAG compliance failures they detected on the eighteen home and separate search engine pages (Wilcoxon T = 39.5 and 46.5, respectively), although the Bobby result is on the border of the 5% significance level. The range of the number of compliance failures detected within these pages was 4–10 and 3–11 for Bobby and A-Prompt respectively, but the range of differences between the home and search pages was only 0–3 and 0–5, respectively. The number of ties is likely to decrease the statistic's sensitivity. Comparison of the fourteen home pages with search engines included to the eighteen where the search facilities are separated found no difference in the number of compliance failures detected (Mann-Whitney U = 106.5 and 92 for Bobby and A-Prompt, respectively). Given the lack of difference between these two styles of Web page, then all subsequent analyses are on all 32 Web sites tested.

Bobby found some compliance failures on every Web site and A-Prompt on all but two of the sites.

Table 1 shows the average number of WCAG check point compliance failures detected per site, at each priority level, for each tool individually and the total number that are detected by both tools. NB the first two figures in each column do not sum to the third, 'Total Different', because the same failure detected by each tool is counted only once, i.e. a perfect R1 result would make the three figures in each column identical.

Combining the results across all three priority levels, then A-Prompt finds many more compliance failures than Bobby (Wilcoxon $z = 3.89$, $p < 0.001$). There are too few failures detected at priority 1 for statistical analysis purposes and a worrying number of ties at priorities 2 and 3. Inspecting the data, A-Prompt gains its clear superiority over Bobby at detecting WCAG compliance failures at priority 3: A-Prompt detects more failures than Bobby on 29 Web sites; they tie on one; and Bobby does better than A-Prompt on the remaining two sites.

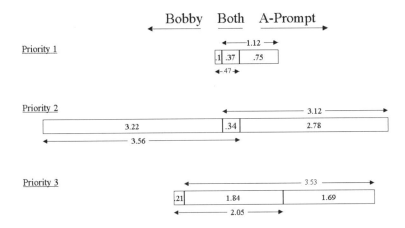

Figure 1: Mean number of WCAG compliance failures, per Web site, detected at priorities 1, 2 and 3 which: only Bobby detected, on the left hand side of the bar; only A-Prompt detected, on the right hand side of the bar; and the compliance failures detected by both tools, in the centre of the bar. The arrow above each bar represents the mean number of WCAG compliance failures detected by A-Prompt and the arrow below represents this for Bobby.

Figure 1 shows graphically and numerically the average, per Web site, number of check point failures detected by each tool at each priority level. The central portion of the bar represents the average number of check point failures that both tools detected and the outer portions those detected only by either Bobby, on the left, or A-Prompt, on the right: the length of the bars is consistently proportional across all three priority levels. The arrow above the bars represents the average number of check point failures per site detected by A-Prompt and the arrow below the bars, the average detected by Bobby (see also Table 1).

Figure 2 shows the same data as Figure 1, but representing the average number of check point failures per site as a percentage of the number detected at each priority level, hence the bars are all the same length.

Given that the university Web sites were selected as quality ones that publish some concern about disability issues, then it is good news for the universities that only a small number of compliance failures were found at priority 1: on average, just over one failure per site (1.21). Of the 17 check points at this priority, only three different ones were detected by the tools (17.6% coverage). The three check points were:

Check Point 1.1 Provide a text equivalent for every non-text element.

Check Point 6.3 Ensure that pages are usable when scripts, applets, or other programmatic objects are turned off or not supported. If this is not possible, provide equivalent information on an alternative accessible page.

Check Point 8.1 Make programmatic elements such as scripts and applets directly accessible or compatible with assistive technologies.

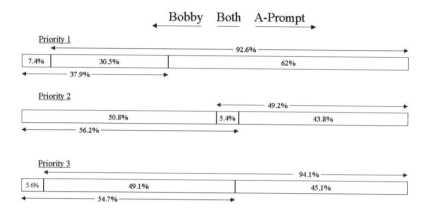

Figure 2: Percentage of WCAG compliance failures, per Web site, detected at priorities 1, 2 and 3 which: only Bobby detected, on the left hand side of the bar; only A-Prompt detected, on the right hand side of the bar; and the compliance failures detected by both tools, in the centre of the bar. The arrow above each bar represents the percentage of WCAG compliance failures detected by A-Prompt and the arrow below represents this for Bobby.

At priority 1, Figure 2 clearly demonstrates a strong type R2 result in that A-Prompt detects virtually all of the check point 1.1 failures that Bobby detects and, unlike Bobby, it also detects check point 6.3 and 8.1 compliance failures. The latter two are obviously closely related, although A-Prompt sometimes detected only one of them on some sites. We were not surprised at finding a few check point 1.1 failures as sites, particularly around their home pages, tend to have a lot of images and occasionally it is easy to forget to provide the additional ALT text. Both Bobby and A-Prompt provide a valuable check that there is some text but, as discussed earlier, they don't ensure that the text is suitably equivalent, or even meaningful. Our suspicion from looking at the Web sites with the 'programmatic' failures detected is that these are sometimes invisible to Web developers, particularly when many developers are involved and our 'falling between the cracks' hypothesis is the one we advance as their most probable cause.

The number of types of compliance failure detected is small, but with quality Web sites, particularly at priority 1, this is to be expected. Bobby's complete failure to detect the 'programmatic' compliance failures supports using A-Prompt rather than Bobby if a site is only interested in covering priority 1 compliance and only one assessment tool is to be used. Furthermore, A-Prompt's ability to detect D-link compliance failures, which Bobby does not detect and which were ignored in our research, also thus favours choosing A-Prompt over Bobby at priority 1.

The priority 3 results, while three times as many compliance failures were detected as at priority 1 (3.75 vs. 1.21), are very similar to the priority 1 results in that A-Prompt detects all the failures that Bobby detects (taking the 5.6% in Figure 2 to be effectively 0%) and detects a similar number that Bobby fails to detect. Also like the priority 1 results, the coverage of all priority 3 check points is relatively small, with only 5 out of a possible 20 types of failure being detected. At the priority 3 level, however, we suspect that the tools are actually weaker at detecting compliance failures, not just because priority 3 is of lesser consequence than priority 1, but also, we suspect, because some of the priority 3 check points are harder to interpret, by person or machine. If only one accessibility assessment tool was to be used, then the evidence again strongly favours A-Prompt over Bobby.

The priority 2 results are quite different from those found at the other two levels. Five times as many failures are found at priority 2 compared to priority 1 (6.34 vs. 1.21) and not quite twice as many as at priority 3 (6.34 vs. 3.75). Between them the tools found 15 different types of check point failure out of a total possible at priority 2 of 29 (51.7%). Critically, the results show a strong type R3 result in that the two tools detected completely different types of error; only 5.4% of the failures were detected by both tools.

In summary, the pattern of the results is: type R2 at priorities 1 and 3, favouring A-Prompt; and type R3 at priority 2.

4   Discussion and Conclusion

The only way to properly assess a Web site's accessibility is to undertake some approach like Sloan et al.'s, but quite a number of people were involved in a range of methods in their work and we don't think most organizations have the resources, and particularly the expertise, to assess their Web site's accessibility in such a thorough way. While one might imagine organizations hiring an expert accessibility team, against such a one-off approach is that large Web sites tend to evolve continuously so there is a strong case for in-house expertise to ensure that accessibility is maintained. There must be a strong temptation for organizations to rely more on accessibility assessment tools than they should because the tools are supposed to encapsulate and apply knowledge about the WCAGs and check points. Accessibility tools have their own knowledge over-heads concerning how to use the tools and, vitally, interpret their outputs. Indeed, it may well be that at present the tools' related knowledge is additional to a sound understanding of the WCAG by the tools' users, i.e. you need to know more to use the tools, not less. This still makes accessibility tools valuable as a contribution to efficiently finding possible WCAG compliance failures, which are difficult for people to always find reliably, provided that the tools do find most of them.

For anyone wishing to assess the accessibility of their Web site using either Bobby or A-Prompt, then our results should give them cause for concern. Even though A-Prompt better performs at both priorities 1 and 3, detecting virtually everything Bobby detects and quite a lot more, the results at priority 2, where both tools detect a large number of types of compliance failure but with no agreement between them, would make the sensible advice to be to use both tools. Furthermore, generalizing these results, we might suggest that until further research is conducted on other tools, then the best strategy is to use as many Web accessibility assessment tools as possible. While sensible, we doubt that the 'use many tools' advice will be adopted, not least because of the overheads associated with using each tool and, sometimes, there may be conflicting advice between the tools. Our comparative approach to tool evaluation is cheap by comparison to other approaches and we think it provides a paradigm example that can, and should, be extended to many such related tools.

One reason for publishing our research is that we were shocked by the results. What we had expected when we started was that we would find type R1 results, with the tools mostly agreeing but with a few exceptions, which we had expected to investigate in detail. We were interested in looking at the performance of these tools on real Web sites of reasonable quality with respect to accessibility because we have assumed that the tools will have been tested on blatant examples of compliance failures during their development, i.e. we intended to investigate the utility of these tools to organizations that had probably tried to support universal accessibility and we wanted to know if the tools could help in such cases. Noting that Bobby is probably the most well known Web accessibility assessment tool, then our results show that A-Prompt is a better tool at priorities 1 and 3. The priority 2 results are a mess and, we think, reflect a nascent technology. The priority 2 results suggest that the tools functionality, i.e. their compliance failure detecting abilities, needs further development and we think that the tools warrant some improvement in their usability. We also think that further work is needed on the WCAGs and check points; to us they look like something designed by a committee and could do with some simplification, perhaps by reducing the number of check points by making greater use of the many relationships that already explicitly exist between the check points. We favour abandoning WCAG 14 regarding keeping everything as clear and as simple as possible as the concept of simplicity is not simple.

Overall, if you are only going to use one Web accessibility assessment tool then, based on our research, use A-Prompt rather than Bobby. Much more importantly, we don't recommend placing too much trust in either tool, particularly below priority 1.

Our research cannot stand the 'test of time' in that the WCAGs, Bobby and A-Prompt, and other Web accessibility assessment tools, continue to be developed. Our research, however, represents a 'shot across the bows' to organizations who are perhaps over confident of the performance of tools such as Bobby and A-Prompt and it offers a warning to such tool developers of both the difficulty and distance they still have to cover before their tools are functionally sufficiently adequate that they can be relied on. Our comparative approach to testing is efficient, easy and cheap and we hope that others will apply it to a wider range of assistive technologies.

References

Bergman, E. & Johnson, E. [1995], Towards Accessible Human–Computer Interaction, *in* J. Nielsen (ed.), *Advances in Human–Computer Interaction*, Vol. 5, Ablex, pp.87–112.

Colwell, C. & Petrie, H. [1999], Evaluation of Guidelines for Designing Accessible Web Content, *in* C. Buhler & H. Knops (eds.), *Assistive Technology on the Threshold of the New Millennium*, IOS Press, pp.39–47.

Diaper, D. [1989], Giving HCI Away, *in* A. Sutcliffe & L. Macaulay (eds.), *People and Computers V (Proceedings of HCI'89)*, Cambridge University Press, pp.109–20.

Hailes, S. & Hazemi, R. [1998], Reinventing the Academy, *in* R. Hazemi, S. Hailes & S. Wilbur (eds.), *The Digital University: Reinventing the Academy*, Springer-Verlag, pp.7–24.

Miller, S. [1975], *Experimental Design and Statistics*, Methuen.

Nielsen, J. [2000], *Designing Web Usability*, New Riders.

Siegel, S. [1956], *Nonparametric Statistics for the Behavioural Science*, McGraw-Hill.

Sloan, D., Gregor, P., Booth, P. & Gibson, L. [2002], Auditing Accessibility of UK Higher Education Web Sites, *Interacting with Computers* **14**(4), 313–26.

Smith, D. C., Irby, C., Kimball, R., Verplank, B. & Harslem, E. [1982], Designing the STAR User Interface, *Byte* **7**(4), 242–82. Reprinted as Smith et al. [1987].

Smith, D. C., Irby, C., Kimball, R., Verplank, B. & Harslem, E. [1987], Designing the STAR User Interface, *in* R. M. Bæcker & W. A. S. Buxton (eds.), *Readings in Human–Computer Interaction: A Multidisciplinary Approach*, Morgan-Kaufmann, pp.653–61. Reprint of Smith et al. [1982].

Waddell, C. [1999], The Growing Digital Divide in Access for People with Disabilities: Overcoming Barriers to Participation in the Digital Economy, http://www.icdri.org/CynthiaW/dig_div1.htm (last accessed 2003.05.26).

'Look at Me': Emotions, Faces and Eyes

Expressive Image Generator for an Emotion Extraction Engine

A C Boucouvalas, Zhe Xu & David John

Multimedia Communications Research Group, School of Design, Engineering and Computing, Bournemouth University, Fern Barrow, Poole, Dorset BH12 5BB, UK

Email: *{tboucouv, zxu, djohn}@bournemouth.ac.uk*

We report an expressive image generator suitable for an emotion extraction engine which we have developed for a real-time Internet text communication system. Real-time expressive communication provides aspects of the visual clues that are present in face-to-face interaction. We have demonstrated an engine that can analyse the emotional content of text input and can deliver the emotional parameters necessary to invoke an appropriate expressive image in a real-time chat environment. The engine requires a set of emotionally expressive images from each participant for the display of emotions. The aim of this paper is to present a fast and user-friendly method to automatically generate the set of expressive images from a single default image. Using a combination of warping and morphing, images belonging to six expressive categories are generated from one original neutral image provided by each user. In each expressive category, three different intensities can be depicted. The method only requires a single default image per user, six control points and two control shapes. In a series of experiments we have tested the effectiveness of the generated images. The preliminary findings are also presented in this paper.

Keywords: emotion, expression, warping, morphing.

1 Introduction

Real-time expressive communication is beneficial as it provides some aspects of the visual clues that are present in face-to-face interaction but are not available in ordinary text only-based communications.

This paper is concerned with the generation of expressive images that are displayed in a specially developed text input communications system which automatically detects the emotions expressed by the users. The associated emotion extraction engine identifies the emotions expressed by individuals in their text communications, and the output displays the appropriate expressive images.

The specific problem addressed in this paper is how to generate the unique set of expressive images for individual users without the need for them to pose for photographs portraying all categories of emotion. We present a quick and user-friendly method to generate the expressive images from a single neutral image. Images can be generated for six emotion categories, and for each category, typically we achieve three different emotion intensities. Users need to define only six control points and three control shapes in order to generate all the images. This paper also presents the findings from a series of experiments that have been carried out to test the effectiveness of the generated images. Users correctly identify the emotion expressed by the majority of images. The level of recognition improves by increasing the emotion intensity and by adding a suggestive text label.

This paper is organized as follows: In Section 2 the emotion extraction engine is reviewed. In Section 3 the background knowledge of image generation is discussed. In Section 4 the motion image generator is described in detail. In Section 5 the test strategy for the expressive image generator is given. Section 6 illustrates possible applications using the engine. Finally in Section 7 conclusions are presented.

2 The Real-time Emotion Extraction Engine

We have developed an emotion extraction engine [Zhe et al. 2002] that can analyse user text input in real time, and has been applied to an Internet chat environment. The engine uses a client/server architecture. The client side engine analyses the user input sentences and searches for emotional content. Subsequently, the emotional parameters detected are sent to the server. The server will forward these parameters to the related clients. When the client receives the parameters, the engine analyses the parameters, selects and displays corresponding expressive images. The server-side engine will send the parameters needed for selecting the images. In this way, image transmissions are avoided since the only data transmitted over the network are the parameters. As a result the network bandwidth requirement is extremely low.

Two sub-systems constitute the emotion extraction engine: the emotion analysis system and the expressive image generator. The emotion analysis system includes three parts: *input text analysis, tagging system* and *parser* (Figure 1).

2.1 Input Analysis Function

The engine provides a user interface similar to ordinary chat rooms. However the user interface first splits user input into sentences and each sentence will be sent to *the input analysis function*. The *input analysis function* will replace all the punctuation with pre-defined characters and remove the blank and space characters. The analysed sentences will be sent to the *tagging system*.

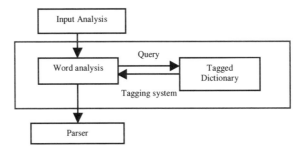

Figure 1: The working flow of the emotion analysis system.

2.2 The Tagging System

The tagging system includes two components: the *word analysis function* and the *tagged dictionary*. The *word analysis function* splits the sentences into words and searches the *tagged dictionary* to find the corresponding tag category.

From [Kuehn 1993] daily communications involve about two thousand words. A dictionary that includes around 16400 words was set up. In order to identify the words, the dictionary was tagged. The dictionary tagged each word entirely in order to keep the response time to a minimum, which is different from the tagging methods in some existing systems, e.g. BNC [Leech 1997] and Brown Corpus [Francis & Kucera 1979].

The created dictionary database includes three fields: *word field*, word *category field* and *emotional tag field*. The *category* field contains the corresponding word category (noun, verb, adjective etc.) and the *emotional tag* field describes whether that word belongs to one of the six emotion types.

Those sentences containing emotional words will be sent to the *parser* for further analysis.

2.3 Parser

The parser's analysis is accomplished through the use of rewrite rules and tree representations [Russell & Norvig 1995]. According to pre-defined rules, the parser will search for the current emotional words, the person to whom the emotional words refer to and the intensity of the emotional words.

The output from the parser will be sent out through the network to related users. When receiving the output, the corresponding expressive images are selected from a database and displayed. Two possible approaches have been implemented to generate expressive images. The first is a static approach, in which users upload their default facial images together with all other expressive images generated photographically. The second approach using the expressive image generator is a dynamic approach that is discussed here.

2.4 The Effectiveness of the Expressive Interface

Zhe et al. [2002] demonstrated an effectiveness experiment. In that experiment, testers were asked to watch the three interfaces (an interface with expressive image, voice and text, an interface with expressive image, text and an interface with text only). The results show that most testers prefer the interface with expressive image, voice and text. A significant number of subjects like the interface with expressive image, voice and text much more than the text only interface. This means that with the expressive images, the effectiveness of the human interface can be considerably improved. The problem remaining in that experiment is how to generate the expressive images for each user in a fast and user-friendly way.

3 Expressive Image Generation

2D and 3D images are both commonly used in facial image generations. For 3D facial expression generations, current methods are based on different 3D face models. [e.g. Magnenat-Thalmann et al. 1988; Parke & Waters 1996]. The common problems are the long computation time and poor user interface interactions.

2D approaches are attractive, free from computational complexity and are supported by psychophysical theories [Bulthoff & Edelman 1992; Riesenhuber & Poggio 2000]. For real-time communication, a fast and efficient approach is most desired. We have adopted 2D approaches for the expressive image generation engine.

Six universal categories of facial expressions have been suggested in facial expression research [Parke & Waters 1996]. The categories are *happiness, sadness, anger, fear, disgust* and *surprise* and are recognized across cultures. A wide range of expression intensity and variation of detailed expression exists within each of the categories. The emotion extraction engine requires a set of expressive images for each of these categories to represent the emotions found in the sentences.

There are number of techniques used to solve the problems of reducing the computation time and providing a user-friendly interface. For example, some programs hold large databases of facial expressions and when presented with a new image the program will search for matches. Alternatives build complex models of the face, and users are required to identify between twenty to thirty control points to define the location of facial features. The main problems with this type of program are that it is difficult for users to select all of the required points accurately, and it is not always possible to generate images fast enough to be used in real-time communication systems.

In contrast to the systems that use complex facial models that require a high degree of computation to generate the finished image, we developed a simple algorithm based on image warping and image morphing. The facial model requires users to identify only six control points and draw two control areas on the original neutral image. The engine then automatically generates 18 images corresponding to the six expression categories, each with three different emotion intensities. These images are distributed among the users of the system and stored for future use.

In image warping a source image is distorted into a destination image according to a transformation between source space (u, v) and destination space (x, y) [Wolberg 1990]. The transformation function $f()$ describes the destination (x, y) for every location (u, v) in the source. To apply warping to an image, we may apply the transformation function $f()$ to each pixel. Some well known techniques include radial functions and spline lines. The pseudocode is shown in Figure 2.

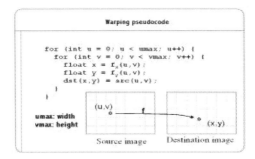

Figure 2: The warping pseudocode.

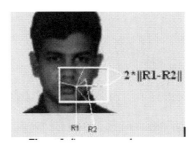

Figure 3: Segment warping area.

According to Ekman et al.'s [2001] *Facial Action Coding System* and Parke & Waters's [1996] Computer Facial Animation, specific muscles on the faces are responsible for the expression generations. For example only four muscles contribute to expressing happiness. Limited parts of muscles on the face are involved in generating different facial expressions. It is much more efficient to carry out manipulation only in those areas.

According to the above analysis, we suppose that in some segmented areas exist the noticeable facial distortions, while in the other part of the image the distortion should be so small that it can be neglected.

The segmented area is a square that covers the facial distortion area. To choose the segmented area, two anchor points (R_1, R_2) are needed. R_1 represents the edge before transforming and R_2 represents the edge after transformation. The width of the segment area is $2 \times ||R_1 - R_2||$ and the central point is the point R_2. For example to create a happy expression, the anchor point R_1 is the right edge of the mouth and R_2 is the finish point. An example of segmented area is shown in Figure 3.

We use image morphing, an image processing technique applied for the metamorphosis from one image to another. The usual morphing technique is to generate a sequence of intermediate images which when put together with the original images would represent the change from first image to the last [Zhang 2001].

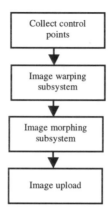

Figure 4: Expressive image generator structure.

4   Expressive Image Generator

To generate expressive images, users need to upload a neutral face image to the expressive image generator. The generator is based on combining local area warping and morphing technologies. The expressive image generator is implemented as a Java applet and can be used in an Internet Explorer or Netscape environment. The structure of the expressive image generator is shown in Figure 4.

4.1   Expressive Categories

To generate expressive images for the six emotion categories, the characteristics of each category are evaluated. Ekman et al. [2001] and Parke & Waters [1996] demonstrated that 64 action units on the face generate the facial expressions. However determining the actual positions for the 64 action units require tedious human operator interaction and it is not practical in real-time communication. In our expressive image generator, for each emotion type the action units were summarized and simplified from Parke & Waters [1996] to be applied in a real-time communication environment. Specifically we adopt the following rules:

Happiness: The eyebrows are relaxed, the mouth is wide with the corners pulled up toward the ears.

Sadness: The inner portions of the eyebrows are piled up above the upper eyelid and the mouth is relaxed.

Anger: The eyebrows are pulled downward and together. The mouth is closed with the upper lip slightly compressed or squared off.

Disgust: The middle eyebrows are pulled upward and the mouth is slightly opened with the upper lip squared off.

Fear: Eyebrows are raised, pulled together and bent upward. The mouth may be dropped slightly open.

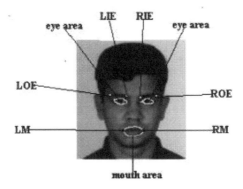

Figure 5: Example of control points.

Surprise: The eyebrows are raised up, the upper eyelids are opened and the mouth is dropped open.

For each expression category, three different emotion intensities are automatically produced. Based on the above rules, the movement of mouth, eyebrows and lips are quantified. From low intensity to high intensity, the movement is enlarged.

4.2   Control Points

To generate different expressions, two sets of parameters: start points and finish points are required. Users only need to select the start points. The finish points are calculated automatically based on the user's selection.

After uploading the neutral image to the system, users will be guided to select six start points and three control areas. The six start points include: left corner of the mouth (LM), right corner of the mouth (RM), outer edge of the left eye (LOE), inner edge of the left eye (LIE), outer edge of the right eye (ROE) and inner edge of the right eye (RIE).

The three control areas include the outer edge of the lips, and the inner edge of the eyelids for the left eye and right eye. These areas will be used in image morphing subsystem.

An example of control points and control areas is shown in Figure 5.

These parameters will be sent to the image warping subsystem to generate the expressive images.

4.3   Image Warping Subsystem

The image warping subsystem implements the model based warping. Instead of interactive manipulation, the destination positions will be calculated according to pre-defined rules. Users only need to define the start positions. The model based warping subsystem has the advantages of accuracy and speed.

To generate the model, the facial action coding system and several different expressive images from different persons were analysed. We have named the kernel

	Happiness Int1	Happiness Int2	Happiness Int3	Sadness Int1	Sadness Int2	Sadness Int3
FLM. x	LM. x-2	LM. x-3	LM. x-4	LM. x-1	LM. x-3	LM. x-4
FLM. y	LM. y-2	LM. y-4	LM. y-6	LM. y+2	LM. y+3	LM. y+4
FRM. x	RM. x+2	RM. x+3	RM. x+4	RM. x+2	RM. x+3	RM. x+4
FRM. y	RM. y-2	RM. y-4	RM. y-6	RM. y+2	RM. y+4	RM. y+6
FLOE. x	LOE. x-0	LOE. x-0	LOE. x-0	LOE. x-0	LOE. x-0	LOE. x-0
FLOE. y	LOE. y-0	LOE. y-0	LOE. y-0	LOE. y-0	LOE. y-0	LOE. y-0
FLIE. x	LIE. x	LIE. x	LIE. x	LIE. x +2	LIE. x+4	LIE. x+6
FLIE. y	LIE. y	LIE. y	LIE. y	LIE. y-2	LIE. y-4	LIE. y-6
FROE. x	ROE. x-0	ROE. x-0	ROE. x-0	ROE. x-0	ROE. x-0	ROE. x-0
FROE. y	ROE. y-0	ROE. y-0	ROE. y-0	ROE. y-0	ROE. y-0	ROE. y-0
FRIE. x	RIE. x	RIE. x	RIE. x	RIE. x	RIE. x-4	RIE. x-6
FRIE. y	RIE. y	RIE. y	RIE. y	RIE. y	RIE. y-4	RIE. y-6

Table 1: Control points value for emotion 'happiness' and 'sadness'.

that generates the images as the 'expression model mask'. The mask is constituted by two sets of points. The first set is the start points selected by users. The second set is the control points of the start points, which we call the finish points. The values of the finish points are calculated relative to the start points. By applying the masks to images of individual faces, corresponding expressions can be generated.

The first step of the image warping subsystem is to choose the segment area. On choosing the segment area, the finish points will be calculated. The six finish points are FLM, FRM, FLOE, FLIE, FROE and FRIE (FLM = finish point of LM, FRM = finish point of RM, FLOE = finish point of LOE, FLIE = finish point of LIE, FROE = finish point of ROE and FRIE = finish point of RIE).

The functions to calculate the finish points are the same. The finish points are calculated as the start points plus an integer value that depends on the emotion being generated.

$$\text{Finish. } x = \text{Start. } x + a$$

$$\text{Finish. } y = \text{Start. } y + b$$

The actual values for all the finish points are shown in Tables 1–3. (Int1, Int2 and Int3 correspond to the intensity level of each emotion category).

When the segment area is selected, some parts of the segment area are stretched while other parts are suppressed, thus making facial expressions achievable. In Figure 6, it can be seen that the segment areas 3 and 4 are compressed and areas 1 and 2 are stretched. By stretching areas 1 and 2, the lip was moved to upper right, which simulates the smile effect.

For the expression categories of *happiness*, *sadness*, *anger* and *disgust*, the image warping subsystem can create the corresponding facial characteristics. The weakness of the image warping subsystem is that it can not generate new pixels. For the expressions of *fear* and *surprise*, opened mouth and widened eyes are important characteristics that can not be achieved by the warping subsystem.

	Surprise Int1	Surprise Int2	Surprise Int3	Anger Int1	Anger Int2	Anger Int3
FLM. x FLM. y	LM. x LM. y	LM. x LM. y	LM. x LM. y	LM. x+2 LM. y	LM. x+3 LM. y	LM. x+4 LM. y
FRM. x FRM. y	RM. x RM. y	RM. x RM. y	RM. x RM. y	RM. x-2 RM. y	RM. x-3 RM. y	RM. x-4 RM. y
FLOE. x FLOE. y	LOE. x+8 LOE. y-3	LOE. x+8 LOE. y-6	LOE. x+8 LOE. y-8	LOE. x+0 LOE. y-0	LOE. x+0 LOE. y-0	LOE. x+0 LOE. y-0
FLIE. x FLIE. y	LIE. x LIE. y	LIE. x LIE. y	LIE. x LIE. y	LIE. x+2 LIE. y+2	LIE. x+4 LIE. y+4	LIE. x+6 LIE. y+6
FROE. x FROE. y	ROE. x-8 ROE. y-3	ROE. x-8 ROE. y-6	ROE. x-8 ROE. y-8	ROE. x-0 ROE. y-0	ROE. x-0 ROE. y-0	ROE. x-8 ROE. y-0
FRIE. x FRIE. y	RIE. x RIE. y	RIE. x RIE. y	RIE. x RIE. y	RIE. x-2 RIE. y+2	RIE. x-4 RIE. y+4	RIE. x-6 RIE. y+6

Table 2: Control points value for emotion 'surprise' and 'anger'.

	Disgust Int1	Disgust Int2	Disgust Int3	Fear Int1	Fear Int2	Fear Int3
FLM. x FLM. y	LM. x-2 LM. y+2	LM. x-4 LM. y+4	LM. x-6 LM. y+6	LM. x LM. y	LM. x LM. y	LM. x LM. y
FRM. x FRM. y	RM. x+2 RM. y+2	RM. x+4 RM. y+2	RM. x+6 RM. y+2	RM. x RM. y	RM. x RM. y	RM. x RM. y
FLOE. x FLOE. y	LOE. x-0 LOE. y-0	LOE. x-0 LOE. y-0	LOE. x-0 LOE. y-0	LOE. x+8 LOE. y-4	LOE. x+8 LOE. y-7	LOE. x+8 LOE. y-10
FLIE. x FLIE. y	LIE. x-8 LIE. y-3	LIE. x-8 LIE. y-5	LIE. x-8 LIE. y-8	LIE. x LIE. y	LIE. x LIE. y	LIE. x LIE. y
FROE. x FROE. y	ROE. x-0 ROE. y-0	ROE. x-0 ROE. y-0	ROE. x-0 ROE. y-0	ROE. x-8 ROE. y-4	ROE. x-8 ROE. y-7	ROE. x-8 ROE. y-10
FRIE. x FRIE. y	RIE. x+8 RIE. y-3	RIE. x+8 RIE. y-5	RIE. x+8 RIE. y-8	RIE. x RIE. y	RIE. x RIE. y	RIE. x RIE. y

Table 3: Control points value for emotion 'disgust' and 'fear'.

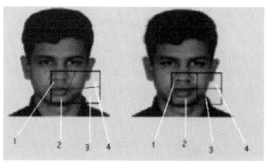

Before warping   After warping

Figure 6: Local area warping example.

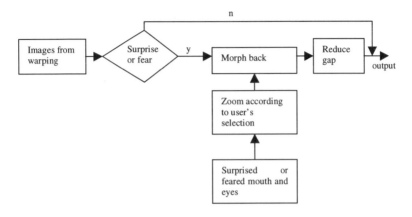

Figure 7: Structure of the morphing subsystem.

To generate *fear* and *surprise* images, the generated images are sent to the image morphing subsystem.

4.4   Image Morphing Subsystem

To achieve characteristics for expressions *surprise* and *fear*, an image morphing subsystem is implemented.

First several different image clips of mouths and eyes are selected from different surprised and feared facial expression images. When the morphing subsystem receives the intermediate images, it will first find all the images belong to the emotion categories *fear* and *surprise* and then replace the mouth and eyes with the pre-selected mouths and eyes. The user selected mouth and eye areas are the keys for the morphing subsystem. The morphing subsystem first zooms the pre-selected mouth and eyes according to the size of the corresponding selected area and then replace all the pixels in the selected area with the pre-selected images. One common defect of morphing technology is the gap between the replaced part and the pre-prepared images. To fill in the gaps that are generated when the mouth is opened or the eyes are widened, a Gaussian blur operation is applied. The structure of the image morphing subsystem is shown in Figure 7.

Examples of expressive images generated by our expressive image generator are shown in Figure 8.

5   Experiments

5.1   Experiment Strategy

The generated expressive images can be used in isolation or in text-accompanied environments, i.e. chatting rooms or online games. Two types of experiments were carried out in order to test the quality of the generated images by the expressive image generator.

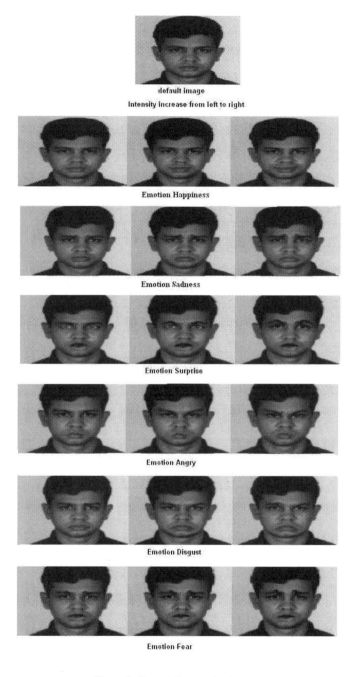

Figure 8: Generated expression images.

The first experiment presented the expressive images only, in which the test participants viewed the generated expressive images in isolation and had to recognize the emotion. The second test presents the image plus suggestive text, to the users to agree or not on the intended emotion.

5.2 Test Participants and Methods

Thirty-five individuals participated in the experiments. Participants were from Bournemouth University. There were nine women and twenty six men.

In first experiment, participants viewed the synthesized images and were asked to choose the one best describing the emotions expressed in the images from six expression types.

In second experiment, participants viewed the default images, synthesized images with suggestive text. For example, the accompanying text for the generated sad image is 'I am sad'. Then participants answered the question: compared to the default image, are the corresponding pictures appropriate to the text?

5.3 Image Only Test Result Analysis

The results are shown in Figure 9 (1, 2, 3 in the x axis represent the intensity in the corresponding emotion category. 1 is the lowest and 3 is the highest; the y axis shows the percentage of participants, who identified the emotion correctly).

The χ^2 test result shows that for the six emotion categories *happiness, sadness, surprise, anger, fear* and *disgust*, the corresponding obtained values are 245.3, 456.1, 563.2, 123.4, 245.7 and 156. The values mean that they are extremely significant $p < 0.01$. In this case users did not classify the images randomly.

5.4 Image Plus Text Result Analysis

The results are shown in Figure 10 (in these figures, 1, 2, 3 in the x axis represents the intensity in the corresponding emotion category. 1 is the lowest and 3 is the highest; the y axis shows the percentage of the participants who agree that the image is appropriate with the text).

The χ^2 test result shows that for the emotion categories *happiness, sadness, surprise* and *anger*, the corresponding obtained values 8.257, 24.03, 9.91 and 9.94. The values mean that they are extremely significant $p < 0.01$. For categories *fear* and *disgust*, the obtained values are 3.671 and 4.82, which are marginally significant $(0.05 < p < 0.1)$. For each case there is evidence that users did not classify the images randomly.

It is shown that by accompanying text context information with the expressive images, the participants correctly recognized more expressive images than in the first test. By increasing intensity, even more participants also correctly recognized the expressive images. For emotion categories *happiness, sadness, surprise* and *fear*, more than 70% images were correctly recognized. For emotion categories *fear* and *disgust*, on average more than 60% images were correctly recognized. For all images with medium and high intensity, more than 78% are recognized correctly.

This experiment shows that by increasing the emotion intensity, acceptable expressive images can be obtained. In this case, the expressive image generator can be used together with the emotion extraction engine in a chatting environment.

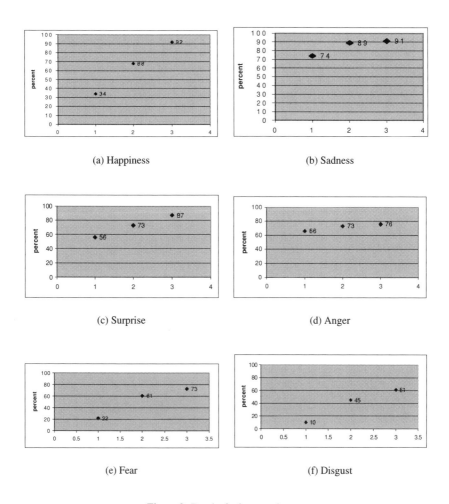

Figure 9: Results for image only test.

6   Conclusions

Generating facial expression images will always be a challenge. The expressive image generator generates a discrete set of expressive images of varying expressive intensity using warping and morphing technologies. The process is fast and user-friendly. Once the control points are selected the algorithm is very fast and could be used in real-time applications.

The expressive image generator is an inherent part of the emotion extraction engine. With a neutral facial image uploaded by each user, the generator in its current form creates eighteen different expressive facial images. The generated facial images belong to six universal categories: *happiness, sadness, disgust, anger, surprise* and *fear*. For each category, three images with different emotion intensities are archived.

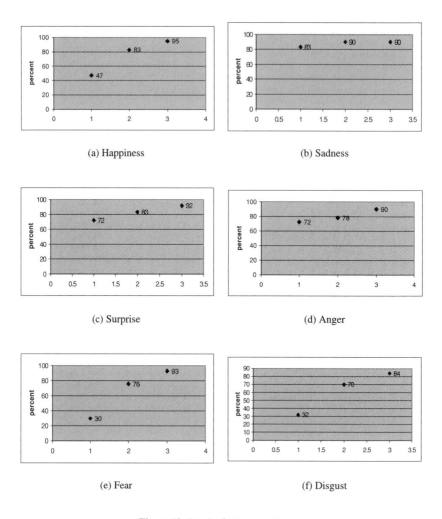

(a) Happiness

(b) Sadness

(c) Surprise

(d) Anger

(e) Fear

(f) Disgust

Figure 10: Results for image only test.

The generator can be used within the emotion extraction engine in a number of environments that require text input information e.g. chatting room, story reader and online games. It is possible that the generator's effectiveness may be enhanced with improvements to the expression model mask. Possible refinements include adding more control points and more control areas, although this should not be at the expense of reducing the ease of use of the system.

The experiments demonstrated that more acceptable expressive images could be obtained by increasing the emotion intensity.

The test results also proved that the generator could create satisfactory expressive images for a chat environment which are easily recognizable, and even more so when accompanied by suggestive text, which is normal in chat environments.

References

Bulthoff, H. H. & Edelman, S. [1992], Psychophysical Support for 2D View Interpolation Theory of Object Recognition, *Proceedings of the National Academy of Sciences* **89**(1), 60–4.

Ekman, P., Friesen, W. V. & Hager, J. C. [2001], Facial Action Coding System, CD-ROM. Network Information Research Corporation, 545 East 4500 South E-160, Salt Lake City, Utah, USA 84107.

Francis, W. N. & Kucera, H. [1979], Brown Corpus Manual, http://www.hit.uib.no/icame/brown/bcm.html (last accessed 2003.05.26). Department of Linguistics, Brown University. Originally 1964, revised 1971 and 1979.

Kuehn, S. A. [1993], Communication Innovation on BBS: A Content Analysis, *Interpersonal Computing and Technology* **1**(2). http://jan.ucc.nau.edu/~ipct-j/1993/n2/kuehn.txt (last accessed 2003.05.31).

Leech, G. [1997], A Brief Users' Guide to the Grammatical Tagging of the British National Corpus, http://www.natcorp.ox.ac.uk/what/gramtag.html (last accessed 2003.05.26).

Magnenat-Thalmann, N., Primeau, E. & Thalmann, D. [1988], Abstract Muscle Action Procedures for Human Face Animation, *The Visual Computer* **3**(5), 290–7.

Parke, F. I. & Waters, K. [1996], *Computer Facial Animation*, A. K. Peters.

Riesenhuber, M. & Poggio, T. [2000], Computational Models of Object Recognition in Cortex: A Review, Technical Report CBCL Paper #190/AI Memo #1695, Massachusetts Institute of Technology.

Russell, S. & Norvig, P. [1995], *Artificial Intelligence — A Modern Approach*, Prentice–Hall.

Wolberg, G. [1990], *Digital Image Warping*, IEEE Publications.

Zhang, Y. [2001], Image Morphing, http://www.fmrib.ox.ac.uk/~yongyue/morphing.html (last accessed 2003.05.26).

Zhe, X., John, D. & Boucouvalas, A. C. [2002], Text-to-Emotion Engine: Tests of User Preferences, http://dec.bournemouth.ac.uk/staff/tboucouvalas/ILMENAU.pdf (last accessed 2003.05.27). Paper presented at the IEEE International Symbposium on Consumer Electronics 2002 (ISCE'02).

An Exploration of Facial Expression Tracking in Affective HCI

Robert Ward, Dennise Bell & Phil Marsden

Department of Multimedia and Information Systems, School of Computing and Engineering, University of Huddersfield, Huddersfield HD1 3DH, UK

Tel: *+44 1484 472000*

Email: *{r.d.ward,d.bell,p.h.marsden}@hud.ac.uk*

We report an investigation exploring facial expression tracking in the evaluation of software usability and content. Participants' faces were videoed whilst taking a Web-based quiz. The quiz contained two relatively ordinary HCI events as stimuli: a surprise alert (the stronger stimulus intended to evoke surprise) and questions with high affective content (the weaker stimulus intended to evoke amusement). Physiological arousal was also recorded. The videos for the periods around each event were analysed by commercially available facial movement tracking software, and the output used to drive a 3D virtual head. The movements of the real and virtual faces were assessed by human judges. Users' real faces were judged to have responded to both stimuli, but more to the stronger stimulus than the weaker. Facial response did not always concur with physiological arousal. Judgements of the virtual faces indicated that the tracker successfully detected responses to the stronger stimulus but had mixed success with the weaker stimulus. The track data appeared to distinguish between amusement and surprise. These results suggest that facial expression tracking can be a viable and useful technique for affective computing. We suggest that the intentional and communicative use of facial expression may be a fruitful domain for future applications.

Keywords: facial expression, affective computing, anthropomorphic interfaces, usability, facial modelling.

1   Introduction

This paper explores whether automatic facial expression tracking could be a viable addition to the repertoire of techniques used in affective computing. We report an investigation in which facial expression tracking software was used to monitor the facial movements of participants engaged in a Web-based task. We wished to explore the incidence of facial responses to relatively ordinary computer-based events, and the detection of these responses by movement tracking software.

Much of the work in affective computing to date has relied upon physiological sensing. For example, Scheirer et al. [2002] used skin conductance and blood volume pulse in developing a technique for automatically detecting software-induced frustration. Many other physiological signals, including heart-rate variability, respiratory activity, pupillary size, voice quality and electrical activity in brain, muscle and the peripheral nervous system, have been shown to be sensitive to various kinds of cognitive activity [Andreassi 2000] and have therefore been either used or proposed as data sources for use in affective sensing [for example, Picard 1997].

There are however both practical and theoretical problems with many of these measures, especially in situations of computer use. In practice, physiological sensors and electrodes can be restrictive or uncomfortable. Some measures, such as blood volume pressure and skin conductance, usually involve the attachment of sensors and electrodes to the fingers, which precludes the use of one hand for task purposes. Facial muscle electromyography (EMG) involves the attachment of electrodes to the face. Wearable devices containing inconspicuous sensors are a partial solution [Picard & Healey 1997], but these still usually require specialist skills and equipment. From a theoretical perspective, there are problems in interpreting the meaning of physiological signals. Different reactions can produce similar signals, and there is much debate in the literature as to whether or not there are distinct emotions with distinct physiological profiles [Ekman 1992; Caccioppo et al. 1993]. Hudlicka & McNeese [2002] recommend the adoption of an approach that restricts the assessment of emotion to a two dimensional pleasure-arousal space [Russell 1997] which distinguishes only between high and low arousal, and positive and negative valence, rather than a large set of distinct emotions. Nevertheless, their preferred techniques, heart-rate variability for arousal, and facial muscle EMG for valence, do not avoid the practical problems.

Facial expression recognition may offer a means of addressing some of these shortcomings. EMG studies have provided strong evidence of the reliability of facial expressions, demonstrating brow (corrugator) activity to be associated typically with negative or unpleasant stimuli, cheek and mouth (zygomatic) activity with positive stimuli, and wrinkling of the nose (levator) movement with disgust. Andreassi [2000, pp.182–7] provides a review of these studies. Although these muscle activities may sometimes be too small or rapid to be seen [Caccioppo et al. 1993], many of course are visible and therefore potentially available to provide information about users' affective reactions.

Advances in computer vision, increases in the power of everyday computers and price reductions in digital video have removed many of the barriers to computer vision applications that once existed. Essa [1999] describes systems able to recognize various facial expressions deliberately made by people to represent different emotions. Bianchi-Berthouze & Lisetti [2002] describe a system that refines its classification of users' expressions through dialogue. However in systems like these, facial expression is the subject of interaction rather than an inherent aspect of it. In genuine applications, software would detect and classify facial expressions for purposeful use.

Recently, software for tracking the facial movements of unmarked faces in live or recorded video signals has become commercially available and affordable. Typically, this software identifies a face in the video signal, assigns virtual markers to various points around the face, and monitors changes in the relative positions of these markers. An example is described in Section 3.2.

To summarize, facial expression monitoring would appear to be less restrictive and invasive than other physiological techniques, to use standard video equipment rather than specialist sensing, to provide information about some of the qualities of users' emotions, and to have recently become accessible and affordable.

But how viable actually is it? This investigation was designed to begin to explore the following preliminary questions:

1. Do facial expressions change during ordinary computer use?

2. Do these facial expressions reflect physiological arousal?

3. How successfully are these facial movements detected by facial movement tracking software?

4. To what extent does the software distinguish qualitative differences in facial movements?

2   Functional Context

Affective Computing can be divided into two main application areas:

1. the use of emotions to inform software behaviour in emotionally responsive machines [for example, Picard & Klein 2002]; and

2. the use of emotional reactions to help identify usability and content issues such factors that cause high workload, surprise, stress or frustration [Ward & Marsden 2003; Wilson & Sasse 2000].

The work discussed here relates to this second area, the evaluation of content. Facial expressions are therefore considered as potential indicators of HCI events that may be of significance to users. For the moment we consider this a simple and easily understood domain in which to explore facial expression recognition.

To place this in context we offer a functional categorization of facial expression recognition in human-computer interaction, summarized in Table 1. Software may either simply monitor users' facial reactions to HCI events (Column 1) or permit users to communicate with it intentionally through facial expressions (Column 2). Reactions to events will be mainly subconscious, whereas communicative facial movements will be mainly conscious, acting as a direct input device. In either case,

	(1) User reacts to HCI events	(2) User has communicative intent
(a) Software does not adapt its behaviour.	Usability and content evaluation, e.g. this paper.	Controllable software e.g. virtual puppeteering.
(b) Software does adapt its behaviour	Adaptive software e.g. adaptive CAL.	Anthropomorphic interaction.

Table 1: Functions of facial expression recognition in HCI.

on detecting a change in its user's facial expression, software may either be able to adapt its subsequent behaviour (Row b) or not (Row a).

In the investigations reported here, the software used in the experimental task does not adapt its behaviour in any way, nor do users' facial expressions directly control the software. It therefore falls into Category 1(a). An example of Category 1(b) software that does adapt its behaviour to users' facial expressions would be an adaptive computer-assisted learning program able to detect users' levels of understanding, motivation, feelings of failure, loss of interest, and so on, and individualize its teaching strategies accordingly [for example, Picard 1997, pp.93–4; Conati 2002]. An example of Category 2(a) software, where users' facial expressions afford direct, intentional control and manipulation is 'virtual puppeteering' software, where the face of an avatar copies the face of an actor (see Section 3.2). However, apart from copying the user's facial movements, virtual puppeteering software does not adapt its subsequent behaviour. Ultimately we may see software of Category 2(b) that both allows the user the intentional and communicative use of facial expression, and also adapts its behaviour in response. This could enable users to manage their collaborations with computers through the communicative use of emotion. According to some theorists, communicative emotion is very important in managing human-human collaboration [Oatley & Jenkins 1996; Oatley 2000]. The investigations reported here are a step towards this more genuinely anthropomorphic form of interaction.

3   Experimental Design and Materials

3.1   Experimental Task

Participants completed a multiple choice quiz based on the UK driving theory test. The quiz was written in JavaScript and delivered in Internet Explorer on a Windows PC. The task presented 35 questions drawn from the genuine test bank, and participants were informed that, as in the real test, the pass mark was a minimum of 30 correct answers out of 35. Questions were presented separately, each with a choice of four possible answers, as shown in Figure 1. Answers were selected by clicking on the associated box which then changed colour. Provided the 'Next' button had not been clicked, this selection could be reviewed and changed as many times as desired. 'Next' proceeded to the next question. The beginning of the quiz presented an initial trial screen for the purpose of familiarizing participants with the

Figure 1: The experimental task showing the first of the questions with affective content.

look and feel. After the final question, a panel appeared showing the number of correct answers and the 'Pass' or 'Fail' outcome, and prompting participants were to inform the experimenter they had finished.

The task differed from the real theory test in several minor ways: the questions were the same for all participants, there were no pictorial questions, questions offered only a one from four choice, previous questions and answers could not be revisited, and answers were selected by mouse click rather than touch screen. Otherwise the experimental task was quite similar to the real test, and very similar to published preparation and revision software.

The task was however fixed to contain two specific stimuli: a surprise event and questions judged to have high affective content. The surprise event was the appearance of a standard browser alert box accompanied by a standard Windows sound at moderate volume, containing the message "Reaction Time Test. Click OK to Proceed". Participants were unable to proceed further until the alert box had been cleared. This appeared after question number 27. This kind of event had previously been observed to produce large changes in the arousal levels of most participants [Ward et al. 2002] and can therefore be regarded as the stronger of the two stimuli. The questions with high affective content were genuine questions from the official test bank. Whereas most of the 850 or so questions in the test bank are factual and unexciting, such as questions about speed limits and road markings, a small number of questions appear to have stronger affective content, such as how to deal with accident injuries or bad behaviour in other drivers. The experimental task was sequenced so that only questions 13 to 17 were from those agreed by the experimenters to be of high affective content. Figure 1 shows the first of these. This kind of event had previously been observed to produce changes in the arousal levels of some but not all participants and may therefore be regarded as the weaker of the two stimuli. The software for the experimental task was also programmed to record a timed log of the main events (start, clicking 'Next', answer selection, the appearance and clearance of the surprise alert box, end). This provided information on participants' performance, and allowed synchronization with other data sources.

3.2   Face Tracking Software

FaceStation 1.2[1] was used. This uses 22 virtual facial markers to automatically track the movements of an individual face in a live or recorded video signal, frame by frame. FaceStation is marketed primarily as a facial animation tool: i.e. a virtual face copies the movements of an actor's face in a process coined 'virtual puppeteering' — the face tracker extracts movements from the video signal and passes them into a 3D modelling package which, by means of a proprietary plug-in, transfers the movements on to a virtual head and face. Using inverse kinematics and mesh distortions, the modelling package then manipulates the positions of the head, eyeballs and lower jaw, and modifies the appearance of the eyelids, eyebrows, mouth, upper lip, etc. The results can be very convincing, especially with manual fine-tuning. More importantly for the purposes of this investigation, the data representing these movements and distortions can also be analysed separately. The modelling package used here was discreet 3ds max version 4.3. Recorded rather than live video was used.

3.3   Physiological Monitoring

Physiological arousal was monitored by means of skin resistance (SR). Signals were collected using Lafayette DataLab 2000 running on a separate Windows PC, with recording and analysis through National Instruments BioBench. Blood volume pulse (BVP) was also recorded but did not form part of the analysis presented here. The SR electrodes and BVP sensor were attached to the fingers of participants' non-dominant hands, leaving the other hand free for the experimental task. For SR, standard stainless steel dry electrodes as supplied with the DataLab system were attached to the first and third fingers. The BVP sensor fitted over the end of second finger.

3.4   Participants

An opportunity sample of 17 participants from the general university population took part in the study. Participants were required to have some driving experience, either as a qualified driver or as a learner, so as to have reasonable understanding of the experimental task. Participants with facial hair or glasses were excluded as earlier trials had shown these factors to cause problems for the tracking software. Otherwise age, gender and computing skills were not an issue for participation. Two of the 17 participants were subsequently excluded from the analysis, one who on seeing the task decided that glasses were indeed necessary, and one whose unusual mouth shape (thin lips) caused tracking difficulties. The 15 remaining participants consisted of 5 males and 10 females aged from 21 to 55.

3.5   Experimental Procedure

Experimental sessions took place in a quiet room free from distractions or interruptions. No special lighting was used, only daylight and standard fluorescent tubes. This had previously been found adequate. However, it is worth mentioning that the camera had the standard capacity to adjust automatically to lighting conditions. As recommended by the producers of the software, participants sat in

---

[1]http://www.eyematic.com/products_facestation.html (last accessed 2003.01.10).

front of a white screen in order to aid tracking. Without this we have found the software sometimes to mistake background objects for parts of the participant's face. Once participants were comfortably seated at the task computer, a video camera on top of the monitor was aligned so as to capture the full head, and the physiological sensors were attached to the non-dominant hand. Participants were asked to try not to move this hand during the experiment. Physiological and video recordings were then started and synchronized, the task was explained and the trial screen brought up. The experimenter then moved out of sight, and participants could start when ready. Participants were debriefed at the end of the procedure.

3.6   Measures

There were two events of interest to the analysis reported here:

1. the presentation of the first question with emotive content (Question 13); and

2. the appearance of the surprise alert box.

For each event there were two associated periods of interest: the 10s immediately before the event, and the 10s immediately afterwards. There were therefore four periods of interest for each participant. There were four data sources for each period of interest:

1. physiological arousal;

2. real facial movements;

3. captured facial movements as visualized on a virtual face; and

4. the data underlying the captured facial movements.

3.6.1   Physiological Arousal

To gain an indication of whether participants had genuinely reacted to events (see Questions 1 and 2 in Section 1), the absolute changes in skin resistance before and after each event were extracted. A greater post-event decrease in resistance, indicating increased eccrine activity, was taken as evidence of increased arousal caused by the event.

3.6.2   Participants' Real Facial Movements

To ascertain whether the events of interest had generated genuine changes in participants' facial expressions (Question 1), 10 human judges examined videos of each participant's face for the two 10s periods immediately before and after:

1. the first appearance of affective content; and

2. the appearance of the surprise alert.

Judges were asked to state whether there was more facial movement in the pre-event video, the post-event video, or whether there was no difference. The pre-post-event videos were presented side by side in pairs in as shown in Figure 2 (this actually shows the virtual faces relating to Section 3.6.3). The left and right positions were randomized. The videos in each pair could be run either simultaneously or independently as many times as required.

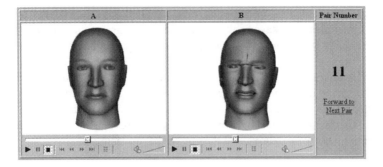

Figure 2: Presentation of paired video sequences for judgement — virtual faces (the same technique was also used in judging real faces).

3.6.3   Movements of the Virtual Face

To gain an indication as to how well participants' facial movements had been tracked by the software (Question 3), judges were also asked to compare the pre-event and post-event movements of the virtual head and face generated from the video data files. The key point to bear in mind here is that the movements of the virtual face form a visualization of the underlying data captured by the facial expression tracker. The virtual head and face used for this purpose was a discreet 3ds max model, 'reference.max', supplied with the FaceStation system. The default movement and morph settings were used. To generate the movements of the virtual face, the video files prepared for the previous measure were passed through the FaceStation FaceLifter utility to create data files for import into the virtual model. Corresponding 10s video sequences of the virtual face were then generated and rendered for judgement as shown in Figure 2.

3.6.4   Data Underlying Movements of the Virtual Face

Also to evaluate the performance of the automatic tracker, and to begin to gain an indication of how well the tracker was able to differentiate quality of facial expression (Questions 3 and 4), an analysis of the data underlying the movements of the virtual face was carried out. Assuming that the predominant response evoked by the surprise event should indeed be surprise, and that the predominant event evoked by the affective content should be humour, then from Andreassi [2000], one would predict increased brow (corrugator) movement in response to surprise events, and increased mouth and cheek (zygomatic) movement in response to affective content.

The reference.max model makes use of 16 morph data tracks. Here, five sample morph tracks were examined: Smile, Disgust, 'Ah', Eyebrow Raise and Eyebrow Furrow. Smile and Disgust are lower face movements reflecting zygomatic and levator activity. Eyebrow Furrow and Eyebrow Raise are upper face movements reflecting corrugator activity. 'Ah' was also included as one of the tracks that captures opening of the mouth. The reference.max model actually manipulates the left and right eyebrows independently but for this analysis these two data tracks were combined. The reference.max model also uses further data tracks for other

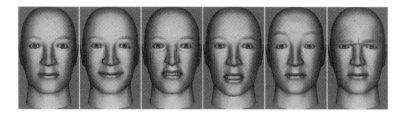

Figure 3: Morph targets selected for data analysis: neutral face, smile 100%, disgust 75%, 'ah' 50%, eyebrows raise 100%, eyebrow furrow 200%.

morph targets and for movements of the head, jaw and eyeballs, but these are not considered here. The five selected morph movements, together with a neutral face for comparison, are shown in Figure 3. In reality these movements would occur in various combinations, rather than in isolation as illustrated. The percentages show the degree of movement that has been applied towards the normal limit of each morph target. Some targets respond to percentages greater than 100%, and also to negatives.

The track data were exported to Microsoft Excel for further analysis. For each morph data track, two summative statistics for the whole of each 10s period were calculated: the mean as an indication of positional change, and the inter-quartile range as an indication of variations in movement.

4 Results

Tables 2 & 3 summarize the physiological and human judgement data relating to the two events of interest: the surprise alert box and the presentation of affective content.

4.1 Physiological Arousal

Tables 2 & 3 show the changes in skin resistance during the pre-event and post-event periods. Participants showed highly significant decreases in skin resistance following both events ($t = 4.213$ with 14 d.f., $p = 0.001$ for the surprise event, and $t = 3.464$ with 14 d.f., $p = 0.004$ for the affective content). This implies that both events caused increased levels of arousal. However, it can be seen that participants' responses varied considerably in magnitude. In 3 participants there was no increase in arousal in response to presentation of affective content. As it is always possible that a post-event decrease alone may simply reflect an underlying downward trend, the net decreases were also considered, although here this gives the same indication.

Twelve participants responded more strongly to the surprise event ($p = 0.035$), which supports the assumption that the surprise event was a stronger stimulus than the presentation of affective content.

4.2 Participants' Real Facial Movements

In dealing with judges verdicts, if 6 or more judges were in agreement that the post-event sequence showed more facial movement than the pre-event sequence, then this was taken as indeed the case (binomial $p = 0.076$ for 6/10 with a test property

P#	Change in Skin Resistance (kOhm)				Increased Facial Movement		Increased Virtual Movement	
	pre-event	post-event	net	shows decrease	judges agreed	agreed by 6 or more	judges agreed	agreed by 6 or more
1	-7.9	-17.9	-10.0	Yes	10	Yes	6	Yes
2	0.9	-4.9	-5.8	Yes	7	Yes	6	Yes
3	3.7	-2.7	-6.4	Yes	9	Yes	2	fneg
4	1.8	-17.9	-19.7	Yes	10	Yes	8	Yes
5	-1.5	-12.2	-10.7	Yes	10	Yes	10	Yes
6	0.0	-10.6	-10.6	Yes	10	Yes	5	fneg
7	4.3	-6.4	-10.7	Yes	10	Yes	8	Yes
8	0.3	-27.4	-27.7	Yes	10	Yes	8	Yes
9	1.8	-29.2	-31.0	Yes	7	Yes	10	Yes
10	0.9	-19.5	-20.4	Yes	6	Yes	3	fneg
11	2.1	-84.3	-86.4	Yes	10	Yes	10	Yes
12	0.0	-28.9	-28.9	Yes	10	Yes	9	Yes
13	3.0	-7.6	-10.6	Yes	9	Yes	10	Yes
14	3.0	-23.7	-26.7	Yes	10	Yes	7	Yes
15	3.7	-60.8	-64.5	Yes	10	Yes	10	Yes
mean	1.1	-23.6	-24.7	N=15	N=15			
s.d.	3.0	22.1	22.7		15/15 arousal		12/15 positives	
		p 0.001						

Table 2: Results of the appearance of the surprise alert box.

---

of 0.333). By this criterion, Tables 2 & 3 show that all 15 participants' real faces were judged to have shown greater movement in response to the surprise event (binomial $p = 0.000$ for 15/15 with a test property of 0.5), but only 5 in response to the first affective item (binomial $p = 0.302$ for 5/15).

In the case of the surprise event this leaves little scope for disagreement between physiological and facial measures. In the case of affective content only 4 of the 12 arousal responses were accompanied by greater facial movements in the post-event period. There was also one occasion where facial movements appeared not to have been accompanied by increased arousal.

4.3 *Movements of the Virtual Face*

Movements of the virtual face may be regarded as a visualization of the facial movement data captured by the tracker from participants' real faces. The same threshold of 6 or more judges in agreement was used as in judging the real faces. With respect to the surprise event, the post-event sequences for the virtual face were judged in agreement with the real face for 12 out of 15 participants (binomial $p = 0.000$ with a test property of 0.333), with 3 false negatives. With respect to affective content, judges agreed that 3 of the 5 cases in which the real face had shown greater post-event movement were picked up by the face tracker, with 2 false negatives. The face tracker also showed false-positive post-event movement for 6 of

P#	Change in Skin Resistance (kOhm)				Increased Facial Movement		Increased Virtual Movement	
	pre-event	post-event	net	shows decrease	judges agreed	agreed by 6 or more	judges agreed	agreed by 6 or more
1	9.1	-28.3	-37.4	Yes	1		9	Yes-fpos
2	-4.3	2.1	6.4		8	Yes	0	fneg
3	-0.3	-4.3	-4.0	Yes	2		9	Yes-fpos
4	3.3	-2.1	-5.4	Yes	0		9	Yes-fpos
5	6.4	-22.2	-28.6	Yes	10	Yes	10	Yes
6	2.1	-4.9	-7.0	Yes	10	Yes	10	Yes
7	10.6	-35.0	-45.6	Yes	2		7	Yes-fpos
8	-0.6	-25.9	-25.3	Yes	2		9	Yes-fpos
9	5.8	-3.0	-8.8	Yes	8	Yes	2	fneg
10	0.0	0.0	0.0		0		1	
11	12.8	12.8	0.0		1		0	
12	5.8	-22.2	-28.0	Yes	10	Yes	6	Yes
13	3.7	0.0	-3.7	Yes	1		10	Yes-fpos
14	5.2	-2.4	-7.6	Yes	1		4	
15	3.0	-7.9	-10.9	Yes	2		0	
mean	4.2	-9.6	-13.7	N=12	N=5		3/5 positives	
s.d.	4.6	13.6	15.3		4/12 arousal		4/10 negatives	
		p 0.004					9/12 arousal	

Table 3: Results of the presentation of affective content.

the remaining 10 participants. Judges therefore considered the movements of the real and virtual faces in agreement in only 7 of the 15 pairs.

There were however signs of additional agreement between the virtual faces and the arousal data. The physiological responses of 5 participants (1, 5, 7, 8, 12) were considerably great than those of the others. All 5 of these participants generated greater post-event movement in their virtual faces, despite 3 of them not having been judged to have done so in their real faces.

4.4   Data Underlying Movements of the Virtual Face

The raw tracking data represents the degree to which each morph target has been applied in each video frame, in effect a percentage of the range of movement (see Figure 4). Values are influenced by default settings in the virtual model, and can occasionally be negative or greater than 100%. Settings were constant throughout the investigation. The Smile, Disgust and 'Ah' data tracks for all participants were fully populated by the tracker for all the periods examined. However, the brow furrow track for some participants contained sequences of zeroes covering several seconds worth of data. Also, the brow raise values were entirely zero for half of the participants. Certainly there is noise in the system because the virtual markers were sometimes observed to drift off-target and then back during analysis by the software. However, no data were excluded from analysis.

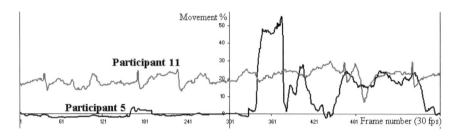

Figure 4: Smile track data for Participants 5 and 11 for the 10s before and after delivery of affective content.

	Smile	Disgust	'Ah'	brow Furrow	brow Raise
Surprise Alert					
pre-event mean	9.36	14.01	-1.23	57.34	3.08
post-event mean	13.48	23.90	-0.30	80.37	6.95
p	0.061	* 0.015	0.334	* 0.012	* 0.050
pre-event IQ range	7.03	11.05	1.66	30.48	3.27
post-event IQ range	12.85	24.51	5.60	41.15	8.89
p	* 0.015	* 0.011	* 0.002	0.191	* 0.028
Affective Content					
pre-event mean	8.89	19.33	-1.39	70.62	8.40
post-event mean	12.70	23.63	-1.39	76.88	4.09
p	0.191	0.191	0.609	0.776	0.249
pre-event IQ range	5.33	12.47	2.26	36.05	8.02
post-event IQ range	9.91	15.37	2.35	23.88	4.70
p	* 0.036	0.140	0.609	0.733	0.398
Affective Content (6 participants excluded)					
pre-event mean	7.03	16.15	-0.87	55.58	10.11
post-event mean	15.61	26.55	-2.53	74.98	4.57
p	* 0.028	0.139	0.059	0.441	0.647
pre-event IQ range	3.26	9.07	2.01	30.87	5.72
post-event IQ range	11.11	17.14	2.00	22.38	5.76
p	* 0.017	* 0.011	0.445	0.767	0.893

Table 4: Summary of virtual face movement data for selected morph tracks.

Table 4 summarizes the data from the morph tracks examined. Thus, the mean of participants' mean brow furrow values over the 10s prior to the surprise alert was 57.34%, and 80.37% over the succeeding 10s. Other morph tracks had lower mean values. Also for the surprise alert, the mean of participants' brow furrow inter-quartile range values were 30.48 over the pre-event period and 41.15 over the post-event period. Table 4 also shows that the mean brow furrow, brow raise and disgust values showed statistically significant increases in the period after the surprise alert (Wilcoxon signed ranks test). Similarly for the surprise alert, the smile, disgust, 'ah' and brow raise tracks showed statistically significant increases in post-event inter-quartile ranges. Mean differences are rough indicators of changes in the positions of these features. Inter-quartile range differences indicate greater variation of movement.

For affective content, only the smile track variability showed a statistically significant difference, with some differences in the wrong direction. However, if the six virtual faces judged not to have shown greater post-event facial movement are excluded from the analysis (i.e. those derived from participants 2, 9, 10, 11, 14 and 15) then most of the statistics move towards significance.

Figure 4 shows the smile track data for two participants shown by Table 3 to fall at the extremes of individual response to the presentation of affective content. Participant 5 showed strong post-event physiological and facial responses that were judged present in the virtual face. Participant 11 showed no physiological response and judges did not distinguish any differences between the pre-event and post-event facial or virtual videos. These observations appear to be clearly reflected in the data traces.

5 Discussion

On the whole, the face tracking software performed well, although there were some questions about the reliability of the upper-face tracking in the software used, under the circumstances in which it was used, which warrants further investigation. Possibly the software emphasizes lower face tracking because of its importance in lip synchronization in virtual puppeteering. The software also had difficulty in tracking participants with facial hair and spectacles who were excluded from the investigation, and one participant with an unusual mouth shape whose data was not used. These problems would need to be solved for the approach to have more general applicability.

The upper face data tracks contain a large proportion of zero values. Unlike eye-gaze tracking where periods of data-loss are common and can confidently be identified [Mullin et al. 2001; Renshaw et al. 2002], it is not so clear whether zero values in face tracking data represent data loss or simply that participants did not move their eyebrows (or other facial feature). Similarly, just because a data track is fully populated does not mean that a feature was tracked accurately, without marker drift. These concerns may diminish in future as facial movement tracking improves, but it also seems likely that uncertainty will always be a factor in the system, requiring probabilistic interpretation [Conati 2002].

In the investigation, physiological responses to the stronger stimulus occurred in more participants and were stronger than responses to the weaker stimulus. There was an even more marked difference between the two stimuli in the judgements of facial movement. Judges considered the weaker stimulus to have produced increased facial movement in only 5 participants, one of which was not accompanied by increased physiological arousal. This suggests that judgement of facial expression is a less sensitive response indicator than physiological measures, particularly with weaker stimuli. However, the judgement conditions may have been too exacting. Judges were asked simply to compare the amount of facial movement, rather than to judge aspects of the quality of expression (e.g. "Which of the two faces shows the greatest degree of amusement or surprise?"). Also, the fact that a participant's face showed less post-event movement than pre-event movement does not necessarily imply little or no post-event movement. Furthermore, responses to surprise events may be faster than responses to affective content, and physiological reactions may in some circumstances be faster than facial ones. Some participants did not smile or laugh until after the end of the 10s analysis period, but the physiological response may have been present sooner. More precise discriminations, more neutral baselines and more relaxed time constraints might have produced more favourable verdicts.

What can be concluded is that users' facial expressions can and do change in response to relatively ordinary computer-based events, and that the numbers of users that respond facially to an event is related to the stimulus strength of that event. Bearing in mind that research into affective computing to date has tended to focus mainly on strong stimuli such as the failure of a mouse to operate correctly during a competitive game [Scheirer et al. 2002, for example,], or on accentuated emotions deliberately generated by actors [Essa & Pentland 1997; Vyzas & Picard 1999], the fact that these results have been obtained with more ordinary computer-based events is promising.

Turning to the performance of the face tracker, there was a high degree of agreement with both the physiological and real facial data with respect to the stronger stimulus. The three cases apparently not detected by the face tracker were amongst the weaker physiological responses. However, performance was again less convincing with respect to the weaker event. Judgements of the virtual face agreed with judgements of the real face in only 7 of the 15 cases. Again, however, the judgement criteria may have been over-demanding. For example, in the two false negative cases (participants 2 and 9), the differences in the movements of the real faces were slight, despite most judges being in agreement about them.

Therefore, although the face tracker performed well in detecting responses to the stronger stimulus, it had mixed success with the weaker stimulus. This may in part be due to individual differences, which were more wide-ranging with the weaker stimulus. In fact, those 5 participants who showed the strongest physiological responses to the weaker event all showed greater post-event movement in their virtual faces, despite 3 of them not having reflected this in their real faces. Perhaps therefore the tracker accentuated differences that were not so obvious in real faces.

Evidence for this would lie in the track data. In fact, any emotionally aware agent or system would have only track data on which to base its interpretations. Here, in the case of the surprise alert (the stronger stimulus), there were differences between the pre-event and post-event movements in both the upper and lower regions of the face. These differences suggest changes in brow position held over a number of seconds, which appears to support the prediction that a surprise event should produce corrugator activity. There were also suggestions of variability of movement in the mouth area. In the case of the affective content (the weaker stimulus), after excluding participants whose virtual faces did not show post-event movement, there appears to have been increased variability of movement in the lower face area, but little in the brow region. This appears to support the prediction that the affective content should result in zygomatic movements (e.g. smiling) but not corrugator movements. A further comparison of the post-event upper face movements revealed a significant difference between the two events in participants' brow furrow inter-quartile ranges ($Z = -2.666$, $p = 0.008$). This is of course a simple analysis that takes no account of the sequences of changes in facial expression over the periods examined, but is nevertheless highly encouraging, particularly when individual data, as in Figure 4, also appears to make sense.

6 Conclusions

We consider the general substance of these results to be positive. They indicate that, even with a currently available off-the-shelf facial movement tracking system, facial expression recognition has the potential to be a viable tool in affective computing research. The study raises perhaps as many questions as it answers, requiring further analysis and investigation.

The performance of facial movement trackers will undoubtedly improve, and analytical techniques for extracting meaning from their data will continue to be refined. The extent to which this will permit better facial expression recognition is uncertain. Even human observers do not always find it easy to interpret the meaning of facial expressions.

It may be that where users work mainly alone and in private with the kind of office software currently in widespread use, changes in facial expression will be few. Those that do occur may be more useful when considered alongside other sources of information. Thus, in the results reported here, the smile and brow furrow data together with skin resistance data could provide a useful indication of both valence and strength of response. This may be the way forward in the evaluation of usability and content, and possibly also in adaptive software, as conceptualized in Table 1.

It may also be that new kinds of applications in which users' facial expressions are intentional and communicative could provide a more fruitful domain for facial expression recognition. Here users' facial movements would be deliberate and more obvious, and simpler to recognize and interpret. Such applications might permit users to manage collaborations with computers more in the way that human-human collaborations are managed, possibly through the expression of emotions such as assertiveness, affection and anxiety. However we believe the development of these kinds of ideas requires groundwork research in simpler domains first.

Acknowledgements

Part of this work is supported by EPSRC project grant GR/N00586. The authors would also like to thank Dr John Blacktop for advice on statistical issues.

References

Andreassi, J. L. [2000], *Psychophysiology : Human Behavior and Physiological Response*, fourth edition edition, Lawrence Erlbaum Associates.

Bianchi-Berthouze, N. & Lisetti, C. L. [2002], Modelling Multimodal Expression of Users' Affective Subjective Experience, *User Modelling and User-adapted Interaction* **12**(1), 49–84.

Caccioppo, J. T., Klein, D. J., Bernston, G. G. & Hatfield, E. [1993], The Psychophysiology of Emotion, *in* M. Lewis & J. Havilland (eds.), *Handbook of Emotions*, Guilford, pp.119–42.

Conati, C. [2002], Probabilistic Assessment of Users' Emotions in Educational Games, *Applied Artificial Intelligence* **16**(7/8), 555–75.

Ekman, P. [1992], Are there basic emotions?, *Psychological Review* **99**(3), 550–3.

Essa, I. [1999], Computers Seeing People, *AI Magazine* **20**(2), 69–82.

Essa, I. & Pentland, A. [1997], Coding, Analysis, Interpretation and Recognition of Facial Expressions, *IEEE Transactions on Pattern Analysis and Machine Intelligence* **19**(7), 757–63.

Hudlicka, E. & McNeese, M. [2002], Assessment of User Affective and Belief States for Interface Adaptation: Application to an Air Force Pilot Task, *User Modelling and User-adapted Interaction* **12**(1), 1–47.

Mullin, J., Anderson, A. H., Smallwood, L., Jackson, M. & Katsavras, E. [2001], Eye-Tracking Explorations in Multimedia Communications, *in* A. Blandford, J. Vanderdonckt & P. Gray (eds.), *People and Computers XV: Interaction without Frontiers (Joint Proceedings of HCI2001 and IHM2001)*, Springer-Verlag, pp.367–82.

Oatley, K. [2000], Emotion and Distributed Cognition, Invited talk to the 2000 Annual Conference of the British Psychological Society. Summarized by Fiona Jones in The Psychologist 13(6), pp.290-291.

Oatley, K. & Jenkins, J. M. [1996], *Understanding Emotions*, Blackwell.

Picard, R. W. [1997], *Affective Computing*, MIT Press.

Picard, R. W. & Healey, J. [1997], Affective Wearables, *Personal Technologies* **1**(4), 231–40.

Picard, R. W. & Klein, J. [2002], Computers that Recognise and Respond to Human Emotion: Theoretical and Practical Implications, *Interacting with Computers* **14**(2), 141–69.

Renshaw, T., Finlay, J. E., Ward, R. D. & Tyfa, D. [2002], The Impact of Object Dimensions upon Eye Gaze, *in* H. Sharp, P. Chalk, J. LePeuple & J. Rosbottom (eds.), *Proceedings of HCI'02: Volume 2*, British Computer Society, pp.86–89.

Russell, J. [1997], Reading Emotions From And Into Faces: Resurrecting a Dimensional–Contextual Perspective, *in* J. Russell & J. Fernandez-Dols (eds.), *The Psychology of Facial Expression*, Cambridge University Press, pp.295–320.

Scheirer, J., Fernandez, R., Klein, J. & Picard, R. W. [2002], Frustrating the User on Purpose: A Step Towards Building an Affective Computer, *Interacting with Computers* **14**(2), 93–118.

Vyzas, E. & Picard, R. W. [1999], Offline and Online Recognition of Emotion Expression from Physiological Data, Technical Report TR-488, Affective Computing Group, MIT. ftp://whitechapel.media.mit.edu/pub/tech-reports/TR-488/abstract.html. Paper presented at Workshop on Emotion-Based Agent Architectures held at the Third International Conference on Autonomous Agents, Seattle.

Ward, R. D., Cahill, B., Marsden, P. H. & Johnson, C. A. [2002], Physiological Responses to HCI Events — What Produces Them and How Detectable Are They?, *in* H. Sharp, P. Chalk, J. LePeuple & J. Rosbottom (eds.), *Proceedings of HCI'02: Volume 2*, British Computer Society, pp.90–93.

Ward, R. D. & Marsden, P. H. [2003], Physiological Responses to Different Web Page Designs, *International Journal of Human–Computer Studies* **59**(1–2), 119–212.

Wilson, G. M. & Sasse, M. A. [2000], Do Users Always Know What's Good For Them? Utilising Physiological Responses to Assess Media Quality, *in* S. McDonald, Y. Waern & G. Cockton (eds.), *People and Computers XIV (Proceedings of HCI'2000)*, Springer-Verlag, pp.327–39.

Could I have the Menu Please? An Eye Tracking Study of Design Conventions

John D McCarthy, M Angela Sasse & Jens Riegelsberger

Department of Computer Science, University College London, Gower Street, London WC1E 6BT, UK

Tel: *+44 20 7679 3644*

Email: *{j.mccarthy, a.sasse, j.riegelsberger}@cs.ucl.ac.uk*

Existing Web design guidelines give conflicting advice on the best position for the navigation menu. One set of guidelines is based on user expectation of layout, the other on results from user testing with alternative layouts. To resolve this conflict we test whether placing the menu in an unexpected position has a negative impact on search performance. The results show that users rapidly adapt to an unexpected screen layout. We conclude that designers should not be inhibited in applying design recommendations that violate layout conventions as long as consistency is maintained within a site.

Keywords: Web design, design guidelines, information architecture, visual scanning, eye movements, eye tracking.

1 Introduction

A problem facing users in a wide variety of interfaces is locating the right option to achieve their goal. This problem is especially acute on Web interfaces, where users are presented with a large number of simultaneous choices. The user's task can be simplified by designing Web sites that conform to conventions or expectations. For example, Nielsen [1999] shows that success rate for product search is 80% when menu labels conformed to expectations. This drops to 9% with unfamiliar menu labels. From this finding and others Nielsen develops '*Jacob's Law of Web user experience*':

> "Users spend most of their time on **other** sites. Thus, anything that is a convention and used on the majority of other sites will be burned into the users' brains and you can only deviate from it on pain of major usability problems."

Conventions play an important role in Web design guidelines. For example, the IBM design guidelines [IBM 2003] suggest that persistent navigation links should be placed on the left or top of the page *'because these are the areas users expect to find them'*. But is expectation alone justification for a design guideline? The National Cancer Institute Guidelines [NCI 2002] give different advice. These suggest that the navigation menu should be placed on the right of the page. From a study of extended use of a portal they observed that users clicked on topics much more efficiently with a right-justified menu, as it was located close to the scroll bar. The advantages observed were even more pronounced on laptop computers [Bailey et al. 2000].

But if user testing shows better performance and greater user satisfaction with right-justified menus, why are they not more widespread? If guidelines are based on current conventions, how can new interfaces be introduced? The QWERTY keyboard is just one example where culturally endemic expectations are non-optimal in terms of task performance, user satisfaction and user cost [Shneiderman 1998, pp.307-15]. Clearly, user expectation needs to be challenged if interfaces are to change. But what exactly is the impact of placing the menu in an unexpected location?

In this paper, we investigate the impact of challenging user expectations by measuring search performance with the menu in three different locations. To examine in detail where people look, we utilize eye tracking to measure their search process as it proceeds.

2 Background

Patterns of searching Web interfaces are governed by both the display and the expectations of the user. The display exerts a *bottom-up* influence. Expectations exert a *top-down* influence. Careful manipulation of static display factors such as layering, separation, colours and contrast can draw the eye to important pieces of information and reduce competition between display elements [Tufte 1990]. Motion or animation is also an effective cue to capture attention [Hillstrom & Yantis 1994]. Rensink [2000] claims two types of information can be extracted from bottom-up processing without attention. One is the abstract meaning or 'gist' of the scene. 'Gist' would distinguish the particular type of interface facing the user, e.g. Web Page, Word Processor, Spreadsheet. The other type of information is the spatial arrangement or layout of objects in the scene. This representation is vital to integrate information from individual eye fixations into a structure capable of *directing* subsequent eye movements.

But search behaviour is also governed by expectations about *what* is being looked for, and *where* it might be found. For example, if I'm looking to find a share price on a Web site — I might look for an option labelled 'shares' or 'business'. But, evidence from studies of search indicates that *what* a target looks like exerts very little influence on search or eye movements. Unless a unique physical feature (*bottom-up*) — such as colour, contrast or motion — identifies the target, search proceeds by selecting the screen elements one by one [Treisman & Gelade 1980]. By contrast, an influence *could* be exerted by an expectation of *where* a target might be found. The available evidence supports the claim that users have prior expectations about where things are. For example, in a study of people's schemata for Web pages

Influence	Processing	Origin	Factors
Display	Bottom Up	Current Interface	Contrast Colour Motion Grouping Layout Labelling
Expectation	Top Down	Memories of past interfaces and target representation	Contrast Colour Motion Grouping Layout Labelling

Table 1: Factors governing search behaviour.

Bernhard [2001] found that most users expected the navigation menu to be found on the left of the screen. Such expectations are *top-down* factors based on memories of '*what is where*' from previous interactions and are a defining feature of a convention.

These two processes, *top-down* and *bottom-up*, exert an influence on search behaviour (see Table 1). An important interaction between them results in what has been described as *information scent* [Pirolli 1997]. Scent is perceived when the proximal cues (*bottom-up*) provided by page elements such as such as WWW links, graphics, icons or menu items are evaluated relative to the current goals (*top-down*). This gives an indication of the value, cost, and location of the distal content on the linked page. Thus, information scent is a *basis for selection*, but it cannot be perceived unless an element is actually looked at. It therefore cannot guide the visual search process itself. To understand the factors that influence search behaviour we need to examine the eye movements of the user.

3 Eye Tracking Usability Studies

On the empirical side, there is surprisingly little published research on how people actually do conduct search within a Web page. Perhaps the best-known eye tracking study of Web use is the Stanford-Poynter study [Lewenstein et al. 2000]. This examined how users read news articles online and measured where users looked on a page in the first three glances. Their results show that users' attention was drawn to text over graphics and photos, and run against findings from traditional print media which suggests that users are attracted to photo elements first [Kroeber-Riel 1996].

In an excellent review article, Jacob & Karn [in press] summarize 21 usability studies since 1950 incorporating eye tracking. The earliest study, by Fitts et al. [1950], used cine cameras to study the eye movements of pilots landing planes. Of the studies conducted since, only 3 explicitly examine search of Web pages.

Cowen [2001] used eye tracking to evaluate the usability of four sites under two search task conditions. Significant differences between the sites were found

#	Where would you go on this site to...	Menu Labels
1	Browse the latest Playstation games	Auctions
2	Get the latest football results	Business
3	Find the current share price for British Airways	Careers
4	Get info on the new MG sports car	Cars
5	Find a two bedroom flat in Camden	Games
6	Sell something on the Web	News
7	Find reports on recent bombings	Property
8	Book a flight to Paris	Sport
9	Find a new job	Travel

Table 2: Search tasks given to users and menu labels on the sites.

with both a standard task performance measure (time) and the number of fixations. Other work has shown that the number of fixations is strongly correlated with task duration, and this measure has been used as a proxy for measures of task performance [Goldberg & Kotval 1998].

Ellis et al. [1998] examined search for textual information on a page layout with a two-column, graphic-text block design. Performance was compared to three alternate designs, one with more hyperlinks, a second with text descriptions instead of pictures, and a third with a 'book-like layout' containing no graphics and text across the width of the page. Their results show that the 'book-like' layout led to faster and more efficient processing of information on the page although it was liked the least by users.

Goldberg et al. [2002] used eye tracking to examine a Web search conducted across several screens of Web portal application. They found little evidence of a change in strategy across different screens and a bias towards horizontal search of screens (across columns) rather than vertical search (within a column). They also found evidence that strong *information scent* heading labels were largely ignored in the search process. The Goldberg et al. [2002] result illustrates that *information scent* based on label identity is not actually a driver for eye behaviour.

4 Menu Study

To investigate the impact of top-down and bottom-up factors on search, we examined performance on 9 different search tasks across different sites (see Table 2). On all tasks, the task target was an option on the navigation menu. The menus labels were identical across all site variations and were derived from the most frequent menu options found across the top 5 UK Internet Service Providers (ISPs). Menu labels where ordered alphabetically (see Table 2). Each participant was given nine tasks, each one relating to an option available on the menu.

To examine the *top-down* influence on search, we manipulated the position of the navigation menu. All participants were tested across three sites with the menu positioned either to the *left*, *top* or *right* of the page. We predicted that participants would be unable to locate the menu directly from *bottom-up* processing and that

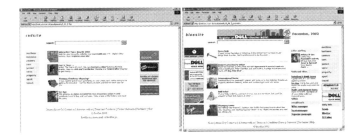

Figure 1: Screen shots of Simple and Complex sites with different menu positions.

search would be driven by expectation about *where* the menu would be located. As users expect the menu to be located on the left of the screen [Bernhard 2001], we predicted that performance would be better for menus located in this position.

H1: Search performance is better with left navigation menus.

To examine the influence of *bottom-up* factors, we manipulated the number of screen objects that would compete for users' attention. Two types of site were used — *Simple* and *Complex*. Simple Sites had only four content areas and four banner ads (see Figure 1). Complex Sites had 9 content areas and 9 Banner Ads (see Figure 1). We predicted that search performance would be better on the simple sites, as there would be less competition for attention from other screen elements.

H2: Search performance is better on simple sites.

4.1 Method

4.1.1 Participants

We used an eye tracking system that does not require head restraint. This meant that when participants changed their body posture too quickly or moved out of the tracking field, data was lost. To ensure high-quality data, we excluded from the analysis any participant who was tracked less than 90% of the time. This strict criterion left 31 subjects with tracking rates of 90% or greater. Of these 31 participants, 17 were male and 14 female. The mean age of the participants was 22 years. All participants were experienced Web users who used the Internet at least 3 hours/day. Participants were paid £5 Sterling.

4.1.2 Stimuli and Equipment

The template for the interfaces presented to participants was based on the design of a large Internet Service Provider (ISP) in the UK. Content and ads for the site were taken directly from the ISP homepage. Eye movements were measured using the EyeGaze system from LC technologies. The system samples eye position at a rate of 50Hz (60Hz in the US). Raw eye coordinates are converted to fixations using an algorithm that assumes a fixation time of 100ms and gaze deviation of 7mm. We

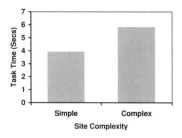

Figure 2: Task performance on simple and complex sites.

used the EyeBrowse[1] software to display stimulus pages and to define functionally distinct areas that could be analysed separately, called *regions of interest*.

4.1.3 Design

All participants performed 9 tasks in total, three tasks on each of three types of sites. All tasks involved finding a target on the navigation menu. The three types of site had a navigation menu on the *left, right* or *top* of the page. The effects of presentation order were counterbalanced between-subjects using presentation sequences based on a Latin squares design. The experimental design was a $2 \times 3 \times 3$ mixed design. The between-subject variable was **Site Complexity** — *Simple vs. Complex*. Within subject variables were **Menu Position** — *Left, Right* and *Top*, and **Page Visit** — *First, Second* and *Third*.

4.1.4 Procedure

Participants were briefed about the nature of the experiment and the measures that were going to be taken. The eye tracker was then calibrated to the participant's eye movements. They were then presented with an alternation of instruction and test screens. Instruction screens provided participants with the current goal — e.g. "Where would you go on this site to search for something on the Internet?". They were then presented with the page on which to complete the task. All participants received a single practice trial.

4.2 Results

4.2.1 Task Completion Time

To examine differences in task performance, we conducted an ANOVA on task completion times. The raw scores were transformed using a natural log transformation to approximate a normal distribution. The reported results are transformed back into seconds to simplify interpretation.

The ANOVA revealed three findings of interest. Firstly, there was a significant difference between *Simple* and *Complex* sites (see Figure 2), with participants taking almost 50% longer to complete the search task on the complex site, $F(1,29) = 7.33$,

---

[1]EyeBrowse is Open Source software developed as part of this research project. Please contact j.mccarthy@cs.ucl.ac.uk for further information.

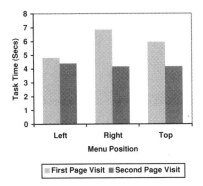

Figure 3: The effects of expectation on the first page visit.

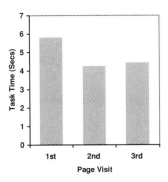

Figure 4: Decrease in task time after first page visit.

$p < 0.05$. This supports H2 — that search performance is better on simple sites — and shows how *bottom-up* display factors influence search performance.

The effect of *Menu Position* was not significant, $F(2,58) = 1.31$, n.s. In other words, averaging across tasks and site complexity, there was no evidence that performance was better when the menu is placed in the expected position on the left. This result suggests that expectation of *where* the menu is placed does not affect task performance. However, closer examination of the results revealed an interaction between *Menu Position* and *Page Visit*. Specifically, on the first page visit, performance is indeed better with a left navigation menu than with a right menu, $F(1,29) = 6.26$, $p < 0.05$ (see Figure 3). However, this difference disappears on the second page visit.

Thus, we have evidence for H1 — that performance will be better with the left menu — but only on the first page visit. Prior expectations do have an influence on the search but these expectations are rapidly updated to reflect the layout of the current page. Rapid learning of layout is also supported by a main effect of Page

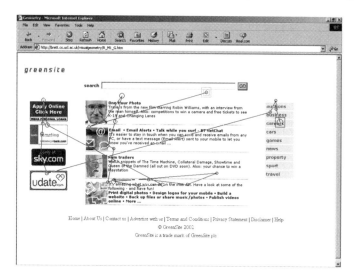

Figure 5: An example scan path from a search task.

Visit (See Figure 4) — showing a significant decrease in task completion time after the first page visit, $F(2,58) = 8.75$, $p < 0.05$. No other effects or interactions where significant.

4.2.2 Where do People Look?

To examine where people look when searching, we used location information from the eye tracker. Figure 5 illustrates a sample trace from one of the participants. The search *scan path* starts just below the search box and terminates on the right menu bar. The circles on the scan path in Figure 5 represent fixations — the larger the circle the longer the fixation.

According to Fitts et al. [1950], frequency and duration of eye movements should be treated as separate metrics, with duration reflecting difficulty of information extraction and frequency reflecting the importance of that area of the display. As we were primarily interested in the importance or attraction of different screen positions, we adopted a frequency measure. Our basic unit of analysis is *glance frequency* where a glance is defined as one or more successive fixations to the same screen object. Seven types of screen object where identified as the basis for this analysis. The categorization scheme for objects was a hybrid of the schemes used by Nielsen & Tahir [2002] and Krug [2000] to classify screen objects on Web pages. The objects were — Logo, Search Box, Menu, Content Text, Content Picture, Ad, Quick Links (Complex Site only) and Page Footer.

Across all subjects, sites and tasks, a total of 3767 glances were recorded. Figure 6 shows the proportion of searches completed by the number of glances taken. The graph illustrates that 55% of all searches take 10 glances or less, and that 95% of all searches are completed in 38 glances or less. As the glance sequence gets longer

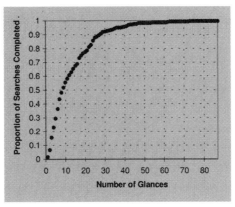

Figure 6: Proportion of searches completed by glance number.

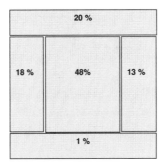

Figure 7: Glance distribution across all site variations.

we have fewer data points (i.e. a smaller sample size) to estimate the probability of glancing at different screen regions. Consequently, the subsequent analysis is restricted to the first 23 glances to ensure a reasonable sample size (> 50).

To give an indication of the spatial distribution of search, we categorized screen objects according to their position on the screen. Figure 7 shows the distribution of gaze to the Top, Left, Middle, Right and Bottom screen. Across all sites and tasks, there were very few glances to the bottom region of the screen (~1%), and although task targets where always to be found either top, left or right — these screen regions do not receive the most glances. Somewhat surprisingly, the eye tracking data shows that people focus the bulk of their search in the middle content area.

To examine how search proceeds through time we calculated the *Attraction* (*A*) of each screen area, where:

$$A = \frac{\text{Glances accumulated in target region}}{\text{Glances accumulated across all regions}}$$

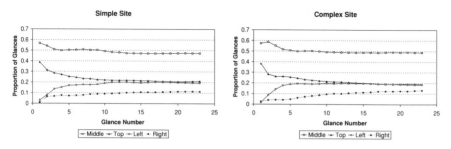

Figure 8: Attraction of screen regions on Simple and Complex sites.

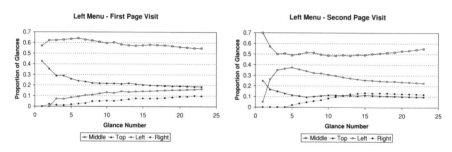

Figure 9: Attraction of areas on sites with a LEFT navigation menu.

A measures the proportion of glances made to a screen region and varies between 1 and 0^2. Figure 8 shows the attraction measures for *Simple* and *Complex* Web sites throughout the search sequence. Most striking about this figure is the similarity in search patterns. Although on the task performance measure there are clear differences in search time with *Simple* and *Complex* sites, the eye tracking data shows that although search is slower on the *Complex* site, the search process is the same. Therefore the difference in speed is not driven by a difference in strategy.

Figures 9–11 show the changes in search strategy for sites with *Left*, *Right* and *Top* menus across the *First* and *Second* page visits. Across all variations the middle (content) region of the page attracts the most glances. On the *first* page visit, the *left* menu sites receive a surprisingly small proportion of glances on the left hand side of the page, with most glances being directed to the middle and top of the page. The immediate response of the subjects is to search the middle of the page for the target. By the *second* page view, however, the strategy has changed, with more glances earlier on to the left region of the page. (See Figure 9.)

---

[2]Previous work has used a binary measure of *attraction* to indicate whether a region is glanced at or not [Riegelsberger et al. 2002]. This is simply a transformation of the continuous measure used here where:

$$attraction = \begin{cases} 0 & \text{if } A = 0 \\ 1 & \text{otherwise} \end{cases}$$

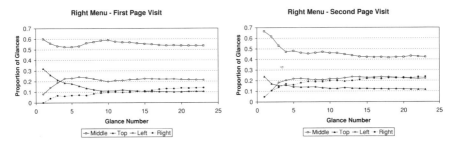

Figure 10: Attraction of areas on sites with a RIGHT navigation menu.

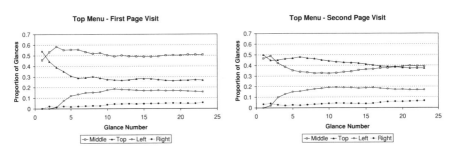

Figure 11: Attraction of areas on sites with a TOP navigation menu.

For sites with the navigation menu on the *right*, there is a large proportion of glances on the left hand side on the *first* page visit — particularly in the first ten glances (see Figure 10). This is interpreted as the search for the left menu driven by a mismatch with expectation. By the *second* page visit, the proportion of glances to the right has doubled, although there are still a significant number to the left hand side. On sites with the right-justified menu, the left side the page only contains banner ads — yet the fact that participants are glancing at these on the second visit — does not appear to affect task completion times (see Figure 3).

Results on sites with a *Top* navigation menu show a similar adaptation across *Page Visit*, although the change in search pattern is much more pronounced (see Figure 11). By the *second* page view, the top region of the page is attracting more glances than the middle region in the search for the target.

5   Discussion

On the measure of task performance, we found that sites that conform to expectations do indeed lead to faster search times, but this advantage is short-lived. The second time a site is visited, search times are equivalent irrespective of menu position. This shows that violating the expectation or convention of the left menu bar has little long-term effect on task performance.

The task performance measure also shows that search times are significantly affected by site complexity. Here there is a trade-off between making options available to the user while keeping the complexity low enough that they can still find what they are looking for. While a detailed evaluation of this issue would require another study, the present results support the design heuristic for search — simple is better.

The eye tracking measures give an extra dimension to the results above and beyond task time. Where differences in task time where found between *Simple* and *Complex* sites, there were no differences in search strategy revealed in the eye behaviour. By contrast, on the second page visit, the task performance measures show no significant differences between different sites, yet analysis of the eye data shows marked differences in search strategy — clearly mirroring changes in the interface. From this data we find clear evidence of expectation driving search behaviour with first impressions of a site. The data also gives insight into the rapid adaptation to the unexpected layout as new tasks are performed. This could not be seen from measures of task time alone.

6 Conclusions

The results show that violating expectation of menu position on Web pages has little long-term impact on task performance when searching a single page. The user quickly adapts to designs violating layout conventions. This should encourage design practitioners to take on board findings that menus on the right, close to the scroll bar, are better when searching across several pages [Bailey et al. 2000]. On this particular design feature, it is the internal consistency of a site that is important, rather than consistency with other Web sites. Practitioners should not be inhibited from applying guidelines based on evidence because of deviation from the standard.

Although the present investigation is limited to search of Web pages, the methodology can be applied to wide range of use cases with different tasks and interfaces. For researchers, the study demonstrates the value that eye movement studies add to evaluation methodologies. The eye data provides a detailed picture of where people look, when, and is sensitive to interface changes where task completion time is not. This level of detail can only benefit the design and development of future tools by challenging the assumptions implicit in craft design approaches. The most surprising result of the current study for us was the bias toward searching the middle of the screen. As the task is a search task, our 'folk' assumption was that people would look to the navigation menus first. The data obtained from eye tracking does not support this belief. Eye tracking allows researchers to evaluate and test beliefs implicit in the design process so that future developments proceed on a firm empirical foundation.

Acknowledgement

The research was funded by BT as part of the HIGHERVIEW Project http://www.cs.ucl.ac.uk/research/higherview/.

References

Bailey, R. W., Koyani, S. & Nall, J. [2000], Usability Testing of Several Health Information Web Sites, Technical Report 7-8, National Cancer Institute.

Bernhard, M. L. [2001], Developing Schemas for the Location of Common Web Objects, *in Proceedings of the Human Factors and Ergonomics Society 45th Annual Meeting*, Human Factors and Ergonomics Society, pp.1161–5.

Cowen, L. [2001], An Eye Movement Analysis of Web Page Usability, MRes Thesis, Department of Psychology, Lancaster University.

Ellis, S., Candrea, R., Misner, J., Craig, S., Lankford, C. & Hutchinson, T. [1998], Windows to the Soul? What Eye Movements Tell Us about Software Usability, *in Proceedings of the Usability Professionals' Association 7th Annual Conference*, Usability Professionals' Association, pp.151–6.

Fitts, P. M., Jones, R. E. & Milton, J. L. [1950], Eye Movements of Aircraft Pilots during Instrument-landing Approaches, *Aeronautical Engineering Review* **9**(2), 24–29.

Goldberg, J. H. & Kotval, X. P. [1998], Eye Movement-based Evaluation of the Computer Interface, *in* S. K. Kumar (ed.), *Advances in Occupational Ergonomics and Safety*, IOS Press, pp.529–32.

Goldberg, J. H., Stimson, M. J., Lewenstein, M., Scott, N. & Wichansky, A. M. [2002], Eye Tracking in Web Search Tasks: Design Implications, *in* A. T. Duchowski, R. Vertegaal & J. W. Senders (eds.), *Proceedings of the ETRA 2002 Symposium*, ACM Press, pp.51–8.

Hillstrom, A. P. & Yantis, S. [1994], Visual Motion and Attentional Capture, *Perception & Psychophysics* **55**(4), 399–411.

IBM [2003], Web Design Guidelines, http://www-3.ibm.com/ibm/easy/eou_ext.nsf/ Publish/572 (last accessed 2003.05.26).

Jacob, R. J. K. & Karn, K. S. [in press], Eye Tracking in Human–Computer Interaction and Usability Research: Ready to Deliver the Promises (Section Commentary), *in* J. Hyona, R. Radach & H. Deubel (eds.), *The Mind's Eyes: Cognitive and Applied Aspects of Eye Movements*, Elsevier Science.

Kroeber-Riel, W. [1996], *Bildkommunikation: Imagerysysteme für die Werbung*, Vahlen.

Krug, S. [2000], *Don't Make Me Think: A Common Sense Approach to Web Usability*, New Rider Publishing.

Lewenstein, M., Edwards, G., Tatr, D. & DeVigal, A. [2000], The Stanford Poynter Project, http://www.poynter.org/eyetrack2000/ (last accessed 2003.05.26).

NCI [2002], Research Based Web Design and Usability Guidelines, http://usability.gov/guidelines/ (last accessed 2003.05.26).

Nielsen, J. [1999], Do Interface Standards Stifle Design Creativity?, Jakob Nielsen's Alertbox, August 22. http://www.useit.com/alertbox/990822.html (last accessed 2003.05.26).

Nielsen, J. & Tahir, M. [2002], *Hompage Usability — 50 Web sites Deconstructed*, New Rider Publishing.

Pirolli, P. [1997], Computational Models of Information Scent-following in A Very Large Browsable Text Collection, *in* S. Pemberton (ed.), *Proceedings of the CHI'97 Conference on Human Factors in Computing Systems*, ACM Press, pp.3–10.

Rensink, R. A. [2000], Seeing, Sensing, and Scrutinizing, *Vision Research* **40**(10-2), 1468–87.

Riegelsberger, J., Sasse, M. A. & McCarthy, J. D. [2002], Eye-catcher or Blind Spot? The Effect of Photographs of Faces on E-commerce Sites, *in* J. L. Monteiro, P. M. C. Swatman & L. V. Tavares (eds.), *Proceedings of the 2nd IFIP Conference on E-commerce, E-business, E-government (i3e)*, Kluwer, pp.383–98.

Shneiderman, B. [1998], *Designing the User Interface: Strategies for Effective Human–Computer Interaction*, third edition, Addison–Wesley.

Treisman, A. & Gelade, G. [1980], A Feature Integration Theory of Attention, *Cognitive Psychology* **12**(1), 97–136.

Tufte, E. R. [1990], *Envisioning Information*, Graphics Press.

Author Index

Keyword Index